The Middle Ages

An Encyclopedia for Students

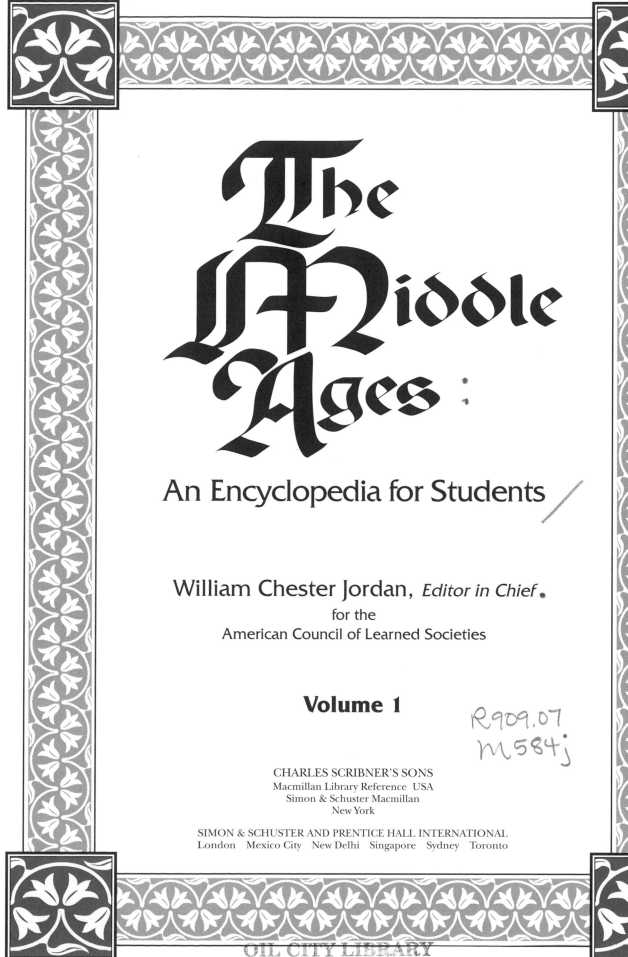

The Middle Ages:

An Encyclopedia for Students

William Chester Jordan, *Editor in Chief* .
for the
American Council of Learned Societies

Volume 1

R909.07
M584j

CHARLES SCRIBNER'S SONS
Macmillan Library Reference USA
Simon & Schuster Macmillan
New York

SIMON & SCHUSTER AND PRENTICE HALL INTERNATIONAL
London   Mexico City   New Delhi   Singapore   Sydney   Toronto

Developed for the American Council of Learned Societies by Charles Scribner's Sons and Visual Education Corporation.

For Scribners
PUBLISHER: Karen Day
SENIOR EDITOR: John Fitzpatrick
COVER DESIGN: Irina Lubenskaya

For Visual Education
PROJECT DIRECTOR: Jewel G. Moulthrop
WRITERS: Blair Bolles, Cindy S. George, Charles Patterson,
Adriane Ruggiero, Rebecca Stefoff, Richard Steins
EDITORS: Charles Roebuck, Robert Waterhouse
ASSISTANT EDITOR: Jeanine Evans
MAP AND ART EDITOR: Christine Osborne
COPY EDITOR: Margaret P. Roeske
INDEXER: Sallie Steele
RESEARCHER: Carol J. Ciaston
PHOTO RESEARCH: Martin A. Levick
PRODUCTION SUPERVISOR: Anita Crandall
INTERIOR DESIGN: Maxson Crandall
ELECTRONIC PREPARATION: Cynthia C. Feldner
ELECTRONIC PRODUCTION: Elise Dodeles, Lisa Evans-Skopas

PRINTING
3 4 5 6 7 8 9 10

Library of Congress Cataloging-in-Publication Data

The Middle Ages / William Chester Jordan, editor in chief for the American Council of Learned Societies.
    p. cm.
  Includes bibliographical references and index.
  ISBN 0-684-19773-1 (hard/libr. bind. : alk. paper)
  1. Middle Ages—Encyclopedias, Juvenile.   I. Jordan, William C., 1948– .   II. American Council of Learned Societies.
D114.M54 1996
909.07´03—dc20   95-49597
                                     CIP

ISBN 0-684-80483-2 (vol. 1)
ISBN 0-684-80484-0 (vol. 2)
ISBN 0-684-80485-9 (vol. 3)
ISBN 0-684-80486-7 (vol. 4)

Table of Contents

Volume 1

A
Aachen
Abbasids
Abelard and Heloise
Abu Bakr
Adrian IV, Pope
Agriculture
A'isha
Alamanni
Albertus Magnus
Alchemy
Alcuin of York
Alfonso X el Sabio
Alfred the Great
Alhambra
Ali ibn Abi Talib
Allegory
Anatolia
Angels
Angevins
Anglo-Saxons
Anointing
Anselm of Canterbury
Anti-Semitism

Aquinas, Thomas, St.
Aquitaine
Arabia
Arabic Language and Literature
Arabic Numerals
Aragon
Archives
Aristotle in the Middle Ages
Armenia
Armor
Arthurian Literature
Artillery
Astrolabe
Astrology and Astronomy
Asturias-León
Augustine in the Middle Ages
Austria
Avignon
Ayyubids

B
Bacon, Roger
Badr, Battle of

Baghdad
Bailiff
Bailli
Ballads
Baltic Countries
Banking
Barber-Surgeons
Barcelona
Bard
Baron
Bartolo da Sassoferrato
Basil I the Macedonian
Basil II "Killer of Bulgars"
Bastide
Bavaria
Bayazid I, Yildirim
Baybars al-Bunduqdari
Bayeux Tapestry
Becket, Thomas, St.
Bede
Beguines and Beghards
Bells
Benedict of Nursia, St.
Benedictines

Volume 2

Volume 3

Volume 4

Volume 4

Preface

Professional interest in the Middle Ages—conventionally the years 500 to 1500—has grown tremendously in the last half-century. While continuing to stress traditional themes of the importance of the Middle Ages both as a bridge between ancient and modern civilizations and for its special significance in the history of the West, recent writers have expanded beyond the traditional focus of scholarly interest on northern and western Europe. Of course, earlier scholars were aware that northwestern Europe constituted only a fragment of a larger picture, and they pointed to the significance of contacts between this region and the Byzantine and Muslim worlds, especially during the crusades. Even so, relatively little attention was paid to the multiple interactions—political, social, economic, and religious—among the various civilizations of the medieval world. Moreover, within each cultural environment scholars tended to highlight great men and elite culture, to the exclusion of studies of the poor, women, minorities, and popular culture.

The achievement of the last 50 years has gone a long way toward rectifying these imbalances. Recognizing the need for a comprehensive work on the Middle Ages that would incorporate the new insights, the American Council of Learned Societies (ACLS) and Charles Scribner's Sons published the *Dictionary of the Middle Ages (DMA)* in the 1980s. The *DMA* is an authoritative 13-volume reference work for advanced students and professional scholars.

In recent years, librarians, educators, and parents have expressed a growing need for reliable, accurate, and authoritative reference works that younger students can use in research projects and to supplement their textbooks. The range, depth, writing style, and cost of the *DMA*, however, make it inaccessible to some younger readers and to many school libraries.

In response to the requests for an attractive, smaller, less-detailed, and less-expensive version of the *DMA*, Scribners approached the ACLS with the idea for a scaled-down version. Scribners then asked Visual Education Corporation, a development house with years of experience producing high-quality reference works and textbooks, for a proposal to develop a version of the *DMA* for younger readers. The result of this three-way collaboration is *The Middle Ages: An Encyclopedia for Students,* a work that carries the authority and accuracy of the parent work, but in a form more suitable to a less-advanced readership.

An editorial board, composed both of scholars who had contributed to the original *DMA* and specialists on middle school and high school curricula and needs, discussed several key issues during the planning stages: (1) how the work should be organized; (2) how to use the material in the *DMA* to its best advantage; and (3) how to meet the needs of the intended audience.

Since accessibility is the hallmark of a useful reference work, the traditional alphabetical organization of the parent work was retained. Students, already familiar with other encyclopedic works and reference books, would find the A–Z format easy to use. The entry list for *The Middle Ages: An Encyclopedia for Students* was based on that of the *DMA*. Because of the comprehensive and in-depth nature of the parent work, it was generally assumed that a topic not covered in the set was peripheral to an understanding of the Middle Ages, although the editors were flexible on this point. The final entry list was based on the following overlapping criteria: coverage in the *DMA*, interest to students, relevance to the curriculum, importance to the medieval period, representation of a broad cultural range, and representation of women and issues related to women. The result is a balanced, concise, curriculum-related list that includes focused articles addressing significant facets of medieval life in brief; half-page article profiles (e.g., *Beowulf, Medici Family,* and *Relics*); and more-extensive articles on broader, important topics (e.g., *Agriculture, Feudalism,* and *Islamic Art and Architecture*). Many of these longer articles are subdivided into easy-to-understand units. *Schools,* for example, is split into six subtopics (*cathedral, monastic, grammar, palace, Islamic,* and *Jewish*).

In addition to creating an appropriate entry list, the *DMA* text itself had to be significantly abridged and recast to convey the essential information to a younger audience. To accomplish this, a team of experienced writers with strong backgrounds in history was assembled to rewrite the articles using an easier vocabulary and generally shorter sentences.

To produce a reference work that appeals to today's students, a new page format was designed and color was added. The new format consists of a major column, in which the entries lie, and a minor column that enhances the visual appeal of the page. The minor column is a functional part of the page, holding many of the special features of the work—entry titles, brief definitions of important terms in the main text, small illustrations and captions, time lines, and interesting sidebars that expand the main text. Cross-references to related articles in *The Middle Ages* are provided within the text and at the end of most entries. The new format, it is hoped, will not only capture the reader's interest but also aid in increasing comprehension of the material.

More than 300 illustrations enhance the visual appeal of *The Middle Ages.* These include photographs of medieval art and architecture; maps showing trade routes, migration patterns, changing boundaries, and other geographically significant concepts; diagrams showing the layout of a feudal manor and the construction of castles and fortifications; and drawings of medieval clothing, armor, and heraldic insignia. Three sections of brilliant full-color plates illustrate topics of special importance—Daily Life, Art and Architecture, and People of the Middle Ages.

The Middle Ages is a period that continues to capture the imagination of young people and adults around the world. It is our hope that, as a serious but accessible reference work, *The Middle Ages* will allow youthful enthusiasts to follow up their initial interest and ground it in the best information scholars now have on medieval life.

A large number of people have played particularly important roles in bringing this project to completion. The president, Stanley Katz, and the board of directors of the American Council of Learned Societies, as well as Michael Holzman, who served as liaison between the ACLS and the editorial board, were always supportive. At Scribners, Karen Day and John Fitzpatrick were sympathetic and encouraging spirits from the beginning. At Visual Education Corporation, the project initially came under the direction of Robert Waterhouse. He and his successor in this role, Jewel Moulthrop, along with Anita Crandall, were instrumental in keeping everything on schedule—not always an easy or enviable task—and making sure that the final product was of the highest possible standard, intellectually and aesthetically.

At the earliest stage, when we were first sitting around the table mapping out the project, it was suggested that a member of our intended audience of students might look at some sample entries. Lorna Janice Jordan, then 12 years old, accepted the responsibility. She enjoyed the articles, made numerous suggestions, and encouraged us to complete the project. Heartfelt thanks to everyone who helped us fulfill her wish.

William Chester Jordan
Princeton, New Jersey

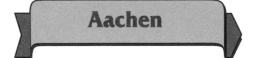

Aachen

Located in northwestern Germany, the city of Aachen, or Aix-la-Chapelle, is noted for its warm natural springs. It was the royal city of CHARLEMAGNE and of the German Holy Roman Emperors.

Before the Middle Ages began, Aachen was a Roman military settlement. In the 400s, the area was taken over by the FRANKS. Frankish power grew, and after Charlemagne became ruler of the Franks in 771, he made Aachen the capital of his kingdom. It was conveniently located for his war against the Saxons, and close to his family estates. He built a palace at the old Roman site. The palace included a great hall with living quarters and government chambers, a large warm bathhouse, and a chapel* that is still standing. In spite of later additions, the chapel's structure is unchanged.

During the first half of the 800s, the Frankish Empire expanded to include Saxony, and Aachen became an important center. It was the place where the emperors were crowned, and royal assemblies and religious meetings were held there. Charlemagne invited many scholars to Aachen, whose work led to a cultural rebirth known as the Carolingian renaissance. Charlemagne was buried in the palace chapel in 814.

Near the end of the 800s, the Carolingian Empire collapsed, and Aachen lost its importance. The dukes of Saxony replaced the Carolingians as rulers of Germany. But in 936, the Saxon ruler OTTO I decided to hold his coronation in the palace chapel at Aachen. By doing so, he hoped to link himself with the reputation of Charlemagne. Otto was later crowned at Aachen as Holy Roman Emperor. From then until the 1500s, nearly every Holy Roman Emperor was crowned at Aachen.

The memory of Charlemagne continued to play an important part in Aachen's history. Otto III, grandson of Otto I, had Charlemagne reburied in a splendid tomb; then he decided to be buried in the chapel himself. In 1165, Emperor FREDERICK I BARBAROSSA had Charlemagne canonized*, drawing pilgrims to the city. Aachen received royal protection, and its churches and monasteries were generously supported by the monarchs.

The citizens of Aachen included a community of merchants and artisans who ran a profitable trade between FLANDERS (the Belgian coast) and the Rhine valley. In the late Middle Ages, the influence of this group grew, and the city was granted increasing control over its government. A city council of elected merchants and citizens was formed.

Aachen continued to prosper in the 1300s and 1400s. The city walls were enlarged, an impressive city hall was built, and a Gothic choir was added to Charlemagne's chapel. There were occasional conflicts between the rich merchants who controlled the city council and the guilds* of craftsmen. Nevertheless, Aachen remained a wealthy imperial city throughout the Middle Ages. (*See also* **Carolingians; Germany.**)

Abbasids

The Abbasids were an Arab family descended from an uncle of the prophet MUHAMMAD. They ruled the Islamic Empire from 750 to 1258. At their peak, they governed an area stretching from central Asia to North Africa.

In the early 700s, the Abbasids joined other groups who were opposed to the UMAYYAD dynasty*. After waiting for the right opportunity, Abbasid armies took advantage of tribal rivalries in Persia (Iran) to gain greater

* **caliph** religious and political head of an Islamic state

* **orthodoxy** strict adherence to the established traditions and beliefs

* **succession** the transmission of authority on the death of one ruler to the next

See map in Fatimid Empire (vol. 2).

support, then defeated the Umayyads in Iraq and Syria. The head of the Abbasid family, Abu'l-Abbas, became the first caliph* of the Abbasid dynasty. All but one of the Umayyads were executed. The one who escaped fled to Spain, starting a new Umayyad dynasty there that ruled until 1031.

Abu'l-Abbas died in 754, and different people in the family struggled for power. The caliph's brother al-MANSUR emerged as the new leader. He made many changes. The caliphate, or government, had been based on special powers for a small Arab aristocracy. Al-Mansur expanded it and appointed new officials, including non-Arab Muslims, to his court. He also brought a Persian military force to his new capital of BAGHDAD. This formed the core of a well-disciplined army, which was at first loyal to the caliph.

The Early Abbasids. To lessen religious fighting and unify the empire, the early Abbasid caliphs stressed religious orthodoxy* and conformity. Conflicts still occurred, however, which eventually led to the dynasty's decline. One reason for the conflicts was the struggle for succession* among family members whenever a caliph died. These struggles led to divided loyalties in the army, as different generals tried to back the winner.

The situation was particularly severe after the reign of HARUN AL-RASHID, the fifth Abbasid caliph. Al-Rashid attempted to satisfy all his heirs when he died, but his plan failed. A long civil war followed, in which the victor was al-MA'MUN, al-Rashid's second son. Al-Ma'mun's rule brought a new element into Muslim politics: Turks from central Asia.

Al-Ma'mun and his successor, al-MU'TASIM, began to develop a new style of slave army. During the civil war, even the Persian troops had divided into rival armies, each supporting a different heir. They had been useless for keeping order in the Islamic Empire. During his reign as caliph, al-Ma'mun won victories against Turkish tribes east of the Aral Sea, and he brought their noted cavalry to Baghdad as slaves. Al-Mu'tasim, who succeeded his brother as caliph, began to wield them into a slave army that would be loyal to him alone. However, like the Persian troops before them, the Turkish army later began to operate out of self-interest rather than merely supporting the caliphs.

The building of the Great Mosque at Samarra began in 848. Covering more than ten acres, it is the largest mosque in the Islamic world. The detached circular minaret has a spiral ramp running counterclockwise to the top. The minaret has survived to the present day, but only the outer walls of the mosque remain standing.

Persian Splendor

The Abbasid court was heavily influenced by the traditions of Persian royalty. The old Persian capital was less than 18 miles from Baghdad, and Persia's kings had ruled one of the most powerful empires of the ancient world. When the Arabs brought Islam to Persia, they borrowed many aspects of Persian culture. One of the first new officials of the Abbasid court, and one of the most powerful, was the vizier, believed by many to have been based on a Persian dignitary. Persian architecture, art, and clothing also had a strong influence on the cosmopolitan style that developed in the Muslim world's great cities.

Decline of the Abbasids. After al-Mu'tasim, the Abbasid caliphs gradually became less influential in the Muslim world. They squandered tax revenues building a second magnificent capital at SAMARRA, less than 100 miles north of Baghdad. The decline in their wealth meant that power in the empire became divided among the caliph, the bureaucracy, and the Turkish generals.

The empire also declined. A series of revolts led to the creation of several independent, smaller states, especially in Arabia. In 969, the African FATIMID dynasty took over Egypt, gained control of Syria and the Arabian peninsula, and worked to undermine the Abbasids in Iraq. In 1055, the SELJUK Turks rescued the Abbasids, but from that time on the caliph was never able to regain full power. The Seljuks gave still more power to the military by creating the position of SULTAN, or military leader.

In 1258, the Mongols conquered Baghdad and executed the caliph, thus bringing the Abbasid dynasty to a dramatic end in its native region. One member of the family escaped to Egypt, however, and was recognized there as caliph. This Egyptian caliphate continued until 1517. But the Abbasids ruled Egypt in name only. Real control was in the hands of the MAMLUK sultans, a slave dynasty that became the military rulers of Egypt. With the Ottoman conquest of Egypt in 1517, the Abbasid caliphate was finally abolished. (*See also* **Mongol Empire; Ottoman Empire.**)

Abelard and Heloise

Peter Abelard
ca. 1079–ca. 1142
Philosopher, teacher,
and author

Heloise
ca. 1101–ca. 1164
Abbess

* **philosophy** study of ideas, including science

* **theology** study of the nature of God and of religious truth

* **Trinity** God as Father, Son, and Holy Ghost

* **oratory** chapel dedicated to prayer

Peter Abelard was born in BRITTANY, France. His father was a minor lord. Abelard studied philosophy* at Anjou and Paris. During his 20s and 30s, he taught philosophy in Paris and began to publish his first works on philosophy. He attracted many students because of his brilliant logic and wit, but he also made enemies because of his arrogance.

Around 1112, Abelard expanded his interests to include theology*. After a period of study at Laon, he returned to Paris and taught at the cathedral school at Notre Dame. During this time, Abelard became the tutor of Heloise, the niece of a church official at Notre Dame. Abelard was about 40 years old, and Heloise was 20. The couple fell passionately in love, Heloise had a child, and they were secretly married. Heloise's father, Fulbert, was outraged by the affair and the secrecy. He suspected that no marriage had actually taken place. In revenge, Fulbert hired two thugs, who attacked Abelard and castrated him.

Publicly humiliated, Abelard entered the Benedictine monastery at St. Denis and insisted that Heloise enter a nearby convent at Argenteuil. But Abelard found the rules of monastic life hard to bear, and he was permitted to leave and establish a school of theology. There he wrote a work about his view of the Trinity*, in which he attacked the ideas of his old teacher in Anjou. Because of this work, Abelard was charged with heresy, which means holding false beliefs. He was tried at the Council of Soissons in 1121 and found guilty. After a short time in prison, Abelard was released and returned to St. Denis.

Abelard left a year later to build an oratory* outside Paris. He called the oratory Le Paraclet (the Holy Spirit), and he established a convent

The love between Abelard and Heloise was depicted in this 14th-century manuscript of *Le Roman de la Rose*.

* **abbess** female head of an abbey or monastery. The male equivalent is an abbot.

* **ethics** study of morality and what makes actions good or evil

there as well. In 1129, Heloise joined the convent, where she became the abbess*. Abelard wrote many hymns for the nuns at Le Paraclet. His writings also include personal letters and sermons, some of which he dedicated to Heloise. During this time, he wrote an important work on ethics* as well.

Once again, Abelard's work had some influential critics, including the well-known Cistercian monk BERNARD OF CLAIRVAUX. When Abelard was brought before a church council, he was again condemned. His sentence was to join the Cluny monastery as a monk and to stop teaching. At Cluny, Abelard became ill and died.

Heloise was a notable person in her own right. She was respected by other scholars for her learning and was an excellent administrator. Under her leadership, the abbey at Le Paraclet grew and flourished, and new convents were established elsewhere. At her death, she was known as a pious and effective abbess and was honored by popes and other church officials.

According to tradition, Abelard and Heloise both died at the age of 63. Abelard was buried at Le Paraclet, and Heloise was later buried beside him. In 1817, they were reburied at Père Lachaise Cemetery in Paris. The love affair between Abelard and Heloise became a noted theme in European literature. It inspired a number of writers, including Petrarch, Alexander Pope, and Jean-Jacques Rousseau.

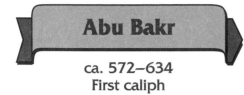

Abu Bakr

ca. 572–634
First caliph

* **hegira** celebrated emigration of Muhammad
from Mecca in 622, which marks the first year
of the Islamic calendar. It can also be spelled
hijra.

* **hajj** pilgrimage to Mecca that Muslims are
required to make once in their lifetime

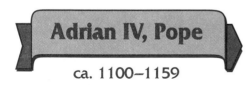

Adrian IV, Pope

ca. 1100–1159

* **abbot** male leader of a monastery or abbey.
The female equivalent is an abbess.

* **interdict** papal decree that forbids an entire
district from participation in the sacraments
and from Christian burial

See
color plate 10,
vol. 3.

Abu Bakr was an Arabian merchant from a leading Meccan tribe, the Quraysh. He was the most trusted adviser of the prophet MUHAMMAD. The two men became even closer when Muhammad married Abu Bakr's daughter A'ISHA in about 618.

Abu Bakr stayed with Muhammad through his years of persecution in Mecca and accompanied the Prophet on his hegira* to Medina in 622. There he helped Muhammad build a base of political support among the tribes in ARABIA. He planned Muhammad's military strategy and, at the Prophet's request, sometimes carried a banner and led the army into battle. In 631, Muhammad appointed Abu Bakr to lead the hajj* to Mecca. When Muhammad became ill, he told Abu Bakr to lead the group prayers in his place.

When Muhammad died in 632, there was a crisis over Islamic leadership because Muhammad had not named anyone to succeed him. Some Arabs suggested they should have two rulers, one from each of the two most important groups in the community. But Abu Bakr advised against this, saying it would weaken the community. In the end, Abu Bakr was elected caliph, the political leader of the Islamic world. His wisdom, loyalty to Islam, and ties to the Prophet earned him wide support.

Several Arab groups, however, tried to break free of Abu Bakr's rule from Medina. Abu Bakr concentrated on crushing this opposition. He swiftly subdued all the tribes in the Arabian peninsula. Abu Bakr then turned his attention north to the Euphrates region and Syria. In 634, with his forces battling the BYZANTINE EMPIRE, he fell ill. Remembering the crisis that had followed Muhammad's death, he chose UMAR I IBN AL-KHATTAB to succeed him as caliph. When Abu Bakr died, he was buried beside Muhammad in the mosque at Medina.

Abu Bakr's election as caliph held the Islamic community together at a critical moment. By uniting Arabia, he prepared the Muslims for their later conquests in the Middle East and North Africa. (*See also* **Caliphate; Islam, Conquests of.**)

Adrian IV, an Englishman, was born Nicholas Breakspear. He joined a community of priests near Avignon in France, where he rose to abbot*. During some local disputes, Breakspear was noticed as a strong leader by the pope's court in Rome. He was appointed CARDINAL bishop of Albano in 1149. One of his missions was to reorganize the church in Scandinavia.

When Pope Anastasius IV died in 1154, Breakspear was elected to succeed him. He took the name of Adrian IV. At the time, the citizens in Rome were fighting for independence. The new pope placed the city under an interdict* during Easter Holy Week. It was too much for the people to bear, and the revolution collapsed. The leader, named Arnold of Brescia, was hanged.

As pope, Adrian came into conflict with many political rulers. The king of Germany, FREDERICK I BARBAROSSA, had been in Rome to support the papacy during the revolution. Adrian crowned him as emperor of the Holy Roman Empire, but later they turned against each other. The pope

Adrian IV was a talented preacher and administrator. As cardinal bishop of Albano, he reorganized the church in Scandinavia. He was the only Englishman ever to serve as pope.

ADRIANO IIII. PONT. CLXXI. Del 1154.

also supported rebels in southern Italy against Sicily's King William I; however, in 1156 William and Adrian agreed to an alliance.

Toward the end of Adrian's rule, a struggle arose between the papacy and the Holy Roman Emperors over who had final power over the empire. Each side started to set up alliances with the other's enemies. In the midst of this conflict, Adrian died, but the conflict continued for many years after his death. Adrian is noted for his talent as an administrator, preacher, and singer, and as the only Englishman ever to serve as pope.

Agriculture

* **nomadic** wandering from place to place to find food and pasture

See color plate 12, vol. 1.

Farming to produce foods and clothing materials was central to the major cultures in the Middle Ages: the Byzantine world, the Islamic world, and western Europe. Some of the peoples of the medieval world had long traditions of agriculture. Others had formerly led nomadic* lives and began to farm as a result of contact with more settled cultures. Methods of agriculture developed, especially as Muslims and western Europeans worked to adapt farming to the lands they settled.

The Byzantine World

During the early years of the BYZANTINE EMPIRE (from 330 to about 700), Egypt and other parts of North Africa were the major sources of grain for the empire. By the 700s, however, these areas had been conquered by the

Arabs. In the 1000s, the agriculturally rich region of southern Italy was also lost to Byzantium. This restricted Byzantine agriculture in the later Middle Ages to ANATOLIA (Asia Minor) and the Balkan peninsula between the Adriatic and Black Seas (with Greece at its southern end).

These land areas consisted primarily of forested mountains and highlands. Large plains and meadows were rare, and many regions had stony ground. In coastal areas, the summers were hot and dry. Rainfall was seasonal, usually coming during the spring and fall planting periods. Some regions required irrigation. Others were swampy and needed to be drained to grow crops.

Despite the loss of their most fertile provinces, the Byzantines still managed to produce large amounts of agricultural products. In the 1100s, they were exporting grain, wine, and meat to Italy.

Principal Crops. Byzantine agriculture was characterized by a variety of crops. The most important were grain and grapes. In the Balkans, the principal grain crop was barley; in Anatolia it was wheat. Millet and oats were grown primarily as animal food. In addition to grapes, other fruits such as apples, peaches, pears, figs, cherries, and pomegranates were grown. Small garden crops included cabbages, onions, leeks, carrots, garlic, squashes, melons, and cucumbers. In some regions, olives, poultry, honey, and fish were important products.

The Byzantines also cultivated flax (used for making linen), cotton, and sesame. Silkworms were raised in southern Italy. Little is known of crop yields, but in some regions the mild climate and fertile soil made it possible to have two harvests in a year.

Animal grazing was also an important agricultural activity in the Byzantine world. Herds of sheep and cattle reached huge numbers in some areas. Since good pastureland was scarce, these herds often had to be taken to distant pastures each day. This was a job for young boys, who left at dawn and did not return until evening. Some herds were also moved from summer to winter pastures and back again.

Technology. The agricultural methods of the Byzantine world were similar to those of ancient Rome. In fact, the Byzantines often relied on ancient sources; in the 900s they compiled the *Geoponica,* a collection of old Roman agricultural writings. Byzantine farmers practiced two-field rotation*, meaning that they left fields unplanted in alternate years to preserve the soil and save its moisture.

Byzantine farmers employed a number of tools. One was the ard plow, a wheelless plow fitted with a simple iron blade. It was pulled by a pair of oxen. This type of plow was cheap to make, easy to use, and inexpensive to operate. It was ideal for use in semiarid* areas where the soil required light, frequent plowing. If a plot was small or too rocky to plow, farmers relied on a variety of spades and hoes.

During harvesting, workers typically cut the plants with a sickle*, leaving half of the stem in the soil so that it could be used as straw for fertilizer. After the harvest, animals were also allowed to graze in the fields and vineyards.

The harvest was threshed* by having oxen crush the sheaves under foot, or by making the animals drag a wooden board over the crop. The board was often embedded with pieces of iron. Then the grain was ground in mills. Throughout the Middle Ages, both hand- and animal-powered

* **rotation** using land differently each year so that the soil has a chance to recover its nutrients

* **semiarid** with little rainfall

* **sickle** large short-handled curved blade, sharp on the inner edge of the curve, designed to cut grain-bearing stems efficiently

* **thresh** to crush mature wheat or other grain plants so that the seeds or grain are separated from the stalks and the husks

Three-Field Rotation System
The farmers of northern Europe adopted a three-field system of rotation. Each year one field was planted with grain in the autumn for harvest in the spring, a second was planted with grains or legumes in the spring for harvest in the autumn, and a third was left fallow. The use of the fields was rotated each year.

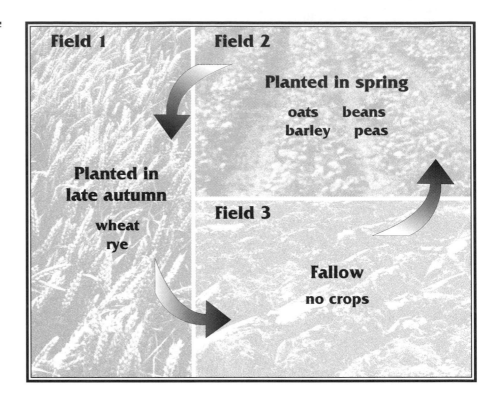

grain mills were used. But water mills were also used in some areas starting in the 600s, and in the late 1200s, windmills began to appear.

Byzantine agriculture was affected by a number of social factors. During the 600s, for example, a decrease in urban population reduced the constant demand for bread, which had been a problem up to that time. Most farm labor was carried out by free workers rather than by slaves. A typical farmer cultivated dozens of small parcels of land scattered around the community area.

Villages were not closely knit; the houses were spread over a wide area, and the people were independent and self-reliant. The only land that villagers commonly shared were the border zones between communities. Though villages were loosely organized, neighbors had many legal obligations to one another. These created links among the independent property owners and helped foster a sense of community feeling.

The Islamic World

In the medieval Islamic world, the two main aspects of agriculture—growing crops and raising animals—remained quite distinct. Farmers who grew crops kept few large animals. Herders raised few crops and relied mostly on natural pasturelands for feeding their animals. Two distinct ways of life developed in the Islamic world because of these two separate activities. Each had its own social and political systems, culture, and values. In some areas, the boundary between cropland and pastureland shifted back and forth. This was a result of changes in laws, leaders, population, technology, soil, and climate.

Overall, crop farming spread during the early centuries of Islam at the expense of herding. This was largely the result of policies that favored city life, settled agricultural communities, and private ownership of land.

Development of agricultural technology made crop farming more profitable. A rising rural population and the growth of large cities also increased the demand for crops.

legumes vegetables such as peas and beans that are rich in protein

Principal Crops. Muslims grew the traditional crops of the Mediterranean area, including wheat, grapes, olives, figs, millet, and legumes*. Arab conquests and trade during the Middle Ages also brought a number of new crops into the area. Some of the most important new crops were sorghum (a sweet food crop similar to corn); sugarcane; rice; citrus fruits such as oranges; bananas; watermelons; artichokes; spinach; and eggplants. Other crops were grown to make condiments such as mustard and pepper, medicines, dyes, and perfumes. Together they helped enrich the lives of the people in the Islamic region.

The cultivation of new crops helped nearby cities become more prosperous. As harvests increased, more food was available for urban markets. Some crops, such as sorghum, could grow in dry or less fertile areas. Others, such as sugarcane and rice, could grow in salty soil. As a result, croplands expanded, and grazing was pushed back onto more arid land.

Livestock. Islamic herders kept large flocks of sheep, goats, camels, horses, and cattle. Some of these animals were used for transportation, and they all produced meat, milk, wool, or hides. Herders used these products themselves and sold some to villagers and city dwellers. Wool and hides provided the raw materials for a large and growing textile industry within the Islamic world. These raw materials and the finished products of the textile industry were also exported to Europe.

The lives of herders were dominated by the need to compete for good pastureland. This problem was especially difficult in the dry summer season and in drought years. Often herders had to kill or sell many animals in the spring and move the remaining ones long distances to new grazing lands. In some regions, this problem was lessened by a tradition called *hima,* which encouraged tribes to share pasturelands.

But demand for animal products from the expanding population of city dwellers and farmers often led to excessive use of the pasturelands. Such overgrazing damaged the soil, allowing it to be eroded by wind and rain. This increased the pressure on herders and may have caused some to settle as crop farmers themselves.

Technology. Choice of tools and use of land in the Islamic world were influenced by the availability of water, the quality of soil, and climate. Most croplands in the region received little annual rainfall. Islamic farmers employed many tools similar to those used in the Byzantine Empire. They plowed with the ard plow. They threshed grain by driving oxen across a threshing ground called a *baydar,* often pulling a threshing board that was studded underneath with flint stones. Another tool used for threshing consisted of heavy beams fitted with toothed disks that were dragged over the crop by an ox. On smaller farms, grain was threshed by hand using wooden flails or sticks.

The ard plow is suited to a dry climate because it stirs the surface soil. This allows soil to absorb and retain as much water as possible. In addition to the ard plow, Islamic farmers used several other techniques to handle the semiarid conditions. Farmers left fields fallow* in some years. They

fallow unplanted, so that moisture and organic processes can replenish the soil's nutrients

Islamic farmers who grew crops kept a few large animals, which they used for plowing the fields. Herders, however, raised livestock for milk, meat, wool, and hides.

built terraces on hillsides to reduce the runoff of water. Most importantly, they developed the use of irrigation.

By the end of the 700s, new irrigation techniques were giving farmers different ways of capturing, storing, lifting, channeling, and spreading water. One important technology was the use of *qanats*. These were underground canals that captured groundwater and carried it long distances. Farmers also used water-powered or animal-powered wheels that could lift water in boxes, buckets, or pots. By the end of the 900s, most parts of the Islamic world had extensive irrigation systems.

Improved cultivation of land was also made possible by using the new crops as well as the old ones. Because farmers could choose from a broader range of crops, they could rotate crops more easily to suit the conditions. Islamic farmers grew crops in a great variety of soils, including soils that farmers in other areas might have considered infertile. As a result, the Muslims could cultivate more land.

Because heavy farming uses up important nutrients in the soil, Islamic farmers took steps to maintain the soil's productivity. They employed many different substances for fertilizer. Animal manure, blood, urine, olive oil sediment, dust, chalk, crushed bricks, broken tiles, and powdered bones, horns, and ivory were all used. Islamic farmers recognized that different crops used up different nutrients in the soil. The right choice of crop rotations was another way that they maintained productivity.

Despite the use of such measures, many agricultural lands were overfarmed by the 1000s. Egypt and parts of Muslim Spain remained productive, but much of the Islamic world experienced a slow decline.

Farms and Agricultural Labor. Traditionally, Islamic agriculture consisted of small farms operated by single families. These farms raised produce both for the family and for sale in urban markets. The size of farms could vary, however. In addition to small owner-operated farms, there were large estates. Labor for these estates was often provided by tenant farmers, who shared part of their harvest with the estate owner. Estate owners also hired farm laborers for wages.

During the centuries of agricultural decline caused by overuse of the land, the number of small farms decreased, and large estates became more common. In many places, tenant farmers became legally bound to landowners because of high taxes or rents. This further affected their agricultural productivity. Other factors also contributed to agricultural decline, including reduced security in rural areas, a shrinkage of the money economy, and a decline in trade.

Western Europe

Western Europe can be divided into two major agricultural regions—south and north. The differences between the two regions are the result of such natural factors as rainfall, soil, and terrain, as well as farming methods. Southwest Europe has dry, hot summers, light and sandy soils, and irregular, often mountainous terrain. In contrast, the north has considerable rainfall with frequent summer rains, rich heavy soils, and rolling plains.

Traditional crops and methods of agriculture in southwest Europe were based on practices from the old Roman Empire. During the Middle Ages, many agricultural practices developed by the Arab world were adopted in the area. This resulted in rich sources of food for the south's numerous villages and cities.

Agriculture was at first less productive in the north. This was partly because many of the crops introduced there could not grow well in its different climate and soils. During the Middle Ages, new methods of food production developed that were more suited to the region's environment. The process was so successful that the center of European prosperity eventually shifted from southern Europe to the north.

Principal Crops and Animals.   Throughout western Europe, the main crops were grains, such as wheat, barley, rye, and oats; various legumes; and some fruits. Because of its milder climate, the south also grew olives and various crops introduced by the Arabs, such as sugarcane, rice, citrus fruits, bananas, watermelon, artichokes, and eggplants. Southern Europeans did not eat a lot of meat, relying more on cereals, olive oil, and small amounts of cheese. By contrast, the people of northern Europe ate considerable quantities of meat, butter, and cheese.

Farmers throughout Europe kept livestock. Some of the animals were used as food. Certain animals were used as sources of milk, eggs, cheese, wool, and other products. Others were used as draft animals to pull plows or wagons. Southern Europeans had sheep, goats, oxen, cattle, horses, pigs, geese, and chickens. Fishing and beekeeping were also important in some areas. Northern Europeans had similar livestock, although there were fewer sheep and goats and more horses and cattle. In some heavily forested parts of northern Europe, there was also abundant wildlife—such as deer, bear, and rabbits—that could be hunted for food.

Technology.   Variations of soil, climate, and tradition between the south and the north resulted in the development of different combinations of farm customs and implements as well as crops.

Islamic influence in southwest Europe gave the agriculture of that region a number of distinctive characteristics, at first in Muslim Spain and then in northern Spain, southern France, and Italy. Techniques such as irrigation and the terracing of fields required many agricultural workers. This led to a pattern of densely populated towns surrounded by irrigated garden plots. Beyond the towns were sparsely populated areas devoted to dry farming* and grazing. In fact, the contrast between intensive irrigation near towns and dry farming practices in between became even more pronounced than in the Islamic world.

Other features of southern agriculture included the use of many types of soil and the ability to grow a great variety of crops. As in the Arab world, farmers of southwest Europe improved the fertility of different soils with different types of fertilizers. Many of the crops, including the hard durum wheat used for pasta, had also been introduced by the Arabs. Some crops, such as rice, could be grown only with irrigation.

In some parts of southwest Europe, Islamic techniques of agriculture spread slowly. There are several possible reasons for this. Peasants may have lacked the skills for new crops that were difficult to grow. Another factor may have been a lower population density. This made it more difficult to develop irrigation systems and other techniques that required many workers.

As in the Byzantine Empire and the Arab world, the soil in southwest Europe was light, well suited to the ard plow. In the north, however, most

Remember: Consult the index at the end of Volume 4 to find more information on many topics.

* **dry farming** farming that relies on natural moisture only and does not use irrigation

soils were moist, thick, and heavy. The ard-type plow was not strong enough to work these types of soils. What was needed was a larger, heavier plow that could cut deep into the earth and turn up lower layers of dirt, helping to drain away excess moisture. It is not known exactly when this type of plow was developed. But the transition from the ard plow to the wheeled, heavy plow seems to have taken place in some regions between 600 and 900.

The heavy plow placed new demands on farmers in northwest Europe. It was more difficult to maneuver than the ard plow, and this caused the shape of fields to change. With an ard plow, fields could be cross-plowed, or plowed with short furrows perpendicular to one another. Small, square fields were, therefore, common in the south. But a heavy plow pulled by a large team of oxen was difficult to turn. It was easier to plow long, straight furrows instead of short, crossed ones. For this reason, the most efficient shape for a field that was to be worked with a heavy plow was a long, rectangular strip. As a result, long strip fields became common in many parts of the European north.

The heavy plow also brought other changes. It was more expensive to operate than the ard plow, requiring costly wheels and iron parts and often a large team of oxen to pull it. This made cooperation among many people important—farmers had to share the costs and the tasks for plowing. In addition, cooperation was needed because European farmers practiced mixed farming*. Fences were vital to keep animals from damaging crops. Small, square plots of land were quite easy to fence, and farmers in southwest Europe could do this by themselves. With long strip fields, however, it was easier to fence in large areas of a village's arable* land than to fence the individual strip-shaped plots.

Cooperation was also important in northern villages because of the need to decide which areas should be planted, what crops should be used, and when fields should be left fallow. Community meetings to discuss these types of questions helped start a strong tradition of rural democracy in northwest Europe.

Crop Rotation. European farmers recognized the importance of rotating crops so that the soil nutrients would not be depleted. In northern Europe, farmers gradually adopted a three-field system of rotation instead of the traditional two-field method. With this system, rural villages divided their arable land into three large fields. Each year one field was left fallow, a second was planted with grain in autumn for harvest in the spring or summer, and a third was planted with grains or legumes in the spring for harvest in autumn. The use of the three fields would be rotated each year for three years.

This three-field system seems to have begun sometime in the 700s. It was possible only in areas with rich soils and enough summer rains. This ruled out most of southern Europe, which had dry, hot summers. As a result, most farmers in southern Europe used a two-year rotation of crops.

The three-field system had several advantages. First, the increased production of legumes helped improve the fertility of the soil and also provided a better diet. Second, having two seasons of planting and harvesting each year reduced the risk of famine, since it was unlikely that both crops would fail. Third, the cycle of planting distributed the labor of plowing more evenly over the year. This kept farmers, plow animals, and costly

* **mixed farming** raising both animals and crops on a single farm

* **arable** suitable for plowing and producing crops

Sowing and Reaping

For farmers who grow grain, the hardest tasks are sowing the seed and reaping, or gathering, the grain. Even before modern machines, each task needed special tools. The plow was the main device used to prepare for sowing. It loosened the soil so the scattered seeds would take root. Farmers used sickles and threshing tools for harvesting, gathering the ears and separating the grain from the rest of the plant. The final step was milling, or grinding the grain into flour. During the Middle Ages, the technology for all these tasks advanced.

plows from standing idle for a long period, thus benefiting the landowners. It also gave peasant farmers a larger surplus of products after they paid their dues to the lords of the manors. Another advantage of the three-field system was that it meant farmers could cultivate more land each year with the same amount of labor.

The three-field system also increased the supply of oats (the best food for horses). This was important because it enabled farmers to use horses rather than oxen for pulling plows and wagons. A horse was more expensive to keep than an ox, but it could work longer and move faster, especially after the development of a new type of horse collar. Horses allowed peasants to cultivate more land, thus increasing harvests and the food supply. The main shift from oxen to horses occurred in the 1000s and 1100s in northern Europe. In some less fertile parts of the region, however, the benefit of plow horses was not worth their added expense, and farmers continued to use oxen until well after the Middle Ages ended.

Even by the 700s, the three-field system was spreading rapidly throughout much of northern Europe. It allowed greater production of food, encouraging increases in population. Those increases, in turn, helped stimulate the adoption of more efficient agricultural methods. One of these was the use of the jointed flail for threshing. Instead of the single flail used in the Arab world, farmers used two rods joined by a leather thong. This permitted an efficient, circular motion.

A setback in agricultural development occurred in much of northern Europe during the 800s as a result of invasions from outside the region, mainly by VIKINGS from the north and by SLAVS from the east. Thousands of villages were burned, plow animals were killed, and countless peasants died. But after these invasions stopped, population increase and agricultural change continued.

By the early 1300s, there was very little new land to be farmed. Population began to exceed the food supply, and the standard of living of peasants declined. At about the same time, changes in climate caused floods and drought, which led to great famines. In addition, the BLACK DEATH wiped out as much as 30 percent of Europe's total population between 1347 and 1350. This and other catastrophes lowered the population in 1400 to about half of what it had been in 1347. Thousands of villages stood abandoned, and there was a scarcity of labor. Northern European agriculture did not recover until after the Middle Ages were over.

A'isha

ca. 614–678
Third wife of the prophet Muhammad

* **harem** place where the wives of a Muslim leader lived

Born in Mecca, A'isha was the daughter of ABU BAKR, one of MUHAMMAD's earliest and most trusted followers. She was married to Muhammad when she was about six years old. The marriage was arranged to strengthen social and political ties between Muhammad and her father. A'isha grew into an intelligent and determined woman. These qualities, along with her devotion to Muhammad, made her his favorite wife.

When Muhammad moved to Medina in 622, A'isha was less than ten. She lived beside the main mosque in an apartment next to Muhammad's quarters, spending most of her time with her family and Muhammad's other wives. Relations within the harem* were generally quite good, but there were rivalries. These often resulted from political arguments between the different wives' families.

A'isha's position as Muhammad's favorite wife was threatened only once, when she was accused of being unfaithful. Her rivals and Muhammad's political opponents encouraged the gossip, and even the Prophet's son-in-law, ALI IBN ABI TALIB, hinted that she might be guilty. This made her bitter against Ali. For a while, Muhammad acted coldly toward A'isha, but she was cleared of the charge. When Muhammad became ill in 632, he asked to be taken to A'isha, and he died in her arms. In accordance with Arabian custom, his body was buried beneath the floor of A'isha's chamber.

After Muhammad's death, A'isha continued living at the mosque with the other wives. They were all forbidden to remarry, but they held high status in the Muslim community. They were called "mothers of the believers," and they received a pension until death. When her father died in 634, A'isha took over her own affairs and supervised her family's interests.

* **caliph** religious and political head of an Islamic state

In 656, when Ali ibn Abi Talib had become caliph*, A'isha joined a rebellion against him. Ali defeated his opponents at the Battle of the Camel, so called because the camel A'isha rode became the focus of the fighting. Ali treated A'isha graciously and persuaded her to return to Medina and to end her participation in politics. For the rest of her life, she remained an influential person, eagerly sought out for personal, religious, and political advice. A'isha died at Medina in July 678. She is remembered in Arabic literature for her eloquence and for the many hadith* that she is said to have preserved.

* **hadith** collected traditions of the words and deeds of Muhammad

Alamanni

* **Frankish** referring to the Germanic tribe called the Franks, who dominated western Europe in the early Middle Ages

The Alamanni were a group of German-speaking tribes. They were one of the roving peoples that had been pressuring the Roman Empire for land in western Europe. In 500, they were settling along the upper part of the Rhine and were pushing west into France. At that time, France was dominated by King CLOVIS, an early Frankish* ruler from the MEROVINGIAN family. Clovis defeated the Alamanni at a battle at Bonn in southwestern Germany, and most of the Alamanni came under Frankish rule.

Under the Franks, the Alamanni settled in southern Germany and northern Switzerland. At first, they cooperated with the Frankish kings. In 554, two leaders of the Alamanni joined with Franks and Goths to fight Byzantine* forces in Italy.

* **Byzantine** referring to the Eastern Christian Empire that was based in Constantinople

* **pagan** word used by Christians to mean non-Christian and believing in several gods

Clovis and the Franks became Christian, and their language was greatly influenced by Latin. But the Alamanni remained largely pagan* until the late 500s, when the Irish missionary St. COLUMBANUS was exiled from Frankish lands by Merovingian queen Brunhilda. Columbanus came and preached to the Alamanni, and they began to embrace the Christian faith.

The Alamanni became separate from the Frankish kingdom again when the CAROLINGIAN Franks began to take over power from the Merovingian dynasty* soon after 687. The Carolingians reconquered the Alamanni, but the Alamanni remained rebellious. They clung to

* **dynasty** succession of rulers from the same family or group

See map in Migrations, Germanic (vol. 3).

their ancestral Germanic language, and the region where they settled, Swabia, later became part of the kingdom of Germany. (*See also* **Migrations, Germanic.**)

Albertus Magnus

ca. 1200–1280
Philosopher, theologian, and bishop

* **friar** member of a religious brotherhood of the later Middle Ages who worked in the community and relied on the charity of others for his livelihood

* **theology** study of the nature of God and of religious truth

* **priory** small monastery or convent headed by a prior or prioress

Albert, born in southern Germany, was considered the leading scholar of his day. As a young man, he studied at the University of Padua, Italy. In his early 20s, he became a Dominican friar* and for 15 years taught theology* at several places in Germany. Then in 1241, he was sent to the University of Paris to study further. There he became interested in ARISTOTLE, the ancient Greek philosopher, and he began lecturing and writing on philosophy and religion. In Paris, Thomas AQUINAS was one of Albert's students. Aquinas became one of the leading philosophers and theologians of the Middle Ages.

In 1248, Albert went to Cologne, Germany, to establish a Dominican center of learning. There he began the major work of his life, an interpretation of Aristotle's philosophy. His aim was to make the ideas of Aristotle acceptable to Christian scholars. The project took more than 20 years.

Albert was later elected religious superior over the province of Teutonia in Germany. The priories* of his district were spread across great distances, but he visited all of them, always traveling on foot. As bishop of Regensburg in 1260, he continued to travel on foot and became known as "Boots the Bishop." Three years later, Pope Urban IV gave Albert a special commission: he was to urge people in German-speaking lands to join a new crusade. But Pope Urban died the next year, and the crusade was called off.

Albert died in 1280 and was buried in Cologne. He was declared a saint in 1931. Because he was held in such esteem as a scholar, Albert was known in his lifetime by the name Albertus Magnus, which means Albert the Great. (*See also* **Friars; Scholasticism.**)

Albigensians

See *Cathars.*

Alchemy

* **artisans** skilled craftspeople

Alchemists were the chemists of the Middle Ages. One of their main goals was to create gold and silver from less precious metals such as copper and lead. This was called transmutation. In addition to chemistry, their work related to such fields as pharmacy, medicine, geology, and physics. However, alchemy was quite different from modern science. Alchemists often believed they would succeed in their experiments only if they themselves were spiritually pure.

The theories of alchemy probably grew from the ideas of artisans* in the ancient world as they tried to imitate precious metals and stones and rare dyes. These ideas were refined by Greek and Byzantine philosophers, who examined natural substances and processes from their understanding of mathematics and human thought. Medieval alchemists often wrote

Medieval alchemists often recorded their work in secret codes and signed their work using the names of scholars of ancient times. Although their theories were later disproved, alchemists developed some of the basic techniques and apparatus of chemistry.

* **sublimation** using heat to make a dry substance evaporate without becoming a liquid first. The word means the same in modern chemistry.

* **distillation** extracting a pure substance from a mixture

* **elixir** powerful substance with magical properties, such as the ability to change metals into gold or to prolong life

their work using the names of scholars of ancient times, and some wrote in codes to keep their work secret, out of the hands of unqualified people.

Byzantine alchemy reached its peak just before 400 with the work of Zosimus of Panopolis. Zosimus worked on sublimation* and distillation*. His theory used Christian beliefs: changes in matter were related to sacrifice, death, resurrection, and salvation. After Zosimus, Byzantine alchemy was mostly theoretical, explaining processes through Greek and Christian ideas.

Islamic Alchemy.   Beginning in the 700s, knowledge of alchemy spread to the Arabic world through translations of Greek texts. The first important Muslim theories that we know of were those of Jabir ibn Hayyan, an alchemist from Baghdad in the early 800s. Jabir's works discuss the composition of metals and how to use distillation to create elixirs*.

Other notable Islamic writers on alchemy include, one century later, the physician al-RAZI, who stressed practical science and experiments in his works on alchemy. At the start of the 1000s, the renowned philosopher IBN SINA said that metals would never be transmuted until they were broken down to a prime matter, a matter more basic than the elements then believed in.

European Alchemy.   Beginning in the 1200s, translations of Arabic texts on alchemy spread to the West. European scholars conducted new experiments based on what they read. In the mid-1200s, both ALBERTUS MAGNUS and Roger BACON wrote important works on alchemy. Albert examined alchemical techniques and discussed the properties of metals. Bacon divided alchemy into two branches: theories about the world and experiments to test the theories.

From about 1300, in Europe as in the Islamic world, alchemy came under attack. The idea of producing gold raised concerns about counterfeiting. The pope condemned the spiritual ideas of alchemy, and

Alchemy in Action

Here is a Byzantine alchemist's technique for purifying silver: "Take a part of silver and an equal part of lead; place in a furnace and keep melting until the lead has been consumed; repeat the operation several times until it becomes brilliant." This description comes from a text called the *Leyden Papyrus*, which includes several such recipes.

certain religious orders were forbidden from studying it. Alchemists' writings from this period often defended alchemy by arguing for its status as a science.

In the next century, alchemy became less experimental and more symbolic. Christian symbolism again became common in the texts on alchemy. Alchemy also appeared as the subject of poetry, which dwelt upon the spiritual and mystical aspects of the alchemists' work.

Theory and Technique.   Alchemists studied the properties of metals and chemical substances. They believed that all matter consisted of four basic elements—fire, air, earth, and water—in different combinations.

Most metals were considered imperfect. If they could be perfected, they would become gold, which had the ideal balance of the four elements. Many alchemists believed they would succeed in transmutation if they could find an elixir that they called the philosopher's stone. In addition to sublimation and distillation, their methods included dissolving, powdering, evaporating, and other processes that change the state of a substance.

Because it involved experiments with matter, alchemy contributed knowledge and techniques to the development of modern scientific research. Its theories, though later abandoned, were an important part of a philosophical tradition that helped to shape modern science.

Alcuin of York

ca. 730–804
Educator and theologian

See color plate 8, vol. 3.

* **liturgy** form of a religious service, particularly the words spoken or sung

* **abbot** male leader of a monastery or abbey. The female equivalent is an abbess.

* **scriptorium** workshop in which books were written or copied, decorated, and bound

Alcuin was born in Northumbria, England. He studied at the cathedral school of York, which was the leading center of religious and classical studies in the Christian world at that time. Alcuin became a teacher at the school and had many noted students. He also loved books and traveled through Europe to collect them. On one of his journeys, he met the emperor CHARLEMAGNE.

In 778, Alcuin was promoted to be headmaster of the cathedral school. But soon after, Charlemagne invited him to head the imperial palace school at AACHEN. Alcuin accepted the offer and introduced the program of education that was used at York. This program was a blend of religion and the seven classical liberal arts: grammar, rhetoric (the study of speech and composition), logic, arithmetic, geometry, astronomy, and music.

Under Alcuin's guidance, the palace school attracted important visiting scholars. Charlemagne himself, the queen, and their family studied there. Besides teaching and supervising the school, Alcuin wrote textbooks and many letters. Under his supervision, the liturgy* used in the Frankish church was revised. Alcuin also defended Charlemagne's position in several religious debates in the late 700s.

In gratitude, Charlemagne made him abbot* of an abbey at Tours, in France. There Alcuin helped develop a scriptorium* that produced copies of the Bible. These became known as "Alcuin Bibles," and he sent one to Charlemagne as a personal gift. Alcuin died at Tours in 804, having composed his own epitaph: "Alcuin was my name and wisdom always my love."

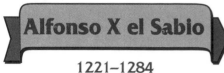

Alfonso X el Sabio

1221–1284
King of Castile and León

* **patron** person of wealth and influence who supports an artist, writer, or scholar

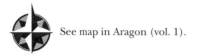

See map in Aragon (vol. 1).

Alfonso X was the son of Ferdinand III, the king of CASTILE and León in Spain. His mother, Beatrice, was the niece of Holy Roman Emperor Henry VI. When Ferdinand died in 1252, he left Alfonso the entire kingdom.

Alfonso was known as a patron* of the arts. During his reign, the royal court of Castile became an important cultural center, attracting educated Christians, Jews, and Muslims. Latin was the usual language for scholarly books, but Alfonso encouraged the use of Castilian, the Spanish dialect spoken at the court. Scholarly ideas thus became available to more people, and Castilian became a more extended and polished language—it was soon the standard for educated Spanish.

Alfonso's scholars produced a history of Spain and a world history from the Creation of the earth to the birth of Christ. They collected a code of the laws and customs of the different peoples of Castile, which became one of the foundations of later Spanish law. Important translations were made of Arabic works on astronomy and astrology, and Alfonso's astronomical tables were standard in Europe for centuries. Alfonso also welcomed TROUBADOURS to his court and collected an important book of their songs, *Songs to the Virgin Mary,* some of which he may have written himself.

In contrast to its cultural achievement, the reign of Alfonso X was a time of political upheaval. He continued the Christian campaign against the Muslims, helped by ARAGON's James the Conqueror, whose daughter he married. However, he had to deal with revolts in al-Andalus, the large territories in Spain that his father had won from the Muslims.

Alfonso was also involved in a crisis in Germany. After the death of the Holy Roman Emperor in 1254, *two* rulers were elected to succeed him. Alfonso was one of the choices, and for 20 years he tried to pursue his claim, but in 1273 the first HABSBURG monarch, Rudolf I, was finally elected king of Germany and leader of the empire.

The end of Alfonso's reign was marred by family conflict. He was undecided about who should succeed him to the throne. This created strife in his family as well as international problems with France and Aragon. Alfonso's son Sancho rebelled against his father and nephews, who also had claims to the throne. Alfonso died in the midst of this civil war. Despite the political turmoil during Alfonso's reign, however, the learning and art at his court were a bright spot in Spanish history. (*See also* **Holy Roman Empire.**)

Alfred the Great

849–899
Anglo-Saxon King

Alfred was the fifth son of Ethelwulf, king of Wessex, a kingdom in the south of ENGLAND. He did not learn to read until he was 12, but he was responsible for starting the English tradition of education. Though he is said to have suffered from many illnesses during his life, Alfred also played a key part in keeping Danish VIKINGS from overrunning all of England.

Each of Alfred's older brothers ruled Wessex during their lifetimes. After the death of his brother Ethelred in 871, Alfred became king. During most of Alfred's reign, his kingdom was at war with the Danes, who had captured a large part of the north of England. In fact, the year that he

See map in Vikings (vol. 4).

came to power there were nine major battles as well as numerous minor raids. The Vikings won most of these battles and captured LONDON from the neighboring kingdom of Mercia. This allowed them to sail up the Thames River and harass Wessex.

In 878, Alfred organized a large army and defeated the Danish king Guthrum. Eight years later, Alfred's forces helped to recapture London, and the fighting stopped for a time. Alfred made an important treaty with Guthrum, which established rights for Anglo-Saxons in Danish territory and granted rights to Danes in Anglo-Saxon territory. The Vikings resumed their raids in the 890s under different leaders, but Alfred began constructing forts in the countryside and ordered larger, faster ships built. With these new defenses, he trapped the Danish fleet up the Thames and again drove the invaders from his kingdom.

Alfred became an accomplished scholar. Although he did not study Latin until his late 30s, a few years later he began translating important Latin works into English. His translations included writings of St. AUGUSTINE, Pope GREGORY I THE GREAT, and the historian BEDE. Alfred saw that making more books available in English would encourage wider literacy.

Alfred is known as "Alfred the Great" because his military victories protected England from falling under foreign rule, and his learning improved the education of his people, introducing them to Latin culture. (*See also* **Anglo-Saxons; England; English Language and Literature.**)

Alhambra

See map in Islam, Conquests of (vol. 3).

* **Qur'an** book of the holy scriptures of Islam

* **aqueduct** channel, often including bridges and tunnels, that brings water from a distant source to where it is needed

The Alhambra is an Islamic palace in southern Spain. It is considered a masterpiece of medieval Islamic art and architecture. Located on a high plateau in the city of Granada, its name comes from an Arabic phrase meaning "the red castle." This describes the color of its outer walls.

Built on the site of an older Muslim fort, the palace was started in the 1200s, well after the Christian kings of Spain had started recapturing Muslim territory to the north. The Alhambra includes three major sections: a citadel (or fortress), a palace complex, and a private residential section for the sultan and his wives. There are also many private and public buildings there, set amid extensive and beautiful gardens and parks.

Several major buildings in the Alhambra are especially noteworthy. The Court of the Myrtles is a huge marble courtyard with a pool in the center and stone columns of alabaster and jasper along the sides. The Court of the Lions has a central fountain supported by 12 marble lions. An arcade of 124 slender columns gives the court a delicate beauty. The ceiling of the Hall of the Ambassadors (the throne room) is decorated with crowns, circles, and stars like those mentioned in the Qur'an* in descriptions of the heavens. The Hall of the Two Sisters is crowned with an intricate dome that appears to be in motion and suggests the revolving heavens.

Water, brought in by an aqueduct* from a river nearby, appears in many parts of the Alhambra. There are canals, pools, and fountains. The architecture emphasizes contrast and variety. For example, the plain outer surface contrasts with the rich interior decorations, and heavy roofs are supported by seemingly delicate walls and columns. The interiors are

The Alhambra served as a palace for the Muslim rulers in Granada. The Court of the Lions is named for the central fountain, which has an alabaster basin supported by 12 marble lions. The lions spout water into a canal that leads to other chambers of the palace.

decorated with a wealth of Islamic ornaments, such as geometric patterns, floral decorations, and Arabic inscriptions. Washington Irving, the American author of the early 1800s, was impressed by the palace. He wrote a book of short stories called *Tales of the Alhambra*. (*See also* **Granada; Islamic Art and Architecture; Spain, Muslim Kingdoms of.**)

Ali ibn Abi Talib

ca. 600–661
Fourth caliph and first
Shi'ite imam

* **caliph** religious and political head of an Islamic state

* **Qur'an** book of the holy scriptures of Islam

Ali ibn Abi Talib was a cousin and son-in-law of the prophet Muhammad. He is viewed by Shi'ite Muslims as their first IMAM, or religious leader.

Born in Mecca, Ali grew up in Muhammad's house and at the age of 11 became one of the Prophet's first followers. According to tradition, Ali slept in Muhammad's bed on the night the Prophet fled to Medina. This helped to trick and delay enemies who sought to murder Muhammad. Ali later joined the Prophet in Medina and was one of his most trusted soldiers. Muhammad honored him as a member of his household, calling him "free from every impurity." Ali married Muhammad's daughter Fatima.

After Muhammad died, Ali withdrew from military life. Though he often disagreed with the first two caliphs*, he supported them. However, his relations with Uthman, the third caliph, were very bad and grew worse. Ali and others accused Uthman of disobeying the teachings of the Qur'an* and Islamic tradition. They called on Uthman to step down as caliph.

Uthman was assassinated by his political opponents in 656, and Ali accepted their invitation to become caliph. However, he was unpopular with several powerful Muslim groups. One of these was Uthman's family, the

UMAYYADS, a wealthy clan in Mecca with strong trading connections. Uthman's cousin, MU'AWIYA ibn Abi Sufyan, had become governor of Syria. He refused to accept Ali as caliph and accused him of involvement in Uthman's death. As Mu'awiya prepared for war with Ali in Syria, Muhammad's widow A'ISHA and other opponents started another rebellion against him in Iraq.

Ali's success against the rebellions was mixed. He defeated A'isha at the Battle of the Camel, so called because A'isha rode on a camel in the fighting. But a fierce battle against Mu'awiya at SIFFIN, Iraq, in 657 had no winner. Both sides suffered heavy losses; then, to avoid defeat, Mu'awiya had his men raise copies of the Qur'an onto their spears. Many of Ali's soldiers saw this and dropped their weapons. They asked Ali to negotiate, and he agreed, leaving the battle's outcome to be settled later.

One group of Ali's supporters were angry at his willingness to negotiate. This group, known as the Kharijites, turned against Ali and called him an unbeliever. In 658, Ali fought a battle against this group, killing many of his former supporters. This added to his unpopularity.

The situation between Ali and Mu'awiya remained uncertain. Ali continued to receive support as caliph in some regions. But Mu'awiya took control of Egypt as well as Syria, and his supporters claimed *he* was the caliph. Then, in 660 or 661, Ali was wounded by a poisoned arrow while in a mosque. His attacker was a Kharijite seeking revenge for the killing of Kharijites by Ali's army in 658. Ali died a few days later, and Mu'awiya became sole leader of the Islamic state. This started the Umayyad dynasty* of caliphs.

In addition to being caliph and a noted soldier, Ali was a gifted orator, very knowledgeable about the Qur'an and about Islamic law. His followers, known as the Shi'ites*, stayed active as an opposition group to the Umayyads and later caliphs, and they became the main alternative sect of Islam. They remained loyal to Ali's children, regarding them as the true spiritual leaders of the Islamic religion. (*See also* **Qur'an.**)

* **dynasty** succession of rulers from the same family or group

* **Shi'ites** Muslims who believed that Muhammad chose Ali and his descendants as the rulers and spiritual leaders of the Islamic community

Allegory

An allegory is a type of symbolic story widely used in the Middle Ages. It resembles the literary device called metaphor, in which one word is used in place of another to suggest a likeness between them (such as "the evening of life" to mean "the end of life"). Allegories, however, are whole stories that can be enjoyed as stories but can also be read on another level. For example, a person's whole life might be described as a single day using the dawn, midday, and evening as symbols for different stages.

The basic principles of allegory were familiar to early Greek and Roman writers. Old FABLES such as The Hare and the Tortoise use this technique. Also, myths about the gods were often looked on as allegories. For example, the Greek goddess Athena usually stood for wisdom.

Medieval religious writers used allegorical stories to refer, on a deeper level, to the life of Christ, moral values, or the final judgment and the afterlife. In fact, many famous allegories can be read on all three of these levels, in addition to the story on the surface.

Bridge over Troubled Waters

The Middle Ages were a time when many bridges were built in Europe. Bridges also had a strong allegorical meaning. Pope Gregory I the Great told a story about a dreamer's vision of the bridge from this world to heaven. The bridge, like many small medieval bridges, was very narrow and had no railings. It crossed the dark and gloomy stream of Hell. As the dreamer crossed, he felt his foot slip, but good spirits came and rescued him. According to Gregory, this simple allegory tells how hard it is to reach heaven, and how one needs divine help to succeed.

A famous allegory often read in the Middle Ages was the *Psychomachia,* written in Latin by the Spanish poet Prudentius in about 400. Prudentius depicts human virtues and vices (such as Hope and Pride) as characters; he tells the story of a battle between them, which the virtues win.

The Consolation of Philosophy, by the Roman writer Boethius (ca. 480–524), is an allegory in which the narrator has a vision of a character called Philosophy and has a conversation with her. The narrator is in prison, and Philosophy comes to advise and teach him. Boethius was one of the first writers to present an allegory in dialogue form.

As the Middle Ages continued, many authors began to write in their local languages—for example, French, German, and Spanish—rather than in Latin. In addition to religion and philosophy, they also wrote allegories about romance.

The Romance of the Rose is an allegorical love poem in French, begun in the 1230s by Guillaume de Lorris and completed by Jean de Meun. It tells the story of a romance in the form of a dream, in which the beloved woman is symbolized by a vision of a rose. The poem became well-known, and many later writers adopted the dream vision form in their works.

Another common allegorical theme is a journey, in which the narrator learns from the characters and scenes he encounters. The finest example of this is *The Divine Comedy,* written in the 1300s by the Italian poet DANTE. Dante's narrator visits the places inhabited by the souls of the dead, from hell through paradise. The story of his journey is carefully woven together with moral and religious themes to create a complex and powerful poem.

Piers Plowman is an important allegory written in English in the 14th century by William Langland. It makes use of most of the popular allegorical devices and themes, such as a dream vision, a voyage, and a battle between virtues and vices, to tell a tale of spiritual discovery. (*See also* **French Language and Literature; Rhetoric; Roman de la Rose.**)

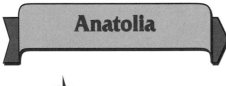

Anatolia

See map in Byzantine Empire (vol. 1).

* **Roman Empire** ancient Mediterranean empire of Rome that became the Byzantine Empire

* **Persian** referring to the ancient culture of Iran that continued to rival Greek civilization during the early Byzantine period

* **plague** disease that swept across the medieval world several times, including the Black Death in the mid-1300s

Anatolia, also known as Asia Minor, is now the western end of Turkey. It is a broad peninsula stretching toward the Aegean Sea. To its north is the Black Sea, to its south the Mediterranean. The importance of Anatolia was due largely to its strategic location on land and sea routes connecting Europe and Asia. During the earlier Middle Ages, it was one of the main territories of the BYZANTINE EMPIRE, important because of its closeness to Constantinople and because of its agricultural and mineral wealth. It was, however, open to attack from the east, across the Euphrates River.

In 500, Anatolia had many old Greek trading cities around its western shores. The interior region, part of ancient ARMENIA, had been within the Roman Empire* for 400 years, separated by the Euphrates from Persian* territory. Anatolia was ruled by civilian governors and had enjoyed more than five centuries of peace and prosperity.

This began to change in the 500s. The emperor JUSTINIAN I rebuilt defenses on the eastern frontier and constructed large churches and public works. High taxes to support these projects ruined many cities and districts. Military officials took control in some areas to try to restrain rural bandits. Also, the plague* struck several times, killing many people.

Then, in 611, Persians attacked Anatolia from the east. They captured, plundered, and destroyed cities and villages. The network of cities that had been the basis of Anatolian civilization became weaker. The Byzantines built many fortresses to protect their land, but the Persians were soon followed by the warlike Muslim Arabs from the southeast, who raided Anatolia for 200 years. Military districts called themes replaced the old civil provinces, and the ancient cities declined further.

The Byzantines regained much territory under the Macedonian dynasty* in the early 800s. There was a return to peace and limited prosperity; villages and monasteries grew and flourished. Then Turks began invading from the east, and a Turkish victory at the Battle of Manzikert in 1071 started a slow change from Byzantine Christianity to Turkish Islam.

After Manzikert, Anatolia was split into several states, as SELJUK and OTTOMAN Turks, Greeks, Christian crusaders from the west, and Mongols fought for power. But after 1337, the Ottomans gained control. By the middle 1400s, they ruled all of Anatolia. Their empire introduced a greater unity in the region, which became the center of the Turkish Empire. (*See also* **Plagues.**)

* **dynasty** succession of rulers from the same family or group

Angels

See color plate 15, vol. 2.

Angels are heavenly beings found in the Jewish, Christian, and Islamic traditions. They usually act as messengers between God and human beings—the word *Angelos* means messenger in Greek. Angels were important to thinkers in the Middle Ages, who devoted considerable study to them.

In the Old Testament (Jewish Scriptures), angels are the attendants and agents of God. The Angel of the Lord speaks to Jacob in a dream, and the angel Gabriel explains the meaning of Daniel's visions. In the New Testament (Christian Scriptures), angels are mentioned at many of the important moments of Christ's life; they comfort Christ in the wilderness and announce his birth and his Resurrection.

Angels also appear in the Qur'an (Islamic Scriptures), where they act as messengers and worship God. Angels throng around the throne of the Lord, and the angel Gabriel delivers God's inspiration to the prophets. However, in Islam, angels are seen as inferior to humans; they are ordered by God to fall down before humankind.

In the Scriptures, angels usually have no wings, but by the 800s they were described as youths with wings, sometimes with halos over their heads. An Islamic scholar in the 1100s wrote that all things are created by the sound of Gabriel's wings. In Europe, angels were often pictured in clothing of ancient style, with symbols of knowledge or power such as scrolls or staffs. Some angels, such as Gabriel and Michael, are mentioned by name and have individual personalities. Most of the angels are virtuous, but some fallen angels, including one known as Satan or Lucifer, rebel against God.

An important theory about angels was developed in the 500s by Pseudo-Dionysius the Areopagite, a writer based in Syria. His book, *The Celestial Hierarchy,* describes nine levels (or choirs) of angels grouped in sets of three, from the highest to the lowest, as follows: (1) seraphim,

Angels usually were depicted as the attendants of God or as messengers between God and humans. Fra Angelico's famous fresco, *The Annunciation,* painted in Italy in the mid-1400s, shows the angel Gabriel announcing to the Virgin Mary that she will be the mother of Jesus.

cherubim, thrones; (2) dominations, virtues, powers; and (3) principalities, archangels, angels. Only the archangels and angels have contact with human beings.

Later philosophers and theologians in the Middle Ages discussed the physical form of angels. In Islamic thought, they were beings of light. In western Europe, they were seen as spiritual beings who could take bodily form. The nature of that form was disputed, however. Thomas Aquinas argued that they assumed real fleshly bodies. But Duns Scotus wrote that the bodies were of a special type of matter that could take up no space—meaning that two angels could be in the same place at the same time.

Angevins

* **dynasty** succession of rulers from the same family or group

 See map in England (vol. 2).

The Angevins were two important family dynasties* that began in the French province of Anjou. The first Angevins came to power in the 900s and went on to control all of England and a large part of France. The second Angevins emerged in the 1200s and held territory in France, Italy, Sicily, and other places around the Mediterranean.

The early Angevins were involved in a long-term feud with the neighboring dukes of Normandy. The feud continued when the Normans took over the throne of England in 1066. Finally HENRY I, king of England and duke of Normandy, arranged a peace. In 1128, his daughter Matilda married the Angevin heir, Geoffrey Plantagenet. This united the ruling families of England and Anjou.

When Henry I died seven years later, Matilda expected to become queen of England. However, Henry's nephew Stephen de Blois seized the crown, and England entered a period of civil war. Matilda fought in England. Her husband, Geoffrey, now the count of Anjou, conquered Normandy, passing it on to their son Henry. When Stephen died in 1154,

Henry also became King HENRY II of England. He and his descendants were known as the Plantagenets. They held onto the English throne until RICHARD II, the last English Angevin, was deposed in 1399.

In France, the Angevins had lost most of their lands to the French king in the early 1200s. King Louis IX gave Anjou to his youngest brother, Charles. Charles founded the second great Angevin dynasty. He increased his holdings in France by marrying the daughter of the count of Provence, and he conquered SICILY and southern Italy by force in the 1260s. Charles also gained influence over Albania and Tunisia and in the Kingdom of Jerusalem. Charles was unable to hold on to all of this territory—he lost Sicily in 1282—but some of his descendants ruled Naples until 1435, and for a time others became kings of HUNGARY. The Angevin dynasty in France died out in the 1480s, and their lands were taken over by the French king. (*See also* **England; France; William I of England, the Conqueror.**)

Anglo-Saxons

* **Celts** ancient inhabitants of Europe and the British Isles

Anglo-Saxons are the people on whose language modern English is based. They began to settle in the British Isles during the 400s. For three centuries before that time, England had been part of the Roman Empire, and most of its inhabitants were Celts*, who had converted to Christianity. Roman rule weakened in the 400s, however, and the invasion began.

Anglo-Saxons were a group of Germanic peoples living in coastal areas of Denmark and Germany. The earliest to come to England may have been troops invited by the Romans to help defend the region. The settlers came from two main tribes, the Saxons and the Angles. They were joined by the Jutes from Denmark and the Frisians from islands in the North Sea.

The Anglo-Saxon settlers formed farming communities in the eastern part of Britain. They worshiped Germanic gods, such as Woden and Thor, and their rulers were tribal kings supported by bands of fiercely loyal warriors. The arrival of these pagan* invaders drove the Celtic Christian population into Wales and the west of Britain.

* **pagan** word used by Christians to mean non-Christian and believing in several gods

There are almost no records of the Anglo-Saxons as they arrived. But in 597, when a monk named Augustine was sent to England by Pope GREGORY I THE GREAT, he found that much of England was no longer Christian. There were still some Celtic kingdoms in the far west and north, but the east was solidly Anglo-Saxon. St. Augustine established his church at Canterbury in the southeast and began to convert the Anglo-Saxons to Christianity. (*See also* **England.**)

Anointing

Anointing means applying olive oil in sacred rites that dedicate a person to the service of God. In the Middle Ages, anointing was part of the ceremony to ordain church leaders such as priests and bishops. The oil was usually applied to the person's head. It was blessed on Holy Thursday celebrating Jesus' Last Supper, and it was often kept in a sacred vessel. For the holiest rites, it was mixed with balsam.

Kings were anointed by priests in ancient Hebrew times, and this practice was revived by Christian bishops in the 600s. Early Anglo-Saxon

* **coronation** ceremony during which a leader, king, or queen is crowned

coronation* rites also included an anointing ceremony. This practice indicated that the ruler was chosen by God to rule over the people.

In the middle 700s, anointing was used to crown Pepin, the first Carolingian king of the Franks. It became a part of crowning Holy Roman Emperors in 816. Because anointing was used both for ordaining clerics and for crowning kings, kings soon came to be seen as having both political and religious authority. By the 1200s, it was an accepted part of coronations in the kingdoms of Spain, as well as in France and England.

Coronations in France and England used special sacred oils. In France, the oil was poured from a sacred vessel said to have been sent from heaven for the baptism of King CLOVIS in the early 500s. For English kings after Henry IV, a special oil was used that had supposedly been given to the martyred archbishop Thomas BECKET by the Virgin Mary. These oils were believed to grant miraculous powers. (*See also* **Kingship, Theories of.**)

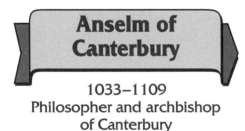

Anselm of Canterbury

1033–1109
Philosopher and archbishop of Canterbury

* **abbey** monastery under the rule of an abbot or abbess

* **prior** second most important monk in an abbey (after the abbot); leader of a priory or small monastery

* **archbishop** head bishop in a region or nation

* **saint** Christian who is officially recognized as a holy person by the church

Anselm was born into a noble family in Aosta, northern Italy. In his 20s, he became a monk, studying with a teacher named Lanfranc at a Benedictine abbey* in Normandy, France.

Anselm was made prior* and then abbot of the abbey. During this time, he wrote some of his major philosophical works, including the *Proslogion*. In the *Proslogion*, he argued that God's existence could be proved by the idea that there must be a being "than which a greater cannot be thought."

While Anselm remained in Normandy, his teacher Lanfranc became archbishop* of Canterbury, England. Lanfranc died in 1089, but King William II of England, who often did not agree with the church, chose not to replace him. However, William fell gravely ill, and he was finally persuaded to name Anselm as archbishop. Anselm was surprised by this offer and reluctant to accept it, but the English bishops pressed the archbishop's staff into his clenched fist.

As archbishop, Anselm had many disagreements with William and his son HENRY I, especially about kings' right to choose bishops and abbots. At the same time, Anselm continued his scholarly writing, including his great work *Cur Deus homo* (Why God Became a Man), which discusses some central questions about the nature of God. Anselm is considered one of the great philosophers of the Middle Ages. Thomas BECKET, a later archbishop of Canterbury, arranged for Anselm to be made a saint*.

Anti-Semitism

Anti-Semitism describes the harmful belief that Jews are an evil people who threaten society and Christianity. The word was first used in the 1800s. But attitudes similar to anti-Semitism have existed for much longer and were common in the Middle Ages.

The first Christians were Jews who believed that Jesus was a holy leader predicted by earlier Jewish prophecies. These Christians felt that they upheld the true faith, while the ruling Jewish authorities had distorted it. When Christianity spread to other peoples and became a separate religion, these beliefs and feelings remained.

 See map in Crusades (vol. 2).

* **crusader** person who participated in the holy wars against the Muslims during the Middle Ages

* **banish** to force a person to leave the country

By the Middle Ages, many Jews had traveled far from Palestine into other communities. The belief that Jews had rejected the true faith, coupled with suspicion of them as an alien people, became the basis for violent anti-Jewish feelings. These feelings were especially prevalent when economic life was difficult.

Medieval anti-Semitism was strongest in northern Europe, which had been converted to Christianity later than the Mediterranean area. Northern Europe also had less contact with people from non-Christian cultures because they were far from the busy trading routes of the south. Jews were invited to come to northern Europe to live and work in the growing cities. But from the start, efforts were made to limit their religious freedom.

When the First Crusade passed through the Rhineland in 1096, many of the crusaders* attacked the Jews who had recently moved there. The crusaders, on their way to drive the Muslims from Jerusalem, said the Jews either had to convert to Christianity or they would be killed. Many were massacred, and others killed themselves and their families to avoid conversion.

Though official church doctrine protected Jews and their religion, it was still widely believed that Jews were the enemies of Christianity. The belief also developed in the 1100s that Jews mutilated and killed young Christian children and poisoned wells. When the BLACK DEATH broke out in the middle of the 1300s and later, Jews were blamed. The most common accusation was that Jews were involved in large-scale plots that could endanger the Christian community. Such ideas spread quickly.

Growing out of these types of accusations was the belief that Jews were in some way less than human. That view was widely reflected in medieval art and folklore, which depicted Jews with animal features and animal forms. Even more damaging was the view that Jews were linked in an unholy, inhuman alliance with the forces of evil and the devil.

As the Christian faith grew more widespread, Christians increasingly believed that theirs was the only true religion. The failure of most Jews to accept Christianity willingly was considered additional evidence of their evil nature. These beliefs developed throughout the Middle Ages, intensifying in times of economic trouble or social unrest. France, England, and Spain actually banished* all Jews for several centuries. Medieval anti-Jewish beliefs certainly had an impact on modern anti-Semitism, though the degree and nature of this influence is uncertain. (*See also* **Jewish Communities; Jews, Expulsion of.**)

Aquinas, Thomas, St.

1224–1274
Theologian and philosopher

* **theology** study of the nature of God and of religious truth

Thomas Aquinas was born into a noble family at Roccasecca, Italy. When he was five years old, his family sent him to a monastery at Monte Cassino in Italy. The whole family would benefit if he became a priest. In his teens, however, he decided to join the DOMINICANS, a newly formed order of friars who took a vow of poverty. His family objected and kept him home for a year.

At the age of 20, he joined the order and began the traveling life of a friar. He moved north to France, where he studied in Paris and Cologne with philosopher ALBERTUS MAGNUS. Under Albertus's guidance, he began to appreciate the works of the ancient Greek philosopher ARISTOTLE. Aquinas became a master of theology* in 1256.

Thomas Aquinas was one of the most important men of medieval Christianity. He spent his life writing and teaching about the Scriptures and grappling with questions about the Christian faith. He is shown here surrounded by Christ, the apostles, and members of his order, the Dominicans.

* **analogy** explanation of a difficult, abstract idea by comparing it with a simpler and often concrete image

As a theologian, Aquinas wrote and taught about the Scriptures and grappled with questions about the Christian faith. He also wrote commentaries on important works of Aristotle. Some of these works had only just been discovered in western Europe through contact with the Islamic world. Aquinas used Aristotle's ideas and methods of philosophy in his own works, which are among the most important writings of later medieval theology, also called SCHOLASTICISM.

Aquinas followed Aristotle's view that most knowledge of truths is gained through the senses and then analyzed by the mind. He wrote that some truths are observed directly; others are deduced from observations. Aquinas also accepted that still other truths are revelations, revealed by God, and he argued that these can never be in conflict with knowledge from the senses. Much of his work explores questions that arise from these issues.

Aquinas's proofs for the existence of God in his work the *Summa theologiae,* completed around 1270, are a famous example of this approach. One of these arguments, borrowed from Aristotle, is the argument from motion. An object moves only if there is someone or something to move it. Whatever causes the movement must itself have moved; that movement had to be caused by something else. Ask the question "What caused the movement?" over and over again, and you either have to keep asking it forever or accept that there is an "original mover," God, to set everything moving.

All people, argued Aquinas, can recognize certain basic principles of practical reasoning. For example, people can agree that knowledge is a good thing, to be pursued whenever possible. These basic principles provide the foundation for a system of natural law to guide human behavior.

To discuss concepts beyond the reach of the senses, such as the nature of God, Aquinas used analogies* with human experience. For example, thinking about the highest level of wisdom achieved by human beings helps us to imagine, by analogy, the perfect wisdom of God.

Aquinas's life took him back and forth from Italy to France several times. He was attached to the pope's court in Rome for a while, and he taught at various Dominican study centers. He spent the last few years of his life teaching at Naples, Italy. He was on his way to attend a council of church leaders at Lyons, France, when he fell ill and was taken to a monastery south of Rome. He died there in March 1274. Aquinas's greatest achievement was his integration of Aristotle's philosophy into medieval thought.

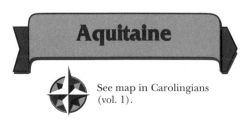

Aquitaine

See map in Carolingians (vol. 1).

* **duchy** territory ruled by a duke or a duchess

* **principality** region that is ruled by a prince

Aquitaine is a region in southwestern France. During the Middle Ages, it was a Frankish kingdom, a French and English dukedom or duchy*, and an English principality*. Aquitaine was at various times also known by the names Guyenne and Gascony.

At the start of the Middle Ages, Aquitaine was in the hands of the VISIGOTHS. They had captured Spain and southern France from the Roman Empire. In the early 500s, however, the Franks pushed the Visigoths south and out of France. As the Frankish Empire grew, the Franks respected and preserved many parts of the old Roman culture in the region.

* **homage** formal public declaration of loyalty to the king or overlord

* **feudal** referring to the social, economic, and political system that flourished in western Europe during the Middle Ages

In 781, the Franks were ruled by the emperor CHARLEMAGNE. Charlemagne made his three-year-old son, Louis the Pious, king of Aquitaine. Louis's kingdom covered a region stretching from the Atlantic to the Mediterranean coast. Later, Louis made his own son king of Aquitaine. He himself became emperor of the Franks, ruling over all of France and Germany and much of Italy. But when Louis died, the Frankish Empire split up. Aquitaine soon became a duchy in the kingdom of France, owing homage* to the French king.

By the early 1100s, the duchy of Aquitaine had become important because of its wealth. It contained valuable salt mines. (Salt was a precious substance in the Middle Ages.) More important, there was a thriving wine industry centered in the city of Bordeaux. In 1137, Duke William X of Aquitaine died with no sons to inherit from him. He left his large dominions to his daughter, ELEANOR OF AQUITAINE.

When Eleanor married King Louis VII of France, the rich duchy of Aquitaine came more closely under the control of the king. Eleanor established an elegant court that became a center for artistic activity. However, her marriage to Louis was dissolved 15 years later. The duchy of Aquitaine was restored to Eleanor, as feudal* law demanded, and she then married Henry of Anjou and Normandy, who became King HENRY II OF ENGLAND.

This marriage formed a link between Aquitaine and the English crown. It meant that England now controlled three French regions: Normandy, Anjou, and Aquitaine. Governing these regions of France caused major problems for the English kings. They were independent sovereigns in England, but in France they were lords who legally owed homage to the French king. The French king could decide legal cases in their French territories, so the kings of England had to appoint a lawyer in the court of France to look after their French interests. The English kings objected to paying homage to the French kings on behalf of their lands in France.

The feudal links between the English dukes of Aquitaine and the kings of France were broken and restored repeatedly in the 1200s and early 1300s as a result of disputes between France and England. Several treaties were negotiated, only to be broken again. In the 1200s, Henry III of England had to give up the titles of duke of Normandy and count of Anjou, and the English holdings in France gradually reduced in size. Finally, the French claimed the duchy of Aquitaine in 1337, one of the causes of the HUNDRED YEARS WAR.

During this war, the English invaded France and took back much of their old territory. In 1360, they signed a treaty with France that brought a period of relative peace. King Edward III of England made Aquitaine into a principality by giving it to his son, EDWARD THE BLACK PRINCE. Prince Edward had won important victories for England, and he set up a luxurious court in Aquitaine.

The court was very expensive to run, however, leading the prince to tax the people of Aquitaine heavily. This caused a general revolt, which ended his reign and also ended the treaty. The Hundred Years War continued, and the French had other setbacks, but they persisted in their campaign to win back Aquitaine. Finally, in 1453, Bordeaux was captured, and nearly all of England's territory in France was returned to the French crown. (*See also* **Angevins; Suger of St. Denis.**)

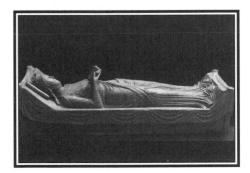

In the Middle Ages, nobles were often buried inside important churches. The gisant, or sculpture, of Eleanor of Aquitaine lies in Fontevrault Abbey near the city of Tours. In her lifetime, Eleanor was duchess of Aquitaine and queen, in turn, of both France and England. Buried near her are her husband Henry II of England and her son Richard I the Lionhearted.

Arabia

* **oasis** fertile area in a desert

* **monsoon** rainy season in India and in regions around the Indian Ocean

* **irrigation** farming technique in which water is brought in channels from rivers to supplement natural rainfall

* **monotheism** belief that there is only one God

* **caliph** religious and political head of an Islamic state

The dromedary, or one-humped camel, has been the chief mode of transportation in desert countries, such as Arabia, for many centuries. In the Middle Ages, traders used caravans of dromedaries to carry goods from one place to another. Army commanders used them to carry supplies. This manuscript page shows a guard tending several dromedaries.

Arabia is a peninsula in the Middle East that stretches southeast from the Mediterranean toward the Indian Ocean. It lies between North Africa and central Asia. The northern and central parts of Arabia are very dry, though scattered oases* provide some land for farming. The southern part of the peninsula receives more rainfall because of summer monsoons* from the east.

Pre-Islamic Arabia. Little is known about the early inhabitants of Arabia. The southern part of the peninsula and the oases farther north probably had farming populations from an early date. But people could exist in the desert only after the camel was domesticated in about 2000 B.C.

The farmers of southwest Arabia had achieved a high level of culture by the A.D 500s. They built impressive buildings and used irrigation* systems and other advanced farming techniques. Their social structure was based on the village community—people felt their main responsibilities and loyalties toward their local regions, not toward Arabia as a whole.

Southwest Arabia was on the trade route between the Mediterranean Sea, India, and nations in northeast Africa. Trade links kept the area in contact with the Greek-Roman-Byzantine world. In Arabia, there were religious groups that worshiped a single deity called *al-Rahman,* the merciful one. Jewish and early Christian traders also brought their own monotheism* into the area.

The people in the central and northern parts of the peninsula, though culturally similar to the people in the south, were very different socially. They were called bedouins, and their lives were largely based on raising camels and trading through the desert. They were warlike, often fighting with one another over territory and trade routes, and their main loyalties were toward their families, tribes, and chieftains rather than toward regions. Farmers of oases in these areas were considered socially inferior to the bedouins.

There were several kingdoms in the wealthy areas of southern Arabia and in the north near the Byzantine and Persian Empires. The central area around MECCA was less organized. But during the 500s, the Persians defeated kingdoms in the north and south. The area around Mecca became more important. Mecca was on important trade routes and was an important religious center. It was under the control of a tribe named the Quraysh.

Arabia and the Rise of Islam. The cults in Mecca worshiped many gods. But in the 600s, MUHAMMAD, a member of the Quraysh tribe, began to preach monotheism. Other powerful Quraysh in Mecca opposed his teaching. Many felt threatened by Muhammad's religious beliefs; others feared his growing power. Muhammad and his followers were forced to flee the city. They went north to Medina in 622, and Muhammad gained many new converts. The year 622 is considered the first year of the Islamic calendar. Mecca and Medina became Islamic holy places, and Medina became Muhammad's capital.

During Muhammad's lifetime, the authority of Medina was recognized through much of western and central Arabia, and Islam began taking root in those areas. Some Arab tribes rebelled against this authority when Muhammad died, but the caliphs* who succeeded him won them back by persuasion or often by force. The early Muslim caliphs brought all of Arabia under their control and extended Islamic rule to lands beyond Arabia.

* **cosmopolitan** having an international outlook, a broad world view

 See map in Islam, Conquests of (vol. 3).

* **dynasty** succession of rulers from the same family or group

Twelvers and Seveners

The followers of Ali never had control over the Islamic Empire, but they formed many small dynasties of their own. The main branch of the Shi'ites, strongest in Iran, became known as twelvers because the first twelve imams came from their dynasty. Another group, called seveners or Ismailis, split from the twelvers because they supported a brother of the seventh imam, named Ismail. The Qarmations and the Egyptian Fatimids were Ismailis or seveners.

Muslims from Arabia migrated to these foreign lands, and non-Arabs came to Arabia to visit the holy places and to settle. These contacts with other cultures helped make Arabia more cosmopolitan*. But it also decreased the power of native Arabs within the Islamic Empire, because more and more Muslims were non-Arabs.

Split Within Islam. The election of the fourth caliph, ALI IBN ABI TALIB, led to a serious split within Islam. A powerful Muslim group rebelled, and Ali had to move his capital out of Arabia. Struggles between the rival groups finally led to Ali's assassination. His death caused a split in Islam, creating two major religious sects—the Sunnites and Shi'ites.

After Ali's death, the Sunnites, who had opposed him, said that the caliph could be any member of the Quraysh, Muhammad's tribe. The Shi'ites held that the spiritual leader of Islam, whom they called the imam, should be a direct descendant of Muhammad. Ali, who had married the Prophet's daughter Fatima, was the father of those descendants.

The caliphate went to the man who had defeated Ali, the previous caliph's cousin. He began the UMAYYAD dynasty*, which moved the empire's capital to Damascus in Syria. The Sunnites slowly became a majority in the Islamic Empire. Parts of Arabia itself, however, remained strongly Shi'ite, as did parts of eastern Iraq and Iran. This split between Sunnites and Shi'ites destroyed the original unity of Islam. It also lessened the influence of Arabia within the Islamic Empire.

Arabia and the Islamic Empire. During the Umayyad dynasty, the Islamic state continued to expand. Muslim rule soon reached from central Asia and the borders of India in the east across North Africa to the Atlantic Ocean in the west. Most of Spain and Portugal were added to the empire as well. Umayyad power declined in the 700s, and the ABBASID dynasty arose. At first aided by Shi'ites, the Abbasids became Sunnite and moved the capital to Baghdad in Iraq. While Medina and Mecca remained the holiest cities of Islam, these cities never again became the seat of the caliphate.

During Umayyad rule, the Shi'ites in Arabia caused few problems. They became more active, however, after the Abbasids took power in 750. One Shi'ite group, the Qarmations, established an independent state in eastern Arabia in the 800s. Members of this group preached revolution, causing problems in Arabia and Iraq. They appealed strongly to oppressed and discontented groups in society. Another Shi'ite group moved to Egypt and founded the FATIMID dynasty, which took its name from Muhammad's daughter Fatima. In the 900s, other Shi'ite dynasties were established in Mecca, Medina, and the southwest of Arabia.

Sunnite Muslims were unwilling to accept these Shi'ite dynasties. The SELJUK Turks, who took over much of the Islamic Empire in 1055, began reestablishing Sunnite control in Arabia. By the middle 1100s, most of the small Shi'ite states there had been overthrown. The AYYUBIDS and later the MAMLUKS, two Sunnite dynasties, controlled Arabia and much of the empire up to the 1500s. Beginning in that century, Arabia was more influenced by the OTTOMAN Turks (also Sunnite) and by European nations seeking trade and territory. (*See also* **Islam, Conquests of; Islam, Religion of.**)

Arabian Nights

See *Thousand and One Nights.*

Arabic Language and Literature

* **bedouin** nomadic Arab of the deserts, especially in Arabia

* **Qur'an** book of the holy scriptures of Islam

At the beginning of the Middle Ages, Arabic was a fairly simple and vivid language. It was spoken by the bedouin* tribes in Arabia and was used in their oral poetry. Then the language became the official language of the Islamic religion, and it spread as the faith advanced around the Mediterranean Sea. Arabic became an international language, and with its development came an extensive body of poetry and prose.

Language.   Arabic belongs to the Semitic family of languages, which also includes Hebrew and some languages from Ethiopia. It is written with an alphabet very different from that used for English and other Western languages. Vowel sounds are not written down at all, and several consonants occur that have no equivalent in the letters used for Western writing, including some glottal stops sounded in the throat. Over the years, scholars have used several methods of representing Arabic sounds in the Western alphabet. This has resulted in a variety of ways of spelling Arabic words in English. In this book, the apostrophe mark represents either of two glottal sounds, called hamza and ayn, which are used in Arabic.

The first speakers of Arabic were mostly the bedouins of ARABIA. Their language had a simple vocabulary that allowed them to communicate about their own particular way of life. This was the original language of Islam, similar to that used in the Qur'an* and in the Hadith, the collected sayings of the prophet Muhammad. However, during the Islamic conquests, contact with other cultures caused a gradual change in the language. When the Muslims conquered areas such as Egypt and Iraq, the conquered people began to speak Arabic and used words from their own languages to express local ideas. As more city dwellers began to use Arabic, further words were brought into the language to meet the needs of urban life.

In addition, translations of books from Greek and Persian during the 700s and 800s contributed other new ideas and words. Arabic scholars also made significant discoveries of their own in philosophy, science, and mathematics. When their works were translated into Latin in the Middle Ages, European scholars became familiar with ancient Greek authors such as Aristotle, and they also learned about Arabic culture. As a result, such words as *admiral* and *algebra,* originally Arabic, spread to other languages.

Some areas of the Muslim Empire—such as ANATOLIA, parts of the Indian subcontinent, and the East Indies—retained their original languages. In these places, Arabic was used only for religious or scholarly purposes, but not for everyday speech. Today, formal written and spoken Arabic is very different from informal everyday speech even in Arabic-speaking countries. This gap may have existed in the Middle Ages as well.

Poetry.   The tradition of Arabic poetry dates from before the beginning of Islam. The nomadic desert tribes listened to poems that were memorized and performed by professional reciters. Some poems sang the praises of the poet's tribe. Others told the adventures of a particular hero or mourned the death of a friend or relative.

These early bedouin poems emphasized virtues such as courage and generosity. Both the action and the setting, such as a camel ride through forbidding deserts, were vividly described. Powerful images were used. In one poem, palm trees are described whose "topmost heads of foliage waving in every wind are like girls that pull at one another's hair." The most famous poet from this period was named Imru'al-Qays. Grandson of a

tribal chief, he led a wild life that supposedly took him to the court of Emperor JUSTINIAN I at Constantinople. One of his most famous poems describes his grief on visiting the deserted camp of the girl that he loved.

During the early Islamic period, scholars wrote down this pre-Islamic poetry to preserve it. Poets also imitated the works, and they began writing other types of poetry, such as love lyrics*. These new poems at first described traditional bedouin settings, but later they began to reflect the poets' elegant new lives. Themes of the Islamic religion were sometimes borrowed, with love depicted as a holy war.

In the 700s and 800s, as the Muslim Empire grew, new intellectual centers developed, such as BAGHDAD in Iraq. Poets flocked to these cities, where they could find patrons* and meet other writers. Lyric poetry was especially popular. Bashshar ibn Burd wrote delicate love poems. Abu Nuwas wrote brilliant lyrics of love, wine, and the hunt, and he showed great imagination in his use of Arabic. Religious poems such as those of Abu'l-Atahiya were also popular during this period. Two centuries later, the blind Syrian poet Abu'l-Ala al-Ma'arri took up similar solemn ideas; one of his poems says, "Like coins in its hand, time spends us as it will."

Another type of poem that grew more popular was poetry that praised powerful rulers or patrons. These poems used stately language and a grand style to celebrate the subject's virtues. A patron might be described as "a sea of generosity" or "a lion in battle."

Prose. Arabic prose developed with the beginning of Islam. The first work written down was the Qur'an. Scholars became interested in recording the events and ideas of the new Islamic culture. As a result, many texts about religion, law, and history were produced during the first centuries of Islam. And the Hadith, or Tradition, was also written down—sayings of Muhammad and the early caliphs that had at first been passed on by word of mouth.

Arabic literary prose flourished in the 800s. The Muslim Empire soon grew wealthy, and learning and the arts were well supported in the growing cities. Writers were drawn to these cities, where they could study and work. Rather than writing fiction, they commonly wrote about history and philosophy as well as biography and autobiography. They often mixed their scholarly discussions with stories to illustrate an idea.

The writer al-JAHIZ came from Basra, Iraq, one of the main cultural centers of the time. He wrote lively books about a wide range of topics, including human nature and natural science. He especially enjoyed mixing the serious and the entertaining in his work. His works cover various subjects, such as types of animals, why babies cry and how they should be soothed, and the nature of fire.

Ibn Qutayba, slightly younger than al-Jahiz, created a type of book that had many imitators. His *Choice Stories* are a collection of *adab,* brief tales and sayings that describe types of people and teach correct behavior. The characters used as examples include the prophet Muhammad, famous bedouin chiefs, slave girls, and Muslim princes. Soon other writers began compiling books of *adab,* such as books of manners for drinking companions, or longer and broader works covering many aspects of life. After the 900s, these storybooks began to be written as much for amusement as for instruction. In the 1100s, Ibn al-Jawzi wrote two such

* **lyric** poem expressing personal feelings, often in a form similar to a song

* **patron** person of wealth and influence who supports an artist, writer, or scholar

Remember: Words in small capital letters have separate entries, and the index at the end of Volume 4 will guide you to more information on many topics.

books illustrating certain types of people, *Fools and Gullible People* and *Clever Men and Women.*

After the Mongols destroyed Baghdad in 1258, Arabic prose writing seemed to be less inventive. However, significant works were still written in the later Middle Ages. In the 1300s, the great Arab historian IBN KHALDUN developed a complete philosophy of history. The *THOUSAND AND ONE NIGHTS* was also written down during this period. (*See also* **Qur'an.**)

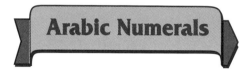

ARABIC NUMERALS

Early	Spanish Muslim	Modern
(	)	1
۲	٢	2
۳	٣	3
٤	۹	4
୫ or ∅	५	5
٦	6	6
✓	٨	7
٨	8	8
٩	٩	9
	·o· or ·t·	0

Arabic numerals have their roots in Hindu numerals. In the late 1100s, the system reached western Europe, with the addition of a symbol to represent zero. At first, there was resistance to using the new system, and it was not widely accepted until the late 1300s.

Arabic numerals are really Hindu-Arabic numerals. The system originally developed in India during the 500s or earlier, then spread to the Islamic world. In the late 1100s, it reached western Europe via Muslim Spain. The Byzantines did not learn about the system until a century later.

Arabic numerals are the ones commonly used today. They have played a crucial part in the development of mathematics and science. The system has three important features. First, it is a decimal system, based on powers of ten. Next, it uses place value, meaning that the order of symbols in a number indicates their values. Finally, with only ten symbols (numerals), any quantity can be represented. Originally there were nine symbols; the zero, added by the Arabs in the 1100s, made computation easier to perform.

Before the Arabic system, calculations were commonly done with an abacus (a frame with counters or beads that slide back and forth). The solutions were recorded using numbers written out in words, Roman numerals, or other symbols based on the alphabet. Such traditional ways of noting solutions were at first also utilized by those who used the Arabic system. They drew and erased the numerals on a board covered with sand, keeping only the solutions. However, the use of Arabic numerals in calculations later led to significant mathematical advances.

The first Arabic work about the new system was *Calculation with the Hindu Numerals,* written by al-KHWARIZMI in the 800s. (The mathematical term *algorithm* means method of calculating and is derived from his name.) The numerals of the system soon began to appear in tables of numbers for astronomy or for numerology (the "magic" use of numbers).

The numeral symbols were different in different parts of the Muslim world. In eastern regions, they remained similar to their original Hindu forms, but in Spain they changed under European influence—versions of Roman numerals were substituted for some values. The Spanish set of numerals began to spread to Europe as Spain's Christian kings conquered Muslim territory.

Arabic numerals took some time to find acceptance in Europe, however. At first, only specialists and scholars used the new system. Roman numerals and the abacus remained popular for trade. It was not until the late 1300s that Arabic numerals became widely accepted throughout Europe.

Unlike the abacus, the Arabic system allows the steps in a calculation to be easily recorded on paper. This made Arabic numerals ideal for developing new mathematical techniques. Once the Arabic system was adopted, mathematics and science began to progress rapidly. (*See also* **Mathematics.**)

Aragon

* **tribute** payment made to a dominant foreign power to stop it from invading

See color plate 8, vol. 3.

During the Middle Ages, Aragon grew from a small area in northeastern Spain into an important power. It became one of two major kingdoms that combined to create modern Spain.

When the Muslims invaded the Spanish peninsula in 711, they forced the Visigothic rulers to retreat to the northern coastal and mountain areas. With the help of the Franks under CHARLEMAGNE, however, the Muslim advance was halted. The northern areas had to pay tribute* to the Muslims, but they remained independent. Aragon, in the middle of the mountains, became known as a land of barons and lords, because it had no king.

For a while, Aragon was dominated by the neighboring mountain kingdom of NAVARRE, which had also resisted the Muslim advance. The lords of Aragon kept peace with the kings of Navarre by accepting dependence and through marriage ties. However, their lands were virtually part of Navarre until the end of the 900s. During this period, the population in northern Aragon was growing—so much so that a bishop was established there in 922. Aragon was also increasingly protected from the Muslims by fortified military settlements in the south.

Establishment of the Kingdom of Aragon.   Aragon became a kingdom in the 1000s. Sancho III of Navarre appointed his son Ramiro as deputy ruler over Aragon. When Sancho died, Ramiro pledged loyalty to his brother, who became the new king of Navarre; in return, Ramiro kept control of Aragon. He proceeded to extend his authority into frontier areas formerly controlled by his brother. This made Aragon more than six times its original size.

In 1044, Ramiro won territory to the east from CATALONIA, another neighboring state. He also fought in the growing struggle against the Muslims, whose strongholds faced his southwest frontiers. Ramiro never actually claimed to be king. Yet he acted like a king, uniting the barons and lords of Aragon.

Ramiro died in a battle with the Muslims in 1063. His son Sancho Ramirez took over the fight. French knights and knights from Catalonia were soon fighting alongside the Aragonese. The kingdom of Navarre, however, sometimes supported the Muslims against Aragon. But in 1076, Sancho's cousin, who was now king of Navarre, died, and Sancho succeeded him. As a result, Aragon and Navarre were united as one kingdom.

During Sancho Ramirez's reign, military raids by the Christian knights continued to put great pressure on the Muslims. This forced the Muslims to begin paying tribute. The kingdom of Aragon was also becoming an important trading center. Its mountain passes brought merchants from the Frankish Empire seeking Muslim spices, fruits, and manufactured goods. In addition, pilgrims from the north traveled through Aragon and Navarre to the shrine of St. James at Santiago de Compostela in ASTURIAS-LEÓN. Tribute from the Muslims and money spent by traders and pilgrims brought great profits.

Prosperity and Expansion.   Economic prosperity and religious revival led to further expansion. A new wave of Aragonese conquests began in the last years of Sancho Ramirez. A number of Muslim cities were taken, opening the way to further advances. By 1101, Sancho's son, Pedro I, had reached the Muslim stronghold of Saragossa.

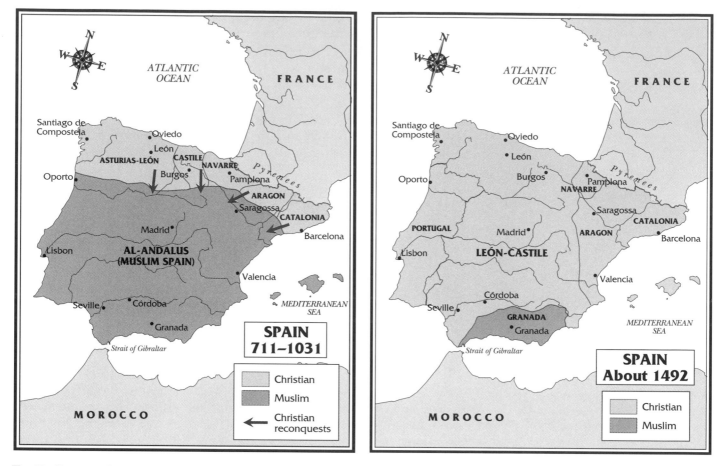

The Muslims invaded the Spanish peninsula in 711 and ruled most of Spain for three centuries. As the northern kingdoms became more powerful, however, they joined forces to push the Muslims southward. Until 1492, only Granada remained under Muslim control.

* **crusades** holy wars declared by the pope against non-Christians. Most were against Muslims, but crusades were also declared against heretics and pagans.

The campaign against the Muslims then slowed, however, due to shifting alliances among the Christian kingdoms. Pedro had been helping King Alfonso VI of CASTILE to attack other parts of Muslim territory. But Alfonso began to feel that Castile was threatened by Aragon's growth, and he provided aid to the Muslims against Aragon. This stopped Pedro from advancing farther.

Concern about Castile continued when Pedro's brother, another Alfonso, became Alfonso I of Aragon. However, Alfonso I renewed the drive against the Muslims in 1117. In doing so, he won the full support of the pope, so that the war against the Muslims virtually became a crusade*. Many foreign knights joined the campaign.

Between 1118 and 1120, Alfonso I captured Saragossa and other Muslim areas to the south and east. Known as "Alfonso the Battler," he was one of the great kings of the Spanish Reconquest. His victories over the Muslims defined the medieval kingdom of Aragon by establishing its western borders. However, he died in 1134, shortly after losing a battle to the Muslims at Fraga. The defeat touched off Muslim uprisings and threatened Aragon's southern frontier. Saragossa was saved from recapture only by the forces of Alfonso VII of Castile.

At this point, it seemed that the king of Castile might claim the throne of Aragon and Navarre, because Alfonso I had no heir and his brother Ramiro was a monk. However, the leaders in Aragon arranged for Ramiro to leave the monastery and marry a princess of Aquitaine. Ramiro was king for only three years, until he had fathered a daughter. The princess was immediately betrothed to Count Ramon Berenguer of neighboring Catalonia. Ramiro was able to rejoin the monastery, and in 1137, Berenguer became the first "count-king" of the combined state, now known as the crown of Aragon.

The Crown of Aragon.   The nobles in Navarre refused to be ruled by a Catalonian and selected a king of their own. But the loss of Navarre was more than made up for by Catalonia. The name of the combined state was Aragon, but the Catalonian district had more people and usually had greater influence in making policies. Catalonia was on the Mediterranean coast. It had a thriving seaport, Barcelona. It also had great influence in the south of France, until Berenguer's grandson Pedro II was killed there by French forces in 1213. He had tried to support the CATHAR heretics* against the French king during the Albigensian crusades.

This reversal in France came just one year after a combined Christian victory over the Muslims at Las Navas de Tolosas in central Spain, at which Pedro had been one of the main leaders. The forces of the crown of Aragon continued to press southward. A third major area was added to Aragon in 1245, when Pedro's son James I finally captured all of the Muslim kingdom of VALENCIA. James I, also called "the Conqueror," was an outstanding ruler in an age of famous kings. In addition to subduing Valencia, he helped the king of Castile capture other parts of Spain from the Muslims. He also conquered the island of Majorca, a Muslim stronghold in the Mediterranean. This set the stage for expansion across the seas. As a ruler, he respected the customs of the people in different parts of his kingdom, allowing Muslims who stayed in Aragon to keep their religion and many of their laws.

James's successors expanded the realm of Aragon still farther. His son Pedro III claimed Sicily from the ANGEVINS in 1282. During the reign of Pedro's son James II, Aragon also had influence in Sardinia, Naples, Tunis, Athens, and even Egypt—all around the Mediterranean Sea. It was a far-flung kingdom. But James II, like his grandfather James the Conqueror, was careful to respect the competing interests of different areas.

While Aragon gained power and wealth in the Mediterranean, the kingdom of Castile was expanding in the rest of Spain. Ties of marriage between the two states had prevented any major wars up to this point. But the ties would also give Castile grounds to claim the throne of Aragon.

In 1336, a daughter of the king of Castile married Alfonso IV of Aragon, James II's son. She hoped her children would inherit the crown of Aragon. Alfonso's older son Pedro IV managed to keep the throne, but Pedro later had to deal with an invasion from Castile. This invasion captured much of the original mountain land of Aragon for Castile.

Pedro's second son died in 1410 without a male heir. This made Castile's claims to the crown of Aragon stronger. The king who was finally chosen, Ferdinand I, was a grandson of Pedro but was also a prince of the royal family of Castile. Ferdinand and his sons ruled Aragon for the next 60 years, but they favored Castilians as officials. Finally, Ferdinand's grandson, also called Ferdinand, married Isabel of Castile in 1474 and thus controlled the Castilian throne. Five years later, he himself inherited the crown of Aragon. The two kingdoms, which now covered most of the

* **heretic** person who disagrees with established church doctrine

United Yet Divided

The Christian kingdoms of Spain were not always united against the Muslims. Rivalries between them sometimes caused them to make alliances with Muslim states and against each other. In Christian and Muslim territories, believers in both religions often worked together and respected each other. However, at other times, Christians and Muslims were bitter military enemies.

See color plate 15, vol. 3.

peninsula, were joined. Their children became kings of all Spain. (*See also* **Pedro IV the Ceremonious of Aragon; Santiago de Compostela; Spain, Muslim Kingdoms of.**)

Architecture

See *British Isles, Art and Architecture; Byzantine Architecture; Gothic Architecture; Islamic Art and Architecture; Romanesque Architecture; Spanish Art and Architecture.*

Archives

Archives are collections of records saved for legal or historical purposes. Many archives were kept during the Middle Ages. Those that survive provide valuable information about many different aspects of medieval life.

The word *archive* comes from the ancient Greek word *archeion,* which means a ruler's document collection. The term now includes any significant set of records, whether saved by the state, the church, or a private individual or institution. Collections of books are usually not counted. Sets of books kept for study or interest are known as libraries, even though many books are actually kept with everyday archival material.

The Byzantine Empire is known to have kept extensive archives, including laws, wills, contracts, and historical records. Keeping such records was the custom in ancient Rome, and it was required by the Code of Civil Law written under Emperor Justinian I. However, nothing appears to have survived the sack of Constantinople in 1437. The Muslims kept similar records in cities, such as Alexandria, that they took from the Byzantines, as well as in other communities. Only the Ottoman Empire, however, left records in significant quantities.

The situation is different in the European west, where many archival collections have survived. Together, the documents can be used to fill out the picture of events large and small that shaped western European life.

In much of the West, the Christian church played an important part in preserving old records. The church used many of the archiving techniques of ancient Rome. It kept documents that proved church ownership of land and buildings in secure, dry rooms, copying them by hand when they became too old. It also preserved other documents—during unsettled times monasteries were the safest places for rulers to keep their records. In many areas, too, clerics were the only people who could read and write.

In addition to religious archives, where many types of documents were stored together, three other types of collections developed. First, there were state archives, which kept records related to acts of government. These included laws and decrees, judicial records, treaties, letters between rulers, records of taxes, and lists of government personnel. State archives were kept by the HOLY ROMAN EMPIRE and by some kingdoms. For example, England has regular records that date back to 1130.

A second type of archive was the notarial* archive, where local legal records were held—such as contracts of partnership and sale, marriage settlements, wills, and adoptions. Notarial records could be used as legal proof of a claim in place of evidence from original witnesses.

The third type of archive was private or dynastic archives. Here noble families might store their own documentary evidence of property ownership, rights, rank, and powers. Commercial families and companies might also keep correspondence and financial records, though these were often destroyed when they were no longer needed.

After the Middle Ages, preservation of ancient archives was handled differently in different countries. In northern Germany and Spain, there was little centralization. Most archives remained in the regions where they were originally collected. In France and Scandinavia, however, large central archives were set up to preserve both religious and civil documents. (*See also* **Christianity.**)

Aristotle in the Middle Ages

Aristotle was an ancient Greek philosopher who lived in the 300s B.C. His ideas had a profound influence on medieval Islamic and Christian scholars. Much of Aristotle's thinking was based on analysis and observation. He explored principles of logic, and he studied the natural world. He also speculated about morality and about the nature of existence.

Aristotle's approach was attractive to many medieval thinkers, who appreciated his logic and attention to detail. It was also threatening because his ideas appeared to challenge religious writings and beliefs; Aristotle did not even mention God in his work. Muslim scholars wrote works that developed Aristotle's ideas further, making them more compatible with Islam. In western Europe, a movement called SCHOLASTICISM developed, in which scholars tried to show that Aristotle's thought could support Christianity.

Two of Aristotle's works were of particular importance in the Middle Ages because of their relation to religious themes. In *Metaphysics,* where he discusses existence, Aristotle examines the idea of a supreme intellect. This supreme intellect had attributes that many medieval thinkers equated with God. Aristotle also suggests in this work that there was a "first mover" who set the universe in motion. In *On the Soul,* Aristotle describes ideas about human knowledge to explain how people come to know universal truths. Because Aristotle suggests that there is a human soul that is not made of matter, medieval scholars used his ideas in debates on the immortality of the soul.

In the Byzantine* world, Aristotle's ideas influenced Christian theology as early as the 400s. By the 800s, there was an Aristotelian Christian movement that continued through the 1100s. Arab scholars learned about Aristotle from the Byzantines. In the 800s, his works were translated into Arabic, and noted scholars developed his ideas in their own writings—al-Farabi in Syria in the early 900s, IBN SINA in Iran around 1000, and IBN RUSHD in Spain in the late 1100s. MAIMONIDES, a Jewish philosopher who lived in North Africa in the late 1100s, also explored Aristotle's thinking.

Some of Aristotle's works on logic were known in the West, largely through Latin translations by a Roman scholar of the early 500s named

Boethius. But during the early Middle Ages, Western scholars largely ignored Aristotle's work. In the late 1000s, the philosopher Peter ABELARD took a logical approach to theology based on Boethius, but it was not until the era of the crusades* that interest in Aristotle blossomed.

Increased contact with the East and with the Muslims of Spain made people in the Western Christian world aware of the works in Arabic, and scholars went to Constantinople to translate the original Greek. This coincided with the founding of the first universities at Bologna, Paris, and Oxford. Scholasticism began to gain momentum in the West. Between 1250 and 1350, many Western interpretations of Aristotle were developed. The theologians ALBERTUS MAGNUS and Thomas AQUINAS used Aristotelian ideas in their works on Christian theology. The English Franciscan John Duns Scotus and William of OCKHAM proposed new interpretations of Aristotle. Aristotle's work exerted a tremendous influence on later medieval thought, and it continued to be important well beyond the Middle Ages. (*See also* **Crusades; Plato in the Middle Ages.**)

* **crusades** holy wars declared by the pope against non-Christians. Most were against Muslims, but crusades were also declared against heretics and pagans.

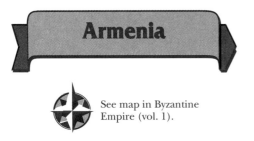

Armenia

See map in Byzantine Empire (vol. 1).

The Armenians were a people of eastern ANATOLIA. Their homeland was located between some of the medieval world's greatest powers, and they were frequently without land to call their own. Theirs was the first state to adopt Christianity as its official religion, and their beliefs differed from those of the Byzantine and Roman Churches. In the later Middle Ages, Armenians played an important part in several of the CRUSADES.

The ancestral territory of Armenia is centered on a high plateau southeast of the Black Sea. River valleys linked the plateau with Byzantine Asia Minor to the west and with Persia (Iran) to the east. While the mountains of the plateau provided excellent refuge from attack, they also divided the area into small isolated units, hindering growth of a centralized state. The valleys allowed Armenians to act as traders between their powerful neighbors, but they also made the region vulnerable to invasion.

When the Middle Ages began, Armenia was already occupied by the Christian BYZANTINE EMPIRE and pagan* Persia. The Byzantines heavily fortified a frontier across the middle of the Armenian plateau. They also tried to convert the Armenians to their own Christian beliefs. The independent-minded Armenians responded by moving the patriarch, or head, of their church from the Byzantine to the Persian, or eastern, sector of Armenia. However, Persian power was declining, and it seemed in the early 600s that the Byzantines would soon take over the whole of Armenia.

By 640, however, the Arab invasions had swept through SYRIA and had reached Armenia. Once again, many Armenians preferred a tolerant non-Christian overlord to demands for Byzantine orthodoxy*. They accepted the Muslim Arabs as their rulers and even contributed their famed cavalry to the Arab forces. As war between the Muslims and the Byzantines continued, Armenians generally prospered under their new Arab conquerors. However, the Byzantines briefly reconquered Armenia and pillaged it as though it were an enemy state.

A change in Muslim leadership from the UMAYYADS to the ABBASID dynasty* led to a pronounced change for Armenia. The Muslims began to demand that Armenians adopt the Islamic faith. By the year 800, there

* **pagan** word used by Christians to mean non-Christian and believing in several gods

* **orthodoxy** strict adherence to the established traditions and beliefs

* **dynasty** succession of rulers from the same family or group

had been three Armenian rebellions against the Arabs, and several national martyrs. Many Armenians moved from their homeland to areas nearby: north to the Caucasus Mountains and south to the Mediterranean coast opposite Cyprus. Farmers from Syria, Arabia, and other Muslim countries settled in their place.

In the early 800s, the Syrian Arabs began to be threatened again by the Byzantine Empire and decided to allow the Armenians greater independence, under a leader from the Armenian north called Asot I. For about 150 years between the 800s and the 1000s, Armenia had some degree of self-rule under Asot and his descendants, the Bagratids. During this period, Christian monasteries sprang up throughout the region, and a number of cities grew and prospered. By the middle of the 1000s, however, the region had been reconquered. At first, it was the Byzantines who took over the land, but the Byzantine domination of Armenia was brief. SELJUK Turks invaded the region and captured most of Armenia by 1071.

Various small Armenian principalities continued to survive, however. One of these was the Christian state on the coast of the Mediterranean called Cilicia. This state played an important part in the crusades to the Holy Land, often helping the knights from the West in their battles against Muslims and Byzantines alike. In the end, however, Cilicia proved impossible to defend, and it, too, fell to the Seljuk Turks.

That was not the end of Armenia's woes. Mongols invaded Armenia in the 1200s. More Armenians fled, and many who stayed were massacred by the Mongol conqueror TAMERLANE. After the region was conquered by the OTTOMAN Turks in the 1400s, Armenians maintained their independence only in the mountains of the Caucasus, their homeland today.

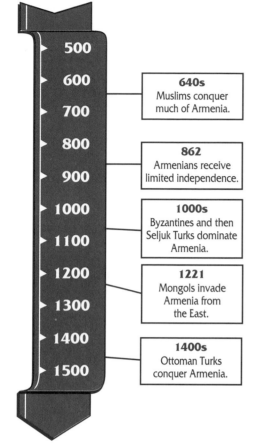

640s
Muslims conquer much of Armenia.

862
Armenians receive limited independence.

1000s
Byzantines and then Seljuk Turks dominate Armenia.

1221
Mongols invade Armenia from the East.

1400s
Ottoman Turks conquer Armenia.

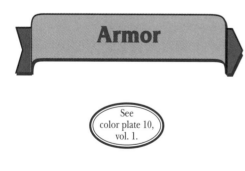

Armor

See color plate 10, vol. 1.

* **tournament**   contest between knights that was staged in peacetime as a sport

* **chain mail**   flexible armor made of small metal rings linked together

Knights in armor are one of the most common symbols of the Middle Ages. The armor pictured is usually from crusading times or later. However, like everything else, armor changed between 500 and 1500. This can be seen from armor that has survived until now and from art created at different times.

Armor changed as techniques of fighting changed, with mounted knights replacing men on foot as the most potent force in fighting. It changed in response to weapons, as the crossbow and later the musket transformed the nature of war. It also changed as the mystique of chivalry developed. The honors and glory to be earned in wars and in peaceful tournaments* led nobles' armorers to put much effort into designing and making armor.

Early Middle Ages.   The armor of the early Middle Ages descended from the protective clothing worn by soldiers in Roman times. Roman foot soldiers wore chain mail* tunics made of interlocked steel rings. Chain mail was flexible, was fairly light to wear, and gave excellent protection against knives and swords. The barbarian warriors who subdued the Western Roman Empire wore heavier armor, with plates of metal or horn laced together by thongs or riveted to a sturdy jacket. They could wear the extra weight because they fought on horseback. Their horses also often wore similar armor.

Throughout the early Middle Ages, these types of armor provided basic protection against the weapons commonly used in war—the sword, the spear, the ax, and the bow and arrow. Helmets and shields were used for added protection. Typical helmets were modeled on those used by tribes in the East, with a solid iron or bronze framework covered by plates of iron or horn. Such helmets were worn from Persia to Denmark. Shields were circular or oval, made from light but tough wood covered with leather and reinforced with bronze or iron. A knob in the middle, which gave extra protection for the hand, was sometimes sharpened as an extra weapon.

Armor During the Early Crusades.   As fighting on horseback became more important, defensive armor began to adapt. At first, the preference was for the lighter chain mail tunic, or byrnie, with slits in the front and back to make sitting in a saddle easier. Most byrnies also had hoods of mail attached. Helmets were cone shaped, with short pieces of metal in the front to protect the nose. They were worn over the chain mail hood and were now sometimes made from a single piece of metal.

Shields were also adapted for horseback. The BAYEUX TAPESTRY of the late 1000s shows a few round shields being used, but most shields are a long, pointed, "almond" shape. They protected the entire side of a knight, from eyes to knee. They were held in place by both a handgrip and a sling that went around the knight's neck and shoulders. The same type of shield is shown being used by foot soldiers.

This was the type of armor taken to Palestine for the First Crusade (1096–1099). There another adaptation occurred. The blazing sun of the Holy Land could make chain mail byrnies uncomfortably hot. So crusaders* began to wear sleeveless coats called surcoats over the armor to keep the sun's rays off the metal. Decorated with crosses and other designs that were the badge of the crusaders, surcoats remained popular when the knights returned to Europe. This was the origin of the term *coat of arms.*

Increasing Protection.   During the later crusades, other changes took place. Byrnies began to have longer sleeves. Chain mail mittens sometimes were added to protect the hands. Because mail offered little protection against crushing blows from axes or other weapons, a padded undergarment called an acton was worn under a byrnie. Actons were very warm, however. Knights sometimes fainted from heatstroke caused by their armor's undergarments.

By the end of the 1100s, leg armor had become more common, and helmets also developed. Mail chausses—chain mail stockings or long strips of mail buckled on the leg—were worn by most knights. Increasingly through the 1200s, leather or solid-metal knee protectors were added to the chausses. In addition, a new type of helmet was introduced that gave greater protection. Instead of a simple nose guard, it included a full face mask with thin rectangular eye slits and some breathing holes.

Protection for the knees and face made the almond-shaped style of shield unnecessary. Shields became lighter, with straight tops and with shorter points below. This triangular shape is what is usually associated with medieval knights. In addition, shields were painted with bright colors and easily recognizable designs. These ensured that knights could be identified in battle—which was important now that their faces could not be seen. They would not be mistaken for the enemy, and, as important, they

> **Remember:** Words in small capital letters have separate entries, and the index at the end of Volume 4 will guide you to more information on many topics.

* **crusader**   person who participated in the holy wars against the Muslims during the Middle Ages

Typical 15th-Century Armor

Complete Plate Armor, ca. 1450

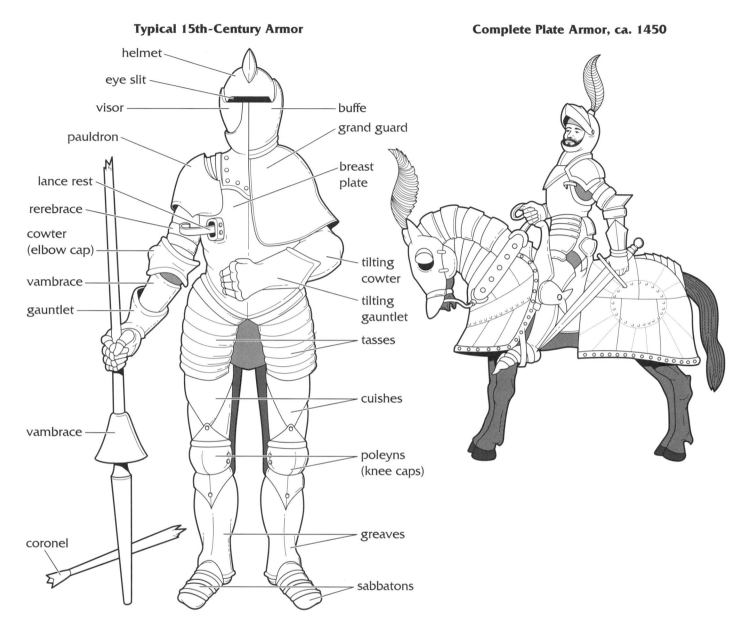

helmet

eye slit

visor

pauldron

lance rest

rerebrace

cowter
(elbow cap)

vambrace

gauntlet

vambrace

coronel

buffe

grand guard

breast
plate

tilting
cowter

tilting
gauntlet

tasses

cuishes

poleyns
(knee caps)

greaves

sabbatons

As the Middle Ages progressed, suits of armor became heavier and more elaborate. Improvements in the crossbow made that weapon more dangerous, and armor was needed to deflect arrows before they penetrated. Typical 15th-century armor consisted of plates of solid iron to protect the arms, legs, knees, and feet. The solid breastplate was often "puffed out" in design, and knights would tilt forward in the saddle to try to catch the lance full in the chest in order to shatter the tip.

would be credited for brave feats they performed. For even clearer recognition, identifying crests were added to the helmets. This is why the shield and crest are important emblems in heraldry*.

Horse armor, unused since Roman times, was also reintroduced in the 1200s in western Europe as a cloth of chain mail over the horse's body.

Deadlier Weapons. During the 1300s, improvements to the crossbow made it a much deadlier weapon. Its arrows could pierce a wooden shield and burst through the meshes of a mail shirt. Armor was needed that could deflect the arrows before they penetrated. This brought back designs similar to the old barbarian armor. Coats with iron plates laced together were used again. More commonly, surcoats were lined with small rectangular metal plates on the inside. These reinforced coats were often loose, to be pulled over the head and buckled at the sides. They sometimes had a single metal plate across the chest, with chains attached to hold shield, weapons, and helmet.

* **heraldry** rules for creating and recording the designs that knights used for recognition

Helmets began to show greater variety. One type, called the great heaume, was like a huge bucket with eye slits that covered the head and neck. Others were more like sturdy iron hats, with broad brims that kept sword strokes further from the head. Others covered the face with attached chain mail or with a solid, movable visor*.

* **visor** part of a full helmet that had narrow holes so that knights could see

Armor for the legs and arms also changed. Solid iron protected the shins, thighs, and feet as well as the knees. Arms were similarly covered. Special attention was paid to the left shoulder, because that was where the spear carried by knights (called the lance) did the most damage. Attacks usually came from the left, away from the knight's right, or weapon, arm. A large left shoulder plate called a grand guard was sometimes provided; and the shield also gave protection.

Because armor had became heavier and stronger, shields became still smaller. The new type of shield was known as a targe. It was squarish in shape and concave. Sometimes it was ridged so that the lance of an opponent would stay on the shield instead of sliding to the more vulnerable body. If the shield was handled correctly, the foe's lance could be made to shatter.

The Full Suit of Armor.   The final step toward full suits of armor occurred when solid breastplates were developed. At first, the reinforced surcoats were made tighter fitting, to be closed in front like modern jackets. (Like modern jackets, they closed from left to right, to protect the all-important left side.) Next, solid, one-piece breastplates were introduced. These were often designed with a puffed-out chest to catch the tip of an opponent's lance. By now, shields were rarely used, but knights could shatter an opponent's lance by taking it on the breastplate at the right angle.

Surrounding the breastplate, other plates of steel were fitted to make a full suit of armor. A backplate was slotted in over the knight's back, and there was a "skirt" of overlapping metal plates below. Full armor was worn on the arms and legs, once again fitted carefully so that there were no open areas. There was also a collar of close-fitting plates combined with a shoulder piece, to protect the area between the breastplate and the helmet.

Helmets also underwent further changes. They began to be fitted to the suit of armor so that there was no lack of protection. Many helmets were more angular, with fewer flat surfaces that might catch an arrow or a bullet. Helmets began to be designed according to themes: there was a type called a *barbute,* which looks like an imitation of an ancient Greek model.

Full armor was worn only by men on horseback (and horses, too, now wore their own fitted armor); it was too heavy and bulky for foot soldiers. Shields, rarely used by mounted knights, were still important for foot soldiers. Swordsmen carried bucklers, small round shields much like those of the early Middle Ages, for deflecting sword strokes. Crossbowmen had pavises, roughly rectangular shields with a protruding ridge down the middle. About breast high, they could be set on the ground for protection while reloading a crossbow.

The "Lighter Side" of Armor.   When the Middle Ages ended, armor was not only a weapon of war, it was also an important part of the culture. Tournaments had become a popular sport, and armor was designed specifically for this "peaceful" use. (Some suits of armor have less mobile protection for the left arm because it never had to be used.) Also, magnificent suits of armor were given as diplomatic presents. Decoration of armor was no longer done merely for identification; it had become an end in itself.

There were famous armorers who specialized in ceremonial armor. They made fancy, antique styles; they polished armor brightly and tinted it with different colors. They could also etch patterns in it or inlay metals such as silver or gold. Another type of decoration was embossing: detailed designs were hammered out in relief from the inside of the armor plate. Embossing was the most prestigious and lavish type of decoration, but it was rarely used in battle armor because raised designs would not deflect enemy weapons. (*See also* **Heraldry; Knighthood; Warfare; Weapons.**)

Art

See *British Isles, Art and Architecture; Byzantine Art; Gothic Painting; Gothic Sculpture; Islamic Art and Architecture; Romanesque Art; Spanish Art and Architecture.*

Arthurian Literature

The legends of King Arthur of Britain and his knights of the Round Table, among the most popular and romantic stories of all time, started in the Middle Ages. As they do today, people then listened with fascination to accounts of Arthur and those close to him: Guinevere, his wife and queen; his closest friend, Lancelot; his evil son, Mordred; and Merlin, the magician. The medieval world viewed much of the Arthurian legend as a part of history. Writers of the time built into it many of their highest ideals—deeds of chivalry, courtly and tragic love, and religious quests of honor.

The History.   Arthur was supposed to have fought at the Battle of Mount Badon in 516, an important victory won by the Celtic Britons against the Anglo-Saxons. But the first undisputed mention of Arthur does not appear until the early 800s in a history of the Britons by a writer named Nennius. In 540, earlier and closer to the time, another historian called Gildas also described the Battle of Mount Badon but made no mention of Arthur. He named the victor in the battle as Ambrosius Aurelianus. Could this have been Arthur? Writers in the later Middle Ages thought so, but modern scholars are not so sure.

It is certain that popular folktales were told about a hero called Arthur throughout the Celtic parts of the British Isles and France, especially in Wales, Cornwall, and Brittany. Other stories of chivalry that did not include Arthur, such as the tragic love story of Tristan and Isolt, became a part of the tradition. Although these stories were not written down at first, they were known as far away as Italy, where mosaics and carvings depict Arthurian characters. The tales are often mentioned by early writers, including William of Malmesbury, who distrusted them as "lying fables." Today we know that such folktales are sometimes based on real characters, but the stories about them change greatly as they are passed from one generation to the next.

The stories of King Arthur and his Knights of the Round Table are some of the most famous and beloved tales in world literature. Arthurian literature expresses the medieval ideals of chivalry, courtly love, honor, and the quest for the Holy Grail, the cup used by Christ at the Last Supper.

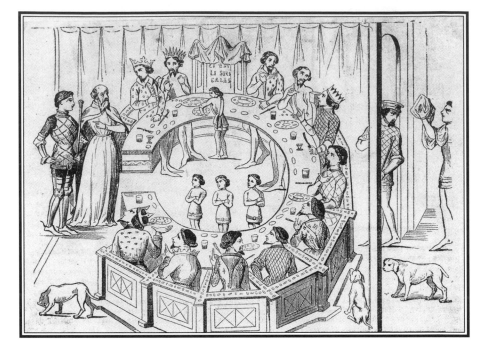

In the 1100s, Arthur and his knights were clearly thought of as historical figures in Britain. A very popular history written at that time was Geoffrey of Monmouth's *History of the Kings of Britain.* Geoffrey gives a detailed account of Arthur's reign, presenting Arthur as a heroic king. But much of his story is clearly influenced by the old folktales. Written in Latin, the work was translated and adapted into other languages—for example, a Norman French version called *Roman de Brut* was written by a poet named Wace in 1155. Another version in Middle English, simply called *Brut,* was written by Layamon a few years later. These works became as important as the folktales to the imaginative writers who followed.

The Arthurian Romances. The earliest literary works about the legend of Arthur were written not in England but in France. The stories were known there from Wace's *Roman de Brut,* and through Breton poet-musicians who traveled across the English Channel from Wales and Cornwall in Britain to Brittany in France. Between 1160 and 1180, French poet CHRÉTIEN DE TROYES wrote five major Arthurian works based on history and legend. These works are among the finest of all Arthurian literature.

Chrétien's romances dealt with the knights of Arthur's court and with such Arthurian themes as courtly love*. His work unified many existing Arthur stories and established a model that influenced much of the Arthurian literature that followed. His was also the first work to include the story of *Perceval,* or the quest for the Holy Grail. In this quest, Arthur's knights search for the cup that Christ used at the Last Supper in Jerusalem, which had been brought to Britain. The religious theme certainly added to the popularity of Arthur in the Middle Ages.

Chrétien also wrote a romance about Tristan and Isolt, though this is now lost. Later works survive that detail the story of their forbidden love, caused by a love potion they mistakenly drank while crossing the Irish Sea during a storm. Tristan and the Grail legend continued to be popular topics in the Arthurian literature that developed in France and among the

* **courtly love** mannerly, idealized form of love that became popular in the Middle Ages, especially in literature

French-speaking nobles of England. Close to 20 French works still survive, for example, that are devoted to the Grail legend.

The French Arthurian tales were widely known, and the stories became popular in other languages too. As early as the 1190s, for example, there were German adaptations of the stories. One of the best-known German Arthurian romances was *Parzival,* by the poet and knight WOLFRAM VON ESCHENBACH. The most famous version of the Tristan story is also by a German writer, Gottfried von Strassburg, who wrote in the early 1200s.

By 1225, Old Norse versions had appeared. Arthurian literature also was written eventually in Latin, Hebrew, Italian, and various Spanish dialects. The authors of these works retold the stories in ways that were suited to their own cultures. In Old Norse versions, for example, the themes of courtly love were left out. In some cases, the Arthurian legend played an important role in determining social customs and morals, especially among the nobility.

Arthurian works in Middle English after Layamon's *Brut* also included many features borrowed from the French romances. But English writers evolved their own distinctive type of romance. They avoided the poetic style of Chrétien and others. English works were more realistic and detailed. They generally were presented as stories with simple plots and characters who had experienced unusual adventures. Many of the authors of these works were probably humble, common men, unlike the better-educated authors of the European romances.

Two of the best and most important Arthurian works were written in England. One is the story of *Sir Gawain and the Green Knight,* a frightening narrative poem in which the hero is nearly beheaded by a magical knight but is spared because of his noble behavior. The other English classic is *Le Morte Darthur (The Death of Arthur),* written by Sir Thomas MALORY about 1470 and one of the earliest books to be printed in England. It is a long prose work that includes all aspects of the Arthurian legend. Malory's famous work is the only English version that includes the story of the Holy Grail. It also includes the story of Tristan, who comes to Arthur's court dressed as a poor minstrel and sings about his tragic life. (*See also* **Courtly Love.**)

Artillery

* **artillery** heavy weapons that hurl large missiles, such as stones, at the enemy

* **besiege** surround a place with armed troops to cut off all supplies and force a surrender

Medieval artillery* existed well before cannons were invented in the 1300s. It was used mostly for besieging* CASTLES and other strongholds. Cannons were tried as experimental artillery for about a century. They proved their effectiveness in the late Middle Ages and began to change the face of war.

The ancient Romans had ballistas that threw darts long distances. These used the principle of torsion, or twisting. A mass of ropes was wound into a tight knot as a beam holding the missile was cranked back. When it was released, the dart hurtled toward its target. Other torsion devices, mangonels, could fling heavy stones from large slings or spoonlike devices.

In the early Middle Ages, other throwing machines used tension as the impelling force. Arbalests were huge crossbows that could be mounted on city walls. *Einarms* (one arms) also used bent wood to provide the power but hurled stones—sometimes two stones simultaneously.

All four of these devices were powerful but unreliable. Changes in the weather affected the ropes, and the spring in the wood soon fatigued after heavy use. A more reliable siege engine was called the trebuchet, which worked like an uneven seesaw. A very heavy weight was attached to the short end, and a sling at the long end was loaded with the missile. The long end was pulled down, then released to hurl the missile high into the air. Trebuchets flung heavy stones distances of up to 800 yards, and they were very consistent.

When gunpowder was brought back from Asia by Muslim traders, its first military use was in sapping: blowing up castle walls by tunneling beneath them and placing a charge. In the early 1300s, the cannon was invented; it was used in a siege of Metz, France, in 1324. Twenty-five years later, cannons were being tried throughout western Europe, from Scotland to Spain.

These early uses of cannons seem to have been experimental. Gunpowder was loaded in devices large and small—there was even a multiple gun with many tubes (barrels) that were to be loaded and set off together. Such experiments were not always successful, mainly because of problems with the barrels. The metal often split or shattered at the force of the explosion.

* **recoil** backward thrust of a gun or cannon when the explosion drives the bullet or cannonball forward

These problems were first solved for larger guns—but they were still hard to aim and, because of the recoil*, hard to control. But wheeled gun carriages solved the recoil problem in the 1400s, and as the century progressed, cannons figured in many victories, including the French victory in the HUNDRED YEARS WAR and the Turkish sack of CONSTANTINOPLE (both in 1453).

Astrolabe

The astrolabe is a flat handheld device for making practical astronomical observations by day and night. Experts used them in the Middle Ages to tell time, to find direction, or to discover their position when they were traveling. On one side is a sighting bar, called an alidade, that measures the angle of the sun or a star above the horizon. On the other side are carefully designed rotating plates, which serve as a calculator.

ASTROLOGY AND ASTRONOMY had made scholars very knowledgeable about the movements of the sun and stars. Astrolabes used this awareness, and simple geometric principles, to make calculations that otherwise would have been very difficult. The astrolabe was hung vertically. The alidade was used to find the angle of elevation of the sun or of another particular star. Then the astrolabe was laid flat, and the plates on the other side were set to the same angle and were used to read off the time, direction, or position.

Astrolabes were probably known in ancient Greece, but the earliest surviving astrolabes are Islamic devices from the 900s. The astrolabe was the most widely used astronomical instrument of the Middle Ages.

Astrology and Astronomy

In the ancient world, the slow but not fully regular motions seen in the night skies were felt to be significant by most cultures. The stars circled eternally. The moon and planets appeared to wander across the heavens. Astrology—studying the skies to foretell the future—was a respected profession. Astronomy—finding ways to describe, measure, and predict heavenly movements—was often viewed as a part of astrology.

During the Middle Ages, astrology remained popular but began to meet with disapproval. It conflicted with many religious ideas in Christianity and Islam. Astronomy, too, challenged some of the ideas of religion, especially when it began to become a science on its own. New ideas in astronomy became part of the new worldview that ushered in the modern age.

Astrology and Astronomy in the Ancient and Byzantine Worlds

Astrology can be traced back to the earliest civilizations. It developed alongside religious beliefs, such as those identifying gods with the different planets. Astrologers started by predicting events that affected society as a whole: wars, epidemics, famines, and weather. Later, astrologers also made personal horoscopes, claiming that the positions of the heavenly bodies at an individual's birth affected major events in the person's life.

Astronomy developed in Egypt, Babylonia (in southern Iraq), and Greece during the last five or six centuries B.C. The Babylonians compiled tables, and the Greeks made geometric models. Both could accurately calculate the movements of planets. The techniques were used by astrologers to aid their predictions.

Some thinkers in the ancient world drew a distinction between astronomy and astrology. Cicero, for example, wrote that, while the skies might be predictable, people's lives depended on their own choices, not on the stars. However, there was a strong philosophical movement called Stoicism*, which held that the future, like the movement of the stars, was already fixed. Generally, astronomy and astrology remained linked.

Around A.D. 142, a Stoic Greek astronomer, Claudius Ptolemaeus (known as Ptolemy), wrote the most important astronomical work of ancient times, the *Almagest*. Ptolemy's theories, which gave a complete mathematical account of the heavens, assumed that the earth was surrounded by a set of transparent, hollow spheres that support and move the planets, the moon, the sun, and the stars. Ptolemy also wrote a companion work on astrology called the *Tetrabiblos,* showing how the movements of these spheres affected life on earth. His theories had an important influence on medieval astrology and astronomy in both Europe and the Islamic world.

The Byzantine world continued the dialogue between those who accepted only astronomy and those who believed in astrology as well. Emperor JUSTINIAN I included laws against astrology in the Code of Civil Laws for which he is famed. But because of the Greek traditions behind Byzantine thought, many Christian thinkers in the Byzantine Empire accepted the idea that the stars not only moved predictably and but also influenced human life.

Islamic Astrology and Astronomy

Astrology.   Before Islam, astrological prediction was part of Arabic culture. An Arab diviner priest, or astrologer, is said to have predicted the coming of Muhammad. The Muslim religion, however, abolished the job

* **Stoicism**   popular philosophy of life in the ancient world that urged people to accept life calmly and without emotion

of diviner priest. The Prophet said that astrology was just magical superstition. Muslims believed that only God could know the future; therefore, it was impossible to make predictions by astrology.

Studying the stars remained important in the Arab world, however. Even scholars who disapproved of astrology sometimes wrote books on it to please their patrons* and to earn money. Important astrology books from the Byzantine world were translated into Arabic, especially during the 700s and 800s. These included Ptolemy's *Tetrabiblos*, which became the most influential source for medieval Islamic astrology.

By the 800s, astrology had, in fact, come to be regarded as part of Greek philosophy. Religious leaders could now oppose astrologers because they used "foreign" Greek ideas. The main objection was still that astrology claimed to predict the future. This meant that astrologers were often attacked and charged with being atheists.

Scholars who studied the other sciences that had come from Greece were also attacked by religious leaders. These thinkers—including philosophers, physicians, and especially astronomers—began to distance themselves from astrology. Several of them rejected astrology fully, including IBN SINA (Avicenna) and IBN RUSHD (Averroës). By the 1200s, scholarly arguments against astrology had become well established.

Despite attacks on astrology from these scholars and from religious leaders, astrologers continued to practice their craft. The most common type of astrological work explained how to deal with individual problems through personal horoscopes. Another type of book dealt with determining the best moment for beginning projects—for example, when to start an experiment in alchemy*. Much importance was attached to times when planets appeared together in the same part of the heavens.

Astronomy. Early Islamic scholars used a single term to refer to both astrology and astronomy. This implies that the two subjects were viewed as connected branches of the same science. In the early years, however, most Arabs probably had limited interest in other aspects of astronomy, focusing almost exclusively on foretelling the future.

According to Islamic tradition, an Indian astronomer visited the caliph al-MANSUR in Baghdad in the 760s. He brought along an astronomical text, which was translated into Arabic. However, Byzantine sources were the most important influence on the development of Islamic astronomy. Ptolemy's *Almagest* was translated into Arabic sometime during the early 800s. This book helped to generate a number of new works in astronomy.

At first, these new works were based on the *Almagest* and other ancient and Byzantine texts. In time, however, Islamic astronomy took on a life of its own. Some Islamic works provided critical explanations of the *Almagest*. Others updated Ptolemy's terminology or revised the work's content based on fresh astronomical observations. Islamic astronomers, for example, discovered that Ptolemy was mistaken about the exact movements of the sun. By the 1300s, Islamic astronomers had developed many of their own more accurate descriptions of the heavens.

The most common type of astronomical writings in the Islamic world was astronomical handbooks. These handbooks helped to compute the actual positions of the planets at any given time. They were modeled on the astronomical tables developed by Ptolemy but were more accurate,

* **patron** person of wealth and influence who supports an artist, writer, or scholar

* **alchemy** medieval chemistry that tried to change base metals into gold, discover a universal cure for disease, and discover a means for prolonging life

Remember: *Words in small capital letters have separate entries, and the index at the end of Volume 4 will guide you to more information on many topics.*

During the Middle Ages, some of the findings of ancient astronomy were found to be inaccurate. Newer, more accurate views of the earth, sun, and planets developed. Astronomers are shown here determining longitude by studying lunar changes.

* **pagan** word used by Christians to mean non-Christian and believing in several gods

simpler, and easier to use. Such handbooks were practical guides. Many were probably meant for less educated astrologers who wanted to make horoscopes quickly.

Other Islamic works covered other practical topics—for example, astronomical instruments. These books discussed the construction of large observatories and also the use of smaller instruments such as the ASTROLABE, a device used to measure the altitude of the sun and other stars. Muslim astronomers also devoted special texts to describing the constellations. Some of the names of stars are derived from early Arabic names for them—for example, Aldebaran, the brightest star in the sky.

During the 1400s, the office of *muwaqqit* (timekeeper) was established as part of the mosque bureaucracy. Timekeeping was done by observing the heavens, and it was important because Muslims had to pray at specific times during the day. Muslim astronomers devised ways to determine the time more accurately. Most later medieval astronomical texts were written by *muwaqqits*. Their works placed less emphasis on astrological subjects and showed more concern for religious issues.

Astrology and Astronomy in Western Europe

Early Middle Ages.   Astrology was common throughout much of barbarian Europe. It was believed that medicinal cures and surgical procedures had to be performed on special days when the stars were in the proper positions. Emperors and kings often used astrology as a guide to their actions. Ideas from astrological theory were mentioned in some of the literature of the time. Astronomy, on the other hand, was less favored. Used during Roman times, it was largely forgotten in the early Middle Ages. Many concepts of Greek science were lost in western Europe after Rome fell in the 400s.

The medieval Christian church condemned astrology because of its association with pagan* cults. The Christian fathers, especially those of the Western Church, such as St. AUGUSTINE, had spoken out against it. Church councils had condemned it. Such Christian opposition did not, however, destroy astrology. In western Europe, it survived as a series of superstitious beliefs and practices largely ignored by scholars.

The Muslim Impact.   With the reconquest of Spain and Sicily in the later Middle Ages, western Europe had increasing contacts with the Muslim world. There scholars found Muslim works on astronomy and Arabic versions of the *Almagest,* the *Tetrabiblos,* and other ancient texts. Translated into Latin, these texts found their way into European schools and libraries. A number of Muslim astronomical instruments and devices were also brought to Europe.

The distinction between astrology and astronomy was very blurred at this time, and the church remained opposed to both subjects. But many philosophers and theologians felt it was important to investigate the new ideas that were being brought west. Many theologians accepted the astrological influence of planets over certain conditions of human life, though they denied the possibility of predicting future events. Astronomy was also studied. Attempts were made to introduce the *Almagest* into European universities, but it was too advanced for most students.

This led European scholars to begin writing their own texts on astronomy. Much of this work, like that of the Islamic scholars, was aimed at changing the details of Ptolemy's work to fit their own observations. The result was a number of astronomical texts, calendars, and astronomical tables. Clockwork machines were built that could indicate the positions of the planets. Astronomy began to flourish as a scientific subject.

Later, astrology, too, became more acceptable. In the 1400s, English scholar and philosopher Roger Bacon was a strong believer in astrology. Astrology was used increasingly by the nobility as well as the common people. By the early 1400s, both subjects had become well established in much of western Europe.

The End of the Middle Ages

By the end of the Middle Ages, astrology was flourishing. One factor that contributed to this was the invention of the printing press, which allowed books to be printed in larger numbers. Many more people could now read almanacs and calendars, which often contained predictions of various kinds. This strengthened popular belief in astrology. In addition, the humanistic movement* brought ancient Greek texts to European scholars and awakened their interest in learning, including astrology. The church, and many scholars, too, continued to speak out against astrology, but they were unable to destroy astrological beliefs. It was not until the science of astronomy began to create new views of the heavens that belief in astrology declined.

Astronomical study and observation during the latter part of the Middle Ages led to new views of the earth, sun, and planets. At first, medieval astronomers trusted the model of the universe proposed by Ptolemy. Gradually, however, by making their own observations and developing their own theories, they found that some of the findings of ancient astronomy were wrong. Their work paved the way for the emergence of the new astronomy of Copernicus* in the 1500s. (*See also* **Alchemy; Calendars; Law.**)

* **humanistic movement** interest in classical learning that began to develop during the later Middle Ages

* **Copernicus** Polish astronomer who developed the idea of a universe in which the earth revolves in orbit around the sun

Asturias-León

See map in Aragon (vol. 1).

During a large part of the Middle Ages, most of the Spanish peninsula was in Muslim hands. Asturias was the one area that remained under Christian control. It soon spread to include the city of León and took the name of Asturias-León, or the Empire of León. Later two of its frontier areas became large Christian kingdoms in their own right, and one of them, CASTILE, engulfed Asturias in the 1200s.

Muslim armies invaded Spain in 711, overwhelming most of the Christian VISIGOTHIC Empire. The Visigoths had been rulers of Spain for almost 300 years. However, the Muslims failed to conquer a small mountain region along the north coast. A Visigothic noble named Pelayo supposedly founded the kingdom of Asturias there and led several campaigns against the Muslims.

Other remote parts of the north coast soon proved hard for the Muslims to defend. The area of Galicia, to the west of Asturias, came under Asturian control. Galicia was important as the home of the cult of SANTIAGO (St. James) DE COMPOSTELA. According to legend, St. James brought Christianity to Spain, and he was buried at Compostela. Asturian kings made St. James's tomb the religious focus of Christian Spain.

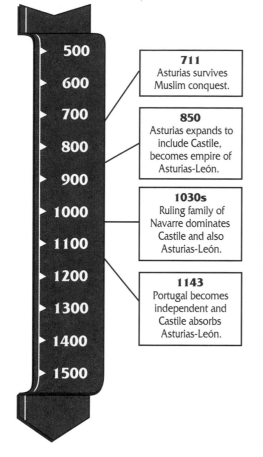

500	
600	**711** Asturias survives Muslim conquest.
700	
800	**850** Asturias expands to include Castile, becomes empire of Asturias-León.
900	
1000	**1030s** Ruling family of Navarre dominates Castile and also Asturias-León.
1100	
1200	**1143** Portugal becomes independent and Castile absorbs Asturias-León.
1300	
1400	
1500	

In the middle 800s, the Asturian king Ordoño I took advantage of divisions in the Muslim part of Spain to expand his kingdom. He spread his influence to the east, setting up a border area with many castles that became known as Castile. He also moved southward to the edge of the Douro River valley, where he captured the old city of León. Ordoño's son Alfonso III drove still farther south, to Oporto in what is now PORTUGAL. The full length of the Douro became Alfonso's boundary with Muslim Spain.

When Alfonso died in 910, he divided his land into separate kingdoms again, for his three sons. This led to rivalries that weakened Asturias, but it was not destroyed: Alfonso's son Ordoño II reunited the land again. At about that time, the ruler of Asturias-León even became known as emperor. But from that time on, the "empire" had mixed fortunes.

A successful campaign against the Muslims took a Leonese army as far south as Lisbon in 955. However, the eastern area of the empire, Castile, became independent under its count Fernán Gonzales. Then a powerful Muslim military leader, al-Mansur, led many campaigns against the Christians. In 997, he attacked Compostela, and he had the bells and the doors of the cathedral of St. James carried away by Christian slaves.

During the early 1000s, there were further troubles. To the west, a series of Viking attacks on the coast had to be repelled. To the east, King Sancho III of NAVARRE gained influence over Castile by marriage, making it a kingdom under his son Fernando. Then Sancho marched through to conquer and claim the Leonese Empire for himself.

When Sancho died, Fernando of Castile became ruler of the empire until 1065. At times during the later 1000s and the 1100s, Asturias-León had independent rulers again. But it was squeezed between Castile and the growing might of Portugal, which in 1143 had also become independent from the empire. Finally, in 1230, Asturias-León became a permanent part of Castile.

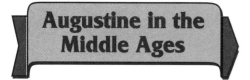

Augustine in the Middle Ages

* **heresy** belief that is contrary to church doctrine

* **pagan** word used by Christians to mean non-Christian and believing in several gods

St. Augustine was a theologian and bishop in North Africa during the 300s and early 400s. As one of the "fathers of the church" in the Latin world, he was a very important figure for medieval Christians. His life set an example that was followed by the monastic orders of the Middle Ages. As a thinker who argued against many religious heresies*, he helped define the nature and beliefs of Western Christianity.

Augustine lived at a time when Christianity was still not established in the Roman Empire. His father was a pagan*, his mother a Christian. He wrote the story of his youth in his famous *Confessions:* as a child he was not baptized; he had a mistress and a son when he was in his late teens; and he became interested in philosophy before he accepted religion. But he underwent a conversion at the age of 31.

From that point on, Augustine led a very religious life, forming many different monastic communities as his life progressed. The Rule of St. Augustine, which was based on his ideas about the early church in Jerusalem, became a model for monasticism in western Europe.

When Augustine became a bishop, the Christian community was still exploring its religious beliefs. Many disagreements had arisen: for example,

Two Augustines

St. Augustine from North Africa was the most celebrated saint of that name, but there was another important Augustine in the church. In the late 500s, Pope Gregory I the Great sent an Italian monk named Augustine to England to convert the Anglo-Saxons. This Augustine is said to have converted 10,000 people in a single day—Christmas Day, 597. He is called Augustine of Canterbury because he decided to make Canterbury the headquarters of England's Christian church.

* **salvation** deliverance from the effects of sin, such as eternal punishment

* **Aristotelian** based on the thought of the ancient Greek philosopher Aristotle

is human nature basically sinful, or does everyone have the free will to be good or bad? Questions of this nature were usually discussed at church councils, where it would be decided which beliefs were correct and which were heretical.

Augustine helped define and then defend the accepted Christian philosophy. For example, on the question of free will, he argued that people were basically sinners, able to gain salvation* not by their own efforts but only through God's grace. His arguments influenced the beliefs of Christians throughout the Middle Ages. For this reason, Augustine is considered by many to be one of the founders of Western theology.

Augustine also defended Christianity against pagan critics. His best known defense, *City of God*, introduced the idea of separation between the realms of politics and religion. This idea played an important part in the history of the Holy Roman Empire and is still very influential today.

The *City of God* is also known for its uniquely Christian view of history. All history is seen as God's preparation of two cities—one of God and one of the devil—to which all humankind will someday belong. *City of God* was one of the most widely read books in the Middle Ages. As a result of this work and others, Augustine became perhaps the most influential author of the medieval Christian world.

In the early 1200s, some of Augustine's ideas about truth and existence were challenged by followers of the new Aristotelian* philosophy—for example, ALBERTUS MAGNUS and Thomas AQUINAS. Augustine had argued that truths are illuminations provided by God. A movement called Augustinianism, led by such thinkers as St. BONAVENTURE, rose to defend Augustine's ideas. However, the arguments of Aquinas became more generally accepted.

Augustine was the great authority on Scripture throughout most of the Middle Ages, and his ideas on such religious issues as grace and free will helped shape medieval and modern theology. (*See also* **Angels; Aristotle in the Middle Ages.**)

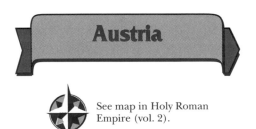

Austria

See map in Holy Roman Empire (vol. 2).

* **duchy** territory ruled by a duke or a duchess

See color plate 3, vol. 2.

The nation of Austria developed during the Middle Ages out of the German HOLY ROMAN EMPIRE. It began as an eastern border territory of BAVARIA along the Danube River north of the Alps. This frontier was contested between Germanic tribes and Slavic and other invaders. By the end of the Middle Ages, Austria had expanded to become one of the richest duchies* under German rule and the major seat of power of the kings of Germany.

Early Years. Most of modern Austria began as a northern edge of the ancient Roman Empire. When Rome was collapsing in the early 400s, Roman soldiers left the region, and waves of Germanic tribes passed through. But a few Roman and Christian centers survived, such as Vienna and Salzburg.

During the 500s, a final wave of these Germanic tribes, the Bavarians, settled in the upper Danube basin, to the west of Austria, while two non-German groups, the Avars and Slavs, occupied the land that became Austria itself. During the next two centuries, the Bavarians were converted to the Christian faith and began sending missions to the Avars and Slavs.

This medieval castle was built on the Danube near Vienna, Austria's capital. Because of its location on the Danube River, Vienna became an important trading city in the Middle Ages. Location on a major waterway provided easy transportation.

---

* **pagan** word used by Christians to mean non-Christian and believing in several gods

* **margrave** noble appointed as military governor of frontier territory

Then, in 788, Emperor CHARLEMAGNE established his lordship over the Bavarians. He began fighting the Avars and conquered much of their territory. Bavaria became a large duchy in the eastern part of Charlemagne's Holy Roman Empire.

Salzburg developed as an important center for converting the Slavic pagans* to Christianity. Christian progress in the borderlands came to a brief halt in 907 when another tribe from the east, the Magyars, defeated the Bavarians. But Charlemagne's German successor, OTTO I THE GREAT, defeated the Magyars in 955 and brought the region permanently into the Holy Roman Empire as an addition to Bavaria.

However, because the Bavarian dukes were becoming very powerful, Otto set up the newly recaptured area as a semi-independent mark, or frontier territory, and in 976 he appointed Leopold of Babenberg as margrave*. The land was within the duchy of Bavaria, but it became known as the Eastern Kingdom—from which comes Austria's modern German name: Osterreich.

Austria Under the Babenbergs. The year 976 is usually considered the birth of Austria. The Babenberg family governed Austria for almost 300 years, as margraves and later as dukes. At first, they were engaged in almost constant warfare with Poles, Czechs, and Magyars along Austria's northern and eastern boundaries. But by the 1050s, German farmers were able to move from the more settled western territories in Bavaria as far as the March and Leitha Rivers. These rivers are still the eastern border of Austria today.

During the next century, the Babenbergs expanded their power through family politics. They became connected by marriage to the

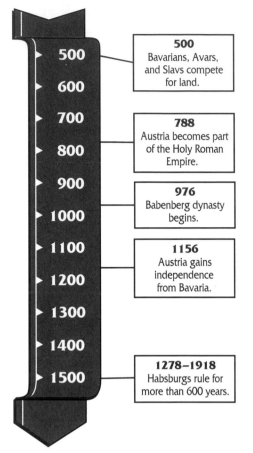

500
Bavarians, Avars, and Slavs compete for land.

788
Austria becomes part of the Holy Roman Empire.

976
Babenberg dynasty begins.

1156
Austria gains independence from Bavaria.

1278–1918
Habsburgs rule for more than 600 years.

* **electors** independent German princes who chose the German kings

* **city-state** independent state consisting of a city and the territories around it

Hohenstaufen family, who during this period were the German kings. FREDERICK I BARBAROSSA, the most famous Hohenstaufen, separated Austria from Bavaria and in 1156 made it an independent duchy. Austria could now be held in the Babenberg family and passed on through both the male and female lines. This was an important step in Austria's growth.

Duke Leopold V of Austria added the southern region of Styria to the Babenbergs' lands in 1192. He further increased the Babenbergs' importance and wealth by capturing King RICHARD I THE LIONHEARTED as he returned to England from the Third CRUSADE, and holding him for ransom. Duke Leopold VI enlarged Austria's capital, Vienna, so that it became one of the most important trading cities on the Danube. His reign is generally considered the golden age of medieval Austria. Leopold gained an international reputation as a leader in the Fifth Crusade (1217).

The power of Austria began to seem too great, however. Holy Roman Emperor Frederick II briefly took over the duchy for himself until other dukes of Germany objected that possessing Austria would make the emperor himself too powerful. Then in 1246, the last male Babenberg died in a war with the Magyars. Austria was without a duke.

Emperor Frederick tried to take over Austria once more but died in 1250. In the chaos that followed, King Ottokar II of BOHEMIA seized Austria and Styria, marrying a female Babenberg to make his claim more legal. Then he pressed farther south into the duchy of Carinthia. These combined lands formed the heart of an expanded Bohemian monarchy, and Ottokar tried to use this power to become elected as the new German emperor. But the electors* instead chose Rudolf of Habsburg, Switzerland, who in 1278 defeated Ottokar and gave the Austrian and Carinthian lands to his sons. This marked the beginning of more than 600 years of Habsburg rule.

Austria Under the Habsburgs.   During the 1300s, the Habsburg family was unable to hold on to the German kingship and lost its original lands in Switzerland. But it enlarged its new Austrian territories by adding the mountain region called the Tyrol and the city-states* of Trent and Salzburg. Duke Rudolf IV added further to Austria's power in the 1360s by simple forgery. He took Frederick Barbarossa's 1156 document that granted Austria to the Babenbergs and had it changed to say that Austria's rulers should have the title of archduke rather than duke. Finally, Rudolf's grandnephew Albert V made a marriage alliance with the German king and Holy Roman Emperor, and in 1438, he became king of Germany himself. From that time until the end of the Holy Roman Empire, Habsburgs ruled both Austria and the empire.

In the early 1400s, also, Austria's southeastern territories were raided by the OTTOMAN Turks, but the Habsburgs succeeded in stopping the Islamic advance into Europe. Before 1500, the Habsburgs had spread their influence far beyond Germany, using family ties to connect themselves with Spain and with a large area of France. The Habsburgs had a motto: "All the world is subject to Austria"; and it almost became true.

Averroës

See *Ibn Rushd.*

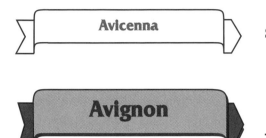

Avicenna

Avignon

* **papacy** office of the pope and his administrators

See *Ibn Sina*.

Avignon is an old city on the east bank of the Rhône River in southeastern France. During much of the Middle Ages, the Rhône was the French border, so Avignon was in the Holy Roman Empire. The city became important in the 1300s and 1400s as a seat of the papacy* and the so-called antipopes.

In 1309, Pope Clement V, who was French, made Avignon the permanent papal residence. There were violent power struggles between church and civil authories in Rome, and Avignon offered better security. The city was enclosed in a sturdy wall, and a new papal palace that resembled a fortress was built there. France, more stable and secure than Italy, was just across the river. Even after 1337, when France became involved in the HUNDRED YEARS WAR against England, Avignon was still considered safer than Rome. The city was officially purchased for the papacy in 1348 from the countess of Provence.

The popes remained at Avignon until 1377. Then Pope Gregory XI returned to Rome, but he died a year later. Because the citizens of Rome feared the papacy would return to Avignon, they pressured the cardinals to elect an Italian pope. However, the new pope, Urban VI, was unruly and offensive, and several cardinals regretted their choice. They declared his election null on the basis that they had been under unfair pressure from the citizens of Rome, and they elected a French pope, Clement VII, to take his place.

Urban VI, however, refused to step down, and his authority was recognized by much of Italy and other parts of Europe, including England. Clement VII fled to Avignon, while Urban continued to rule from Rome. This caused the Great Schism, a split in the Roman Catholic Church that

Avignon first became a papal seat because it was considered safer than Rome. Several popes resided there until 1377, and antipopes lived there during the Great Schism. This photograph shows the papal palace as it looks today.

lasted for about 40 years. During this period, rival popes ruled from both Rome and Avignon. The popes of Avignon are often called antipopes.

The Great Schism was ended by the Council of Constance (1414–1418), when church leaders elected one universally recognized pope. From that point on, Avignon ceased to be a papal residence, and Rome again became the permanent home of the papacy. Avignon remained a papal possession, however, until the 1700s, when its citizens voted to become a part of France. (*See also* **Papacy, Origins and Development.**)

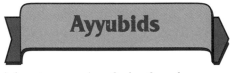

Ayyubids

* **dynasty** succession of rulers from the same family or group

* **crusader** person who participated in the holy wars against the Muslims during the Middle Ages

* **Shi'ites** Muslims who believed that Muhammad chose Ali and his descendants as the rulers and spiritual leaders of the Islamic community

* **vizier** Muslim minister of state

* **caliphate** office and government of the caliph, religious and political head of the Islamic state

* **Sunnite** Muslim majority who believed that the caliphs should rule the Islamic community

* **Mamluk** word meaning slave; later became the name for the dynasty in Egypt that succeeded the Ayyubids

The Ayyubids were an Islamic dynasty* in Egypt and Syria during the late 1100s and early 1200s. This was a period when the Muslims gained many victories over the European crusaders*. The dynasty was founded by SALADIN, the famous conqueror of JERUSALEM, though its name, Ayyubids, comes from Saladin's father, Ayyub ibn Shadhi. Ibn Shadhi and his brother Shirkuh were Kurdish warriors who had won power during earlier campaigns against the crusaders, fighting for the Syrian leader Nur al-Din.

In 1169, Shirkuh and Saladin won a victory for Nur al-Din against the FATIMID dynasty in Egypt. The Fatimids were Shi'ite* Muslims who sometimes acted as allies to the crusaders. Shirkuh died in the battle, but Saladin took control from the Fatimids and became the vizier* in Egypt. Two years later, he abolished the Fatimid caliphate* and started the Ayyubid dynasty, which was loyal to the Sunnite*, Abbasid caliphate. He quickly became a powerful rival to his former commander, Syria's Nur al-Din, and, when Nur al-Din died in 1174, Saladin assumed control of Syria as well.

In the years that followed, Saladin built up strong land and naval forces and won several campaigns against the crusaders, including the recapture of Jerusalem in 1187. Although he protected Jerusalem in the Third Crusade (1189–1192), he failed to defend the important city of Acre and had to sign a truce with England's king, RICHARD I THE LION-HEARTED.

During his reign, Saladin also gained control over northern Iraq and southern Arabia. When he died in 1193, different members of his family ruled different areas. Saladin's own descendants kept control of Aleppo in northern Syria, but they lost Damascus and Cairo, the main seats of power, to his brother al-Adil. Al-Adil was now the main leader of the Ayyubids. He and his descendants ruled Egypt and most of Syria until 1250. During that time, they gained additional victories over the crusaders.

In 1250, during another crusade against Egypt, the Ayyubids' elite Mamluk* regiment rebelled and took command of Cairo and Egypt. This gave Saladin's great-grandson in Aleppo a chance to capture Damascus and all of Syria. He held power for only ten years, however; in 1258 the Mongol king Hulagu sacked Baghdad and by 1260 had destroyed Ayyubid power in Syria. All major centers of Ayyubid rule had now been eliminated.

Despite their short hold on power, the Ayyubids played an important role in the history of the medieval Middle East. At a time when the Fatimids

and SELJUKS were in decline, the Ayyubids brought unity to Egypt and Syria. They transformed Cairo from the capital of Shi'ite Islam to a center of Sunnite Islam. Many mosques, shrines, and colleges were built or renovated and expanded during their rule. This helped improve the relationship between government and religious institutions and created a stimulating intellectual environment. The Ayyubids also used taxes and fees on family lands to support religious, medical, and charitable institutions. (*See also* **Baybars al-Bunduqdari; Caliphate; Crusades; Mamluk Dynasty; Mongol Empire.**)

Bacon, Roger

ca. 1213– ca. 1291
English Franciscan scholar and philosopher

* **friar** member of a religious brotherhood of the later Middle Ages who worked in the community and relied on the charity of others for his livelihood

Roger Bacon was born in southwest England. He studied at Oxford University and the University of Paris. Bacon was a Franciscan friar* who became a celebrated scholar and teacher. His work is firmly rooted in the Middle Ages, but some of his writings seem to foreshadow later scientific ideas.

Like other thinkers of his time, Bacon was deeply interested in the work of ancient Greek philosopher ARISTOTLE. Many of Aristotle's writings had only recently reached western Europe, and the Roman Church viewed them as very controversial. Scholastics such as ALBERTUS MAGNUS and Thomas AQUINAS argued that Aristotle's ideas about thinking and the soul supported Christian doctrine. Bacon went further, saying that Aristotle's view of the natural world should also be part of Christian thought.

Roger Bacon had a keen interest in science. In this diagram from his notebooks, Bacon recorded his theory regarding the refraction of light entering the human eye.

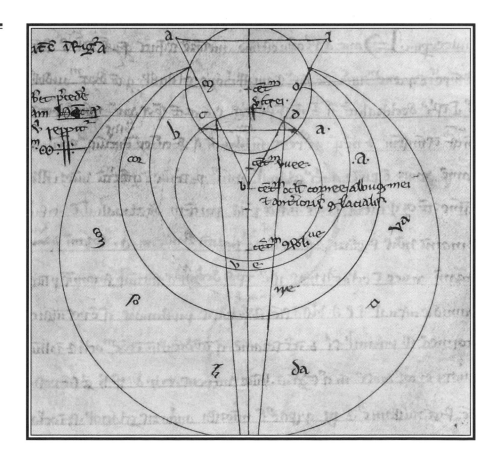

He was interested in optics and natural observations and argued that mathematics was the key to understanding nature. He held that knowledge of nature was an essential part of a knowledge of God. Some scholars today consider Bacon a forerunner of modern applied science because of his stress on observation, experiments, and practical invention.

Bacon's view of science was not our own. He firmly believed that AS-TROLOGY, ALCHEMY, and prediction of the future were practical sciences. But he drew a distinction between the sciences and many magical beliefs that were popular in his time. Bacon strongly supported education that studied nonreligious as well as religious subjects. He believed that the purpose of study was understanding the world in order to lead a good and just life.

Badr, Battle of

Badr was a small village in western Arabia near Medina. It was the site of the first major battle between MUHAMMAD and his opponents in Mecca. The battle helped consolidate support for Muhammad at a critical time.

After escaping from Mecca to Medina, Muhammad and his Muslim followers raided caravans or trading expeditions from Mecca, probably to support themselves economically. This caused hostilities with the Quraysh, Mecca's ruling family. In 624, Muhammad and about 300 followers prepared to raid a caravan returning to Mecca from Gaza. The caravan leader requested Meccan troops as escorts. A Meccan force of 900 to 1000 joined the caravan. They met Muhammad's raiding party at the village of Badr, with disastrous results. The Meccans were routed and lost between 45 and 70 men, including some important leaders. The Muslims suffered only about 15 casualties.

The Battle of Badr brought immediate rewards to the Muslims in the form of booty and ransom for captives. It also had more lasting consequences. It strengthened Muhammad's position in Medina by making the Muslims more certain that God was on their side. It enhanced the Prophet's reputation in Mecca and lessened the power and prestige of the Quraysh family. It helped Muhammad increase his position and influence across all of western Arabia. This brought many converts to the Muslim cause.

Muhammad's victory raised him from a relative unknown to an important figure in west Arabian politics. Those who fought at Badr on the side of the Prophet were later specially honored for their loyalty.

Baghdad

Baghdad was the main capital city of the ABBASIDS, the second dynasty of Muslim caliphs*. It is in the area called Mesopotamia, which means the land between the rivers. Baghdad became a vast city with many palaces. Today it is the capital of Iraq.

The city was founded in 762 at an old village called Baghdad. The site was selected by al-MANSUR, the second caliph in the Abbasid family. Al-Mansur decided to build a new city because his existing capital, al-Kufa,

* **caliph** religious and political head of an Islamic state

From the 700s to the 900s, Baghdad was a prosperous and important city in the Middle East. After that time, the power of the caliphate lessened, causing a gradual decline in political order. In 1258, the Mongols conquered the weakened city, ending the Abbasid regime that had lasted more than 500 years.

See map in Fatimid Empire (vol. 2).

was home to many Shi'ite sympathizers. Shi'ites were a group of Muslims who opposed the Sunnite majority and their caliphs.

The village of Baghdad had many strategic and geographic advantages. It was at the junction of the Tigris River and the Sarat Canal, surrounded on three sides by water. This provided natural defenses. The Sarat Canal connected two major river systems, the Tigris and Euphrates, and was deep enough for cargo-carrying boats. Baghdad was also located on important overland highways. It therefore became a thriving trade center as well as the Abbasid capital.

The first major structure in Baghdad was a famous complex called the Round City, or Madinat al-Salam (the City of Peace). Thousands of workers were involved, and it was more than four years before the Abbasids could move in. The complex included a palace and mosque for the caliph, palaces for his children, buildings for the government, and homes for government officers. However, the area around the walls of the Round City soon developed a sprawling urban complex of mosques, markets, and residential areas. At the end of his reign, al-Mansur moved to a smaller palace, called al-Khuld, located outside the Round City.

Al-Mansur's son and successor, al-Mahdi, completed construction of another palace complex in Baghdad called al-Rusafah. It was on the other side of the Tigris River from the Round City. Once again, manufacturing and trading businesses and large residential neighborhoods developed nearby. The city and its markets continued to undergo major expansion.

The reign of HARUN AL-RASHID, which began in 786, is considered the high point of Baghdad's splendor. The caliph's court was famed for its culture, and the city reached its greatest extent in land area and population. Yet in spite of the magnificence of al-Rashid's court, he and his sons after him often spent time away from Baghdad. In fact, his son al-Mu'tasim, who took power in 883, founded a new capital at Samarra.

The Books of Baghdad

Baghdad, a city of culture, had many libraries—36 are known about today. The grandest was the palace center of learning, built in 830. Called Bayt al-Hikma (the House of Wisdom), it was a library, school, and translation center. Scholars of the caliph did research in it, but it was not open to the public. However, the public could read books in libraries attached to the mosques, or they could buy books in the marketplaces if they could pay enough. The technology of paper had brought prices down—but a book could still cost as much as a farm animal.

Several more palaces were built in Baghdad when the new caliph, al-Mu'tadid, returned there in 892. These palaces featured unusual elements, including a zoological garden and fantastic mechanical devices. However, they were the last major buildings sponsored by the caliphs.

After the early 900s, the caliphate stayed in Baghdad, but its power began to lessen. The city started to shrink in population; neighborhoods became poorer; there was a breakdown of order. Other dynasties, including the Seljuk Turks, began to take over power from the caliphs, but they could do little to stem the decline. When Baghdad was conquered by the Mongols in 1258, it was a hollow shell of the once proud city. It had become a series of separated neighborhoods, much as it is today.

Bailiff

Bailiff is a general word for a lower-level public official in medieval England. Some bailiffs worked for county sheriffs, doing routine administrative tasks—such as signing documents, choosing jurors, and confiscating the possessions of criminals. They also served as local administrators and magistrates over rural districts, or "hundreds."

Bailiffs held similar positions in boroughs and towns. Town bailiffs were originally appointed by the king. In the 1100s and 1200s, as municipal governments grew, town bailiffs began to be elected by the local citizens.

Some bailiffs worked for private landowners, protecting a lord's property rights and collecting the income from his estates. They could sometimes represent the landowner in certain types of legal cases. Increasingly often in the later 1200s, it seems, bailiffs were sued by their own lords for refusing to provide a full account of their activities. (*See also* **Bailli.**)

Bailli

Baillis were administrators in northern France who acted as the king's representatives. At first, they were merely supervisors of the officials who collected royal revenues. Later they began to administer justice. During the 1100s in Normandy, they were assigned to a particular region; elsewhere in France they traveled wherever they were needed.

When Normandy was conquered by the French king in 1204, he adapted the Norman system to help control the new territory. He appointed his own men as regional baillis for Normandy and gave them additional power as military leaders. They became governors of their regions.

This idea spread to the rest of France. Some of the traveling baillis were promoted to positions as regional governors and came to be called grand baillis. Those who were not promoted lost some power, becoming petty baillis. The grand baillis were chosen from the lesser nobility or knightly class and were paid very well for their work. Their income was often higher than that of more noble families. (*See also* **Bailiff.**)

Ballads

Today, *ballad* means a type of traditional song that tells a story. It is similar to the words *ballata* (from Italian) and *ballade* (from French), both of which denoted types of songs that originated in dance music. The ballata was an Italian song form that changed from being a dance song in the 1200s to a solo art song in the 1300s. Then, in the 1400s, it became a form of love poem, to be read and not sung.

French ballades were also usually love songs, for a singer and two or three instruments. Like the ballata, ballades were occasionally written as words without music. Ballades are thought to have developed from the songs of trouvères, the educated poet-musicians in central and northern France (similar to the troubadours of southern France).

Ballades were also known in England—CHAUCER wrote some of his poetry in this form. However, the story songs that we now call ballads are most likely to have developed as the MINSTREL tradition in England declined in the 1400s. They became linked to genuine folk music. Some of the ballads of that time were written down, but many of them survived only because people in each generation memorized them.

Many of these ballads might have been forgotten altogether. But in the late 1800s, an American scholar named Francis J. Child collected and wrote down five volumes of songs, in a work called *English and Scottish Popular Ballads*. It consists of a collection of 305 ballads, some of which probably have origins in the late Middle Ages. (*See also* **Troubadour, Trouvère.**)

Baltic Countries

* **pagan** word used by Christians to mean non-Christian and believing in several gods

* **crusader** person who participated in the holy wars against the Muslims during the Middle Ages

See map in Trade (vol. 4).

The Baltic countries are located in northern Europe around the southeastern shores of the Baltic Sea. This was the last pagan* region in Europe. In the later Middle Ages, missionaries and crusaders* tried to control the tribes there and to convert them to Christianity, fighting the only crusades in the north. The struggle was fierce, but the Christians prevailed, and today's Baltic nations of Estonia, Latvia, and Lithuania began to emerge.

Early History of the Baltic Region. Trading routes had connected the primitive Baltic region with the cultures of the Mediterranean area since the earliest times. Amber was one product from the region that was especially prized. The pagan Balts who lived there—Estonians, Lithuanians, Latvians, and Prussians—developed an orderly political life centered in hilltop villages and castles. They spoke their own languages, and their society was made up of tribal clans ruled by chiefs.

In the early 500s, after the influence of the ancient Roman Empire had declined, the Baltic tribes began to have more contact with western Europeans from Germany and Scandinavia. Trade across the Baltic Sea became important, and there was also a greater need for defense against enemies from the west, particularly the VIKINGS. For protection, the Balts built strong forts and other defenses. They developed a reputation for being hostile and dangerous. Aside from some short-lived Viking settlements, there was no outside rule over any of the Baltic peoples.

By the 1100s, trade had helped the Baltic tribes to improve their standard of living. The Balts had become dependent on imports of cloth,

Marienburg Castle in Poland served as the headquarters for the Teutonic Knights in the 1300s. While Prussia, on the southern Baltic coast, surrendered to the crusaders in 1283, Lithuania resisted conversion to Christianity. In 1410, Lithuania and Poland joined to defeat the Teutonic Knights.

* **icon** Christian religious image of a saint, often painted and placed on a screen in the church, most common in the Eastern Church

metal, and food. Technologies such as the potter's wheel and the millstone were adopted. Baltic forts were enlarged and strengthened as protection against not only the Vikings but also the Danes, Russians, and Poles.

Religious Conflict.   In the early 1200s, border warfare based on religious differences was common in the Baltic region. The Balts, still pagans, were now surrounded by Christians. Baltic warriors reacted to threats by making fierce raids. They frequently looted churches and destroyed altars, icons*, and other holy objects. Writers of the time describe the long lines of prisoners and cattle being herded away by gloating victors. Christians saw the Balts as dangerous foes to be conquered and converted to Christianity.

This conversion was a slow process, however. The first conversions probably occurred along the southeastern borders of the region when princes invaded from KIEVAN RUS. They persuaded local tribes to join the Byzantine Orthodox Church, which had come to Kiev and other eastern regions. However, the number of converts was not great, and pagan traditions continued.

Early attempts by the Roman Church, the church of western Europe, to establish missions in the Baltics were mostly unsuccessful. Though Balts were often willing to be baptized, they were less ready to pay taxes to the church, to give up multiple marriages, and to stop worshiping forest and sky gods. This led to a call for German crusades against the region. Some of these crusades were directed across the Baltic Sea, against the northern areas of Estonia and Latvia. Other crusades were by land, along the southern coast of the Baltic into the regions of Prussia and Lithuania.

A crusading order of knights called the Brothers of the Sword was created in the early 1200s to defend crusader castles in Latvia and to continue fighting tribes that remained pagan. These German crusaders did not approve of Eastern Orthodox Christianity, considering it schismatic*, so they also fought against armies from Rus (Russia). In the southern Baltic, several crusading orders were invited from Palestine to join the attack. The

* **schismatic** causing a schism or deep split, especially in the Christian church

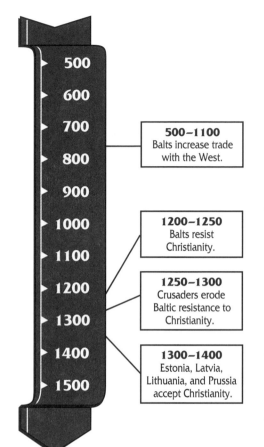

500–1100
Balts increase trade with the West.

1200–1250
Balts resist Christianity.

1250–1300
Crusaders erode Baltic resistance to Christianity.

1300–1400
Estonia, Latvia, Lithuania, and Prussia accept Christianity.

most successful were a small group called the Teutonic Knights, who after the 1250s shifted their main effort to the Baltic region.

Crusaders posed a new threat to the Baltic tribes. Unlike earlier enemies, the crusaders were as interested in spiritual victories as in riches or booty. No matter how hard the Balts fought, crusaders continued their attacks. Eventually, the crusaders' numbers, equipment, and commitment to their cause began to wear down the Baltic peoples.

Response to the crusaders varied. Most Baltic tribes remained neutral until attacked. Some took advantage of the disorder caused by war to attack other local tribes and avenge past insults. A few tribes became allies of the Western Christians so they would be defended against traditional rivals. One tribe, suffering from a famine, surrendered in return for food. Many of the stronger tribes fought fiercely and inflicted defeat on the crusaders. Gradually, however, the Baltic tribes yielded to crusader pressure.

In the northern part of the region, the Estonians resisted strongly until 1227, and they remained dangerous more than a century later. In 1343, they rebelled and killed many Christians. Some Latvian tribes surrendered very quickly; others remained independent until the 1280s. In the south, Prussia slowly surrendered to the Teutonic Knights—the last tribe was finally defeated in 1283, and, even then, half of its members escaped into Lithuania.

By 1300, the Lithuanians were the only Baltic people who retained their independence, their pagan religion, and major aspects of their ancient way of life. Though attacked by Germans, Poles, and Russians, they were better able to resist because of their relative unity, greater numbers, and superior leadership. The area was divided into two kingdoms in the early 1300s, and the people of both halves successfully defended themselves against the Teutonic Knights and Russia, respectively. It was not until 1386 that one of the two Lithuanian kings became king of Poland, joined the other Lithuanian king to defeat the Teutonic Knights, and then voluntarily accepted Christianity.

Increasing Westernization.   During the 1300s and 1400s, the Baltic lands became part of the Western economy. Some Balts moved into German towns and became citizens of the HOLY ROMAN EMPIRE. Meanwhile, German and Polish farmers migrated east into Prussian lands, where they became a majority—the Prussian Balts became assimilated into this population.

Most Baltic natives, however, knew little about Western culture except for taxes, the administration of justice, and the basics of Christianity. In time, the Latvians and Estonians, who were ruled by Germans and who traded with the German HANSEATIC LEAGUE, became increasingly influenced by German ways. The Lithuanians, on the other hand, were drawn to Polish culture. The Roman Church, which the Lithuanians had resisted for so long, became the most important institution in defining their national identity.

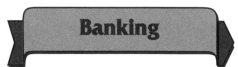

Banking

Banks of the type we have today did not exist in the Middle Ages. Even then, however, money had to be exchanged and loaned so that business and trade could take place. These limited money services were usually handled by wealthy individuals and by companies that had other businesses also.

During the Middle Ages, economic growth and increased international trade slowly led to the development of full banking services and

The development of modern banking began in Italy and spread across the trade cities of Europe. Banking was often a family enterprise. Shown here is a detail from *The Money Changer and his Wife,* painted by artist Quentin Massys in the early 1500s.

banks. Such services were needed first on the busy trade routes of the Muslims, though banks as such did not develop in the Islamic world. The cities of Europe began to feel similar needs in the early 1100s, and these needs were at first met by moneylenders, including Jewish entrepreneurs. But in Italy, companies began to provide complete banking services for local and international trade. From these companies, modern banks developed.

Law played an important part in the growth of banks. All three major religions—Judaism, Christianity, and Islam—prohibited USURY. Usury included charging interest on money that was borrowed. However, without interest, the money needed for business and trade would have been impossible to collect. Therefore, most legal codes allowed forms of interest in their laws about business obligations and repayment of debt.

Islamic Banking

As the Islamic Empire grew, Muslim traders began to sell their goods across great distances. Banking services developed to make this trade easier. Because actual interest was against Islamic law, other alternatives were developed that made payment for money services possible.

For example, credit sales—in which payment is made some time after a purchase—were common. Merchants were allowed to charge more for a credit sale than they did for cash sales. They could also demand advance payment for later delivery. Both methods provided usable cash for other purposes.

Islamic commercial law also provided for payment to be made in far-off areas without having to send cash. Suppose a man wanted to pay a merchant in a distant city and was already owed a debt in the same city. A letter telling the person who owed him money to pay it to the merchant instead was viewed as a legal payment. Such a transaction is a form of credit transfer*.

Paying money over long distances often involved money exchange, too: buying one type of currency with another. The value of each currency was usually open to bargaining, and a fee could be charged for the exchange service. Money changers specialized in this kind of operation, but any merchant who had foreign coins could sell them to others. Thus, most merchants could serve as bankers as well, to some extent.

* **credit transfer** basic technique of banking, in which money can be legally exchanged without actual coins or notes changing hands

Jewish Banking in Western Europe

In the early part of the Middle Ages, Muslim commerce was expanding, but western Europe was in economic decline. By the 900s, however, Europe's population had grown, and the economy was recovering. As in the Islamic world, money services were needed to make business and trade easier.

Several groups provided such services. At times, monasteries would lend large amounts of money, though this was forbidden by the pope after the 1200s. For smaller amounts, wealthy widows and tavern owners were often a good source. But the Jews became known as the specialists in money lending. In northern Europe and especially in England, it was their main occupation, though in southern Europe, Jews had many other jobs also. As in the Muslim world, Jewish and Christian religious law said it was wrong to charge interest for loans. However, the need for financial services encouraged some to ignore the prohibition, and others found ways to modify the loans and disguise the interest payments.

Most Jewish lenders acted alone or as married couples rather than in companies. When large loans were required, groups joined together to raise the money, but these groups were nearly always short-term partnerships.

Jewish loan activities varied from place to place. In England before 1200, Jews often lent money on a grand scale, being protected by the Norman kings. However, during the reign of King John, from 1199 to 1216, heavy taxation ruined many Jewish lenders. On the European continent, a great deal of Jewish lending activity took place. Jews handled large amounts of money for nobles and even the pope. They also made small individual loans to townsfolk and peasants, often acting as pawnbrokers*.

* **pawnbroker** person who makes loans in exchange for valuable items, such as coats and jewelry

In Europe, loans with interest were often legal, or at least tolerated by the authorities. However, in the later Middle Ages, some monarchs tried to abolish money lending and were helped by anti-Jewish feelings. These feelings increased so much in some parts of Europe that Jews were expelled: from England in 1290, from France during the 1300s, and from Spain in 1492. However, the poor of Paris protested in 1306 because they feared that Christian lenders would charge more than the Jews had.

The Development of Modern Banking

Local Banking in Italy. At first, European trade was freest and most active in the coastal cities of Italy. By the 1000s, towns in Italy's interior also experienced growth in trade and industry. This "commercial revolution" spread outward from Italy to the rest of Europe. It provided the basis upon which modern banking developed.

Italian banking began in Genoa, a port city and leader in trade. Money changers there were known as *bancherii* because of the benches or tables at which they worked. In the late 1100s, the *bancherii* began accepting deposits from local individuals and began offering loans. Interest rates are seldom mentioned in early banking records. But there is no doubt that bankers paid interest on deposits and also charged interest on loans, in spite of the Christian church's prohibition of usury.

By 1200, customers of Genoa banks could pay each other by credit transfer. All customers had to do was to tell their banker to transfer funds between their deposit records. They could also make similar arrangements with customers of different banks. Within the next 200 years, exchange banks had spread to all the major European trading centers except Scandinavia, the Baltic region, and northern Germany. In each center, banks generally were located close to one another—this enabled credit transfers involving different banks to be carried out quickly and easily.

Just as today, medieval bankers usually invested the money earned by the bank and much of their customers' deposits by making loans to profitable companies. However, they often invested in risky undertakings and lost money. This led to a high failure rate among the banks. This tendency for private banks to fail led to the first public banks.

The earliest of these, in Barcelona, Spain, was called the Taula de Canvi, or Exchange Table. Founded in 1401, it provided banking services to the city, such as receiving surplus taxes and lending money to the city. It also handled the savings of citizens. Loans to private individuals were forbidden, however. The Taula de Canvi remained in existence until 1853, when it became part of the Bank of Spain. Public banks opened in other parts of Europe also, some more successfully than others.

International Banking.   International banking was invented by large-scale Italian merchant banking* companies. These companies developed in the major trading centers of northern Italy—such as Florence, Milan, Siena, and Lucca—during the 1200s. They consisted of a home office in the city of origin and branch offices in cities throughout Europe, such as Bruges, London, Avignon, and Geneva. This system of banks created an international Italian banking network that determined the structure of international banking in the modern era.

Italian merchant banking companies started as family partnerships. Several family companies competed during much of the Middle Ages. Among the most important were the Bonsignori, the Ricciardi, and the Medici. Merchant bankers worked with their own funds and with money from outside investors. Each partner contributed a sum to the bank and received a share of the profits. Investors received a share of the profits as well.

A primary function of these international banks was to transfer money from place to place and from one currency to another. In the late 1100s and 1200s, these exchanges had been handled at great international fairs, held six times each year in the county of Champagne in France. Toward the end of the 1200s, Italian companies began to bypass these fairs, using their own foreign branches instead.

Remember: Consult the index at the end of Volume 4 to find more information on many topics.

---

* **merchant banking** banking that handles money for international trade

Italian merchant bankers began to handle most of the funds of the pope and performed similar services for royalty. They held church money on deposit and handled its shipment and transfer. They financed crusades and royal activities and served as business agents to monarchies.

In the 1400s, the great Medici bank failed. This ended an era in the history of banking. Although Italian merchant banking obviously continued, its dominance of international commerce and finance was broken. After 1500, the center of international finance began shifting northward. (*See also* **Anti-Semitism; Trade.**)

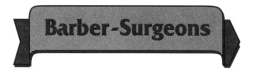

Barber-Surgeons

* **bloodletting** opening a vein to take blood; believed to aid the healing process

See color plate 5, vol. 1.

In the early Middle Ages, most medical care was based on old Greek and Roman medical texts. It was performed by monks and occasionally by other learned people from outside the monasteries. By the late Middle Ages, theoretical medicine had become a specialty of universities, while most practical health procedures were performed by barber-surgeons. Besides cutting hair, barber-surgeons pulled teeth, treated wounds, mended bone fractures, and operated on hernias and hemorrhoids. They also amputated limbs and performed other operations such as bloodletting*. Most learned their trade through experience rather than formal classroom schooling.

There were several reasons why medical care moved out of the monasteries. Church authorities urged clerics to focus on their spiritual duties and to avoid the shedding of blood. For this reason, though the church did not cease to help the sick, church laws began to discourage monks from practicing medicine, especially surgery. In addition, between 1000 and 1300, the medical texts of the ancient world became part of the university curriculum, where lay scholars as well as monks could study them. Theoretical MEDICINE became an intellectual pursuit of high status.

University-trained physicians might have been good at diagnosing some medical problems, but they were rarely good at providing therapy.

Most barber-surgeons did not have any formal medical training. They learned their trade by practical experience. This barber-surgeon is extracting an arrow from the back of a soldier.

Surgery was rarely studied at the university. Like many manual occupations in the Middle Ages, it was considered a lower-class profession. There was a real need for surgeons with practical skills. This need was met primarily by barber-surgeons. The abilities of these surgeons varied greatly, but they were the only people who provided this type of care. Many of their skills, too, were based on the techniques of ancient Greek and Roman doctors.

Barber-surgeons often organized themselves into GUILDS. In many places, only guild members could practice surgery. The guilds set standards of work for surgeons and also provided practical apprenticeships to train new surgeons. Such apprenticeships could take eight years or more.

The special training and skills of barber-surgeons did not, however, earn them higher status in the Middle Ages. Theoretical physicians were considered more learned and respected. At a sickbed, priests were held in higher esteem than barber-surgeons. In fact, barber-surgeons were sometimes accused of interfering with God's work and keeping people alive just for personal gain.

Remember: Words in small capital letters have separate entries, and the index at the end of Volume 4 will guide you to more information on many topics.

Barcelona

See color plate 8, vol. 3.

In the Middle Ages, Barcelona was a leading trade center on the Mediterranean Sea. Located at the northeastern corner of the Spanish peninsula, the city became a major seaport in the 1100s. For 200 years, it flourished as a center of trade and commerce. As capital of CATALONIA and then ARAGON, Barcelona was also an important cultural center.

In the 300s, Barcelona was a colony of the Roman Empire. At that time, it was known as Barcino. When the VISIGOTHS swept into northern Spain in the 400s, Barcino became an early royal center for Visigoth rulers. Later it became a fortress. However, it fell into Arab hands in 716 when the MUSLIMS invaded the Spanish peninsula from northern Africa.

Barcelona was reconquered from the Muslims in 801 by Louis the Pious during an expedition ordered by his father, CHARLEMAGNE. It served as a frontier outpost of the CAROLINGIAN Empire until the 900s, when it gained independence under the powerful counts of Barcelona. The city grew in the mid-to-late 900s. A port was built, the defenses were strengthened, and new buildings were constructed. Barcelona's prosperity at this time was due to local agriculture.

In the early 1000s, the counts of Barcelona succeeded in taking back lands to the south that had been overrun by Muslims. Soon they brought all of Catalonia under their control. Barcelona also began to benefit from its location on the Mediterranean, forging trading links with the Italian cities of Genoa, Pisa, and Venice. Ships traveling from the eastern Mediterranean carried luxuries such as silks and spices from the Middle East and Asia into Barcelona's port, where merchants and traders bought and sold goods. Many of these goods then were carried overland across the Pyrenees mountains to cities such as Paris and London.

In 1137, by a political arrangement, the counts of Barcelona also became the count-kings of Aragon. The city enjoyed a spurt of growth as newcomers were attracted to the city and its lively economy. By 1200,

The Consulate of the Sea

Around 1370, the court of Barcelona decided to standardize its customs regulating ships and shipping. After studying the customs and laws of many countries, it assembled a book called *Llibre del Consolat de Mar (Book of the Consulate of the Sea)*. This collection became the leading authority on maritime law in the later Middle Ages. The influence of the book highlighted Barcelona's position as a center of trade and naval power.

* **guild** association of craft and trade workers that set standards and represented the interests of its members

Barcelona had between 10,000 and 20,000 inhabitants. As in other medieval cities, there were numerous neighborhoods where artisans, merchants, and craftspeople practiced their trades and carried on business. Streets often were named for trades practiced by the craft guilds* located on them. Barcelona also had a Jewish quarter, and Jews worked in various professions in the city. The city's trade and commerce were protected by a strong city government headed by nobles and a council of leading citizens.

During the 1200s and 1300s, Barcelona remained quite prosperous. This led to many city improvements, including paved streets, sewers, and piped-in fresh water. The city also began to take on its special look, with a grid pattern of streets, wealthy palaces, and a large, impressive cathedral. However, by 1400, Barcelona had reached its peak. The court of the kings of Aragon moved to Naples, which had become a part of their empire. Poor harvests and piracy in the Mediterranean hurt the city's economy, and plagues reduced its population. Gradually, too, the kingdom of CASTILE to the west became more powerful. The focus of Spanish trade began to shift to the Atlantic Ocean and soon to the New World. Barcelona, facing the Mediterranean coast, began to enter a period of decline.

Bard

Today the term *bard* simply means poet. Originally it meant a tribal poet of the Celtic peoples of Europe. By the Middle Ages, the Celts had been driven west by Germanic tribes, and bards performed their songs only in the Celtic areas of Scotland, Ireland, Wales, Cornwall, and Brittany.

Like poets in other tribal groups, bards sang the stories of their culture. Before the written word, such songs kept history and traditions alive. Bards in Ireland were trained for up to seven years. There they mastered at least 350 different poems and almost as many types of verse. In Wales, too, poets attended bardic schools. Without Welsh and Breton bards, the ARTHURIAN legends would have been forgotten.

* **patron** person of wealth and influence who supports an artist, writer, or scholar

With musical accompaniment, bards not only celebrated their heroes and gods, they also praised the feats of their patrons* and made fun of some who were less fortunate. They were believed to have magical powers that could make their listeners brave.

Baron

The term *baron* seems to have been used first to mean a warrior and respected man. By the end of the Middle Ages, it was a term of honor for a nobleman. It was a title similar to *knight,* though it generally signified a more senior person, one who ruled and administered land on which serfs lived and worked. Unlike the title *count,* which indicated that a person ruled a specific area called a county, barons could be of greater or lesser status, depending on their position in the FEUDAL system. Counts could be addressed as "Baron." Sometimes the title of baron was given to officials without land. For example, judges and administrators of England's EXCHEQUER were known as barons. (*See also* **Count, County; Knighthood; Nobility and Nobles.**)

Bartolo da Sassoferrato

ca. 1313–1357
Legal scholar, teacher, and author

* **civil law**   body of law that regulates and protects the rights of individuals

Bartolo da Sassoferrato was born in a small village in central Italy. He had a brilliant mind. Bartolo became one of the leading legal scholars of the 1300s, and his work influenced the future of European law.

After studying at Perugia and Bologna, Bartolo held several offices as a legal expert. However, his true callings were teaching and writing. Most of his teaching career was spent at the University of Perugia, about 80 miles north of Rome.

Bartolo had a vast knowledge of the collection of ancient Roman civil law* that was compiled under the Byzantine emperor JUSTINIAN I. These laws—often called the *Corpus juris civilis*—were the rules and regulations that had developed during the history of ancient Rome. Though largely replaced in western Europe by local Germanic laws, civil law began to be studied again in Italy in the 1100s.

Legal scholars before Bartolo held that Roman civil law was based on principles that could not change. Bartolo had a different view, arguing that it should respond to the needs of people living in the present. He found ways to apply some of the old principles to new legal situations of his day, and where ancient Roman laws did not fit the 1300s, he suggested changes. Bartolo's most famous teaching was his theory of the city-state, in which he argued that city governments should have authority to make laws, grant citizenship, and levy taxes. His ideas helped shape legal systems throughout Europe. (*See also* **Law; Law Schools.**)

Basil I the Macedonian

812–886
Byzantine emperor

* **dynasty**   succession of rulers from the same family or group

* **co-emperor**   emperor who shares office with another

* **papacy**   office of the pope and his administrators

Basil was the founder of the BYZANTINE EMPIRE's powerful Macedonian dynasty*, which ruled that empire from 867 until 1056. Basil was an able ruler whose administrative achievements strengthened the empire.

Born in Macedonia, Greece, Basil and his family were carried off by enemy soldiers to Bulgaria, where he spent his youth in captivity. Freed at the age of 25, he impressed the Byzantine emperor Michael III by his horse riding, and he rose to become a high personal servant at the imperial palace in CONSTANTINOPLE. Later Basil accused Michael's chief adviser of conspiracy, won more favor, and became co-emperor* in 865. Two years later, he had Michael assassinated.

Though his path to power was rough, Basil was an effective ruler. He rescued the empire from a financial crisis caused by Michael and started an extensive program of building and restoration. His reign—often called the Macedonian renaissance—was a time of great artistic and literary activity. Basil also began a major revision of the empire's laws, the civil laws first compiled by JUSTINIAN I. He also made peace in a growing conflict between the Eastern Orthodox Church and the papacy* in Rome.

Under Basil, Byzantine naval power increased, and the empire's influence began to spread again. Serbia was converted to Orthodox Christianity by Byzantine missionaries. Decisive victories were won against the Muslims in Asia Minor and in the Adriatic Sea. Basil left a stronger empire, which his successors expanded. (*See also* **Christianity; Law.**)

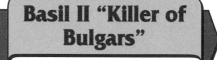

Basil II "Killer of Bulgars"

958–1025
Byzantine emperor

* **regent** person appointed to govern a kingdom when the rightful ruler is too young, absent, or disabled

Basil II was noted for his conquest of BULGARIA and for other great battles during his reign. He died leaving the BYZANTINE EMPIRE at its strongest since the time of JUSTINIAN I, though his rule started with conflict.

He and his younger brother Constantine became co-emperors when Basil was 5 years old. While they were young, the empire was ruled by powerful regents*. At the age of 18, Basil took power. Constantine was willing to let him rule, but Basil suffered a major defeat in 986 from a Bulgarian ruler named Samuil. This led two Byzantine generals to challenge Basil. They took territories in Asia Minor and threatened CONSTANTINOPLE.

Helped by Prince Vladimir of KIEVAN RUS, Basil defeated the generals in 989. In return, Basil arranged for his sister Anna to marry the prince, and Vladimir converted the Russians to Byzantine Christianity. Basil's renewed war against the Bulgarians was again interrupted when an army of Muslims from Egypt attacked the empire's eastern frontier. He drove the Muslims from Asia Minor, strengthening his influence there by forcing large landowners to give up lands they had seized earlier from local farmers.

Basil then returned to Bulgaria, and, by 1014, he recaptured all his territories and defeated the main Bulgarian army. To break their resistance, he had 14,000 captives blinded, leaving one out of every hundred men with a single eye to guide the rest back to Samuil.

Basil made the empire powerful again, but he failed in one regard. He had no children and left the succession to his incompetent brother Constantine. (*See also* **Warfare.**)

Bastide

* **magistrate** ruling official of a town
* **abbey** monastery under the rule of an abbot or abbess

The word *bastide* originally meant stronghold, and it described defensive fortifications in the south of France. Some bastides were merely small forts that defended a village's land. But the name was also given to a successful fortified town called Montauban, built on the border of TOULOUSE and AQUITAINE. Other towns were built to imitate Montauban's success. They, too, came to be called bastides, even though some were not fortified.

Montauban was founded by the count of Toulouse in 1144 on an easily defended high point, to guard the road to Toulouse against threats from the duke of Aquitaine to the north. To encourage people to move to the new town, the count guaranteed freedom for all who would live there. He let them build homes and fixed low land rents. By 1200, Montauban was a thriving community with its own elected magistrates*. They owed allegiance to the local abbey* that had originally owned the land—and also to the count.

In the 1200s and 1300s, local princes and nobles founded similar frontier towns. Like Montauban, these were usually on private property that the founders could share with the former owners. The kings of England, who were also dukes of Aquitaine, also built several bastides in the area.

New bastides were usually started for reasons other than defense. They often became profitable trading communities. Located on busy water and land routes, they attracted local markets and long-distance

The French town of Carcassonne remains one of the best-preserved walled cities in Europe. A portion of the bastide walls of Carcassonne is shown here.

* **artisans** skilled craftspeople

trade. The lords who founded the bastides discovered that they attracted immigrants, including rich merchants and artisans*, from whom fees and taxes could be collected. Thus the bastides provided power and revenue to their founders.

The heart of a bastide was its public square. Sometimes, as in Montauban, this was an area surrounded by a covered walk that contained the market, the municipal offices, and often a well or fountain. But in other bastides, the "square" was a mere widening of the road. Most bastides were fortified and built on a grid plan, but some were circular or irregular in shape. They ranged in size from a few houses to 3,000.

Some immigrants to bastides came from far away—there were English residents in the bastides of Aquitaine—but most were drawn from neighboring towns and villages. To attract residents, bastides offered freedom from arbitrary taxes, protection of property, regulated markets, fixed court fines, limited military service, and an organized city government. (*See also* **Cities and Towns.**)

Bavaria

* **duchy** territory ruled by a duke or a duchess

See map in Germany (vol. 2).

* **pagan** word used by Christians to mean non-Christian and believing in several gods

Bavaria is the southeastern part of modern Germany. It is just north of the Alps, the mountain range that separates Germany from Italy, and it is bounded by the Danube River in the north and its tributary the Lech River in the west. In the Middle Ages, Bavaria was one of the major duchies* of the East Frankish Empire and then of the German kingdom. It played an important part in the politics of Germany and the HOLY ROMAN EMPIRE, and the duchy of Austria was created from its eastern territories.

Early Middle Ages. A Roman province since the first century of the Christian era, Bavaria was invaded by several pagan* Germanic tribes: the Franks, the Alamanni, and the Baiuvarii, for whom the territory was

Dense Forests and Trade

Bavaria's location on the Danube River and its closeness to passes over the Alps to Italy should have made it a major trading center in the early Middle Ages. However, this did not happen. Why? An important reason may have been its vegetation. Roads passing through dense forests were dangerous for traders. Forests also prevented a buildup of agricultural wealth. Land clearance took place in Bavaria as it did in the rest of Europe, but it was slow. By the time Bavaria's roads were safe enough for major trading, western Europe was served by sea routes from the Mediterranean nations.

* **stem duchy** five regions in Germany that were of great importance in the 900s

* **dynasty** succession of rulers from the same family or group

* **margrave** noble appointed as military governor of frontier territory

See color plate 10, vol. 3.

named. These tribes were the main inhabitants from the mid-400s onward. However, the Christian tradition in the area was hardly interrupted. In the 400s, St. Severinus established a monastery near Mautern on the Danube and attended to the needs of the local peasants. In the early 700s, an organized church structure was established by St. BONIFACE, and by the year 800, monasteries dotted the landscape, becoming a focal point for art and scholarship.

In the 500s, Bavaria came under the rule of the Frankish kings of western Europe, known as the MEROVINGIANS. In the main tribal areas of Germany, they installed dukes who ruled on their behalf. These areas, which have become known as the stem duchies*, included Bavaria. Their dukes gained a fair degree of independence, with the right to pass on their titles and privileges to their children. Though the Merovingian duchies were disbanded by the early CAROLINGIANS, they became important units again in about 900. Lorraine, Bavaria, Swabia, Franconia, and Saxony, which had been conquered by CHARLEMAGNE, were vital units in the development of Germany. After the Carolingian dynasty* collapsed, the duchies provided the main electors of the German kings. They were also constant rivals for power over each other and for leadership of the German kingdom and empire.

The Germanic Rulers.   Under the first kings of Germany, whose power base was in Saxony, Bavaria was led by a dynasty called the Liutpoldings (sons of Liutpold). Threatened by the power of the other stem duchies, however, the Saxon kings took several steps to maintain control. They placed their own family members as dukes whenever possible; by 949, OTTO I THE GREAT's brother Henry had become duke of Bavaria. They encouraged changes in ducal families as often as possible; members of the Welf family from Swabia were later installed as Bavaria's rulers. The large duchies were diminished in size. Bavaria was made smaller in 976 when Carinthia became a separate duchy, and smaller still when the duchy of AUSTRIA was founded.

Austria resulted from a great power struggle that developed during the 1100s between the German kings and the Welf dukes of Bavaria. By 1137, Henry the Proud of Bavaria was duke of Saxony as well, and thus he had enough power to be a contender for the German throne. However, the other electors feared Henry's power, and they chose Conrad III instead, the first Hohenstaufen king.

To add insult to injury, King Conrad refused to recognize Henry's claim to Saxony, then granted Bavaria to his own half brother, who was margrave* of the Bavarian border territories that became Austria. Henry's son, Henry the Lion, was able to reclaim his lands only after Conrad's nephew, FREDERICK I BARBAROSSA, became German king and emperor. Frederick, whose mother was from the Welf family, finally permitted Henry to claim Saxony and most of Bavaria. However, he made Austria into a separate duchy to compensate the margrave.

Later during Barbarossa's reign, Henry fell out of favor with the emperor, who broke up the Welf properties in Bavaria for good. Henry was outlawed, and Bavaria was conferred upon Otto of Wittelsbach, a loyal landholder in northern Bavaria. By now, the stem duchies were no longer a major factor in German politics—a new system of electing the German monarchs was developing. More duchies had been created, and the church had gained important influence. An electoral college developed in which only seven princes had votes. The Wittelsbachs kept a vote, but it became associated with royal territories they held on the Rhine. The other electors were Saxony; two new areas, BOHEMIA and Brandenburg; and three bishoprics*, Mainz, Cologne, and Trier.

Louis the Bavarian.   In the 1300s, a descendant of Otto of Wittelsbach became Louis IV the Bavarian, king of Germany. Louis was never recognized as emperor by the pope. In fact, Pope John XXII, who ruled the church from AVIGNON on the French border, used all his power to oppose Louis; he excommunicated* the king and placed an interdict on all of Germany. Louis countered by declaring the pope a heretic* and having himself crowned emperor in Rome "by the Roman People." He also declared that German emperors no longer needed the pope's confirmation—once the seven electors had chosen an emperor, imperial dignity was "bestowed by God alone."

After the reign of Louis, the Wittelsbach family divided the duchy into smaller units to accommodate its many family members. The Rhine territories, called the Palatinate, became totally separate from the duchy. The family remained powerful, however. Most parts of the duchy were reunited under Wittelsbachs in 1505, and the Wittelsbachs remained rulers of Bavaria until 1918.

* **bishopric**   office of or area governed by a bishop

* **excommunicate**   to exclude from the rites of the church

* **heretic**   person who disagrees with established church doctrine

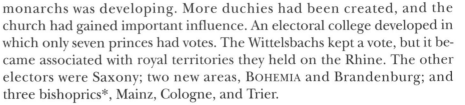

Bayazid I, Yildirim

died ca. 1403
Ottoman Turkish sultan

* **sultan**   political and military ruler of a Muslim dynasty or state

See map in Ottomans and Ottoman Empire (vol. 3).

Bayazid I was ruler of the OTTOMAN Turks. His nickname, Yildirim, means Thunderbolt. He earned it by the speed with which he moved his army within the growing Ottoman Empire. Bayazid played a key role in strengthening Ottoman rule in ANATOLIA (present-day Turkey) and expanding it to the Balkan region of Europe. His own reign ended in defeat, but his actions helped establish the Turkish Empire that lasted until World War I.

Bayazid became sultan* in 1389 when his father, Murad I, died at the Turkish victory in Kosovo, Serbia. Bayazid rushed back to Anatolia, where he defeated a rebellion and extended his borders there. Then he returned to the Balkans, subdued Bulgaria, and laid siege to CONSTANTINOPLE itself. A crusade was organized against him by Venice and Hungary, which he crushed at Nicopolis in 1396. Then he gained still more territory in the East.

In addition to his military success, Bayazid took key administrative steps to strengthen the Ottoman state. He expanded a system in which loyal slaves held power in the government. He also created a naval center at Gallipoli, which began challenging the power of Venice in the eastern Mediterranean.

Bayazid's campaigns in the East angered TAMERLANE, the Mongol overlord of central Asia. Tamerlane considered eastern Anatolia part of his sphere of influence. In 1402, the two leaders clashed in battle outside Ankara. Bayazid was defeated and taken prisoner, dying in captivity soon after. However, the Ottoman state remained largely intact and survived to become a dominant power for 500 years. (*See also* **Byzantine Empire**.)

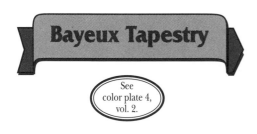

Baybars al-Bunduqdari

ca. 1223–1277
Warrior, ruler, and founder
of the Mamluk dynasty

* **sultan** political and military ruler of a
Muslim dynasty or state

* **crusader states** states established in the East
by Western Christians during the crusades.
They included Jerusalem and Antioch.

Baybars al-Bunduqdari was a Turk who became a prisoner of war in his teens, then went on to become the most successful military commander of his time.

Baybars was born on the plains of southern Russia during the main migration of Mongol tribes from the east. He was captured and sold into slavery in Asia Minor at the age of 14. Soon, however, he was recruited into an Egyptian regiment called the Bahriyya, which was led by the AYYUBID sultan* of Egypt, al-Malik al-Salih. Al-Malik freed large numbers of Turkish slaves to create an elite fighting force that was personally loyal to him.

In 1249, King LOUIS IX OF FRANCE led a well-funded crusade against Egypt. But after some initial success, the crusaders were defeated by the Bahriyya at the Battle of al-Mansura (1250). However, al-Malik al-Salih fell sick and died during this campaign. The victorious Bahriyya was not so loyal to al-Malik's son and successor, Turan-Shah. Led by Baybars, the freed slaves assassinated Turan-Shah and appointed their own MAMLUK, or slave, as sultan.

Strife following Turan-Shah's death forced Baybars to flee from Cairo to Syria. In 1260, the third Mamluk sultan, Qutuz, hired Baybars to lead his army against a Mongol invasion of the Holy Land. Baybars defeated the Mongols at Ain Jalut near Jerusalem, then assassinated Qutuz. He became the next Mamluk sultan, taking the title of al-Malik al-Zahir (the Triumphant King).

During his reign, Baybars' triumphs included the destruction of many of the crusader states* and major victories against the Mongols. A folk epic celebrating his victories was still being recited in Egypt early in this century.

Bayeux Tapestry

See
color plate 4,
vol. 2.

The Bayeux Tapestry is perhaps the best known of all medieval embroideries. Less than 20 inches high but more than 230 feet long, it illustrates the reign of King Harold of England from 1064 until he was defeated at the Battle of Hastings in 1066. His opponent was WILLIAM I THE CONQUEROR, who became England's first Norman ruler. The tapestry includes the battle and Harold's death.

Most scholars think the tapestry was made in England during William's reign, possibly for his half brother, the bishop of Bayeux in Normandy. Embroidered in eight colors of wool thread on linen, it tells the story in full detail, with an explanatory inscription in simple Latin. The vivid pictures of the costumes, armor, ships, and architecture of the time appear to be very accurate. Along the upper and lower borders of the tapestry are animal motifs, fables, and other scenes. The tapestry can still be seen in the town hall at Bayeux, displayed around the walls.

The Bayeux Tapestry contains 72 scenes with more than 1,500 figures. A running inscription in Latin identifies the events. The tapestry is an important historical and cultural document. It provides us with many details about life in the 11th century, including fortifications, shipbuilding, architecture, and clothing.

Becket, Thomas, St.

1118–1170
Chancellor and archbishop of Canterbury

* **chancellor** official who handles the records and archives of a monarch

* **archbishop** head bishop in a region or nation

* **secular** nonreligious; connected with everyday life

HENRY II OF ENGLAND appointed his friend and chancellor*, Thomas Becket, to be archbishop* of Canterbury. He wanted to strengthen royal influence over the church in England, which had gained independence under his predecessor, King Stephen. But Henry found that Becket became a stubborn and powerful opponent, and he ended up calling for Becket's death.

Born in London, Thomas Becket had already been an important official under the former archbishop of Canterbury, head of the church in England. In 1155, King Henry chose Becket to be his own chancellor, a secular* position that could hold great power. Becket became Henry's adviser and close friend, and he was one of the strongest chancellors in medieval English history. In addition to handling administrative, financial, judicial, and diplomatic matters, Becket was a loyal supporter of the king. In Henry's European territories, he acted as a successful military adviser and commander. He also negotiated the marriage of Henry's son to the daughter of the king of France.

After seven years, Henry appointed Thomas as archbishop of Canterbury, expecting him to remain a faithful ally. One goal that Henry had was to gain more control over the church courts, which handled trials of the clergy. Henry thought that, for secular crimes such as rape and murder, clergymen should be accused and sentenced in royal courts under regular English law,

Archbishop Thomas Becket was murdered in Canterbury Cathedral by four of King Henry II's knights. His tomb soon became a shrine and the site of many reported miracles. It became the destination of many pilgrims, including those in Chaucer's *Canterbury Tales.*

instead of in church courts, where penalties were much milder. Henry argued that it was unfair for any murderer or rapist to escape execution by claiming the right to trial in a church court. Becket opposed the king.

During their struggle, Becket changed his position several times, appearing to agree with Henry and then changing his mind. His behavior angered the king. All attempts at compromise eventually failed. Henry tried to put Becket on trial on a trumped-up charge that he took bribes when he was the chancellor. Becket fled to France for safety.

Though the pope now tried to make peace between the two men, the whole English church had become confused. Some bishops supported Henry, others Becket. In 1170, Henry permitted the archbishop of York to crown his son as heir to the throne—a right that belonged to the archbishop of Canterbury alone. Later, Becket appeared to make peace with the king, but he then excommunicated* the archbishop of York and the other bishops who had attended the crowning.

King Henry reacted with rage, asking why no one would serve him by "removing" Thomas. On December 29, 1170, four of Henry's knights attacked and killed Thomas before his own high altar in Canterbury Cathedral.

After Thomas's death, popular support was on Becket's side, and he was declared a saint* after three years. Henry was forced to do public penance* at Thomas's shrine. However, Henry and the pope came to a compromise that allowed the king to have considerable control over the church, though clerics were still able to be judged in church courts. Henry finally succeeded in achieving many of the goals he had sought.

* **excommunicate** to exclude from the rites of the church

* **saint** Christian who is officially recognized as a holy person by the church

* **penance** task set by the church for someone to earn God's forgiveness for a sin

Bede

672/3–735
English Benedictine monk and historian

* **venerable** deserving respect because of age, character, or importance

* **deacon** church officer ranking below a priest

Bede, known in later centuries as the Venerable* Bede, was an early English saint. He was one of the most learned scholars and influential writers between the time of Gregory the Great and that of Charlemagne. The period between 604 and 800 is sometimes referred to as the Age of Bede.

Bede was born in the northern British kingdom of Northumbria. At age 7, he entered a local monastery to be educated, and he remained there for the rest of his life. He became a deacon* at age 19 and a priest at age 30.

More than half of Bede's writings are verse-by-verse commentaries on individual books of the Bible. They are interpreted with reference to the works of early church fathers such as AUGUSTINE, Gregory, and Jerome. He consulted and quoted from many documents as he wrote.

Bede also wrote textbooks on a variety of subjects, including penmanship, spelling, syntax, geography, and natural phenomena. He later developed one of these texts, about the Christian CALENDAR, into a major work. This helped to unify the differing calendars of western Europe, by setting the beginnings of years and the dates of movable feasts.

The work for which Bede is most noted is his *Ecclesiastical History of the English Nation,* published in 731. This work, written in Latin, is the primary source of knowledge about English history from the late 500s to Bede's own time. It describes the triumph of Christianity in England and the development of Anglo-Saxon culture. Because of the importance of this work, Bede is often called the "Father of English History."

Beguines and Beghards

* **apostles** early followers of Jesus who traveled and spread his teachings

* **heretic** person who disagrees with established church doctrine

* **Low Countries** flat coastal lands west of Germany, now occupied by Belgium and the Netherlands

During the 1100s and 1200s, many people sought to adopt a life of simple purity, based on stories of how the apostles* in the early church lived. Several movements arose, ranging from the CATHARS, who were attacked as heretics*, to the FRIARS, new preaching religious orders based on poverty. Another such movement was the Beguines.

Beguines were women who formed devout communities without taking vows or becoming nuns. The movement was at its strongest in the Germanic-speaking Low Countries* between about 1220 and 1320. It was the only medieval religious movement that was not set up and directed by men. However, it was viewed with suspicion by many people, who feared that Beguines were heretics. The church at first supported the Beguines but later prohibited them.

The earliest communities of Beguines appear to have started around Liège, Belgium, in the late 1100s. They were often wealthy or noble women who performed humble tasks such as nursing, housekeeping for others, embroidery, and even funeral services. Some chose to beg for a living. They were committed to chastity but were allowed to leave the movement and marry.

While some Beguines lived in their own homes, many lived together in houses that became called *beguinages*. Cologne in Germany had more than 100 such houses, accounting for almost 15 percent of the adult female population. Ghent and Bruges had whole communities of Beguines, with up to 300 living together in a single section of the city.

The church's official approval and protection was granted to the movement by Pope Gregory IX in 1233, by which time there were communities in many cities of northern France and the Holy Roman Empire. But suspicion was also beginning to surround the Beguines. In that same year, a council in Mainz ordered them to stay in their houses and follow the guidance of their parish priests. They were also warned against the preaching of heresies. In fact, the name *Beguine* is believed to have come from the word *Albigensian*, which was the name given to the Cathars in southern France.

Many Beguines tried not only to imitate the apostles but also to have ecstatic religious experiences. They produced the earliest mystical writings in the northern European languages. Famous Beguine visionaries included HADEWIJCH OF ANTWERP and MECHTHILD VON MAGDEBURG. Their fresh and intense writings probably influenced major mystical theorists such as Meister ECKHART.

There was a parallel but smaller movement among men, who were called Beghards. But neither movement gained full acceptance. In 1310, one Beguine was burned in Paris for heresy. Then, in 1312, a council in Vienne, France, declared that Beguines could face an inquisition* for spreading religious errors and that all Beguines should be banned.

* **inquisition** investigation carried out to discover and punish heresy

Though the council also decreed that truly faithful women could continue to live in communal houses, many Beguines were tried for heresy, and their communities were dissolved. Other communities joined the Third Order of the Franciscan Friars, an organization for laypeople that had spread north from Italy and the south of France. But not all Beguines and Beghards ceased to operate. In the Low Countries, the pattern of walled-in communities continued. The popes of the 1400s finally called for tolerance, and the movement has continued, though without its early life and vigor, until today. (*See also* **Heresy and Heresies; Mysticism; Women's Religious Orders.**)

Bells

During the Middle Ages, the sound of bells was of major importance in telling people the time so that they could organize their days. Bells were also a primary means of transmitting news and information to the people. In addition, they served a number of ceremonial and even magical purposes.

Though tradition says that bells were introduced to Europe by an Italian bishop around 400, bell ringing is believed to have originated in Russia and to have spread into Europe somewhat later. Pope Sabinius, in the year 605, is credited with beginning the use of bells to mark the different hours for prayer in the DIVINE OFFICE. Monastery bells also announced meals and other assemblies.

Bells were important to villagers and townspeople as well as to clerics. They conveyed important information rapidly and simply. In some parts of Europe, the boundary of a lord's domain was determined by the distance at which the manor's bell could be heard. Bells marked the beginning and end of the workday; the opening and closing of city gates; and the opening of the market, town meetings, and other events.

The particular meaning of bells was indicated by the number of rings or the sequence in which different-size bells were rung. During the 900s, many churches began using multiple bells. Some cathedrals had as many as 12 bells in a single tower. In the 1200s, the size of bells, too, began to increase. By the end of the Middle Ages, enormous bells were being made. Such bells were often used to warn of storms, enemy attack, fire, or the approach of wild animals.

Bell ringing was a skilled occupation. The misuse of alarm bells was severely punished by law. Bell ringers, who often came from the lower classes, gained special benefits, such as an exemption from military service and free food and clothing. A bell ringer's duties might include service as town crier or as a singer in the local lord's chapel on feast days.

Bells had a religious significance beyond indicating events or the time of day. They were often made by monks—the Benedictines were active in bell casting—and were used ceremonially during church services. For example, Pope Urban II began a custom of ringing a bell to prompt the reciting of the Ave Maria. The bell used for this was called the Angelus bell. The association of bells with the Ave Maria led many bell casters to engrave the Virgin Mary's name on their bells.

Other bells were consecrated* and "baptized" with the name of a saint, usually the founder or patron saint of the religious institution for which the bell was made. Such bells were treated with reverence because they were thought to possess the mystical power of the saint to punish or heal. Oaths sworn upon these bells were considered more binding than those sworn on the Bible because it was thought that the bells had the power to expose liars.

There was also an ancient belief that bells offered protection against evil spirits. Small bells called tintinnabula were often used as ornaments

Bells and Cannons

Making large bells in bell foundries required great skill. The metal had to be cast flawlessly so the bells would not crack under the stress of being rung.

When cannons began to be made in the 1400s, there was a problem with casting the iron so that it would not crack when the cannons were fired. Where did the military go to find help with this problem? Where else, but to the metalworkers in bell foundries.

* **consecrate** to declare someone or something sacred in a church ceremony

on religious robes. The tolling of a single large bell was thought to provide protection to the souls of the dead as they journeyed to the afterlife. Bells also played an important part in excommunications, when priests drove sinners from the church with "bell, book and candle."

Benedict of Nursia, St.

early 500s
Christian monk and abbot

Since the 700s, St. Benedict of Nursia, Italy, has been considered the founder of the Western monastic tradition. He did not start a religious order himself, founding only a single monastery. But his writings helped shape monastic life in the Western Church up to the present time.

The earliest account of Benedict's life was written by Pope Gregory the Great in the late 500s. Benedict is said to have come from a prosperous family. Sent to study in Rome, he disliked the immoral customs of the city and was attracted to monastic life, which was popular in the East but less so in the West. Benedict spent three years in solitude in a cave near Rome.

After attempting to govern a community of monks nearby, Benedict returned to the cave and formed his own monastic group, loosely organized under his direction. Then he moved with some of his monks to Monte Cassino, between Rome and Naples, where he founded a monastery and preached to the people around it. He became a well-known holy man in the region.

* **abbot** male leader of a monastery or abbey. The female equivalent is an abbess.

Benedict is most noted for his *Regula sancti Benedicti* (Rule of St. Benedict). This document contains Benedict's ideas about monastic life and rules for regulating the activities in a monastery. He wrote that an abbot* must be both a father and a teacher to the monks, caring for their spiritual and earthly needs. For the monks, he stressed the importance of obedience, silence, and humility. The Rule of St. Benedict covers all aspects of monastic life, including sleep, meals, work, possessions, care for the sick and weak, and training of new members.

The Rule of St. Benedict has a sense of moderation that combines firm principles with a willingness to adapt to human weakness and failure. It respects human freedom and the complexity of life. Rather than unbending rules, it provides guidelines and goals for the monks to strive to attain.

The Rule spread to monasteries throughout the Christian world. By the 600s, it was practiced in French and English monasteries. Before the year 1000, it helped produce monastic reforms throughout Europe. Almost all the monastic orders that developed in the later Middle Ages adopted the *Regula sancti Benedicti*. As a result, the years from 800 to 1200 are often known as "the Benedictine centuries." (*See also* **Benedictines.**)

Benedictines

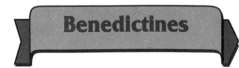

* **habit** costume of a particular group, such as a religious order

The Benedictines were the most influential order of monks in western Europe. All later religious orders in the West descended from Benedictine monasticism. During the Middle Ages, Benedictines were called "black monks" because of the color of their habit*. This distinguished them from other orders of monks, such as the Cistercians, who wore white.

Benedictine life grew from a Christian monastic tradition that started in Egypt and, even before the Middle Ages, had become a powerful movement

St. Benedict of Nursia, founder of the Western monastic tradition, receives bread from the baker while the monks wait for their meal. All Benedictine monasteries were bound together by the Rule of St. Benedict, which involved a daily routine of work and prayer.

* **feudal** referring to the social, economic, and political system that flourished in western Europe during the Middle Ages

in the Byzantine East. Most monks practiced an ascetic, self-denying lifestyle. In the 500s, St. BENEDICT OF NURSIA developed the so-called Rule of St. Benedict, which was more moderate and more flexible.

The Rule of St. Benedict involved a daily routine dedicated to prayer and work. Centered on religious services, each day was divided into several periods in which monks recited psalms and prayers, sang hymns, and read from the BIBLE. In addition, monks grew food, made clothing, and practiced trades; they were totally self-sufficient. At first, the Rule was practiced only at St. Benedict's monastery in Monte Cassino, Italy. But the monks had to flee when LOMBARD invaders from France sacked the monastery.

The Rule spread, first to Rome, then to England, and then to other western European countries. It slowly replaced other types of monasticism that had been centered in France and the British Isles. Benedictine ideas spread because of their humanity, because of support from the popes and feudal* lords, and also because of the missionary work of monks. Augustine of Canterbury, who originally brought the order from Rome to England, and BONIFACE of England, who converted many German tribes, were Benedictines. By 1000, the order had also brought Christianity to parts of eastern Europe.

Benedictine expansion reached its peak about 1070–1130. During these years, the Benedictine abbey of Cluny in France represented the highest spiritual idea of Christian life. Many monasteries were quite prosperous, thanks to income from manorial estates, donations from churches, and other sources of revenue.

Benedictine monks filled various roles in medieval society. Often the monks were the younger children of noble families, and their lives were quite comfortable and safe, and also honorable. People saw them as spiritual soldiers who fought important battles. People believed that the safety of society and individual spiritual welfare depended on monks' prayers and penances.

Benedictines worked in the community, for civil leaders as well as for church officials. Some were royal advisers, judges in civil courts, financial officials and record keepers, leaders of military campaigns, physicians and teachers of medicine, and architects or masons. Benedictine monks also helped develop advanced techniques of farming on their monastic estates.

Benedictines played a crucial role in education and learning. Within their monasteries, they developed schools to teach young monks and the children of local nobles. These schools provided much of the training available in western Europe during the Middle Ages. The preparation of books, necessary for any school, was also important work in a monastery. Monastic teacher-scholars helped preserve the ideas of classical antiquity as well as the ideas of their own times.

Between 1200 and 1500, Benedictine influence began to decline as a result of several factors. One factor was the coming of FRIARS, who were a more dynamic spiritual and intellectual force. In addition, educated laypeople began to rival monks as book copiers and financial administrators. Most important, however, was a decline in revenues. Benedictine monks could no longer live in the comfort they had enjoyed in earlier times. The number of recruits also fell because monasteries could not afford to admit them.

The legacy of the Benedictines has endured to modern times. It includes a tradition of ordered and disciplined living, an appreciation for ancient liturgy, the wisdom of a rich literary culture, and a compassionate understanding of the mysteries and difficulties of the human condition. (*See also* **Monasteries.**)

* **fief** under feudalism, property of value (usually land) that a person held under obligations of loyalty to an overlord

* **feudal** referring to the social, economic, and political system in which vassals gave service to their lord in return for his protection and use of the land

* **papacy** office of the pope and his administrators

A benefice was a gift, of land or of a position, that provided income. Ideally, it was a gift with no strings attached. But in the Middle Ages, as today, givers often expected something in return.

Benefices were often rewards. A lord might give official posts to the children of a loyal supporter. But similar loyalty or support would be looked for in the future. This was especially clear if one person was given several benefices, none of which required much work. Such a person might receive a lot of income. Thus, benefices were often viewed as fiefs* that placed the receiver under a feudal* obligation.

A common type of benefice was the ecclesiastical benefice. This was a gift of income-producing property that could support a church official. Such gifts were usually made by wealthy or powerful people for the sake of their souls. But often donors wanted to appoint the priests or bishops who drew income from the benefices. This caused friction with church leaders, who felt that religious appointments should be made by the church.

One of the most famous disputes about a benefice was between a pope and the Holy Roman Emperor. In 1157, Pope Hadrian IV described the throne of the empire as a benefice granted by the papacy*. Emperor Frederick I Barbarossa took that description to mean that the emperor was under feudal obligation to the pope—an idea that he hotly contested. The pope finally said that he had used the term in its old sense, meaning gift. After 1200, *benefice* was almost never used to mean fief. (*See also* **Church-State Relations; Feudalism.**)

* **pagan** word used by Christians to mean non-Christian and believing in several gods

B *eowulf* is a long, heroic poem, written in Old English. Its author is unknown but probably lived in the 600s or 700s. Only one manuscript of *Beowulf* survives, a copy made by two scribes about the year 1000. The manuscript is kept in the British Library.

The poem describes the fights of the hero, a young warrior named Beowulf, against three different monsters. The story is told against a pagan* background of early Germanic legend and history but also includes some Christian elements and themes. When the poem starts, the kingdom of the Danish king Hrothgar is being terrorized by a monster called Grendel. For 12 years, Grendel has come to the king's magnificent hall each night to kill and eat the king's warriors. News of this trouble reaches Beowulf, who offers to fight Grendel. During the fight, Beowulf tears off Grendel's arm. Grendel goes home to die, leaving a trail of blood across the moor.

One night soon afterward, Grendel's mother comes to avenge her son's death. Beowulf then decides to go out to hunt for her. He swims underwater to her cave. After a difficult fight, Beowulf kills Grendel's mother with a magic sword.

Beowulf's third fight occurs 50 years later. The kingdom he now rules is terrorized by a flying, fire-breathing dragon. Most of his followers flee, and Beowulf fights the dragon with only one young relative. Together, they kill the 50-foot serpent, but Beowulf is mortally wounded.

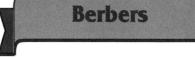

Berbers

* **Phoenicians** important traders in the ancient world, who founded Carthage in North Africa

* **caliph** religious and political head of an Islamic state

* **Kharijite** group of Muslims who broke away from the Arab caliphs at the time of Ali ibn Abi Talib and held that anyone could be elected caliph

* **Shi'ites** Muslims who believed that Muhammad chose Ali and his descendants as the rulers and spiritual leaders of the Islamic community

* **Sunnite** Muslim majority who believed that the caliphs should rule the Islamic community

Berbers were the native inhabitants of North Africa. Before the Middle Ages, the Greeks, Romans, and Phoenicians* had built many communities along the Berber coastline. But the Berber culture survived, leading Europeans to call their country Barbary (for Berbery).

The Berbers became allies of the Arabs during the Arab expansion in the 600s. They helped the Arabs conquer the coastal cities of Africa and then invade Spain. Some Arabs began to think of Berbers as Arabs who had migrated from Yemen in the days before Islam, even though the Berber language was not like Arabic.

Berber society was primarily rural. Like the Arabs, the Berbers were a tribal people, living in small groups with leaders rather than in large settled regions with rulers. During the 800s and 900s, the Berbers developed trade routes across the Sahara desert to Nigeria and other places.

The Berbers were not loyal to the main Arab rulers, the UMAYYAD and ABBASID caliphs*. At first, they joined the extremist Kharijite* movement. During the 800s and 900s, they were converted to Shi'ite* Islam and were a major force in setting up the FATIMID dynasty in Egypt. Though they still opposed the main Sunnite* branch of Islam, this brought them closer to the mainstream Muslim world. They gave up attempts to write their own language in Arabic letters and adopted the Arabic language. Soon Berber was spoken only in isolated parts of North Africa, often by groups that retained their Kharijite beliefs. (*See also* **Spain, Muslim Kingdoms of.**)

Bernard of Clairvaux, St.

1090–1153
French abbot
and religious writer

* **abbot** male leader of a monastery or abbey. The female equivalent is an abbess.

* **asceticism** way of life in which a person rejects worldly pleasure and follows a life of prayer and poverty

As an abbot* in the CISTERCIAN order of monks, Bernard helped shape religious events of his day. He advised two popes, preached the Second CRUSADE, and founded nearly 70 monasteries. Bernard's writings on religious topics were widely read during the Middle Ages.

Born to a noble and pious family, Bernard entered a small Cistercian monastery in his early 20s. The Cistercian order was trying to restore some of the strictness—especially poverty and asceticism*—begun earlier by the BENEDICTINES. Three years later, Bernard went to head the order's new monastery at Clairvaux in CHAMPAGNE. He served as abbot there for 38 years.

To his monks and others who knew him, Bernard seemed both holy and intense. He was a persuasive speaker with a great feeling for words. He used this talent to glorify God in his book *On Loving God* and in 86 SERMONS on the *Song of Songs*.

Bernard was also extremely energetic. In addition to works on monastic life and theology, Bernard wrote hundreds of letters to emperors, kings, popes, abbots, monks, nuns, nobles, and townspeople. He also wrote the rule for the Knights Templars, a religious order of CHIVALRY.

Bernard emphasized the importance of being humble and of loving and praising God. He wrote that the role of monks was in monasteries, yet he traveled extensively, especially after Pope Innocent II made Bernard his adviser. Wherever Bernard went, his power with words impressed his listeners, and new Cistercian monasteries were started.

Bernard's work sometimes involved church controversies. In 1140, the work of theologian Peter ABELARD was brought to his attention. Bernard wrote many letters against Abelard's views, and Abelard, another strong character, was condemned by a council of bishops.

Bernard was not always successful. In 1146, Pope Eugenius III asked Bernard for help in organizing the Second Crusade. Bernard spent months obtaining royal support and raising troops, but the crusade was a dismal failure. Bernard said he would gladly accept the blame if it would spare God's honor.

Bernard remained active in church affairs to the end of his life. After his death, his secretary and companion, Geoffrey of Auxerre, sought to have his abbot declared a saint*; the church approved this request in 1174.

* **saint** Christian who is officially recognized as a holy person by the church

Berserks

The Berserks were fierce warriors in old Germanic tribes. They were said to fight in a frenzied state without armor. Supposedly, they entered battle screaming and biting the rims of their shields, had the power to make their enemies helpless from fear, and fought without being injured. They also fell into a deep sleep after battle. Berserks were as strong as bears and as crazed as wolves. The term comes from the Old Norse words for "bear shirt."

Besides being described in written accounts, Berserks appear in medieval art. On an ancient piece of Germanic armor known as the Torslunda helmet plate, there is a man with a sword wearing only an animal skin. An early medieval chess figure from the Hebrides in Scotland shows a warrior biting the edge of his shield. Belief in Berserks probably came from tribal initiation rites, in which warriors wore animal skins so their spirits would merge with the spirit of the animal. During the deep sleep after battle, these spirits could supposedly change shape and wander freely.

Bertran de Born

ca. 1140–ca. 1215
Medieval troubadour

Bertran came from Born in England's southern French territories. He was a famous writer of heroic and satirical poems and songs on political themes, including war. He became closely involved with HENRY II and his son RICHARD I THE LIONHEARTED, both kings of England. He was later attacked by DANTE as a poet whose writings caused hostility within a royal family.

Bertran's involvement with royalty began because he drove his own brother from a castle that they jointly owned. His brother turned for help to Richard, then the duke of AQUITAINE. Bertran developed a hatred for Richard and allied himself with Richard's older brother Henry, heir to the

English throne. But Prince Henry died young, and his father, King Henry II, settled Bertran's dispute by awarding the castle to Bertran's brother.

Bertran expressed his anger against Richard and Henry II, but he also wrote a touching lament about the young prince's death. This so moved Henry and Richard that they took pity on Bertran and returned his castle to him. From that point on, Bertran's songs supported the two English kings.

Bestiary

Bestiaries are medieval collections of stories about real and imaginary animals. The stories are usually ALLEGORIES that provide moral or religious lessons. Some well-known fantastic beasts described in medieval bestiaries are the griffin, with a lion's body and an eagle's head and wings; the unicorn, with a horselike body and a single horn; and the phoenix, a bird rising from its own ashes. During the Middle Ages, bestiaries were very popular books.

Latin bestiaries began to be written in the 1100s. They seem to have been based mostly on a work written in Greek around 200, called the *Physiologus* (the Physiologist) after its anonymous author. This book collects descriptions of animals from ancient Greek philosophers, from classical myths, from biblical sources, and from animal tales that were handed down orally from one generation to another. Its stories show how the natural world reflects deeper purposes of heaven. They were already well known by the 300s and were translated into many languages, including English, Latin, and Icelandic. The *Physiologus* was often supplemented from other sources—by the 1200s, there were many different bestiaries. Some were in verse, and the longest bestiary was more than three times longer than the original work.

One important source for additions was a work by Isidore, bishop of Seville in Spain in the early 600s. Isidore's book was about the origins of names: for example, he wrote that vipers were so called because they are "violent," and cats got their names because they "catch" things with their claws. Though these origins are nearly all false, they became an important part of bestiaries and led to additional stories about animals.

Like Isidore's word origins, the descriptions given in bestiaries are also frequently inaccurate. Lion cubs are said to be born dead, then brought to life by their parents after three days. Swans are said to make ugly sounds all their life but to sing a beautiful song before they die. Animals and birds such as the phoenix are described even though they never existed.

The people of the Middle Ages did not look to these books for scientific truth. They liked the stories because they were entertaining, and they valued them more when they seemed to illustrate deeper principles. They believed that lion cubs came to life after three days because God had brought Christ back to life after three days. Swans sang because they repented their sinfulness at death and became pure and holy. The phoenix, which burned itself to death and rose reborn out of the flames, symbolized resurrection and everlasting life.

Medieval bestiaries are almost always illustrated. Like the verbal descriptions, their pictures rarely seem real. Except for horses, dogs, and other familiar creatures, bestiary animals are shown as fantastic, often

Medieval Christians attributed religious significance to certain animals. For instance, the lion frequently symbolized St. Mark, one of the four evangelists (authors of the Gospels). This illumination is from the *Echternach Gospels,* written about the year 700.

frightening monsters devouring people. The same is true of the beasts depicted as carvings on medieval buildings.

From the 1100s on, bestiary animals were familiar images to Christians of the Middle Ages. People understood the religious significance even if the animals appeared in a stained glass window rather than in a book. Today much of the medieval lore has been forgotten. We know that the term *swan song* means a last, glorious effort, but do not realize its Christian, allegorical meaning. If we see a phoenix as an insurance company symbol, we may sense that it signifies rebuilding but fail to understand the full story behind the image.

Bible

* **theology** study of the nature of God and of religious truth

* **Aramaic** old Semitic language that was the native language of many Jews in antiquity

* **Gospels** accounts of the life and teachings of Jesus as told in the first four books of the New Testament

ible comes from the Greek word for book and refers to the Jewish and Christian Scriptures. These had a great influence on the Middle Ages. Bible stories and ideas reached people through religious services, sermons, theology*, folklore, art, political thought, and popular literature. No part of medieval life and thought escaped the Bible's influence.

The Bible was originally the Jewish book of Scriptures. Written in Hebrew, it consisted of 24 books and was divided into three parts: the first five books of Moses (Torah or Pentateuch); the Prophets; and the Writings (Hagiographa). Before the year 100, most of the books of the Hebrew Bible had already been translated into Aramaic* and Greek for those Jews who no longer spoke Hebrew.

Early Christians used a Greek translation of the Hebrew Bible that they called the Septuagint. In the 100s, they collected their own writings, which included four Gospels*, the letters of the apostle Paul, and other early Christian letters and writings. They called these documents the New Testament and added them to the Septuagint, creating a complete Christian Bible in the Greek language.

As the Hebrew Bible was translated into Greek and Aramaic for Jews who did not speak Hebrew, so the Christian Bible was translated for people

While vernacular Bible translations gained early popularity in the Eastern Christian Church, they did not receive approval or acceptance in the Western Church for many centuries. The Latin Vulgate remained the official Bible of the Roman Church. This page from the Gospel of St. Matthew, written in Latin, is from a late-tenth-century German manuscript.

Exegesis

Medieval interpretation of the Bible was anything but simple. From the start, many meanings were assigned to the words. In the Talmud, there are four levels of understanding, from the literal to the hidden. Christian scholars also identified three or four levels, including a moral and spiritual dimension. In one type of exegesis, a passage in the Bible was viewed allegorically, as a metaphor for a deeper meaning. Allegory is also a vivid and vital element in medieval literature.

* **vernacular** language or dialect native to a region; everyday, informal speech

* **Reformation** emergence of a new, Protestant Christianity after 1500

who did not understand Greek. For Eastern Christians, the Bible was translated into Syriac, Armenian, Georgian, Coptic, and Ethiopian. In the western parts of the Roman Empire, only Latin was used, but there were several versions of the most popular parts. However, the Vulgate, a Latin translation of the whole Bible by St. Jerome in the late 300s, became the official Bible of the Roman Church in the Middle Ages.

The Bible continued to be translated as needed in eastern Europe. CYRIL AND METHODIOS produced a Slavic version in the 800s, which became the official Bible of the Bulgarian, Serbian, and Russian churches. The Latin Vulgate was the only approved translation in the West. However, unauthorized vernacular* translations of the Bible—in English, French, German, Dutch, Italian, Slavic, and Polish—were increasingly common during the late Middle Ages. In the late 1300s, John WYCLIF's followers created a widely read English version, but they and their book were condemned by the Roman Church. Inspired by their example, Jan HUS, who was condemned as a heretic and later burned at the stake, translated the Bible into Czech. It was not until the Protestant Reformation* that native-language Bibles were widely accepted.

Much medieval writing consists of interpretations of the Bible, called exegesis. Biblical exegesis started with the Jews, who by the year 600 had collected a book of comments on their Scriptures called the Talmud. During the Middle Ages, Jewish scholars continued to interpret their Bible, whether they were writing in Islamic Spain or in Christian France. Notable Muslim scholars also commented on the Bible, since they believed the Hebrew prophets and Jesus were forerunners of Muhammad. Christian exegesis was also an important part of medieval scholarship. In the 1100s, biblical studies were an important reason for the start of UNIVERSITIES and for the rise of SCHOLASTICISM. (*See also* **Allegory; Christianity.**)

Birgitta, St.

1303–1373
Swedish mystic

* **revelation** experience of direct contact with God, frequently accompanied by visions and the conviction that one has been given a divine mission

St. Birgitta's religious life centered on mystic revelations* she received while a nun. These visions were about Christian life and faith, society, and politics. She influenced popes and monarchs and established a religious order devoted to Christ's passion and suffering. St. Birgitta is the patron saint of Sweden.

The daughter of Swedish nobles, Birgitta was married at the age of 13 and had 8 children. Her husband died in 1344, and she entered a Swedish CISTERCIAN convent, where she began to receive her revelations. Five years later, Birgitta went to Rome to work toward goals revealed in her visions.

At this time, the popes were running the Western Church from AVIGNON, on the French border, and one vision led her to urge the popes to return to Rome. Leaders in Rome who supported her called her "protectress of the Holy See." In another vision, she was commanded by Christ to start a new religious order. In 1369, with support from the pope and the king of Sweden, building started on a convent for the order in Vadstena, Sweden.

She made pilgrimages to Trondheim (Norway), Cologne, and Jerusalem, as well as to holy places in Italy and Spain. Birgitta's visions continued until her death. Her accounts of them were gathered together by a Spanish bishop-hermit, who arranged them in a series of books called *Revelations*.

* **saint** Christian who is officially recognized as a holy person by the church

Less than 20 years after her death, Birgitta was declared a saint*. As a result, the monastic order she founded, the Order of the Most Holy Savior, gained many followers. (*See also* **Monasteries; Mysticism; Scandinavia, Culture of; Schism, Great.**)

Black Death

* **bacteria** tiny organisms that cause different types of illness

The Black Death was a terrible disease that ravaged Europe from 1347 to 1351. During those few years, the disease, also known as the plague, killed between 25 and 45 percent of the population of Europe. This huge loss was accompanied by other changes—social and cultural, economic and political—that radically altered life in Europe. In all, the Black Death was the single most important natural phenomenon in European medieval history.

Natural History of the Disease. The plague is a deadly infectious disease caused by a strain of bacteria* called *Yersinia pestis*. These bacteria are usually confined to a type of flea and the small mammals, especially rats, that the flea feeds on. This flea normally inhabits a particular kind of environment found in southern and central Asia, the Arabian peninsula, and east Africa. But sometimes environmental conditions cause the flea to infect humans with the bacteria, which can then spread suddenly over large areas.

In humans, plague can take several forms. The two most common are bubonic plague and pneumonic plague. Bubonic plague is spread by the flea, whose bites infect the bloodstream. Many blood vessels burst beneath the skin, causing large boils called buboes. Half the victims die. Pneumonic plague, which develops if the bacteria attack the lungs, spreads through the air like a common cold and is 100 percent deadly. Both forms of the disease occurred during the Black Death.

How the Black Death Spread Through Europe. In the early 1300s, unusual weather patterns caused the plague bacteria to infect humans. Soon Asia had a serious plague epidemic*. The epidemic followed trade routes toward the west. In September 1346, plague had broken out at the edge of the Black Sea and was caught by Italian merchants trading in the area. It came home with them in their ships.

* **epidemic** disease that affects a large number of people or animals

The first outbreak of the plague in western Europe was at the Sicilian port of Messina in October 1347. By early November, the disease had spread throughout Sicily. Mainland ports were also infected, and in six months the plague was all over Italy. Construction work on the cathedral at Siena was totally halted. The city of Venice lost more than half its population.

By January 1348, the Black Death was in France. Trade carried it northward to Paris in less than four months, and during the following winter, 800 people were said to be dying there each day. The plague quickly moved on to Holland, the British Isles, Germany, Poland, Russia, and Scandinavia. In 1351, it reached the distant ports of Greenland—sailors who later visited those ports found them totally deserted.

Effects of the Black Death. Medieval life was severely disrupted by the Black Death. The most shocking aspect of the plague was the number of people it killed, but it also had dramatic cultural and economic effects.

Culture and religion were deeply shaken. Neither scientific learning nor religious faith was able to save people from the plague. Universities

* **cleric** church official qualified to lead church services

* **penance** an act of repentance for sin

lost many students and some of their most notable teachers. The religious community was also hard hit—more than half of England's clerics* died. No one found any effective remedies.

Believing that the plague was caused by their own sins, many people tried penance*, joining processions led by priests and whipping themselves with painful lashes. Others blamed people in their communities—especially the Jews—and conducted vicious attacks on them called pogroms. But nothing appeared to make any difference. During the plague years, people saw doctors and priests fleeing from victims, unable to use their learning to help.

When the plague was finally over, the church had become less wealthy and less powerful. Plague and death were now pervasive themes in religious art and literature, and some people became more religious. Many others turned away from religion, living luxuriously and recklessly, looking for new approaches to their problems.

This trend was helped by economic factors. Abandoned villages meant unplowed farmland and shortages of food. Death in the cities meant fewer craftspeople to make products. Although such shortages raised prices, the need for workers led to new technologies and great

The spread of the Black Death followed trade routes from Asia to the West. The first outbreaks in Europe occurred in Mediterranean ports. Within six months, the plague had spread all across Italy and France. By 1351, the disease had reached as far as Scandinavia and Russia.

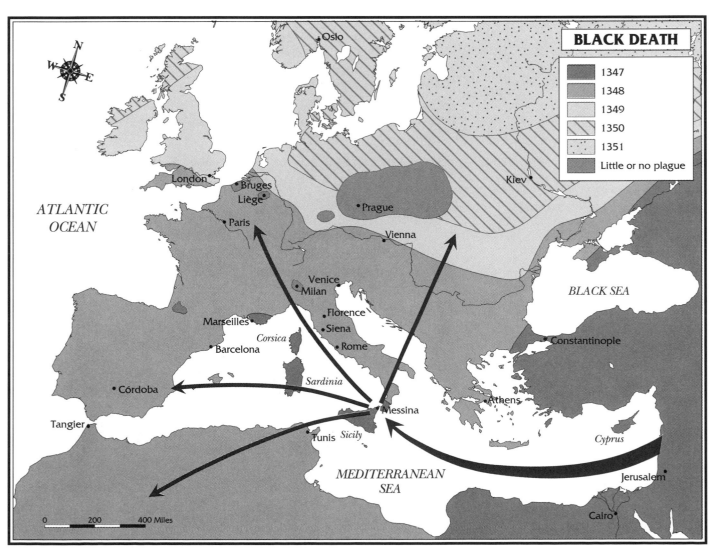

BLACK DEATH

- 1347
- 1348
- 1349
- 1350
- 1351
- Little or no plague

wage increases. The result was a rise in living standards, especially for the less wealthy.

Such changes caused strains in Europe's social structure. There were peasant revolts in France and England. Peasants began to demand written documents from their landlords, spelling out land rights. Some landowners had to rent out their entire estates because they lacked workers. Others turned from producing grain to less labor-intensive types of agriculture such as cattle and sheep farming. This changed marketing and trading practices, and, moreover, it affected the traditional pattern of FEUDALISM. The Black Death sped Europe's change from a medieval to a modern society.

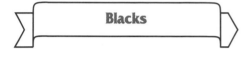

Blacks

See *Ethiopia (Abyssinia); Mali; Slavery.*

Blanche of Castile

1188–1252
Queen of France
and regent

* **regent** person appointed to govern a kingdom when the rightful ruler is too young, absent, or disabled

Blanche of Castile was a powerful regent* of France during the Middle Ages. Her reign was brief, but her rule of the kingdom for her son LOUIS IX was remarkable. She kept order and did much to strengthen the French monarchy.

The daughter of Alfonso VIII of CASTILE, a kingdom in central Spain, Blanche married the future king Louis VIII of France in 1200. When Louis died in 1226, their 12-year-old son inherited the throne. Blanche became young Louis's regent, directing royal affairs and advising him as he came of age.

With a child on the throne and his mother as regent, France's monarchy faced many challenges. Rebellious nobles tried to take advantage of the

The coronation of Blanche of Castile and Louis VIII of France occurred in 1223. After her husband's death in 1226, she remained active in government affairs and became a skillful regent and adviser to her son Louis IX.

king's youth to seize greater power for themselves, but they were opposed and defeated by Blanche. She remained a widow, realizing that marriage to any one of the nobles who were seeking her hand would draw her into conflict with the others. She also skillfully prevented her cousin, King HENRY III OF ENGLAND, from regaining alliances in Normandy, which had once been the possession of their grandfather, England's King HENRY II. She also steered a steady course in disputes between France and the papacy*.

* **papacy** office of the pope and his administrators

Blanche was very devout and tried to pass on her faith to her children. Louis and Isabelle, her daughter, became very religious like their mother. As Louis grew up, however, Blanche had some conflicts with him. She opposed the vow he made in 1244 to go on a CRUSADE to Egypt, and, for a period, she had less influence over him. However, when Louis left for Egypt in 1248, he recognized his mother's power and abilities and made her regent in his absence.

It was during the Seventh Crusade (1248–1254) that Blanche's leadership skills shone. She completed many of the tasks Louis had begun, including construction of a port at Aigues-Mortes in southern France as well as many administrative reforms. She also negotiated with the church for money to finance the crusade. By the time Blanche died in 1252, she had done as much as, or more than, most French kings to establish the foundation of a strong French monarchy. (*See also* **France; Women, Role of.**)

Boccaccio, Giovanni

**1313–1375
Poet, storyteller,
and encyclopedist**

* **plague** disease that swept across the medieval world several times, including the Black Death in the mid-1300s

* **apprenticed** placed in the care of a merchant or craftsman to learn a profession

* **Angevin** referring to a dynasty from Anjou

Italian writer Giovanni Boccaccio is best known for his classic *Decameron*, a set of 100 stories told by ten young people on a journey out of the city of Florence to escape the plague*. During his literary career, Boccaccio composed many other works, including three encyclopedias, but none match his masterpiece. The structure, narrative clarity, and humor of the *Decameron* are still fresh today and the work has served as a model for many other writers.

Early Life. Born in TUSCANY (probably in FLORENCE), Boccaccio was the son of a merchant banker and a mother he never knew. He grew up in Florence, but when he was 14, he and his father moved to Naples. Hoping that he would take up commerce or law, Boccaccio's father had him apprenticed* to a banking house, where he was forced to study arithmetic and law.

However, Boccaccio was much more interested in poetry and in the cultural life Naples had to offer. He went to the library regularly and met many of the city's leading poets and scholars. In Naples, Boccaccio began his literary career by writing poems.

Early Works. Boccaccio's first work was an Italian poem, *La caccia di Diana (Diana's Chase)*, which praises the beautiful women at the Angevin* court in Naples. The poem was heavily influenced by DANTE and by COURTLY LOVE poems from PROVENCE. He also wrote a poem called *Filostrato*, which told the legendary story of Troilus and Cressida. This was the source for later works by CHAUCER and Shakespeare. Another work from Boccaccio's Naples years was *The Theseid of the Marriage of Emilia*, an epic poem in 12 books in imitation of the *Aeneid*, the great Roman epic poem of Virgil. By this time, Boccaccio was an accomplished poet, though to modern ears his early writing may seem rather formal and stilted. Like other writers of his time, he often based his ideas and language on that of earlier poets.

Boccaccio returned to Florence at age 26 and wrote *Bucolicum carmen,* a set of Latin pastoral songs. He also continued his romantic works in Italian, including *Vision of Love, Comedy of the Florentine Nymphs,* and *Elegy to My Lady of the Flame. Elegy* is a psychological romance set in contemporary Naples. It is considered a forerunner of the modern psychological novel and his most successful work before the *Decameron.*

In 1345, Boccaccio's father went bankrupt, leaving him short of money for the rest of his life. Then the BLACK DEATH of 1348 took his stepmother's life, and his father died a year later. He was left alone to raise his half brother Jacopo, a task that was not easy. However, he did not stop his work. He continued collecting material for an encyclopedia he was planning, and he soon wrote his masterpiece.

The **Decameron.**   Boccaccio's prose masterpiece was written in the years following 1350. The stories are told against a background of Italy during the Black Death. Seven young women meet in a church in Florence and leave the city in the company of three young men, to escape the plague's infection. They spend two weeks in the country at three locations, each more remote and peaceful than the last—the gardens of two different villas and a perfect circular garden of delight called "the Valley of the Ladies."

Safe from the plague that is ravaging Florence, the young people amuse themselves for two weeks by walking, singing, dancing, eating, and telling stories for five days, then fasting and bathing over the weekend. Each evening, the group chooses a "queen" or "king" to preside over the next day's festivities. That person selects a topic for the day, and all ten young people have to tell a story connected to the topic. At the end of each day, after the storytelling is over, there is dancing.

The stories told are mostly witty tales about love—in its many forms, from light and funny to serious and sad. Other topics include humor, practical jokes, and various adventures. The tales are mostly ancient and medieval tales from around Europe, Constantinople, and farther east.

The *Decameron* is based on the work of earlier writers, but it is refreshingly natural, free of the awkwardness and formality of Boccaccio's initial work. It has a balanced structure and unity of outlook that make it quite unusual for the Middle Ages. The work was an inspiration and model for many later writers, including the great English writer Chaucer.

Later Life.   In 1350, Boccaccio met the poet PETRARCH, who remained his lifelong friend. Though Boccaccio's later years were troubled by ill health and poverty, he continued to produce significant and popular work. In 1355, he wrote his last work in Italian, a satire on the way women dress. However, he produced important encyclopedias in Latin, which was the literary language of the time and which guaranteed an international audience. His first encyclopedia was a 15-volume work that compiled references to the pagan gods of Greece and Rome appearing in ancient and medieval works. He also wrote a 9-volume work on famous men and a vast geographical reference work. Boccaccio continued to update these works until he died.

See map in Black Death (vol. 1).

Remember: Consult the index at the end of Volume 4 to find more information on many topics.

Boccaccio left behind a body of work that assured him an esteemed place in Italian and world literature. His literary legacy put him in the company of the poets he loved and admired the most—Dante and Petrarch—as one of the "three crowns of Florence." (*See also* **Angevins; Encyclopedias and Dictionaries; Fables; Italian Language and Literature; Latin Language.**)

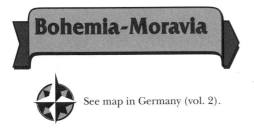

Bohemia-Moravia

See map in Germany (vol. 2).

* **Protestant** referring to movements against the Roman Church begun during the 1400s and 1500s and the religious traditions and churches that emerged

* **duchy** territory ruled by a duke or a duchess

Bohemia-Moravia was an area in central Europe inhabited by a Slavic people who called themselves Czechs. The Czechs joined the Germanic HOLY ROMAN EMPIRE in the late 800s. Their land was recognized as a separate kingdom in 1085—the first new kingdom to be created within the empire. In the later Middle Ages, it became the seat of the empire for a while, and it was the site of one of the first Protestant* uprisings against the Roman Church.

Early History.   Beginning in the middle 800s, the Slavic peoples of Bohemia-Moravia fell under the domination of nearby Bavaria, part of the Frankish Empire. Czech leaders declared loyalty to the lords of Bavaria and may have been converted to Christianity by them.

Involvement with Bavaria joined Bohemia to the kingdom of Germany, which was the dominant force in the Holy Roman Empire. By 1035, Bohemia was recognized as a German duchy*. Then, in 1085, Germany's Henry IV crowned a king of Bohemia, because the Czechs helped him in a conflict with the pope.

Under its kings, Bohemia developed two spheres of government. Areas owned by the Czech nobility were ruled by a "land government," where both the king and the nobles had power. There was even a court to which the king could be summoned. Townspeople in these areas had very limited freedoms, and they had to gain permission from their local lord to sell property. Where land was under the king's direct control, however, he had complete power. He could grant greater freedoms to the towns, and he could also levy taxes without the nobles' consent, thereby gaining great royal wealth.

Bohemia and the Empire.   Under the rule of a dynasty called the Premyslids, Bohemia reached the height of its power. By 1270, King Ottokar

By the early 1300s, Prague, the largest city east of the Rhine River, had become a wealthy and influential city. Emperor Charles IV founded central Europe's first university there. This woodcut shows Prague as it looked in 1493.

Another Moravia?

Byzantine Christians record that Moravia was converted by the famed missionary brothers, Cyril and Methodios from Constantinople. Cyril had invented a special alphabet to write the Bible in Slavic.

Rival Frankish missionaries disapproved of the idea of writing the Bible in a language other than Latin or Greek. But the brothers persuaded the pope to allow use of their Bible.

Today, however, though many Slavs use their own language, the Czechs worship in Latin. Some scholars now argue that "Moravia" in the Byzantine sources was actually Slovenia and parts of Austria and Hungary.

* **artisans** skilled craftspeople

* **archbishopric** church district headed by an archbishop

* **heretic** person who disagrees with established church doctrine

* **crusade** holy war declared by the pope against non-Christians

II was the strongest ruler in central Europe. He had great wealth from the Bohemian royal towns and estates. Ottokar was invited to govern the nearby duchy of AUSTRIA, and he captured several regions farther south. His power was so great that he thought he could act independently from the other Czech nobles.

Ottokar tried to ensure his gains by being elected Holy Roman Emperor. However, the German electors of the time preferred a weak emperor and chose Rudolf of Habsburg, a Swiss duke who was having difficulty holding on to Switzerland. Ottokar rebelled, but his nobles deserted him, while Rudolf was supported by most of the empire. Ottokar died in the war he caused.

The death of Ottokar caused chaos in Bohemia from 1278 to 1310. At that time, at the request of some of the Czech nobles, the German king and emperor Henry VII moved to restore order by putting his son, John, on the throne of Bohemia. John's successor, Charles IV, was elected emperor and brought the imperial residence to Prague.

Prague and the Hussites.   By the early 1300s, Prague had become the largest city east of the Rhine River. Much of its wealth came from its monasteries and other religious foundations, which now owned almost one-third of Bohemia. Over the years, many landowners had donated land to the church in their wills. An estimated 1,200 clergy lived in the city. They spent a good part of the income from their land on the work of local artisans*.

Charles IV arranged for Prague to become an archbishopric*. He also founded a famous university, the first one in central Europe. Prague became a cultural and religious center that attracted scholars, artists, and theologians from all over Europe. The city, and the university especially, became dominated by powerful foreigners from other parts of the empire. At the same time, Prague and other Bohemian towns had large numbers of poor people. Reformers and preachers often criticized the church and wealthy foreigners for gaining their advantage at the expense of the poor.

In the 1400s, an uprising in Bohemia sent shock waves through Europe. Jan HUS, a Czech priest, led a movement urging separation from the church in Rome and from German domination. Hus was burned at the stake as a heretic*. After his death, Hussite armies of peasants and nobles made raids throughout central Europe. A crusade* was called by the pope, involving knights from as far away as England and Spain, but it failed to crush the Hussites. The church made concessions to the Hussites at the Council of Basel in 1433—something never before brought about by a heretical group in the Middle Ages.

Bohemond I, Prince of Antioch

ca. 1050–1111
Leader in the First Crusade

Named Marc at his baptism, Bohemond was nicknamed after a legendary giant because of his great strength and endurance. He was the oldest son of Robert Guiscard, the NORMAN adventurer who drove the BYZANTINES from southern Italy. While still a teenager, Bohemond had been a leader in his father's victorious army, and he expected to inherit the lands he had helped win. However, after the birth of his half brother, Bohemond knew his stepmother would foil these plans. He set out to seize new lands for himself.

At first, he joined his father in campaigns on the Greek mainland, and he won much territory from the new Byzantine emperor Alexios I

Komnenos. But Alexios's forces drove them back and killed Bohemond's father in 1085. Ten years later, Pope URBAN II called upon the Christian leaders of Europe to drive the Muslims from the Holy Land. Sensing a chance for new lands as well as spiritual rewards, Bohemond assembled a band of Normans and joined the First CRUSADE (1095–1099). On his way to the Holy Land, he stopped in Constantinople, the Byzantine capital, and swore loyalty to his former enemy Alexios. Bohemond promised that, if he captured Byzantine lands now held by the Muslims, he would return them to the emperor.

In October 1097, Bohemond's army captured and sacked Antioch, a former Byzantine city held by the SELJUK Turks. He declared himself prince of Antioch in defiance of his promise to Alexios. Though both Alexios and the Turks tried to recapture the city, Bohemond held on by crafty diplomacy and a strong offensive. Antioch became one of the first crusader states*. Within a few decades, the once landless Bohemond had extended his holdings, using the crusades to further his personal ambitions.

* **crusader states** states established in the East by Western Christians during the crusades

Bonaventure, St.

ca. 1217–1274
Franciscan theologian

See color plate 5, vol. 3.

* **theology** study of the nature of God and of religious truth

Bonaventure was one of the prominent thinkers of the Middle Ages. Gifted with a fine memory and a keen intelligence, he was a staunch defender of the order of FRANCISCANS. Bonaventure became head of the order and helped reform it to the original ideals of its founder, St. FRANCIS OF ASSISI.

Born in central Italy, Bonaventure survived a severe illness at the age of ten and believed he owed his recovery to St. Francis. From then on, Francis was an important figure in Bonaventure's life. After studying liberal arts at the University of Paris, Bonaventure joined the Franciscans and studied theology*. By 1254, he was master of the Franciscan school in Paris, lecturing, writing, and delivering sermons at the university.

During his time in Paris, Bonaventure wrote many books on theology and MYSTICISM. In several of these works, he explored his view that theology is the application of human reason to the mysteries of faith, and thus depends on emotion and contemplation as well as logic. Bonaventure also defended the Franciscan vow of poverty against those who said that it contradicted the Scriptures. He based his defense on the idea that humility is the essence of Christianity. Partly because of this defense, Bonaventure was made minister general, or overall leader, of the Franciscans.

When Bonaventure took on his new responsibilities in 1257, conflict was developing within the order. A group called the Spirituals wanted the Franciscans to follow a more austere, rigorous life. Through Bonaventure's wise rule and holy behavior, the opposing factions were reconciled.

In 1259, Bonaventure made a pilgrimage to La Verna, a pilgrimage site for St. Francis. While there, he wrote his best-known mystical work, *The Mind's Road to God,* in which he describes spiritual growth as a seven-stage journey rising from awe at God's works and gratitude to Jesus Christ. He also wrote about the life of St. Francis, using interviews with the saint's surviving companions to depict a spiritual portrait of the man.

Bonaventure continued his religious work, defending the Franciscans and his view of Christian belief to the end of his life. He became cardinal bishop of Albano in 1273 and was declared a saint by the church in 1482.

Boniface, St.

ca. 675–754
English missionary
and martyr

* **pagan** word used by Christians to mean non-Christian and believing in several gods

* **archbishop** head bishop in a region or nation

* **bishopric** office of or area governed by a bishop

St. Boniface spread Christianity among the Germans during the time of the MEROVINGIAN Franks. He is known as the "Apostle of Germany."

Boniface was born near Exeter, in southwest England. His given name was Winfrid. Winfrid's father opposed his son's becoming a monk, but after his father's death, Winfrid joined a monastery and became a gifted scholar.

Winfrid felt drawn to MISSION work, however. In 716, he set out for Frisia in northwestern Germany. The Frisians had rejected earlier Christian missions in the region, and Winfrid's own first attempts also failed. He went to Rome, where Pope Gregory II encouraged him to continue, giving him a new name, Boniface, meaning Good Works. Under the protection of the pope and of Frankish leader CHARLES MARTEL, Boniface was more successful in his next mission to Frisia. He then moved east to work in other pagan* regions of Germany, including Bavaria.

Boniface won converts by his generosity, caring for people who had been made poor by years of Frankish rule. He was also famed for cutting down an oak tree held sacred by the pagan Germans of Hesse, so impressing them that many converted to Christianity right there. The pope made him a bishop in 722, and an archbishop* in 731. Boniface went on to play a vital part in organizing the Christian church in Germany, setting up many of the bishoprics* that later supported the German Holy Roman Emperors.

In his old age, Boniface returned to missionary work, and he was killed by pagans in Frisia at about the age of 79. (*See also* **Franks; Germany.**)

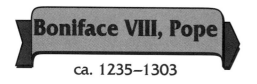

Boniface VIII, Pope

ca. 1235–1303

* **canon law** body of church law

* **clergy** church officials qualified to lead church services

* **ascetic** referring to a person who rejects worldly pleasure and follows a life of prayer and poverty

* **heretic** person who disagrees with established church doctrine

* **excommunicate** to exclude from the rites of the church

The stormy papacy of Boniface VIII was one of the major crises in CHURCH-STATE RELATIONS during the Middle Ages. Boniface was a proud and haughty man, an expert on canon law*, and tactless to a fault. His troubles came to a head when he sought to humble the kings of France over control of the clergy*.

Boniface was born in central Italy. He rose rapidly through church ranks and became a cardinal in 1291. A year later, Celestine V, a saintly hermit of 80 years, was elected pope, but he resigned because of his old age and ascetic* background. Boniface, chosen to succeed him, became pope in 1294.

Boniface's direct style was clear immediately. A group of FRANCISCANS, called Spirituals, still supported Celestine as pope, so Boniface denounced the Spirituals as heretics* and imprisoned Celestine in a castle. Later he argued with the powerful Colonna family, two of whose members were cardinals. They objected to Boniface's use of his power to buy land that they desired. Boniface excommunicated* the family, destroying their palace.

Boniface's greatest conflict began when Cistercian monks protested against paying war taxes to France and asked for his support. He decreed that the clergy should not be taxed without papal approval. The French king, PHILIP IV THE FAIR, then arrested a bishop for treason. Boniface countered by summoning all French bishops to Rome to review Philip's actions and his government. In response, King Philip joined forces with the Colonnas in Italy. Their troops captured the pope, held him prisoner for several days, and then freed him. Boniface was a broken man and died soon after. (*See also* **Excommunication; Heresy and Heresies.**)

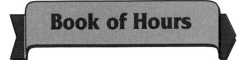

Book of Hours

* **clergy** church officials qualified to lead church services

* **laity** those who are not members of the clergy

One of the most famous books of hours is the *Très Riches Heures* of Jean, duke of Berry. Work on the manuscript began in the early 1400s. More than half of the illuminations were created by the Limbourg brothers, important Flemish manuscript illuminators of the time. This illustration for the month of September shows peasants harvesting grapes near the Château de Saumur.

Books of hours are short, richly illustrated prayer books first made in the later Middle Ages. Unlike BREVIARIES, which were for the clergy*, books of hours were intended for pious laity*. They often contained illustrations of the lives of the saints to inspire devotion and piety in the faithful. A book of hours was the only book in many medieval homes and was often the first book a child learned to read.

The name *book of hours* comes from the Hours of the Virgin, a set of prayers and songs developed in the 800s in honor of the Virgin Mary, the mother of Christ. Like the main monastery services that were called the DIVINE OFFICE, the hours were recited and sung during eight specific periods, or "hours," of the day. By the 1200s, French and English clergy had adopted various versions of the hours for use in churches. As literacy increased, private people had their own books made for personal prayer at home.

At first, the hours were often written down in Psalters, which also contained the Book of Psalms from the BIBLE. Later they were made as special books of hours. In addition to the Hours of the Virgin, these books commonly contained readings from the Gospels, two long prayers to the Virgin Mary, and various other prayers and devotions. There was also a calendar of church feasts and saint's days. Books of hours reached their peak of popularity in Europe in the 1400s and 1500s, when they became the standard private prayer book of the wealthy.

Not surprisingly, books of hours are among the most common medieval books to survive until the present day. In the earlier examples, made before the mid-1400s, the illustrations in books of hours were painted by hand. The number, design, and quality of these illuminations vary according to the wealth and personal taste of the book owner. Rich patrons had famous artists produce elaborate and beautiful books of hours. During the late 1400s, the printing press made it possible to produce books of hours for many more people. Nevertheless, beautiful handpainted books of hours continued to be commissioned by wealthy individuals and members of the nobility. (*See also* **Books, Manuscript.**)

Books, Manuscript

See color plate 8, vol. 2.

Until printing became widespread in the late 1400s, all books were manuscripts—that is, they were written by hand. They were treasured because of their contents: records of the past, ideas of noted scholars, and religious writings. Made with great care and painstakingly written, some books were major works of art and were beautifully illustrated and finely bound. When they became worn out, they had to be replaced by new handmade copies. For that reason, too, books were carefully looked after.

Most of the techniques of bookmaking were inherited from the ancient world. Manuscripts in scroll form had been illustrated since Egyptian times, and the codex, or bound book, was invented in the early years of the Roman Empire. But medieval books represent a high point in bookmaking. The beauty of some of the Jewish, Islamic, and Christian books from the Middle Ages has not been equaled before or since.

* **Torah** sacred wisdom of the Jewish faith, especially the first five books of the Bible

* **scribe** person who hand-copies manuscripts to preserve them

* **illumination** art of ornamenting the pages of a manuscript

* *bifolium* sheet of paper that folds to form two leaves, or four book pages

* **quire** set of *bifoliums* folded together to form a sequence of pages

* **Byzantine** referring to the Eastern Christian Empire that was based in Constantinople

How Books Were Made

By the beginning of the Middle Ages, except for special cases like Torah* scrolls, manuscripts were produced by binding sheets of material together and sewing them into a cover. The sheets were usually made of parchment (animal skin), though paper was occasionally used from the 700s on.

Some books, especially Jewish works, appear to have been created by skilled individuals for their families or communities. Most Islamic and Christian books, however, were put together by teams of scribes*, bookbinders, and sometimes specialists in illumination*.

Setting Up the Pages and Preparing the Manuscript. The first step in creating a book involved smoothing and cutting to size sheets of parchment or paper. Each sheet was then folded to form a pair of facing pages known as a *bifolium*. These pages were carefully numbered so that the scribe would know the order in which the pages would appear in the book. Then they were marked with ruled lines, using ink or a lead point.

The lines were used as guides when the text was copied. Long rules were provided for normal text, and columns of shorter lines were used for poetry. Most of the lettering was done in black ink. In countries of the eastern Mediterranean, scribes generally used a reed pen, while in the West a quill (feather) pen was more common.

If portions of the text were to be decorated—such as chapter titles or the first letters of paragraphs—they were left blank, to be filled in later. After a page of text was written, its *bifolium* was hung up or put aside to dry. It was later returned for the scribe to fill in another page. When all four pages of the *bifolium* were finished, a person called a corrector might proofread the manuscript for errors.

Creating Illuminations. Manuscripts that were to be illuminated required additional steps, depending on the degree of luxury desired. In some cases, all that was necessary was to add certain letters in different colors, or perhaps mark the paragraphs with red and blue ink. Other manuscripts with more elaborate ornamentation needed a specialist known as an illuminator.

Illuminators would start by applying a coat of paint to act as a base for the area to be ornamented. They would then sketch in outlines for the decorated letters, illustrations, borders, and other designs. After that, colors would be painted on, layer by layer. Gold leaf might be applied to make the illustration shimmer with light. Small highlights of white paint might be added. Illuminating a book could take months or even years, depending on the size and complexity of the manuscript.

Binding the Manuscript. The finished *bifoliums* were put together in batches to form quires*. A quire generally contained from 16 to 48 pages. The process for binding manuscripts differed somewhat in the eastern and western Mediterranean. In Byzantine* and Islamic bookbinding, the quires were first stitched together. The entire manuscript was then fastened to the book's cover, often by cords passed through the stitching. In western Europe, each quire was sewn separately onto a strip of cord or leather, and the cords were then attached to the cover.

Covers could be made of leather, cloth, parchment, wood, or metal. Sometimes ornamental metal bindings were folded around the edges to protect the books as they lay on a library shelf. Clasps might be attached to keep the book cover shut when it was not being used. In the Byzantine world, such clasps were usually made of leather or cloth, while in western Europe they were often of metal.

The covers of some Western and Byzantine books, especially sacred works such as the Bible, were lavishly decorated with precious and semi-precious stones. Islamic covers were often decorated with complex geometrical patterns, floral shapes, and arabesques*.

Books and Their Development in the Middle Ages

Illuminated books were one of the great artistic achievements of the Middle Ages. Distinctive artistic styles and techniques emerged in different periods and parts of the medieval world.

Jewish Books.   The survival of Jewish culture after the Jews were scattered across the Mediterranean owes much to its tradition of religious books and learning. However, perhaps because Jewish books were used and produced privately, almost no manuscripts survive from the early Middle Ages. After the Dead Sea Scrolls from the 100s B.C., the earliest complete Jewish manuscript in existence today is from about 900.

The techniques used to make Jewish books varied according to where the books were produced. The type of pen used and the bookbinding, for instance, can provide clues to the origin of a particular volume, as noted earlier. Illustrations, when used, can also help to indicate the type of community in which a book was created.

Illustration of Jewish books was sometimes quite elaborate. Decorated opening letters were rarely used, since Hebrew does not use capitals. But initial words were often paneled and given special treatments. Jewish religious books produced in the Muslim countries follow Islamic practice by showing no human figures or animal forms. In Christian southern Germany and Spain, however, Jewish illuminators developed a style that included human figures with bird or animal heads.

Islamic Books.   The importance of book production in Muslim culture is directly linked to the importance of the QUR'AN, the sacred book of Islam. Copying and illustrating the Qur'an was regarded as an act of piety because of its sacred character. This gave skilled scribes a special status, and it also caused decorative lettering, or CALLIGRAPHY, to have its own religious significance. Though Islamic scribes and illustrators also produced scientific texts, poems, romances, and a vast array of other kinds of books, Islamic book production was closely associated with the Qur'an.

The oldest surviving Qur'ans, dating from the 700s, contain a number of elements that are characteristic of Islamic book design. In addition to the decorative script, the types of illumination used are also highly distinctive. Because Islamic religious practice prohibits showing God or other sacred figures in art, illuminations in Islamic religious manuscripts are mostly abstract. Geometric designs, intricate knotted or floral shapes, and other patterns marked the beginning and end of the text and divided the Qur'an into parts. These ornaments served as an aid to the reader.

* **arabesque** flowing pattern used by Muslim artists to decorate manuscripts

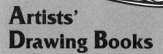

Artists' Drawing Books

In addition to copying pictures from older books, illuminators sometimes used books of exemplars. A book from the 1200s now in Vienna, for example, contains models for decorated initials, ornaments, and animal drawings. There are also collections of sketches that artists made to take back to their workshops. Some were collected during pilgrimages or even during crusades. Such sketches were not only for illuminations but also for church paintings, sculptures, and stained glass windows.

At first, color was used with restraint. Gold often was the most prominent color, with blue and brown added as accents. However, in later centuries, Islamic religious books became more colorful and the designs more intricate. Beautifully illuminated manuscripts were produced in many areas of the Islamic world, from Spain to India. Some of the very finest were made in Egypt and Syria during the MAMLUK dynasty (1250–1517). The symmetry and harmony of these sacred book designs not only influenced other books but also became an example for Islamic design in architecture and other art forms.

In the 800s and 900s, nonreligious Islamic books began to include realistic illustrations. But secular* books did not become popular until increased urbanization and the growth of a prosperous middle class occurred about 300 years later. Educated professionals became more prominent in the arts, and there was an increased demand for fine copies of secular works. The illuminated books of this period often look to Byzantine or Persian* art for their inspiration.

* **secular** nonreligious; connected with everyday life

* **Persian** referring to the ancient culture of Iran that continued to rival Greek civilization during the early Byzantine period

Among the most notable secular works produced at this time were several volumes of the *Maqamat*, illustrated in Baghdad in the 1230s and 1240s. These books tell the story of an old man and his travels, and they contain outstanding examples of realistic illustration. They show strikingly detailed scenes of palaces, mosques, markets, houses, animals, and people engaged in everyday activities.

The greatest achievements in Islamic bookbinding occurred in Persia in the 1400s. During that time, covers were decorated with landscapes and fabulous animals such as dragons. Humans and other animals were also frequently shown. Such designs echoed painted miniatures found inside the books, and they were similar to other forms of Islamic art.

Christian Books. Manuscript books were produced throughout Christian Europe, in the Greek-speaking Byzantine Empire as well as in the Latin* West, which was at first less advanced. The Roman tradition of bookmaking affected both areas: in Constantinople it was largely unchanged, but in the Western nations, institutions for making books changed radically after the Roman Empire came to an end in the 400s.

* **Latin** referring to western Europe and the Roman Church, which used the Latin language for its services

Constantinople and the other cities of the Byzantines maintained a high level of literacy compared to the West. Many books were needed, and they were produced by scriptoria* run by commercial groups, by the government, and, later, within the increasing number of MONASTERIES. In the cities of the West, by contrast, government and other institutions broke down, and book production seems to have almost ceased until the rise of monasticism in the British Isles, France, and Germany.

* **scriptoria** workshops in which books were written or copied, decorated, and bound

The earliest Western medieval books began to be produced in the 600s. Monasteries had their own scriptoria, where monks, nuns, and sometimes lay* workers spent much of their time copying and designing books. In the British Isles, Irish monks produced beautiful copies of the Gospels, which they treasured almost as sacred objects. The Frankish emperor CHARLEMAGNE encouraged book production in France and Germany, mostly in abbey* scriptoria because monks were the people best educated to do the task. Several large Carolingian monasteries became important centers of book production, including the Benedictine abbey of St. Martin of Tours in France.

* **lay** not linked to the church by clerical office or monks' and nuns' vows

* **abbey** monastery under the rule of an abbot or abbess

Until the late 1400s, all books were written and copied by hand. The invention of the printing press made books accessible to more people. This page from the *Sarum Book of Hours* was printed in Paris in 1494.

* **patron** person of wealth and influence who supports an artist, writer, or scholar

For more than five centuries, church institutions were the book keepers for the West. Monasteries made books not only for their own use but also for wealthy patrons* such as kings and bishops. Although the books produced were mostly religious, secular works were also created. These included classics of Latin literature and a few books based on ancient Greek texts that came from the Byzantine or the Muslim world. As the number and size of monasteries expanded from the 700s to the 1100s, their need for books also grew. Monastic scriptoria were kept busy producing these books.

In the 1200s, this era of monastic book production began to end. A new market for books was created as more laypersons began to read and as universities at Bologna, Paris, Oxford, and elsewhere began to offer specialized training in law and theology. New texts were also being discovered and translated from Greek and Arabic. To handle the new enthusiasm for reading, universities began to produce books themselves. A person called a stationer would send out a few pages of a manuscript to be copied by one person, and would then circulate the same pages to another worker. As a result, a number of copies of the manuscript could be made in far less time than it would have taken a monastic scribe.

Even simply ornamented books could be handled in this way. Most university books lacked the beauty and individuality of the best monastery manuscripts. However, the new books served the needs of increasing numbers of students and general readers.

Demand for books continued to increase and soon overwhelmed the capacity of university book producers as well. By the 1300s, commercial production of manuscripts became a profitable trade, centered in such cities as Milan, Florence, Rome, Paris, Bruges, and London. Lay religious groups, such as the BRETHREN OF THE COMMON LIFE, supported themselves through book production. There were also famous workshops where skilled artisans produced beautifully illustrated books for wealthy patrons. The commercial workshops were highly organized and specialized.

Among the earliest such book producers were William de Brailles of Oxford and Master Honoré of Paris. The craftspeople who worked on manuscript production formed their own specialized GUILDS.

Many of the books commissioned by the new secular audience were written in the vernacular* rather than in Latin. Among the most popular vernacular texts were the *Great Chronicles of France* and romantic tales of King Arthur and Alexander the Great. Another very popular type of book was the BOOK OF HOURS, containing private prayers to the Virgin Mary. Books of hours became an essential item in many noble households in the 1400s and 1500s, and they were frequently given to young women as wedding gifts.

*** vernacular** language or dialect native to a region; everyday, informal speech

The Printing Press

In the late 1400s, the production of books was changed forever by the introduction of the printing press. The new technology was greatly needed, since even the newest methods of manuscript production were unable to keep up with the demand for books. Because early printing presses could not produce colored pictures, however, hand-illustrated books continued to be produced for the rich well into the 1500s.

The Islamic tradition of illustrated religious manuscripts also continued to flourish after the medieval period. Persian book illuminators, in particular, produced some of their finest work in the 1500s and later. Other areas such as OTTOMAN Turkey and even Mogul India also continued to draw upon the rich tradition of Islamic manuscript production. (*See also* **Latin Language; Writing Materials and Techniques.**)

Borough

A borough was one of the most important types of local government in medieval England and Wales. Although boroughs existed during the ANGLO-SAXON period, the number of boroughs increased under the Norman and Angevin kings, and their freedoms were expanded. By the end of the Middle Ages, boroughs had become corporations with their own courts, administrators, police, and taxes. They were major centers of trade and of wealth, benefiting their inhabitants and the royal and national economy.

In the early Middle Ages, when England was still overwhelmingly rural, boroughs played a small role in society. They belonged to the monarch like other royal estates, and they were administered by an agent of the king, who received the income from borough lands. But by the time of the DOMESDAY BOOK, boroughs already offered privileges of land ownership that encouraged craftsworkers and merchants to move there to practice their trades.

In the 1100s and 1200s, expanding wealth enabled merchant and craft guilds* in other settlements to purchase town charters from the king. HENRY I, for example, sold borough rights to Newcastle that included the right to collect tolls and the right to choose local leaders.

More borough liberties were purchased under Kings RICHARD I THE LIONHEARTED and JOHN by wealthy townsmen eager to improve their communities. Richard I needed money for his crusade and a ransom when he was captured. John needed money for his campaign to reclaim Normandy.

*** guild** association of craft and trade workers that set standards and represented the interests of their members

Boroughs were now administered by councils of leading gentlemen, merchants, and craftsmen. The council supervised a staff of municipal officials, including lawyers and BAILIFFS. Borough courts oversaw police activities, public health, defense, and local regulations. Boroughs also sent representatives to Parliament, giving them a voice in the national government.

In the later Middle Ages, towns became able to purchase another important privilege, the right to complete incorporation. This allowed the borough council to hold land and divide it, to issue bylaws, and to acquire a town seal. Income from borough-owned lands helped to finance expanding borough governments. With the purchase of these liberties, boroughs became increasingly independent. (*See also* **Bastide; Cities and Towns; Commune; England; Guilds; Law; Trade.**)

Bosnia

Bosnia is a rugged land in the west central region of the Balkan peninsula. Settled by Slavs in the late 500s and early 600s, it has been torn by internal strife since medieval times. Steep mountains and deep valleys have contributed significantly to its internal disunity, separating it into rival areas. Bosnia's neighbors have also dominated it many times in its history. Nevertheless, Bosnia developed a strong economy based on mining in the 1300s, and it was the first Balkan country to make firearms and cannons.

Early Bosnia. In the early Middle Ages, Bosnia was divided into separate areas called *zupas*. Each *zupa* had its own nobles and traditions. The Roman Church was dominant, but many versions of Christianity coexisted. Lack of central authority led to invasions by outsiders, as local nobles shifted allegiances to suit their own interests. Bosnia was briefly part of SERBIA and then part of CROATIA in the 900s. From 1018 to 1101, it came under the power of the BYZANTINE EMPIRE. Then it was annexed by HUNGARY.

For the rest of the Middle Ages, Bosnia was under the nominal control of Hungary, but it had its own ban, or local ruler. The ban's independence led Hungary to launch a holy war against Bosnia in 1235, supposedly to bring the various Bosnian churches closer to Rome. But the Bosnians rallied around their ban, Ninoslav. An independent Bosnian church began about this time, and the Bosnian state itself became smaller. Hungary controlled northern Bosnia during the 1200s, dividing the *zupas* in that area between a former king of Serbia and a local Bosnian noble, Ban Prijezda.

Bosnia Under Kotromanic and Tvrtko. Around 1318, Prijezda's grandson Stjepan Kotromanic became ban of the central Bosnian state. He consolidated his rule because the Hungarian rulers were having internal troubles of their own. In fact, Kotromanic gained their favor by providing them with support.

Under Kotromanic, Bosnia expanded. He took over the Serbian region of Hercegovina. Merchants from Dubrovnik, a major port and trading center on the Adriatic, were attracted to Bosnia and settled there. Silver and lead mines made the town of Srebrnica an important mining center. Kotromanic allowed FRANCISCANS to establish themselves in Bosnia, and he himself accepted the Roman faith in 1347. From that time on,

A Monastic Church

The Bosnians responded to the Hungarian crusade in 1235 by rejecting the Roman Church, but they did not join the other power in Christianity, the Byzantine Church. When the old bishop of Bosnia was forced out of the area, the church existed without bishops and priests, and it was centered in the old monasteries. Worship was probably in Slavic, but otherwise the traditions remained those of Rome.

The Franciscans, who came to Bosnia 100 years later, tolerated the old monastic churches, which were used until after the Ottoman invasion.

most Bosnian rulers were Catholics. However, the independent Bosnian church and the Orthodox Church of Hercegovina were both accepted and tolerated.

During the second half of the 1300s, under Kotromanic's nephew Tvrtko, Bosnia reached the height of its power. He began his reign at age 15. After some initial losses, Tvrtko once again took control of Hercegovina. He then expanded Bosnian influence by claiming the throne of Serbia and later also that of Croatia. Bosnian merchants traded with Hungary, Bulgaria, Constantinople, and beyond. Wealthy towns grew along the trade routes. Bosnian silver buckles and cups became highly prized. Soon Bosnia's mines were a major supplier to all of Europe.

See map in Ottomans and Ottoman Empire (vol. 3).

The Coming of the Ottomans.   When Tvrtko died in 1391, Bosnia began to fall apart. Three powerful families renewed rivalries and, to gain support, became involved in the politics of Hungary and other neighboring powers. Competing claimants to the Hungarian throne gave help to first one and then another of the Bosnian families. Then, in the early 1400s, the OTTOMANS, a nomadic Turkish people from central Asia who were gaining control of Byzantine lands in the Balkans, began to appear on the scene.

At first, the Ottomans were hired as mercenaries* in the Bosnian civil wars. However, Ottoman warriors soon began to invade. They seized the town of Sarajevo in 1451. Bosnian lords became vassals* of the Ottomans. In 1463, the Ottomans sent a large army into Bosnia. They captured the Bosnian king Stefan Tomasevic and beheaded him. The Hungarians tried to rally a counterattack, but they could find no local allies. Bosnia became part of the Ottoman Empire, and many Bosnians converted to the Islamic faith.

* **mercenary** soldier who fights for payment rather than out of loyalty to a lord or nation

* **vassal** person given land by a lord or monarch in return for loyalty and services

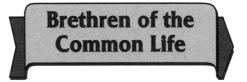

Brethren of the Common Life

* **Low Countries** flat coastal lands west of Germany, now occupied by Belgium and the Netherlands

During the late Middle Ages, people in Germany and the Low Countries* became interested in many religious movements that stressed simple piety and good works. One of the last of these movements was called *Devotio Moderna,* or Modern Worship. It consisted of the Brethren of the Common Life, the Sisters of the Common Life, and the Congregation of Windesheim.

The movement was inspired by the life of Geert de Groote, a rich man who gave up his wealth and traveled through the Low Countries in the late 1300s preaching religious reform. When he died, a group of his students led by Florens Radewijns formed the Brethren. The Brethren were influenced by the monastic atmosphere of the period, but they did not take a monk's vows. They promised only to live purely and harmoniously, with all their property held in common.

The Brethren rose early and devoted much of their day to devotions and the study of Scripture. They cultivated meditation for a spiritual life and wrote books on meditation. Their most important source of income was copying manuscripts. In addition, they acted as spiritual leaders to the Sisters of the Common Life. They also helped young students prepare to be priests or monks. The Brethren were not trained in theology, so they did not run schools of their own. Instead they provided room and board for students and served as counselors and tutors.

The Brethren also started a new monastic order, the Congregation of Windesheim. Members of the Congregation had much the same goals as the Brethren and the Sisters, but they took full monastic vows. In the end, there were many more Windesheim monasteries than houses for the Sisters and the Brethren combined.

The Brethren and the Sisters were not attacked for heresy* as earlier movements such as the BEGUINES AND BEGHARDS had been. But in many ways, they were similar. By 1600, when Protestantism became popular, the movement lapsed. Houses could no longer attract new recruits, and those who might still have joined were drawn to lay orders* that had been established by FRIARS.

Breviary

* **heresy** belief that is contrary to church doctrine

* **lay order** religious group organized by friars for laypersons who did not wish to take full vows

* **abbey** monastery under the rule of an abbot or abbess

During the Middle Ages, the breviary became the official book of the DIVINE OFFICE of the Roman Catholic Church. The Divine Office means the sets of prayers, hymns, lessons, and other readings that celebrate each hour of the day during different seasons and feasts of the Christian year. Reciting each day's Divine Office was a basic task in all religious communities.

In the medieval church, most abbeys* had large libraries of religious books and many monks to help compile each day's Divine Office. But smaller monastic communities had neither the people nor the books for this task. They needed a simpler way to assemble and sequence the texts to be recited. Breviaries arose from this need. The word comes from the Latin *breviarium,* meaning a brief version or summary. The earliest breviaries, dating from about 1100, were large books, but they gathered the items used for each day's Divine Office into a single volume.

In the early 1200s, the Franciscan FRIARS began to travel widely for their missionary work. They requested a smaller, shorter version of the breviary that was easily portable and provided a uniform guide to prayers. This was approved by the pope, and its convenience was soon known throughout Europe. It gradually replaced the many books that had been needed to celebrate the Divine Office. The introduction of the printing press in the 1400s helped extend the use of the breviary. By the end of the Middle Ages, it had become the main prayer book of the Roman Catholic clergy. (*See also* **Book of Hours.**)

Brigit, St.

late 400s to early 500s
Irish abbess

Brigit is the most famous female saint of Ireland. She is second only to St. Patrick in importance and popularity. A biography of Brigit was written in the late 600s, and several others were written later.

The biographies of St. Brigit are full of folklore and myths. They describe how Brigit was born at sunrise; how the house where she lived shone as if it were on fire; and how the sun's rays supported her wet cloak. They tell of Brigit's miraculous powers of healing. These stories were probably borrowed from a pre-Christian Celtic goddess of healing with the same name. Brigit's saint's day was held on the day of an old Celtic spring festival.

There are not many details about the real Brigit's life. She lived in southeast Ireland and came from a minor tribe. Christianity had just begun in Ireland. She founded one of the earliest monasteries, with separate quarters for nuns and monks. The local bishops acted as priests, but Brigit was the abbess*, in overall control. After her death, she was adopted by the leading tribe of the area as its patron saint*.

The cult of Brigit was spread to Britain and the European continent by Irish missionaries and pilgrims from the 600s to the 1100s. Her name was included in many early church calendars, histories of Christian martyrs, and other religious documents. Churches and holy places were dedicated to her, and various folk beliefs and practices were associated with her name. (*See also* **Ireland; Monasticism; Saints, Lives of.**)

* **abbess** female head of an abbey or monastery. The male equivalent is an abbot.

* **patron saint** saint held as guardian of a group's spiritual life

British Isles, Art and Architecture

See map in England (vol. 2).

During the Middle Ages, artisans of the British Isles—England, Scotland, Wales, and Ireland—created distinctive forms of painting, metalwork, stonework, embroidery, and architecture. Their arts were based on several traditions, and their artworks were unique, lively, and diverse in appearance.

Celtic, Saxon, and Irish-Saxon Art.   The work of the native Celtic-speaking peoples of Britain and Ireland formed the basis of art in the British Isles from the 400s to the 1100s. Celtic artists used designs that grew from the traditional motifs of the late Iron Age, which are also found in early Greek and other Mediterranean styles.

Beginning in the 400s, Germanic tribes of Angles, Saxons, and Jutes invaded England. The art of these nomadic peoples focused on personal adornment. Their jewelry, weapons, and tools were often magnificently decorated. Animals, real and fantastic, were a favorite theme and were used extensively to cover surfaces of jewelry and other objects.

By the end of the 600s, the Celtic and Germanic artistic traditions were beginning to blend. In this mixed style, lively beasts were interlaced with scrolls, swirls, and spirals to create dense, colorful designs and patterns of great complexity. Though also influenced by art from the Roman Church, the style is today called Hiberno-Saxon (Irish-Saxon). Irish-Saxon artists produced masterpieces in manuscript illumination, metalwork, and sculpture.

Irish-Saxon art was produced in Ireland and in parts of England. The metalwork used a wide range of materials, such as semiprecious stones and multicolored glass. It involved highly skilled techniques, including filigree* and cloisonné*. The finest pieces are almost unbelievably intricate. Illuminated books such as Bibles, prayer books, and Gospels were another treasured art form. The interlaced animal and spiral designs of Irish-Saxon metalwork found their way into the decorations of these books as well. Among the greatest masterpieces of this art form is the Book of KELLS. Here, interlaced creatures, spirals, and geometric patterns are piled one upon the other in a mass of vibrating visual energy.

Anglo-Saxon Art.   In the early 800s, VIKING invaders from Scandinavia destroyed much of the Irish-Saxon culture. When these invaders were turned back in the late 800s, art in Britain underwent a dramatic change. Artists turned from abstract ornamentation to more naturalistic images that

* **filigree** delicate ornamental work of fine silver, gold, or other metal wires

* **cloisonné** enamelwork in which areas of color are separated by tiny metal bands embedded into the surface

Durham Cathedral, built between 1093 and 1133, was the first Romanesque church to use rib vaulting, which became an element of the Gothic style. This photograph of the cathedral's interior shows the rounded Romanesque arches, rib vaults, and piers that divide the nave into bays.

See color plate 6, vol. 2.

* **bay** section of a church or cathedral, defined by stone supports or columns

* **vault** section of a three-dimensional arched ceiling of stone

showed the influence of the major Christian traditions of Europe—namely, CAROLINGIAN and BYZANTINE art. The new style was noted for its elaborate and dynamic figures, often depicted in frenzied movement. These figures were embellished with flowing lines or zigzag patterns of drapery and leaves, combining to form lively yet unified decorative compositions. In the 900s, painting and line drawing were especially important art forms, and similar styles were used for both. Anglo-Saxon artists also worked in other media, such as ivory and stone carving, metalwork, enamel, and embroidery.

The architecture of the Anglo-Saxon period of the late 800s was regional and diverse. England was divided into seven kingdoms, each with its own architectural customs. Distinctive features of Anglo-Saxon architecture include carved strip work on church towers and triangular-headed windows. The Anglo-Saxons often used the remains of old Roman structures and recycled the stone, brick, and other materials.

Anglo-Norman Art and Architecture. The Norman conquest of England in 1066 marked an important milestone for British architecture. The Normans built many stone fortresses, which were some of the earliest CASTLES. In church architecture, the ROMANESQUE style was introduced, with round-arched windows, vaulted aisles, and long naves divided into bays*. In time, an Anglo-Norman style evolved, in which some Anglo-Saxon decorative elements were added to Romanesque columns, moldings, and other surfaces. The vaults* in the English cathedral of Durham were the first to be clearly defined by the use of ribs arching across the nave. In painting and other art forms, the Anglo-Norman period saw a fusion of Anglo-Saxon practices with European styles imported by the Normans.

Beginning in the late 1100s, France's soaring GOTHIC ARCHITECTURE began to have an increasing influence on English building. Among the

* **tracery** decorative pattern of carved stone separating the leaded glass elements in a church window

earliest English churches to reflect the early Gothic style were Canterbury and Lincoln Cathedrals. This style gradually came to dominate church architecture in the British Isles, with distinctive variations developing. For example, the Decorated style introduced intricate curved lines in the vaulting ribs and the window traceries*. The Perpendicular style, by contrast, emphasized the vertical and horizontal elements in Gothic building. Gothic remained the leading style in England until the end of the Middle Ages. (*See also* **Books, Manuscript; Byzantine Art; England.**)

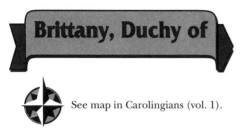

See map in Carolingians (vol. 1).

* **Celts** ancient inhabitants of Europe and the British Isles

When the Anglo-Saxons invaded the British Isles at the start of the Middle Ages, they drove many of the original Celts* west into Wales and Cornwall. Some of the fugitives went farther, escaping by sea to France's western peninsula of Brittany. There they joined mainland Celts, who were defending themselves against the Franks. Together the two Celtic peoples—who came to be called Bretons because the new arrivals were from Britain—established a region that was largely independent of France's national rulers until 1491.

Before the British Celts arrived during the 500s, the region had been known as Armorica. It was a province of the Christian Empire of ancient Rome. The British Celts were also Christian because of their contact with Roman Britain. Both peoples were part of the Celtic Christian church. They set up small Christian kingdoms and made peace with the Franks.

The Franks, under their king CLOVIS, had only recently accepted the Roman branch of Christianity. Frankish and Celtic bishops met together in the 500s and 600s, but they accepted their differences. Then CHARLEMAGNE's son Louis the Pious became emperor in 814 and defeated the Bretons, forcing them to join the Roman Church.

After Louis died in 840, the Frankish Empire began to break up. VIKINGS from Scandinavia were weakening the Franks with raids from the sea. The Breton princes joined together, drove the Franks from their region, and created a unified kingdom of Brittany that lasted until the early 900s. Around 915, however, Vikings' raids threatened Brittany, and many Bretons fled to other parts of France or back to England. The Frankish king made peace by allowing the Vikings to settle on land east of Brittany and west of Paris. The area became known as the duchy* of Normandy, and the Vikings who settled there were known as the NORMANS. The king also made Brittany a duchy. The two new dukes were the king's vassals*, but both held local power.

* **duchy** territory ruled by a duke or a duchess

* **vassal** person given land by a lord or monarch in return for loyalty and services

*homage formal public declaration of loyalty to the king or overlord

In 983, local rulers around France became far more independent. The Breton duke was able to stop paying homage* to the Frankish kings. In Brittany, towns grew, monasteries were founded, and local industries began to trade abroad: shipping and the making of canvas and linen were Breton specialties.

Breton natives joined the Normans in their conquest of England (1066) and in their occupation of Italy and Sicily a few years later. For a time, Bretons became vassals to Normandy and England—Brittany became a Norman county rather than a French duchy. Then the French king Philip II Augustus supported Count Arthur of Brittany as a candidate for king of England. Arthur failed and was murdered; Philip drove the English from northern France in the early 1200s and appointed a French duke of Brittany.

A century later, the Bretons and their dukes objected to taxes imposed by the French king and started to mint their own coins against French royal orders. This was made much easier by the HUNDRED YEARS WAR, during which England invaded France to fight for the return of its old territories. It was not until the later 1400s that the French kings were able to turn their attention to Brittany again. After several years of war, Duchess Anne of Brittany was defeated in battle, and then she was persuaded to marry Charles VIII of France. Brittany had become part of France. (*See also* **France.**)

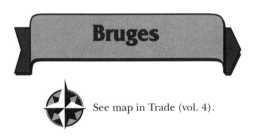

See map in Trade (vol. 4).

* **allegiance** loyalty to a noble or king, who granted property and protection in return for military service in time of war and, often, taxes in peacetime

* **guild** association of craft and trade workers that set standards and represented the interests of its members

Bruges, a city in northwest Belgium, was ideally placed for trade in the later Middle Ages. It was on a narrow bay beside the North Sea, just across from England and close to the Rhine and other great rivers of western Europe. Its citizens conducted trade with England, Germany, Scandinavia, Russia, France, Italy, Spain, and even Africa and other Muslim areas. Merchants and bankers came to Bruges from all over Europe and the Middle East. Just as the city of VENICE dominated trade in countries around the Mediterranean, Bruges was the great commercial center of northern Europe.

Bruges was like Venice in another way too. Situated in low, marshy land that was drained by a network of canals, it was famous for its waterways and bridges. In fact, its name comes from the Dutch word meaning "bridge." The early town grew in the 900s and 1000s, around the castle of the counts of FLANDERS. These counts oversaw clearance of the area's marshes, helping to make Flanders a great agricultural area. Though they technically owed allegiance* to the kings of France and Germany, the counts of Flanders became very wealthy and stayed independent for most of the Middle Ages.

Flanders was famed for wool and cloth, and Bruges soon became a center for merchants trading cloth and other goods. Its people gained considerable freedom because the counts and other noble families needed their support. Bruges soon had its own councilors, called *échevins*, who took care of local government, justice, and public works and who regulated their own commerce and the crafts guilds*. This enabled Bruges to become very prosperous.

Unlike Venice, Bruges never became a naval power. The ships that entered its port were mostly from other nations. The inhabitants of Bruges ran the markets; the foreign merchants who came to trade provided the transportation. In fact, Bruges had such important markets that the city flourished even after it ceased to be a port. In the 1200s, its narrow bay silted up as a result of receding waters and marsh drainage projects in western Flanders. The merchants of Bruges solved the problem by building a canal from the nearby port of Damme.

Bruges reached the height of its power in the early 1300s. At that time, ships from the Italian cities of Genoa and Pisa had begun to sail to the

North Sea. At least 30 Christian and Muslim states traded their goods at Bruges for the world-famous Flemish wool, lace, and textiles. Each state set up a trading house in the city. Bankers from Italy and southern France opened bank branches in Bruges to change money and to give credit.

By 1400, the power of Bruges had declined. Antwerp, a rival city that still had direct access to the sea, took over some of Bruges's trade. Bruges also lost most of its independence. After bitter and sometimes bloody conflicts with the king of France, Flanders became the property of the dukes of Burgundy. The dukes got rid of Bruges's *échevins* and ruled it as a part of the county of Flanders. Many people left the city. They were beginning to call it "Bruges la Morte," or "Bruges the Dead." However, the city's fine churches and public buildings, its castle, its handsome houses, and its canals earned Bruges another role also shared by Venice. It became an artistic center, and famous artists—including Jan van Eyck and Hans Memling—painted the city and its inhabitants. (*See also* **Commune; Trade.**)

Brunelleschi, Filippo

1377–1446
Architect and sculptor

* **baptistery** room or hall for holding baptisms. Early Christian baptisteries were often large, freestanding buildings.

Brunelleschi, now regarded as the earliest great architect of the Italian Renaissance, lived in Florence in the late Middle Ages. He was trained as a sculptor and metalsmith, working mostly in gold, silver, and bronze. Several of his sculptures are still prized today, including a bronze relief from the early 1400s showing the sacrifice of Isaac. The figures of Abraham and the angel are realistically modeled and full of motion; Isaac's body is twisted in fear. The relief was an entry for a competition in Florence to decorate the baptistery* doors, and it was not selected. Other later ornamental work by Brunelleschi can be found in many Florentine churches, however.

One of Brunelleschi's many famous designs was the church of Santo Spirito in Florence. This is an interior view of the nave, the central portion of the church.

In 1402, Brunelleschi visited Rome, where he studied and learned from that city's ancient monuments. These inspired his own work in architecture. One of his first achievements, and that for which he is best known today, is the dome he designed and built to crown the cathedral of Florence. It was the widest dome since Roman times, and the highest ever. It still dominates the Florentine skyline.

Brunelleschi also designed and supervised the construction of many churches in Florence. These show a sense of proportion based on classical buildings, rather than the characteristic vertical thrust of the medieval Gothic style. Because of the slow pace of work and his busy schedule, however, much of Brunelleschi's work was not completed during his lifetime. Even the lantern on top of the cathedral dome was put in place after his death.

The work Brunelleschi left bears witness to his innovative vision and skill. The bold, simple style of his early sculpture may have contributed to his brilliant work as an architect. Using simple forms—the circle, square, hemisphere, and arch—he kept his buildings to a human scale, creating harmonious, rather austere interiors. Brunelleschi's splendid architecture was an inspiration to many later generations of architects, including Michelangelo.

Bulgaria

See map in Ottomans and Ottoman Empire (vol. 3).

* **boyar** Slavic term for powerful lord, similar to medieval baron

* **Frankish** referring to the Germanic tribe called the Franks, who dominated western Europe in the early Middle Ages

Bulgaria, near the southeast corner of the Balkan peninsula, is rich and fertile. It faces the Black Sea to the east. Its northern border is the Danube River. To the west, north of Greece, are other lands of the Balkan peninsula, including Macedonia and SERBIA. In the Middle Ages, Constantinople, fabled capital of the BYZANTINE EMPIRE, was to the south. Bulgaria lay open to invasion from the Mediterranean and from the plains of Europe and Asia.

Slavs and Bulgars.   Before the Middle Ages began, Bulgaria was in the Byzantine Empire. Slavic tribes from eastern Europe north of the Danube began to settle there to farm. Then a group of Turks from central Asia, called the Bulgars, moved south and began to dominate the Slavs.

In the 670s, the Bulgars fought off an attack from the Byzantines and forced them to recognize an independent Bulgarian state, in which the Slavs began to become integrated. Bulgaria started to trade with the Byzantine Empire, and its soldiers helped Constantinople against an Arab siege in 718.

The nation was not a stable unit, however. In 739, the Bulgar king died without an heir, and there were years of civil war among the Bulgar boyars*. During this time, the Byzantines won victories in Bulgaria, though they were unable to conquer the whole land. The great king CHARLEMAGNE also extended the Frankish* Empire into the Balkan peninsula and threatened the northwestern border of Bulgaria.

It was not until 803 that a Bulgar named Krum established firm local rule again. King Krum and his son Omurtag fought back the Byzantines, strengthened the frontier against Charlemagne, and expanded to the north, into Hungary. Then, in the middle 800s, Bulgaria attacked the Byzantine Empire and occupied the west Balkan territory of Macedonia, thus doubling the size of its state.

* **pagan** word used by Christians to mean non-Christian and believing in several gods

* **Orthodox** referring to the Eastern Byzantine Church

* **tribute** payment made to a dominant foreign power to stop it from invading

* **artisans** skilled craftspeople

The Byzantines occupied Bulgaria in the 11th and 12th centuries and greatly influenced the art styles of the region. This icon of the Virgin Mary dates from the 1100s.

Boris and the Christian Bulgarian Empire.

Krum and Omurtag were pagans*, generally opposed to Christians from Constantinople and from the Frankish Empire who were making converts among the Bulgarian people. But in 864, Bulgaria's King Boris expressed interest in converting to Christianity. The Byzantines persuaded him to accept Orthodox* Christianity rather than the Roman Church, which the Frankish missionaries were supporting.

Boris began to model Bulgaria on the Christian Byzantine Empire, realizing this could give him stronger central power and weaken the boyars. The boyars had revolted against him in 866, and he executed 52 of their leaders. Bulgars had by now adopted many Slavic customs, and Macedonia had a large Slav population, so Boris made Slavic the official language of the state. He also used CYRIL AND METHODIOS's new Slavic alphabet to translate Christian services into Slavic, though he was unable to found an independent Bulgarian Orthodox Church.

Boris's son Symeon and grandson Peter ruled after him until 967. Symeon won some great battles against the Byzantines and forced them to start paying tribute* to Bulgaria. He even called himself "Emperor of the Romans," a special title of the Byzantine emperor. Symeon encouraged literature and built MONASTERIES and churches. Artisans* worked in ceramics, stone, gold, and silver. Bulgarian tiles became famous for their beauty and were exported to the Byzantine Empire and to KIEVAN RUS. Bulgaria thrived as a trading center and was described as richer than Rus, with "gold, silks, wine and various fruits from Greece, silver and horses from HUNGARY and BOHEMIA, and from Rus furs, honey, wax, and slaves."

The Russian and Byzantine Conquests.

In 965, the Byzantine emperor refused to pay the Bulgarian tribute and at the same time arranged for a Russian force to attack Bulgaria from the east. By 967, the move appeared to have succeeded; but the Russians then led their new Bulgarian subjects in a war on Byzantine territory. It took six years for the Byzantines to drive the Russians back. This placed Bulgaria under direct Byzantine rule for the first time since the 600s. However, Bulgarians still ruled in Macedonia. From there, they continued to harass Constantinople.

Civil war, meantime, broke out in the Byzantine lands in ANATOLIA. The new Byzantine emperor, BASIL II, quelled the revolt in 1001 and was able to return his attention to the Bulgarians in Macedonia. Basil defeated the Bulgarians in a brutal military campaign ending in 1014, and he became known as the "Killer of Bulgars." Bulgaria remained subdued for 150 years.

The Second Bulgarian Empire.

The second Bulgarian Empire owed more to Byzantine weakness than to Bulgarian strength. The Byzantine emperors had become much weaker after Basil II and were unable to handle Turkish pressure in Anatolia. They had to rely on support from crusading kings and knights from the West to attack the Muslim world. In 1187, Bulgaria was able to revolt, regain its independence, and expand its territories once again.

In 1204, crusaders turned their attack against the Byzantines and captured Constantinople. The Byzantine Empire was fractured into a few states across Greece and Anatolia, and there was no major power in the

* **Latin** referring to western Europe and the Roman Church, which used the Latin language for its services

* **tsar** Slavic term for emperor

region. The new Latin* state of Constantinople was unable to take control, and it became instead one of several local powers that made and broke alliances and fought for territory. In a battle for Thrace in Greece, Bulgaria's King Kalojan, who called himself a tsar*, won a massive victory against the new king of Constantinople.

Constantinople remained in Western hands, however, and the sparring between states continued. Bulgaria's Tsar John Asen II played a major part in the struggles, saving Constantinople in 1230 from a Byzantine army based in Epiros, Greece, and then five years later joining another Byzantine army from Nicaea in an attack on the city. Fearing a new Byzantine dynasty in Constantinople, however, Asen then withdrew his support.

Even after Nicaea finally recaptured Constantinople for the Byzantines in 1261, the military situation in the south Balkans was unstable. However, there was a flowering of Orthodox religious culture across the whole area, during which many fine Byzantine-style churches were built, and monks moved across the national borders spreading scholarly and religious ideas. This cultural flowering continued even as Bulgaria broke into two and then three separate states and Serbia dominated the region in the middle 1300s. But it did not last. The Ottoman Turks conquered the Balkan peninsula at the end of the century, and Bulgaria became a part of the Muslim OTTOMAN Empire until 1878. (*See also* **Anatolia; Christianity; Crusades.**)

* **duchy** territory ruled by a duke or a duchess

See map in England (vol. 2).

See color plate 8, vol. 3.

urgundy is a historic region in eastern France around the upper Saône River. During periods of the Middle Ages, the name covered a much larger area, which included a kingdom of Burgundy, a county of Burgundy, and a duchy* of Burgundy. During the 1100s, all three units existed side by side.

In the 400s, parts of Switzerland and a neighboring portion of France were inhabited by a Germanic tribe known as the Burgundians, from whom the region got the name *Burgundy*. Their kingdom was conquered by the Franks in 534, and it became an area of CHARLEMAGNE's empire. When that empire split apart, Burgundy was divided with it. The eastern section became a kingdom within the German HOLY ROMAN EMPIRE, while the area west of the Saône became a French duchy.

Later, lands in the eastern section began to switch to French rule. The northern part of the kingdom of Burgundy became an independent county, which merged with the French duchy. In the late Middle Ages, the French dukes of Burgundy played a key role in wars between France and England.

The Kingdom of Burgundy. A second kingdom of Burgundy was formed when Charlemagne's grandson Lothar I divided his portion of the empire among his heirs. Lothar's son Charles became king over most of the old Burgundian territory. Because Charles had no children, however, Burgundy's ownership was disputed, first between Charles's brothers and then between other descendants of Lothar. Finally, Burgundy was annexed by a powerful neighboring duke, Rudolf I from the house of Welf, who owed allegiance to the German CAROLINGIANS. Thus, the kingdom of

Burgundy became linked to the German Holy Roman Empire that developed from the lands of Louis the German.

The new Burgundy grew to include not only the eastern lands of old Burgundy but also a southern area called PROVENCE, sometimes known as the kingdom of Arles. Burgundy was important because its mountain passes linked France, Germany, and Italy. Under Rudolf's son Conrad, the kingdom stretched from the city of Basel in the north to the Mediterranean in the south, and from today's Italian-French border to the Saône and Rhône Rivers.

Rudolf's later descendants were weaker monarchs. Provence became virtually independent under the control of powerful archbishops* and counts. Later, when Burgundy was absorbed into the German Holy Roman Empire in 1032, powerful German rulers tried to unify Burgundy again. But their efforts were still hampered by quarrels between the counts of Provence and counts of the neighboring French region of Toulouse.

In 1245, Charles of Anjou, brother of the French king, married the heiress of Provence, thus acquiring control of a large part of Burgundy. The Germans resented this and other annexations of Burgundian land, and Holy Roman Emperor Charles IV finally responded by asserting his rights as sovereign of the region. However, to obtain French support, he appointed the future king of France (Charles VI) as his vicar* in much of southern Burgundy. In doing so, he transferred actual rule of those areas to the French crown, even though legally they remained German territory.

The County of Burgundy. The county of Burgundy began as the northern part of the kingdom of Burgundy. Known as the Franche-Comté, it gained freedom from the Holy Roman Empire in the 1100s as its counts resisted pressures from the kings of Burgundy and the German emperors.

Franche-Comté had important medieval salt mines. It was also on two major trade routes, one from Italy to the north and the other from France to the Rhine River. The eastern part of the county was mountainous and heavily forested, but much of the land was cleared after 1200, and new towns were established. Expanding trade led to the growth of market fairs throughout the county, and many towns were granted charters, increasing the area's wealth. Important ROMANESQUE and GOTHIC churches were built. The period also saw the founding of many monasteries.

During the 1200s, the counts of Burgundy shared power in the area with neighboring French counts. This helped them stay free from the Germans, but it led to stronger ties with France. In the mid-1300s, the county was joined to the duchy of Burgundy under its French duke, Philip the Bold.

The Duchy of Burgundy. The duchy of Burgundy was a land of hills, plateaus, and river valleys. The western end of the original land of Burgundy, it linked the Saône River with the Seine, which passes through Paris. The duchy was originally established in 877 by Charles the Bald, Charlemagne's third grandson, who inherited the western territories of the Franks.

In the 900s, Richard, a duke of the Burgundians, led a successful French defense against Norman invaders. This strengthened the power and influence of the duchy, which was, however, taken over by the counts of Paris in 952. Later, Paris became the seat of Hugh CAPET, first

* **archbishop** head bishop in a region or nation

* **vicar** person granted authority to act in place of another

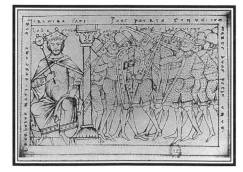

Burgundy has a history as a kingdom, a county, and a duchy. In 841, Lothar I, Holy Roman Emperor, fought against his brothers, Louis II the German and Charles the Bald, for the right to control the kingdom of Burgundy.

Daily Life

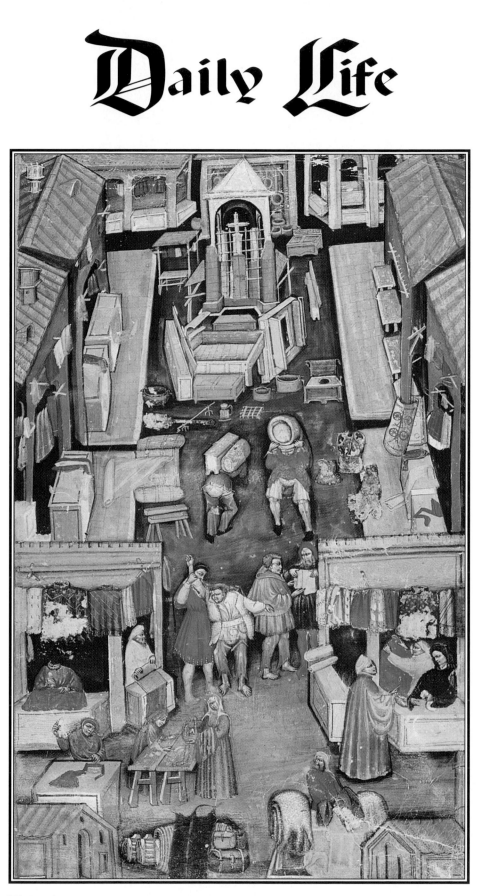

Plate 1

This miniature from the late 1400s shows a busy street scene in the market district of the medieval city of Bologna, Italy. Merchants display their wares for browsing shoppers.

Plate 2

This detail of a Flemish miniature, showing family members by the fireplace, is from the *Da Costa Book of Hours* and was painted in the late Middle Ages. The fireplace-and-chimney system brought great social and economic changes to Europe. By the 1100s, even peasant huts had heating systems.

Plate 3

This Italian fresco from the 1400s shows a bustling fruit and vegetable market. Food trade—the buying and selling of foodstuffs—was the primary activity in the markets of medieval villages, towns, and cities, although many nonfood items were sold as well. Local markets were also places where people came to meet friends, hear news, and be entertained.

Plate 4

This manuscript illumination, from the Rylands Haggadah, shows a Passover seder in Spain in the 1300s. The Haggadah is the special text containing the story of the Exodus of the Jews from Israel. Every spring, Jews commemorate the Exodus by reading from the Haggadah and eating a meal of specially prepared foods.

Plate 5

This illustration shows patients waiting to see the surgeon in his clinic. It is from an illustrated text of *Chirurgia magna* by Guy de Chauliac, one of the most famous surgeons of the 14th century.

Plate 6

Glassmaking was an important industry in the Middle Ages, providing glass for cathedrals as well as for household containers, lamps, and mirrors. Glassmakers used the technique of elongating and shaping a blob of molten glass by blowing through a long metal tube.

Plate 7

Between 1484 and 1485, Bernhard Breidenbach made a trip from Germany to Palestine. Following his return in 1486, he produced a travelogue of his trip. This woodcut from his book shows a galley being built in the shipyards in Venice, Italy.

Plate 8

Stonecutters, or masons, cut stones and prepared them to be used in buildings and monuments. Most stonecutters moved from place to place and found work wherever stone construction was needed. Occasionally, a mason was fortunate enough to work on successive projects in one town. A master mason might spend his entire career on a single project, such as a cathedral.

Plate 9

Medieval musicians traveled constantly, entertaining wherever they could find lodgings and an audience. The instruments being played by this German troupe include the drum, fiddle, horn, lute, and bagpipes.

Plate 10

The knight in armor is one of the best known symbols of the Middle Ages. This detail from a 15th-century English manuscript shows a young man being armed for combat. Arms and armor were elaborate and very costly. The design of armor evolved as new weapons were introduced and as the techniques of fighting changed.

Plate 11

Bread was the most common food in the medieval diet. People spent more of their money on bread or the grain used to make it than on anything else. While noble families feasted on bread made of finely milled grain, peasants' bread was usually dark and very coarse. The commercial sale of bread, controlled by the bakers' guilds, became important in the later Middle Ages. This illustration is from a 15th-century French manuscript.

Plate 12

This miniature from the *Playfair Book of Hours* shows peasants reaping wheat in the month of July. Agriculture was the principal medieval industry. Many peasants and serfs worked long, grueling hours farming the lord's land. In exchange for their services, they were allowed to have a small parcel of land for their own use.

Plate 13

This illumination shows a philosophy class in a French university in the 1300s. Universities spread throughout Europe after the early 1200s. They were semi-independent institutions—similar to modern corporations. While schools played an important role in medieval society, there was no public education.

Plate 14

This illumination from Jehan Froissart's *Chronicles* shows a massacre during the Jacquerie, or peasant rebellion (France, 1358). The harsh demands placed on the lower classes by their rulers and landlords led to discontent and occasionally open rebellion.

Plate 15

Building crews consisted of highly skilled teams that included masons, stonecutters, glassmakers, carpenters, sculptors, and many assistants. This illumination, from a treatise on the art of building, is from a manuscript of *De universo* by Hrabanus Maurus. That treatise is a major encyclopedic work of the Carolingian era that dates from the mid-800s.

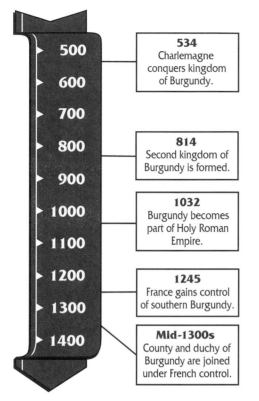

534
Charlemagne conquers kingdom of Burgundy.

814
Second kingdom of Burgundy is formed.

1032
Burgundy becomes part of Holy Roman Empire.

1245
France gains control of southern Burgundy.

Mid-1300s
County and duchy of Burgundy are joined under French control.

* **dynasty** succession of rulers from the same family or group

* **Low Countries** flat coastal lands west of Germany, now occupied by Belgium and the Netherlands

king of France. The duchy of Burgundy was granted to Hugh's grandson Robert, who founded a line of Capetian dukes that continued unbroken until 1361.

The medieval duchy of Burgundy was rich in agricultural resources, and easy access to major land routes and waterways made it very prosperous. The duchy's interior location also protected it from the ravages of outside invaders. As a result, the duchy was one of the first regions in Europe to benefit from increased trade in the 1000s. By 1200, many of its towns had successful markets and fairs, and dozens of towns were granted charters.

The duchy was the birthplace of important monastic reform movements. Reforms begun at the monastery of Cluny, for example, eventually spread throughout Europe. In the 1200s, various monastic orders contributed greatly to the duchy's religious and economic life. The CISTERCIAN order, in particular, played a great role in the development of new agricultural techniques. Monastic buildings in the duchy also had a significant effect on the style of architecture throughout western Europe. For example, the Burgundian Romanesque style was adopted in many places.

After the last Capetian duke of Burgundy died in the 1360s, the duchy was ruled by another highly influential line of dukes, who were related to the Valois dynasty* of French kings. Philip the Bold, the first of these dukes, controlled many parts of the wealthy Low Countries*, and he also took power over the county of Burgundy. His descendants twice changed the course of the HUNDRED YEARS WAR. In 1412, when Burgundy made an alliance with England, England's King HENRY V was able to claim the French throne for his son. However, after a Burgundian alliance with France in 1435, French forces were able to drive the English out of France for the last time.

Byzantine Architecture

The medieval Byzantine Empire, centered on the Aegean Sea and Greece, is famed for its complex domed churches and their magical interior ornamentation. Its buildings were admired throughout the Christian world and beyond. Much of its glory was based on its greatest city, CONSTANTINOPLE, the capital of the empire from its founding in 330 to its conquest by Muslims in 1453. Constantinople was a leading center of Christianity, and Byzantine building styles and workmanship spread throughout eastern Europe and Asia Minor, also influencing some sites in western Europe.

The Heritage of Rome and the Early Church. Byzantine architecture, like the Byzantine Empire, was based on the achievements of ancient Rome. The Romans had built great public buildings with core structures of concrete and faced on the outside with brick or stone. Colored marble was brought from all areas of the Mediterranean to decorate interior surfaces, often creating brilliant effects. In addition to great public buildings, Rome's tradition of civil engineering produced roads and bridges, fortifications, harbors, and aqueducts. Building skills and techniques were brought from Rome to Constantinople when Emperor Constantine I founded his new capital city.

basilica oblong building with rows of columns dividing the interior into a nave, or central aisle, and side aisles

mausoleum memorial building to house a tomb

Christendom name for all the Christian nations of the world

barbarian referring to people from outside the cultures of Greece and Rome who were viewed as uncivilized

mosaic art form in which small pieces of stone or glass are set in cement; also refers to a picture made in this manner

Squinches and Pendentives

Placing a round dome above a square space requires ingenuity. Though domes, like arches, support their centers from below, a firm base is needed all around. Byzantine builders successfully used squinches, arched structures across the square's corners to create an octagonal base.

A second technique worked even if the square had corner columns and no walls. Arches linked the corners and were joined by pendentives, upside-down, curving triangles of masonry. The point of each pendentive was on a corner of the square; its curved sides rested on arches; and its curved base bowed inwards, creating part of a complete circle to support the dome.

Constantine and his successors created the new city to imitate and improve on the old capital. They built broad avenues, marketplaces, and public baths. The new senate was housed in a basilica* similar to the old Roman senate building. In the early 400s, the massive double walls of Constantinople were built. These walls, almost four miles in length and still in existence, protected the city for over a thousand years. No other city in all of the Middle Ages had such well-designed fortifications.

The builders of churches in Constantinople and the other cities of the Byzantine Empire also began by following the models of Rome. In Rome, churches were usually housed in rectangular basilicas. But there were other types of church buildings: round or polygonal churches called "martyr's shrines," modeled after ancient mausoleums*; and in some cities, octagonal "palace" churches, often domed, which appear to have been built for the emperor.

Byzantine churches developed differently from those in other areas of Christendom*. Basilica churches were the main models for later churches in the barbarian*-dominated, Latin-speaking world of Western Christianity. Simple basilicas could be built without advanced techniques. Interior art was normally instructional, usually based on stories from the Bible. Architects in Constantinople, however, favored more challenging structures. Their basilica churches tended to be squarish. The architects also used other geometrical shapes, or they mixed shapes to create intricate internal spaces. Interiors were lavishly decorated, not only with religious images but with leaves, flowers, birds, and animals carved from marble or created in mosaics*.

The Age of Justinian. The largest churches of the Byzantine Empire were built in its early years. During the reign of JUSTINIAN I, who in the 500s recaptured many of the old Roman territories of the West, there was a great wave of church building. New combinations of shapes were used. Large domes crowned otherwise square structures. Domed squares were combined to make churches in the shape of a cross. In one church, an octagonal structure with a circular dome rose from a square exterior. Inside some churches, rows of columns and arches created galleries, leading to intriguing glimpses of one space from another. Marble, mosaics, gold, and silver dazzled the eye.

One church from this period stands out—HAGIA SOPHIA, the Church of Holy Wisdom in Constantinople. Built in only five years (532–537), Hagia Sophia is the largest of all Byzantine churches. While its ground plan still echoes the basilica model, its vaulting is new and technologically daring.

Hagia Sophia is monumental in size and yet has the appearance of lightness. With its central domed space, flanked by smaller half domes, it was admired throughout the world. For 900 years, Hagia Sophia symbolized Eastern Christianity. Too large and too complex to imitate, its splendor nevertheless influenced later building in the Islamic world as well as in Christendom. Hagia Sophia still stands today.

Later Byzantine Architecture. After the great age of Justinian, the Byzantine Empire suffered several setbacks, never quite regaining its former power. The rise of Islam during the 600s shook the empire to its roots and severely reduced its size. Yet Constantinople survived, maintaining extensive lands in eastern Europe and Asia Minor and holding on to the prestige of its Greek roots and its Roman heritage.

Byzantine culture and architecture were deeply affected. The power of the cities, except for Constantinople, began to erode, and large city churches and cathedrals ceased to be a priority. Monasteries gained influence in the religious world, and much care was lavished on the many smaller churches that these communities produced. Private landowners began to gain power, building their own family chapels and mausoleum churches.

Though the focus was now on building smaller churches, architects still favored geometric shapes, domes, and intricate interior spaces. They continued to be creative and to develop new designs. Three basic church types emerged. The simplest was the Greek cross, a design in which the floor plan was a cross with four arms of nearly equal length. The center of the cross was covered with a dome, and there might also be smaller domes above one or more of the arms. Another basic design was called the cross-in-square plan: the floor plan was square, but the ceiling vaults were constructed like a cross. Four columns supported a high dome in the center, and groin vaults* reached out from below the dome to each side of the square. The corner spaces of the square sometimes carried their own smaller domes, making five domes in all. A third type of design was the domed octagon.

* **groin vault**   arched ceiling consisting of two barrel vaults intersecting at right angles

Each of these basic designs had a number of variations. No matter what shape the spaces were, however, all Byzantine churches had in common the most beautiful interior decorations. Precious metals were used. Inlaid marble made geometric designs and mirror patterns. Walls and ceilings were covered with elaborate mosaics. After the end of the iconoclastic* controversy of the 700s and 800s, there was also more emphasis on icons, images of holy figures, in the decoration. Icons and mosaics became the most well-known characteristic of Byzantine church architecture.

* **iconoclastic**   referring to a movement to remove icons (images of Christ and the saints) from all churches

Outside the Byzantine Empire.   Byzantine church designs spread with Orthodox* Christianity into the Slavic nations of eastern Europe. The Greek cross design was popular in Russia, with the basic shape flanked by aisles and galleries to create complex and mysterious interiors. Architects in Bulgaria and Serbia also built many Byzantine-style churches, though Serbians sometimes mixed Byzantine features with a basilica design. In the West, however, only Italy, which traded extensively with Constantinople and had been part of its empire under Justinian, produced many Byzantine-style churches. The church of St. Mark's in Venice, for example, is a Greek cross design. (*See also* **Cathedrals and Churches; Christianity.**)

* **Orthodox**   referring to the Eastern Byzantine Church

Byzantine Art

See color plate 2, vol. 3.

Today only a small amount of the art of the Byzantine Empire survives. Yet in its time, Constantinople, the Byzantine capital, was the leading art center of the medieval world. Its magnificence overawed western European rulers and artists and rivaled the splendors of Muslim Baghdad. Byzantine art also strongly influenced the artistic movement called the Italian Renaissance.

A major cause of the loss of Byzantine art was Constantinople's fall to the Ottomans in 1453. Many Byzantine church buildings survived, but

One of the most richly decorated Byzantine churches is San Vitale in Ravenna, Italy, built in the sixth century. This famous mosaic shows the Byzantine empress, Theodora I, with attendants and the ladies of her court. On the other side of the church is an equally famous mosaic of her husband, Emperor Justinian I, with the bishop of Ravenna and nobles.

See color plate 3, vol. 3.

* **crusader** person who participated in the holy wars against the Muslims during the Middle Ages

* **fresco** method of painting in which color is applied to moist plaster and becomes chemically bonded to the plaster as it dries; also refers to a painting done in this style

* **mosaic** art form in which small pieces of stone or glass are set in cement; also refers to a picture made in this manner

* **Psalter** book containing the Psalms

* **patron** person of wealth and influence who supports an artist, writer, or scholar

artistic decorations were systematically changed. Byzantine Christians valued ICONS, representations of Jesus Christ, saints, and other religious figures. Muslims, however, believed that human images, even of Islamic leaders, had no place in religious buildings.

Before the Ottomans sacked Constantinople, other disasters affected Byzantine art. In 1204, crusaders* captured the city and shipped many pieces of art home to Italy and other parts of western Europe. Earlier, in the 700s, the Byzantines themselves destroyed much of their art during a movement called iconoclasm.

The strength of Byzantine artistic culture was such that these earlier setbacks did not destroy its preeminence. Byzantine icons, like other products of Byzantine culture, owed much to the artistic and technical skills of the Roman Empire. Many artists could still produce the lifelike and naturalistic human figures for which Roman art is famed.

Especially after the iconoclastic period, churches and monasteries throughout the Byzantine Empire were lavishly decorated with icons for meditation and devotion. Some icons were painted on framed panels hung on the sanctuary screens in the churches. Others were emblazoned on the walls, vaults, and domes, as frescoes* or spectacular mosaics*.

Byzantine art was not restricted to icons and religious decoration. There were beautiful illuminated manuscripts. One of the most important works of the 900s to survive is the Paris Psalter*, so called because it is now in Paris, France. It includes 14 miniature masterpieces depicting the life of King David of Judea. Among nonreligious works, the palace of Constantine VII, a great patron* of the arts, was said to be so sumptuous that it surpassed that of the ABBASIDS in Baghdad. His gilded bronze throne, constructed with Arab technology and known as the throne of Solomon, had mechanical lions that roared and birds that twittered.

The "minor arts" also flourished. Byzantine artists made luxurious objects from enamel, glass, precious metals, and ivory. Luxury was very

* **linear** consisting of lines

important. The value of the materials was probably as important to the Byzantine viewer as the artist's skill in using them.

Byzantine art is often said to have a timeless quality, due to the practice of placing figures against plain gold backgrounds. Though this custom did not change, other changes are apparent over time. Early Byzantine art is often simplified and linear*, whereas in later periods figures may be portrayed with softer modeling and visible emotions.

In the 1100s and 1200s, Byzantine art exerted an important influence on Italian art, especially panel painting. The so-called *maniera greca* (Greek manner) was a forerunner of the early Renaissance painting that began to appear around 1260. (*See also* **Books, Manuscript; Calligraphy, Islamic; Crusades; Hagia Sophia; Ravenna; Religious Instruction; Seljuks.**)

Byzantine Church

See *Christianity*.

Byzantine Empire

The Byzantine Empire of the Middle Ages was a bridge between the ancient and modern worlds. Its heartlands included Greece and ANATOLIA, the lands of the ancient Greek civilization that had ringed the Aegean Sea. Its capital was CONSTANTINOPLE, built by the Romans. The Byzantines preserved the ideas of Greece and Rome and passed them on to Arabs, Slavs, and Germanic Europeans. Without the Byzantines, much of ancient science and learning would have been lost.

The Byzantines called their empire the "Empire of the Romans." In Arabic, it was called Rum (Rome). It was, in fact, the direct descendant of the old Roman Empire. Because the Byzantines had adopted the Christian religion, they claimed that their history began with the Old Testament and continued when the Roman Empire converted to Christianity. The empire, they said, had been established by God and would last until the end of the world. Instead the empire collapsed in 1453, when Constantinople was sacked by the OTTOMAN Turks.

History: The Early Middle Ages

Background. The Byzantine Empire took shape gradually. CONSTANTINE I THE GREAT of Rome founded Constantinople in the early 300s on the site of an old Greek trading city called Byzantium. He was the first Roman emperor to accept the new religion of Christianity. He helped settle disputes in the Christian church and received baptism to Christianity on his deathbed.

* **co-emperor** emperor who shares office with another

Originally, and during the reign of Constantine, the Roman Empire was governed as a single unit. But to deal with a growing threat of invasion by European and Asian tribes, it was often divided under different co-emperors*. In the 400s, the western half, ruled from Rome, fell to Germanic tribes. The eastern half, ruled from Constantinople, remained strong.

* **patriarch** head of a large section of the early Christian church

The pope, bishop of the West and traditionally viewed as the senior leader of Christianity, remained in Rome, whose invaders had already become Christian. Rome kept its position as a main center of the church. But now the patriarch* of Constantinople claimed at least a similar status, as spiritual leader of the part of the Christian world still ruled by the emperor.

The Byzantine Empire rose from the old Roman Empire and preserved many of its achievements for several centuries. Hagia Sophia (interior shown here) was the principal church of the Byzantine Christians. After Constantinople fell to the Ottoman Turks in 1453, the church became a Muslim mosque. Much of it was redecorated in Islamic style.

In 527, JUSTINIAN I and his wife, THEODORA I, ruled over the Byzantine Christian Empire. Its powerful navy controlled the eastern Mediterranean. Its capital was the most strongly fortified city in the world. Justinian's territory stretched from Egypt in the south, to Syria and Armenia in the east, and to Greece in the west, and it included the Holy Land of Palestine.

During his 38-year reign, Justinian also recaptured much of the conquered Western Roman Empire, including all of Italy and the whole northern coastline of Africa. The Byzantine Empire now included many peoples—in addition to Latins* and Greeks, there were Armenians, Syrians, Egyptians, and Berbers. Justinian compiled his new empire's laws and created the Code of Civil Law, which later became a model for most European legal systems.

A Threatened Empire. Justinian's conquests were shortlived. The Byzantine army, powerful though it was, could not defend all of its new territories against enemies surrounding it. The Lombards, another Germanic tribe, invaded northern Italy. Slavs from northeastern Europe pressed into the north Balkan peninsula. The Persian Empire, an ancient enemy of the Greek world, threatened from the east. Then the Slavs and Persians formed an alliance, and in 626 they laid siege to Constantinople itself.

With the help of his naval power and heavy cavalry, Emperor Heraklios was able to save Constantinople. He also won a decisive victory over the Persians, making the Persian king his vassal*. However, within the next ten years, the exhausted Byzantines and Persians alike faced a new threat. The Arab prophet MUHAMMAD had founded the religion of Islam, and the Arabs quickly conquered Persia, Syria, the Holy Land (Palestine), and the African coast. In late 674 and again in 717, Arabs attacked the walls of Constantinople.

The city withstood the attacks, but its empire was severely weakened. The Byzantines still held Rome, southern Italy, and parts of the Balkan

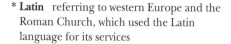

* **Latin** referring to western Europe and the Roman Church, which used the Latin language for its services

* **vassal** person given land by a lord or monarch in return for loyalty and services

See color plate 8, vol. 3.

* **Muslim** word commonly used to describe people who follow the teachings of the prophet Muhammad

peninsula, but the eastern and southern coasts of the Mediterranean were in Muslim* hands. This had a dramatic effect on Byzantine culture. Before, the empire had included peoples with many different languages, religions, and cultures, but now most of its population was Greek speaking. The empire was more culturally unified. Greek replaced Latin as its official language.

Icons and Iconoclasm.   Scholars today suggest many different reasons why the Byzantine Empire was so weak at this time. But in the early 700s, many people believed the empire's weakness was religious. Christians, especially Byzantine Christians, had taken to decorating their churches with ICONS, images of saints and other religious figures. According to Jewish tradition, however, worshiping images was an offense against God. This tradition had been accepted by the early Christians and was also part of Islamic faith.

For such reasons, a movement came about called iconoclasm. Many, including monks who favored icon painting, fiercely opposed this movement, but in the early 700s, Emperor Leo III ordered destruction of all icons. Leo also won military victories against the Arabs, which made iconoclasm appear an effective religious movement. It became the official Byzantine policy.

Leo's son and grandson continued to enforce iconoclasm, and they, too, won victories against the Muslims and against the Bulgarian Slavs. The pope in Italy, however, disapproved of iconoclasm. He also broke from Constantinople at this time and formed an alliance with the Frankish kings. This alliance was a setback that weakened the power of the iconoclasts. At a church council in Nicaea (787), the Byzantine empress Irene agreed that icons should be restored.

Seeking to bring the two halves of the Christian world closer, Irene also approved the marriage of her son to the daughter of the Frankish king CHARLEMAGNE. But in 800, the pope crowned Charlemagne as a Roman emperor, creating a second Christian Empire. Irene and her son fell out of favor. Irene sought compromise with iconoclasm, but this was opposed by the iconoclasts and by supporters of icons alike.

The Golden Age.   During the period immediately after Irene, iconoclasm again became official policy. In 842, however, icons were once again permitted. Byzantine fortunes began to improve. Missionaries sent to Russia and Bulgaria began convincing some of the hostile Slavs to join the Byzantine Church. Then, in the 860s, BASIL I founded a new imperial dynasty, called the Macedonian dynasty after Basil's homeland. Under the Macedonians, who ruled for some 150 years, several very able emperors strengthened the Byzantine Empire. Leo VI the Wise and Constantine VII Porphyrogenitos added to the intellectual prestige of Constantinople. Three strong regents* of this period contributed military victories. Romanos I Lekapenos supported the small farmers who formed the heart of the Byzantine fighting force and stabilized the shifting border with Bulgaria. Nikephoros II Phokas gained victories against the Muslims and became known as the "Pale Death of the Saracens." His successor, John Tzimiskes, led conquering Byzantine armies across Anatolia, through Syria and Palestine, and almost to the gates of Jerusalem.

* **regent** person appointed to govern a kingdom when the rightful ruler is too young, absent, or disabled

Finally, BASIL II defeated Bulgaria, and the Byzantine Empire reached a new pinnacle of power and influence. At the same time, the Byzantine Church was breaking its last ties with Rome. The famous monasteries of Mount Athos in Greece became a major religious center. Further missionary activity, rivaling missions sent out by the pope, helped to establish a Russian church allied to Constantinople. Politically and religiously, the Byzantines again dominated much of the Mediterranean world.

History: The Later Middle Ages

Relations with the Normans and the Latin West.
Basil II was the last great ruler of the Macedonian dynasty*. During the reigns that followed, Byzantine power again declined. There were frequent rebellions among the empire's subject nations. The throne was surrounded by conspirators. Landowners struggled against government officials, and small farmers lost their lands. In the cities, the people and churchmen stormed the palace, and guilds* of craftsmen and merchants often led riots. The empire became weak, and once again it was threatened from outside.

From the north, some Turks called the Pechenegs raided the Balkan peninsula. A navy from KIEVAN RUS challenged Byzantine sea power, almost conquering Constantinople. Norman adventurers attacked the Byzantine Empire from the west. Originally hired as mercenaries* to drive Byzantine forces from Italy, Normans soon took all of southern Italy and Sicily for themselves, and they threatened mainland Greece. Finally, other Turks invaded Persia and Mesopotamia from the east and then attacked Armenia. At the Battle of Manzikert in 1071, the Byzantines lost most of Anatolia.

Such was the situation facing Emperor Alexios I Komnenos when he seized power in 1081. Alexios approached these problems one by one. He persuaded a group of Turks from southern Russia to protect his Balkan frontier. He tried to strengthen his sea power by granting special trading rights to VENICE in return for naval support. He made an alliance with the HOLY ROMAN EMPIRE—now itself threatened by the Normans—to lessen their threat to Greece. Finally, Alexios appealed to Pope Urban II for help against the Turks in Anatolia. This appeal led to the First CRUSADE.

The Crusades and the Fall of Constantinople.
The crusades* were much more advantageous for the armies from the West than they were for the Byzantine Empire. Among those who joined the First Crusade was a Norman adventurer named BOHEMOND, who captured Antioch and made it the first Western Christian stronghold in the eastern Mediterranean. The crusaders also succeeded in capturing other sites in the Holy Land, including Jerusalem. Four crusader states* were created.

The Turks, however, were not dislodged from Anatolia. Instead, the Christian Armenians, who lived in Cilicia in Anatolia under Byzantine control, used an alliance with Antioch to gain independence. In the Balkans, Serbs, Bulgarians, and Hungarians again pressed into Byzantine territory. In 1187, the Muslims, under SALADIN, regained Jerusalem. Alexios's strategies were not saving the empire.

Of all the dangers to the Byzantine Empire, however, the greatest was the presence of the Western Christians. They had discovered the wealth of the East. In 1185, another Norman, William II of Sicily and southern Italy, had attacked Thessaloniki in northern Greece and sacked the city cruelly.

* **dynasty** succession of rulers from the same family or group

* **guild** association of craft and trade workers that set standards and represented the interests of its members

* **mercenary** soldier who fights for payment rather than out of loyalty to a lord or nation

* **crusades** holy wars declared by the pope against non-Christians

* **crusader states** states established in the East by Western Christians during the crusades. They included Jerusalem and Antioch.

See map in Crusades (vol. 2).

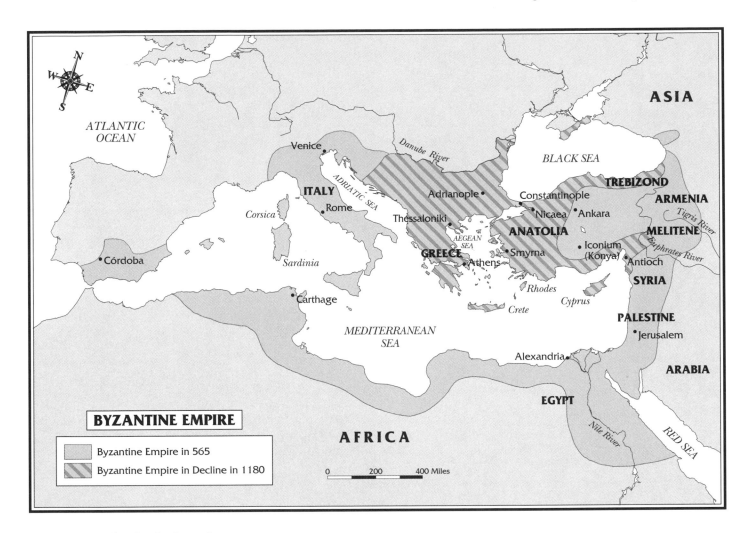

Byzantine Empire

- Byzantine Empire in 565
- Byzantine Empire in Decline in 1180

Under Justinian I's rule, the Byzantine Empire reached its greatest expansion— from Italy in the north to the coast of Africa in the south. By the 12th century, the Byzantine Empire was greatly diminished in area, due largely to Christian invasions from the west.

The ships of Venice began to control trade in the Aegean Sea. CYPRUS, also a Byzantine possession, was captured by RICHARD I THE LIONHEARTED of England on his way to the Third Crusade and then was sold to the French. Great hostility began to develop between the Christians of the West and the Christians of the East. During the same crusade, Byzantine forces even attacked the army of FREDERICK I BARBAROSSA by agreement with Saladin, though Frederick's army repelled the attack.

When the Fourth Crusade reached Constantinople in 1202, both the Byzantine army and navy had become small and weak. Western enemies of the Byzantine state made a show of force outside Constantinople and compelled the Byzantines to change emperors. Then they waited outside the city for nine months to be sure the new emperor was accepted. Instead, he was killed in a revolution. The crusaders attacked Constantinople, and the city fell in 1204. It was severely sacked, and many of its treasures were transported to Venice and to France.

Recovery. In spite of the fall of the Byzantine capital, the empire did not die. The crusaders divided the Byzantine territories, hoping to build a new Latin Empire of Constantinople. But Byzantine refugees fought to restore the empire. Three small Byzantine states emerged, the largest of them at NICAEA in Anatolia. After several years, Nicaea dominated the area, and by 1261 it had recaptured Constantinople from the Western Christians.

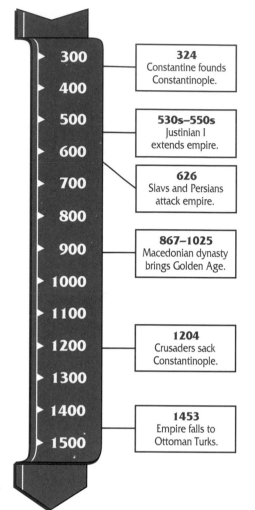

324
Constantine founds Constantinople.

530s–550s
Justinian I extends empire.

626
Slavs and Persians attack empire.

867–1025
Macedonian dynasty brings Golden Age.

1204
Crusaders sack Constantinople.

1453
Empire falls to Ottoman Turks.

* **papacy** office of the pope and his administrators

* **vassal** person or state in the service of a more powerful lord or state

* **bureaucracy** large departmental organization such as a government

In 1258, when Michael VIII Palaiologos became the new Byzantine emperor, Constantinople was in ruins. Most of its wealthy agricultural lands had been lost. Michael controlled only western Anatolia, northern Greece, and land he had captured on the southern Greek peninsula. The Mediterranean trade, which had created a large part of Byzantine wealth, was controlled by western European merchants from Venice and Genoa. One of Nicaea's rival Byzantine states, Epiros in the Balkans, still menaced Michael's new empire. The Bulgarian border also was again being attacked, this time by Mongol tribes.

The greatest immediate danger, however, was from the kingdom of Sicily, now ruled by a brother of the king of France named Charles of Anjou. Like the Normans of Sicily before him, Charles was threatening to invade the Byzantine heartlands, and he gathered powerful allies, including the papacy*. Emperor Michael tried to secure the pope's support with promises to reunite the Byzantine Church with Rome. But the people of Constantinople refused to accept this arrangement, and the threat from Sicily became very serious. So Michael spent large amounts from the imperial treasury to support a rebellion known as the Sicilian Vespers. Charles lost the Sicilian throne, and the Byzantine Empire was saved once again, but vast sums of money had been spent.

The following 150 years saw the empire decline still further, to little more than a minor Balkan state. Greece was overrun by CATALONIAN mercenaries. The growing power of SERBIA on the Balkan peninsula was matched by the growth of the OTTOMAN Turks in Anatolia. Constantinople became a pawn between these two powers. The once famed Byzantine navy was now weak, buffeted between the powerful fleets of Venice and Genoa. To make things worse, civil wars weakened the empire from inside, and the BLACK DEATH also took a major toll.

In the late 1300s, the Ottoman Turks had firmly established themselves in the Balkan peninsula. Byzantine emperor John V made several overtures to the West, appealing to Louis the Great of Hungary and also to Pope Urban V in Avignon. But failing to find help, he became a vassal* of the Ottoman sultan Murad I. Murad was victor at the Battle of Kosovo, after which Serbia also became a vassal state to the Ottomans.

Now the Ottomans were firmly in control in the Balkans. Two other Byzantine emperors went to the West to plead for help as the Ottomans tightened their grip. Finally, in 1453, the sultan Mehmed II began his famous siege of Constantinople. The only Western aid came from some Venetians and Genoese and from the pope. Nonetheless, the city held out for nearly two months before the Turks swept into Constantinople. Constantine XI, who had led the defense, died in the last onslaught.

The Byzantine Empire was crushed. Its legacy may be found, however, in the Orthodox churches of eastern Europe and the modern nation of Greece.

Government and Social Structure

Byzantine Government. The Byzantine system of government employed a vast bureaucracy* inherited from the Romans. This system of government had taken centuries to develop and was continually adapted as the world around it changed. The bureaucracy grew so complex that today the word *byzantine* is used in politics or business to mean overly complex or devious ways of getting things done.

The bureaucracy in Constantinople employed important state officials to handle key tasks for the empire. Among these tasks were arranging for taxes to be collected and providing for supplies for the army and navy. There were also officials, with more prestige than responsibility, holding positions in the royal household, such as doorkeepers or guards. At one point, there was a person with the title "Holder of the Imperial Washbasin." Salaries were not large, but many officials had a great deal of power. Some held more than one office. Graft* and corruption thrived under these conditions.

Outside Constantinople, the provinces were also tightly organized. At first, the system of the old Roman Empire was continued. There were prefectures or military groups that levied taxes, ran the postal service, and maintained roads and bridges. There were provincial governors in charge of all nonmilitary functions, especially legal ones. Sometimes, however, the military and civil authorities were combined, and this arrangement later became standard. By the 800s, the provincial government was rearranged into military units called themes, which supervised local justice as well as handling tax collection and defense of the borders.

In spite of its size and the possibilities for corruption, the Byzantine system of government provided great stability and order. Unlike the developing Western nations, which were ruled mostly by illiterate warriors, the empire's bureaucracy required, and ensured, the existence of a large, literate group of administrators. These people did not represent any one political party or military group, and so, no matter who was in power, an experienced and educated bureaucracy ran the government.

Economy and Society in the Early Middle Ages.   In the early days of the Byzantine Empire, as in ancient Rome, most people had little freedom of choice. Their way of life was determined by their family occupation, often enforced by law. Farmworkers' children had to work in the fields, and a baker's or a sword maker's son was required to follow his father's trade.

The reasons that the government encouraged such stability were complicated. The empire was surrounded by enemies who wished to conquer it. The government bureaucracy, responsible for defense, required great sums of money to operate. Since the chief source of government income was taxes from the land, skilled people were needed to keep the farms profitable. Thus, people were discouraged from leaving the farms for other jobs.

In this way, farming remained a hereditary* occupation. Merchant shipping, food trades, and jobs connected with the military and the imperial court were also controlled by law. Even the nobles who collected taxes had to pass on their positions to their children. While other jobs had slightly more freedom, people rarely left their family occupations.

In the end, however, such stability worked against itself. There was little chance for the poor to escape poverty. In fact, life became worse. Small farmers, heavily taxed, began to sell their farms to larger landowners and promised to work these landowners' fields as serfs* in exchange for protection. This weakened the government in many ways. Large landowners

* **graft**   unfair and often illegal bribes to get special treatment

Greek Fire

The city of Constantinople had three great weapons of defense—its walls, its navy, and a secret weapon. This weapon, a liquid that burst into flame, was used to set enemy ships on fire. The liquid could be fired from a type of nozzle mounted on the bow of Byzantine ships or hurled in pottery hand grenades. Called Greek fire, its formula never fell into enemy hands and is still unknown today.

* **hereditary**   passed on from parent to child

* **serf**   rural worker with little or no freedom who was sometimes sold along with the land he worked

became wealthier and were able to ensure through graft that they would pay less in taxes. Landowners also preferred to pay money rather than lose their serfs for military service. This meant fewer Byzantine recruits for the army, and the government was forced to hire foreign mercenaries who had less stake in the defense of the empire.

Economy and Society in the Later Middle Ages. Life in Byzantine cities was difficult in the later Middle Ages. The weakness of the empire meant that outsiders—Venetians, Genoese, and other Europeans—began to gain the profits from trade in Constantinople. But local people who worked in trade did become somewhat freer. Bakers, for example, might be told how to run their businesses, but positions were no longer hereditary. Compared to the village dwellers, those in cities were well off.

Emperor Romanos I Lekapenos, who had tried to support the small farmers by law, said, "It is the many, settled on the land, who provide for the general needs, who pay the taxes and furnish the army with its recruits. Everything fails when the many are wanting." But by the year 1000, "the many"—small farmers in free villages—had all but disappeared. They had become serfs of the landowners. The landowners used them as they liked. They even had their serfs fight in private armies that defied the central government.

At the same time, monasteries were also gaining power and buying up land. Some emperors tried to check the growth of church properties, but the people in the capital, and most emperors, encouraged it. They believed the safety of the empire depended on the power of the church. So the monks, too, acquired wealth, serfs, and political power.

Villagers, therefore, owed obedience and taxes to landowners or monks. Many were so badly treated that they ran away to the cities. By the early 1400s, nearly every village was in a state of decline, deserted, or in the hands of invaders. The monks were so powerful by then that they controlled almost all of what was left of the empire.

When the Turks conquered Constantinople, they gave the sad state of the villages as one reason for their success. "God has decreed," they said, "that we should take the land from the Christians because they do not conduct their affairs with justice." (*See also* **Christianity.**)

Byzantine Literature

The BYZANTINE EMPIRE was centered in Greece and in ANATOLIA. In ancient times, these were the homelands of classical Greek literature, and they became important regions of the Roman Empire. Byzantine political tradition descended directly from that of Rome, but its literature grew from the literature of ancient Greece. "Byzantine literature" usually means works written in Greek from the late 400s to the 1400s. These included imitations of traditional classical forms, new religious writings such as sermons, and medieval romances—perhaps the first romances ever written.

By the late 400s, the Greek language was no longer the same as that spoken in the great age of the Greek cities. Nevertheless, Byzantine literature continued to be written in classical Greek, which was studied and

* **vernacular** language or dialect native to a region; everyday, informal speech

* **lyric poetry** poetry that has the form and general effect of a song

Action Heroes: Byzantine Style

Digenis Akritas (Born on Two Borders) is about a Muslim prince who loves a Byzantine girl. He crosses the border, marries her, and becomes a Christian. His son, Digenis, fights against Amazons, cattle rustlers, and dragons. He wins his bride in battle and builds a palace.

This Byzantine epic parallels the Old French chansons de geste and the Spanish *Cantar de mío Cid.* It is probably a literary imitation of folk-poems from the wild borderlands of Cappadocia and Armenia, where Muslims and Christians lived together in hostility and friendship. The earliest surviving version of *Digenis Akritas* dates from the 1100s.

* **crusader** person who participated in the holy wars against the Muslims during the Middle Ages

* **oral** by word of mouth rather than in writing

valued. The increasing difference between the vernacular* and the old-fashioned language of most literature caused change, but only slowly.

The best-known examples of classical Greek literature are public speeches, historical writings, poetical dramas, and epic and lyric poetry*. The art of public speaking—rhetoric—remained strong throughout the Byzantine period. Educated people prided themselves on making artful speeches of high praise to emperors and other officials. In these speeches, called panegyrics, what was said often mattered less than how it was expressed. Rhetoric became a display of verbal skill valued in its own right, regardless of substance.

Letter writing was another celebrated form of prose. The letters carried conventional thoughts; once again, they were written mainly to show off the writer's skill. Most were meant to be read aloud to a group of listeners, who might in turn make copies of them. Christianity was also a common theme in speeches. Sermon writing was a major Christian form of Byzantine literature. By the 600s, sermons of earlier days, like other forms of public speaking, were studied as much for their style as for their message.

Concern with religion influenced other types of Byzantine writing. Ancient Greek historians had often written about historical events in terms of human causes and effects, but Byzantines usually sought to describe history in terms of God's will. Writing about the lives of the saints became a small industry; thousands of such texts survive. Even political histories tend to be presented in terms of good and evil. For example, Anna KOMNENA's biography of her father, Alexios—considered one of the most important historical works of the Middle Ages—takes sides and is far from objective.

Poetic drama had almost ceased to exist by 500. Other forms of poetry continued to be written, however. In addition to classical-style odes of praise, a great deal of religious poetry was composed, much of it in the form of hymns. At first, poems continued to be written following the old rules. However, classical verse no longer sounded correct, because word pronunciation had changed considerably since ancient times. Byzantine poetry, therefore, began to be influenced by the medieval Greek language, causing development in the verse forms. There were also reform movements when the old, "pure" poetry of the ancients was brought back. Such reforms occurred in the 900s, in the 1100s, and even later.

In the mid-1100s, some Byzantine writers began to develop informal, popular, romantic poetry. At this same time, crusaders* were active in the East and had begun to write romances. It is unclear whether the Byzantines influenced the crusaders or vice versa; probably each influenced the other. The earliest romances are, however, Byzantine, and they could have been modeled on ancient Greek romances. They also show signs that they may have come from a Greek oral* tradition.

The Byzantine romances are among the earliest examples of invented fiction in modern European literature and sometimes show startlingly modern psychological insight. Within the next hundred years, concepts of Western CHIVALRY began to be brought into Greek romances. One famous romance includes dragons, magic castles, witches, and enchanted maidens. Such poetry shows that the Byzantines were being influenced both by the Latin Christian world of the West and by the Muslim traditions of the East.

Cabala

From its beginnings in the 1100s until the end of the Middle Ages, the cabala was a system of mystical thought known only to a very few. It was used to interpret the Scriptures, history, humankind, and nature.

The cabala first appeared in Provence, in the south of France, in the 1100s and later spread to Spain and Italy. Cabalists (those who studied the cabala) believed that words, letters, and numbers in the Scriptures contained mysteries that could lead to greater understanding by those who knew the secrets. For example, the various names of God were believed to hold miraculous power.

* **oral** by word of mouth rather than in writing

Much of the cabala was handed down orally*. Rabbi Isaac Saggi Nehor (known as "Isaac the Blind") of Provence passed on the knowledge to his students, one of whom, Rabbi Azriel, was from Gerona, Spain. From Gerona, the movement spread to other Spanish cities, such as Burgos and Toledo.

The most important cabalistic book was the *Zohar (Book of Splendor)*, written primarily by Moses de Leon in the late 1200s. This book deals with both philosophy and MYSTICISM. By the early 1300s, Spanish cabalistic works had reached Italy. The cabala soon found followers there. Rabbi Menahem Recanati, an important Italian cabalist, studied the *Zohar* and added his own interpretations to it.

In 1492, the Jews were expelled from Spain, and the Spanish cabalists were dispersed. However, their works did not die. Students of Jewish mysticism in later generations continued to study the writings of the medieval cabalists. (*See also* **Judaism; Toledo.**)

Cade's Rebellion

Cade's Rebellion was an English uprising against King HENRY VI that preceded the WARS OF THE ROSES. People in southeast England were angry at the cost of the HUNDRED YEARS WAR, which had caused the loss of English territory in France and had led to French raids on England's coast. The rebels said Henry's advisers were incompetent and demanded that they be replaced by other nobles such as Richard, Duke of York. Richard was from a family rivaling the king's own.

See color plate 14, vol. 1.

In late May of 1450, thousands of men marched against London under a leader named Jack Cade, who claimed to be related to the duke of York. After the king fled London, leaving the city unprotected against the rebels, city officials imprisoned Henry's treasurer, Lord Say, to please the rebels. A few days later, Cade entered London, declared himself lord of the city, and had Lord Say beheaded. His men burned and looted parts of the city and set London Bridge on fire. Londoners began to resist, however, and Cade agreed to disband his army in return for pardons for all.

Cade's pardon was declared invalid and he fled the city, but he was quickly captured and mortally wounded. His body was returned to London, where it was beheaded and quartered*. The rebellion was over less than two months after it began.

* **quartered** cut into four quarters—a method of dealing with a rebel

Uprisings continued in the south of England throughout that year, and many other rebels were condemned to death. Ill feeling still remained, however, and ten years later Richard of York's son, the future Edward IV of England, marched into London at the head of another rebel army of southeasterners.

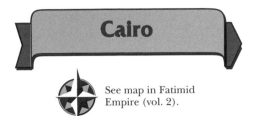

Cairo

See map in Fatimid Empire (vol. 2).

* **Coptic** referring to early Egyptian Christians (Copts). The Coptic church was one of the most important branches of the early church.

* **dynasty** succession of rulers from the same family or group

* **Shi'ites** Muslims who believed that Muhammad chose Ali and his descendants as the rulers and spiritual leaders of the Islamic community

* **crusader** person who participated in the holy wars against the Muslims during the Middle Ages

Cairo flourished through most of the Middle Ages. Many hospitals, schools, and mosques were built to accommodate the growing population. This mosque of Sultan Hasan was built in the mid-1300s.

The city of Cairo, which is today the largest city in the Arab world, has been a center of Arabic and Islamic culture and politics since the middle 600s. It began as an Arab military camp just north of the Byzantine capital of Egypt, at the head of the delta of the Nile River. The camp became a garrison town and continued to grow during most of the Middle Ages, with only a few setbacks from war and disease. In the 1300s, Cairo's population may have reached half a million people.

Before the Arab invasion of 640, Egypt was a Byzantine province, home to the Coptic* church. Coptic Christianity continued under Arab rule, and the new garrison town called al-Fustat attracted a mixed Muslim and Christian population. Textiles, glassmaking, pottery, and shipbuilding were all important industries.

Other garrison centers were established nearby when new Arab rulers took command: the ABBASIDS in the 750s and an independent ruler named Ahmad ibn Tulun in the 870s. These centers, which included palaces and mosques for the Arab leaders, attracted still more residents to the area. Under the Abbasids, many Muslim scholars also came to the city.

When members of the FATIMID dynasty* conquered Egypt in 969, they built a palace city of their own. They called their city al-Qahira, which means "the victorious." (Al-Qahira is the Arabic name for Cairo.) It became a center of Shi'ite* learning. Despite the construction of al-Qahira and the other palace centers, the old city of al-Fustat remained the center of the area's commercial life. However, internal fighting and then struggles with the crusaders* caused major damage to the city, and, in 1168, the Muslims burned al-Fustat to keep it from falling into the hands of Christian invaders.

See color plate 14, vol. 2.

---

* **Sunnite** Muslim majority who believed that the caliphs should rule the Islamic community

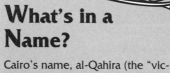

What's in a Name?

Cairo's name, al-Qahira (the "victorious"), seems to refer to the 969 victory of the Fatimids. But a different story is also told. The Fatimids, who believed in astrology, wanted to break ground for the new city when the night skies were just right. They marked the city plan with ropes and hung bells on them. Their astrologers would ring the bells at the time work was to begin. However, a crow landed on one of the ropes and rang a bell accidentally. Ground was broken while the planet Mars (al-Qahir) was ascendant. Thus Cairo could have been named after the planet Mars.

In 1171, the great conqueror SALADIN became ruler of Egypt and founded the AYYUBID dynasty. He built a citadel, other government buildings, and great new walls that circled not only his new center but also al-Qahira and areas to the west and south. Once again the city began to thrive. Many of Cairo's old palaces were replaced by schools and markets, and it became a center of religious revival and scholarship for Sunnite* Islam. Judges and scholars from other parts of the Islamic world came to the new city. Under the Ayyubids, Cairo also continued to be a great commercial center.

The freed slave dynasty of the MAMLUKS took control of Egypt in 1250. Like the Ayyubids, the Mamluks were strong supporters of Sunnite Islam, and, for a time, Cairo was the capital of a large part of the Muslim world. From the mid-1200s to the mid-1300s, the city continued to flourish. There was political peace under Mamluk rule, and a strong international trade brought economic wealth and cultural growth. During this time, Cairo expanded greatly in population, size, and facilities. Hospitals, colleges, and mosques were built, and the population reached some 250,000 to 500,000 inhabitants. The old city center was rebuilt, and neighboring areas were urbanized. New centers of Muslim religious life known as cemetery cities developed when wealthy Mamluks founded colleges to honor their tombs. These cemetery cities became centers of Sunnite religious scholarship.

In the late 1300s and 1400s, life in Cairo began to decline. The BLACK DEATH of 1348 hit hard, and later waves of the plague also occurred. Civil wars added to the city's difficulties, disrupting industry and trade. In addition, agriculture began to decline. Cairo experienced a period of great economic depression. The suburbs of the city became almost deserted. Only the religious cemetery cities continued to grow.

During the 1400s, Cairo's population became still smaller, and, in 1517, Egypt was absorbed into the OTTOMAN Empire. Cairo ceased to be a capital city. It became subject to Constantinople, which under its new name, Istanbul, became the leading city of the Muslim world.

Calendars

Knowing the time of year was as important for life in the Middle Ages as it is today. Farmers, sailors, and others have always needed to know the right time to perform certain tasks: when to plant the seeds or when to bring the boats in from the ocean. In addition, timing was important for religious festivals, especially if they had to be near a full or new moon.

Measuring time is no simple matter, however. As we do today, medieval people used days for short measures of time, weeks and months for longer periods, and years to mark the longest units. While relating days to weeks is simple—there are exactly seven days in one week—relating days to months or years is not so straightforward.

Days are based on the time from one noon to the next; months are based on the phases of the moon; and years are based on apparent movements of the sun from day to day. But the three cycles do not fit together perfectly. From one full moon to the next is not an exact number of days—it is just over 29½ days. A year is actually just under 365¼ days. A year

These calendar pages are from the *Hours of Jeanne d'Évreux,* illustrated by Jean Pucelle in the early 1300s. The page on the left shows the occupation for the month of September; the page on the right shows the sign of the zodiac.

is also 12 months (lunar cycles) plus about 11 days. Adjustments are necessary to make the measures of time fit each other.

Most peoples in the Middle Ages understood the relationships between days, months, and years, but they had different calendars because they did not agree on the best adjustments to make. Today in the Western world, we all use the same system of adjustments or "intercalations." We use a sequence of calendar months, which differ from lunar months, and we intercalate a day every four years, during so-called leap years. In the Middle Ages, the details of the calendar differed according to a people's culture and background.

The Jewish Calendar.   The Jewish calendar used in the Middle Ages is based on a year of 354 days, divided into 12 lunar months of 29 or 30 days. The names of the months are Tishri, Marheshvan, Kislev, Tebet, Shebat, Adar, Nisan, Iyar, Sivan, Tamuz, Ab, and Elul. Notice that this lunar year is shorter than the 365-day solar year.

Reconciling the Jewish lunar year with the solar year was done not with leap days but with "leap months." Whenever a lunar year fell behind the solar year by more than a month, an extra month was intercalated between the months of Adar and Nisan. These leap months were added in a pattern every 19 years—during the 3rd, 6th, 8th, 11th, 14th, 17th, and 19th years.

The week consists of seven days because the Jewish Scriptures say that God took seven days to create the world. In Judaism, these days are given numbers rather than names, although the seventh day is called Sabbath.

The Jewish New Year in the Middle Ages was celebrated at the beginning of Tishri, which roughly coincides with October. Other Jewish feast days and fast days observed in the Middle Ages were Sukkot, Simhat Torah, Passover, and Shavuot.

The Islamic Calendar.   The Islamic calendar, established by the prophet Muhammad, is also based on a pure lunar year with 354 or 355 days. This year is divided into 12 months: Muharram, Safar, First Rabia,

* **hegira**   celebrated emigration of Muhammad
from Mecca in 622, which marks the first year
of the Islamic calendar. It can also be spelled
hijra.

* **saint's day**   anniversary for a saint, when
people would make pilgrimages to the tomb
and listen to an account of the saint's life

Second Rabia, First Jumada, Second Jumada, Rajab, Shaban, Ramadan, Shawwal, Dhu-I-Qada, and Dhu-I-Hijja. The months are alternately 30 and 29 days long.

However, the Muslims did not, and do not, use a leap month. This means that the cycle of months changes each solar year. It takes 19 years for a Muslim month to return to the same season of the year. The Islamic era began on 1 Muharram of the year of the hegira*—July 14, 622, by Christian reckoning. (The date used in most tables for conversion between the Islamic and Christian calendars is, however, July 15.)

Based on a religious tradition similar to the Jewish week, the Islamic week also has seven numbered days. In Turkish and other languages used in Islam, names were assigned to them. The major feast days of Islam, like the months, move from solar year to solar year. They occur at the end of Ramadan, the month of fasting, and in the middle of Dhu-I-Hijja, the month for the hajj, or pilgrimage to Mecca.

The Christian Calendar.   The calendar of ancient Rome, which formed the basis for all the calendars used in the Christian world during the Middle Ages, is called the Julian calendar. It was devised during the time of Julius Caesar, during the 100 years before Christ was born. It fixed a year at 365 days and 6 hours.

Like years in the other calendars, the Julian year was divided into 12 months. Because the division was irregular, however, the months did not match the phases of the moon. In fact, like our months today, they had 31, 28, 31, 30, 31, 30, 31, 31, 30, 31, 30, and 31 days. The names—Januarius, Februarius, Martius, Aprilis, Maius, Junius, Julius, Augustus, September, October, November, and December—are also familiar to us.

The Romans originally viewed Martius (March) as the first month, the beginning of spring. Later they switched to January. In the Byzantine Empire, September 1 was designated the start of the fiscal year. The Western Church used several "styles": in the most common style, the year started on Christmas Day; in another style, used in France after 1215, Easter began the year. January 1 was rarely considered New Year's Day; the French did not adopt it until 1564.

The Romans used the names of their gods for many of the days of the week: *dies Saturni,* the day of Saturn (Saturday); *dies soli,* the day of the sun (Sunday); *dies lunae,* the day of the moon (Monday); *dies Martis,* the day of Mars; *dies Mercurii,* the day of Mercury; *dies Jovis,* the day of Jupiter; and *dies Veneris,* the day of Venus. These names, replaced by their Germanic equivalents, became our familiar days of the week—for example, the day of Wotan, or Wednesday; the day of Thor, or Thursday; the day of Freja, or Friday. Under pressure from the church, some nations named the weekend days the Sabbath *(sabbata)* and the Lord's day *(domenicus).*

The Christian church introduced many saints' days* during the Middle Ages. The most important festivals, however, were Christmas and the weeks leading up to Easter. Easter was a particularly hard feast to time because it is movable within the solar year—it has to fall on the first Sunday following a particular full moon. Elaborate tables were made to help clerics calculate when Easter was due to fall in a particular year. (*See also* **Astrology and Astronomy; Clocks and Reckoning of Time; Feasts and Festivals.**)

Caliphate

* **dynasty** succession of rulers from the same family or group

The caliphate was the main ruling institution in the Islamic Empire. It was headed by the caliph and, at its height, included thousands of officials, clerks, scribes, servants, and slaves. However, the caliphs were seldom in complete command of the Islamic state. They, too, were considered subject to Islamic religious law, which they did not control. Though the caliphs tried to be viewed as leaders of the doctrine of Islam, independent religious scholars, called ulama, were often believed to have superior ability to interpret the holy law. This lessened the power of the caliphate.

The caliphs were an important force in Islam for more than 600 years. Two major dynasties*, the UMAYYADS and the ABBASIDS, played a large part in holding together the huge Muslim Empire. Yet there were also conflicts between rival caliphates, problems with succession, and military takeovers. In the end, the empire was dominated by military rulers. However, for a long time, these rulers preserved the caliphs to ensure their own power.

The Emergence of the Caliphate. The caliphate started in 632, when ABU BAKR was elected caliph after Muhammad's death. This was an important event because no plans had been made for any kind of succession. Muhammad's death could have meant the collapse of Islam and a return to the traditional tribal groups that had controlled Arabia. However, Muhammad's followers managed to reach a peaceful agreement about who should be his successor.

The first caliphs governed more by personal prestige than by official authority—just as the Arab chiefs, or ashraf, had led their people in the years before Islam. These caliphs lived modestly and ruled with small staffs of advisers. Later they were looked back on as the four *rashidun,* "those who follow the right path." The concept behind their authority was that they were "first among equals."

Abu Bakr used his caliphate to unify Islam and suppress tribal rivalries. His successes gave the Islamic movement great power and won tremendous prestige and legitimacy for the caliphate. However, the caliphs who immediately followed, UMAR I IBN AL-KHATTAB and Uthman ibn Affan, had to deal with the expansion of the Islamic state across the Mediterranean basin. This was a difficult adjustment and led to conflict as they tried to maintain their authority across long distances.

Umar was the first caliph to use the title commander of the faithful, to suggest leadership in military and religious life. He developed a flexible policy encouraging the Arabs to let conquered peoples keep their local laws and customs for regulating civilian and religious affairs. The conquering ashraf and their armies ruled from garrison towns, aided by provincial governors who had been appointed by the caliph.

Uthman took a harder line, fearing the independent power of the ashraf. He appointed his own loyal tribesmen as governors and gave them more authority and money. He also gave additional power to some of the conquered peoples. Uthman's policy was unpopular, however. It failed to respect the rights of his "equals," the ashraf. It meant less tax money for powerful people in Medina, the capital. Uthman, who had no palace or bodyguards, was attacked and killed in his own home by angry rivals. His successor, ALI IBN ABI TALIB, was elected by those rivals and inherited a civil war.

At this time, in the middle 600s, several different religious positions began to develop in Islam. Uthman's supporters later became known as

Sunnites because they claimed their authority was based on the Sunna, or traditions of Muhammad's life. Ali's party, called the Shi'ites, became a powerful alternative movement because Ali was more closely related to Muhammad than Uthman was. An extremist group, the Kharijites, broke away from the Shi'ites and started its own traditions.

Each group had a different belief about the caliphate. The Sunnites supported the main line of caliphs. The Shi'ites, though they usually accepted the power of the Sunnite caliphs, believed their own leaders were the true heads of Islam. (They preferred the title IMAM for these leaders). The Kharijites held that anyone could become caliph and could be deposed if he did wrong because the Islamic community was the real source of authority. In fact, the Kharijites chose their own caliph and rebelled. Ali defeated their rebellion and was later killed by a Kharijite assassin.

The Caliphate Under the Umayyads.   Ali was succeeded as caliph by MU'AWIYA ibn Abi Sufyan, a cousin whom Uthman had appointed governor of Syria. He was accepted by the Arabs because he had command of a well-trained provincial army and had the power to restore order. Mu'awiya was the first caliph of the Umayyad dynasty.

Under the Umayyads, the caliphate became a more authoritarian institution. The caliphs moved their capital to Damascus in Syria and increasingly set themselves apart from other Muslims, whose access to them was restricted. They also adopted important symbols, such as a staff, a ring, and a cloak once worn by Muhammad, as signs of their power. The Umayyad caliphate also sponsored building projects on a large scale. These included palaces in the new capital and magnificent Islamic monuments in other places, such as the Dome of the Rock in Jerusalem. These projects expressed the caliphate's majesty, power, and role in the spiritual and material life of the Islamic community.

In addition, Mu'awiya and his Umayyad successors established specific guidelines for dynastic succession. The caliphs would be either sons, brothers, or cousins of their predecessors. This was recognized as the only way to guarantee an orderly transfer of power, though it was against an old Arab tradition in which the tribe elected its new leader.

The Umayyads set up a large imperial government with specialized agencies to handle the affairs of the empire and caliphate. To maintain orderly rule, they appointed loyal Syrian military leaders to govern in the provinces. However, they appointed independent judges and financial officers to balance the governors' power. They had Arabic adopted as the language of administration, and it became easier for Arab Muslims to gain government positions in the provinces. In addition, they held to the principle of priority in Islam—that families that had been Muslim the longest should have preferential treatment. This led, however, to discontent among many later Muslim converts who held power in the provinces.

Finally, the Umayyads surrounded themselves with religious scholars to increase their religious prestige. But this did not always have the intended effects. Instead, it increased the authority of all the religious leaders, or ulama, some of whom supported causes of which the Umayyads did not approve.

The Umayyad caliphate also had other problems. Clan and regional rivalries increased. By the 700s, conflicts arose between civilians in Iraq, which had become the economic heartland of the empire, and the

> *Remember: Consult the index at the end of Volume 4 to find more information on many topics.*

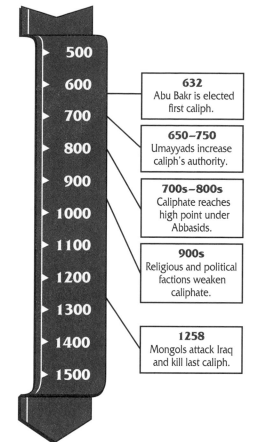

632	Abu Bakr is elected first caliph.
650–750	Umayyads increase caliph's authority.
700s–800s	Caliphate reaches high point under Abbasids.
900s	Religious and political factions weaken caliphate.
1258	Mongols attack Iraq and kill last caliph.

caliph's Syrian army. The Shi'ites and Kharijites felt the caliphate had become a kingship that served the interests of the Umayyad family. In the 740s, a revolutionary movement supported by many different groups swept the Abbasid family into prominence. The Umayyad caliphate collapsed in 749/750.

The Caliphate Under the Abbasids.   The Abbasids, a family whose ancestor had been Muhammad's uncle, took power and moved the center of the Muslim Empire to Iraq. A new capital was built at Baghdad, where it remained until 1258. However, the Shi'ites and other revolutionary supporters of the Abbasids soon became disappointed with their new caliphs.

During the early Abbasid period, tremendous economic growth and social development occurred. The Abbasids had to develop methods for dealing with more complex needs and problems. One result was that the caliphate was forced to give Arab and non-Arab influences equal access. It also expanded, and many more specialized departments and offices were founded. The earliest and most important new office was that of vizier, a position of great power and responsibility. The vizier managed the administration, advised the caliph on policy, and played a major role in relations with the army, provincial governors, and foreign governments.

The office of vizier was probably borrowed from the ancient Persian Empire. Iraq had been an important part of that empire, and the caliphs adopted several ideas about administration, ceremony, and self-image from the old Persian traditions. The Abbasids became even more withdrawn from the people than the Umayyads had been. They held magnificent ceremonies for palace guests and were surrounded by awesome splendor and fantastic wealth. They had lush parks of exotic wild animals, huge arrays of gold and silver objects, gems, precious carpets, and ingenious mechanical devices. The intent of such splendor was to inspire awe and promote loyalty.

In spite of these Persian influences, however, the caliphate remained Arab. The position of caliph was restricted to descendants of the Arab conquerors, and the official language was still Arabic. The Abbasids were guardians of the security and well-being of the empire. They were responsible for commanding the army, supervising officials, stopping internal rebellions, and managing taxes and other revenues. Because the well-being of the empire also involved a spiritual dimension, the caliphs also claimed an important role in protecting the Islamic faith. The era from the 700s to 800s was a high point of caliphal power and prestige.

For all this power, however, the caliphate was still not in full control. Members of the caliph's family, the army, and the bureaucracy also exercised considerable influence. As the administration grew, caliphs found it harder, not easier, to ensure the personal loyalty of those who served them. A caliph had to win and keep the support of officials through presents, patronage, and social obligations. He also had to dismiss, disgrace, punish, torture, and even execute disloyal followers. This made additional enemies for the caliphate.

In addition, the caliph's authority still did not cover religious issues. Though the Abbasids saw that Islam was the one unifying principle of their empire, they did not have the authority to proclaim or interpret religious teachings. In this area, the ulama had ultimate authority because they were the people in the community who developed the shari'a, Islam's holy law. The Abbasids tried to draw the ulama closer to the caliphate, but the scholars remained independent, and this weakened the caliphate.

The Political Decline of the Caliphate.   As early as the 700s, independent states headed by other religious groups rose in several parts of the empire. Their rulers were powerful enough to defy the authority of the caliphs. Kharijites established themselves in Oman, at the south of the Arabian peninsula. Shi'ite governors ruled Mecca and Medina, the two holiest cities. In the late 900s, a Shi'ite group called the Ismaili set up the powerful FATIMID caliphate in Egypt and conquered Syria as well. An Umayyad family member declared himself a caliph in Spain.

Even in Iraq, the Abbasids lost influence. They spent huge amounts of money on the court. They hired an army of Turkish mercenaries as their own personal bodyguard. The caliphate became inefficient and corrupt. Then a caliph was murdered by his Turkish troops in 861, and the caliphate was reduced to almost complete subservience. The Buyids, a Shi'ite group from Persia, occupied Baghdad in 945 and forced the caliph to grant them special privileges and honors. In 946, they deposed the caliph and blinded him.

Despite its loss of power, the caliphate continued for another 300 years. When the Seljuk Turks took over Baghdad in 1055, they regarded the caliphate as a valuable Islamic symbol. In fact, they said they had captured Baghdad to defend the caliphate from its enemies. The final disaster for the Abbasid caliphate occurred in 1258, when the Mongols swept into Iraq, sacked Baghdad, and executed al-Musta'sim, the last Abbasid caliph. The end of the caliphate was a great shock to the Islamic world, but its real effects were quite limited. Military rulers and a governing bureaucracy continued to exercise political power. Islamic culture and values were hardly affected at all.

Calligraphy, Islamic

See color plate 10, vol. 2.

Calligraphy, which means fine writing, has special significance in the Muslim world. Because of the exceptional importance of the Qur'an (Islam's holy book), the written word became a sacred symbol of the Islamic religion and Muslim power. In the Christian world, images played an important role, especially in the decoration of books and religious buildings. However, because Islamic custom did not allow images of people or animals in religious contexts, beautifully designed lettering became the main decorative form of Islamic religious art.

Arabic script is written from right to left. It uses a combination of horizontal, vertical, and diagonal lines and curves in a flowing, rhythmic style. There are 17 basic letter shapes, to which dots are added to create 28 separate consonants. Other small marks indicate short vowels. There are several different styles of lettering, each of which has a different purpose. A style called *Kufi,* stately and angular, was used primarily for decorative religious inscriptions on buildings. Other styles had other purposes—for example, in literature, letter writing, and government documents.

Arabic script spread east and west from the Arabian peninsula during the period of Islamic expansion after 622. A key person in this development was the caliph* Abd al-Malik (685–705). Besides making Arabic the official

* **caliph** religious and political head of an Islamic state

The beautifully written letters of an Islamic phrase form the body of a bird in this Persian manuscript illumination.

* **metaphor**   literary device in which an idea is suggested using words or phrases that literally mean something else

language of the empire, he ordered that script be used instead of images on coins, monuments, and elsewhere. In time, the script could be seen on almost everything in the Islamic world: on banners, ceramics, textiles, even weapons. It was also used for Turkish and Persian, two other important languages in the Muslim world. It became an Islamic script that helped unify the far-flung Islamic lands.

Islamic calligraphy served several important goals. It emphasized important religious teachings, it was a decoration, and it made objects visibly Muslim. It was a clear indication that a newly won area was under Islamic control. For example, in the 1450s, the Muslim Ottoman Turks overran the Byzantine Empire and conquered its capital, CONSTANTINOPLE. One of their first actions was to cover over the mosaic Christian images inside the great church of HAGIA SOPHIA. The Turks replaced these images with quotations from the Qur'an written in decorative Arabic script.

Many Islamic books describing how to do calligraphy were produced. They taught moral virtues as well as manual techniques. The scribes who mastered Arabic script held high positions in Islamic society. They were well-educated professionals, many of whom filled important government posts. Others were teachers, copyists, and booksellers.

Besides being the leading art form of the Islamic world, calligraphy became a metaphor* that added richness to the languages of Islam. Allah was referred to as the supreme calligrapher. The reed pen was one of his first creations, and people were described as the pens with which Allah wrote history. Written letters had a special meaning in Islamic culture, which encompassed more than their formal beauty and the value of the words they conveyed. (*See also* **Writing Materials and Techniques.**)

Canonization

* **martyr**   person who suffers and dies rather than renounce a religious faith

* **sepulcher**   carved stone tomb or coffin for a saint's remains

* **saint's day**   anniversary for a saint, when people would make pilgrimages to the tomb and listen to an account of the saint's life

* **Roman Church**   referring to the Western Church that is based in Rome and led by the pope

When a person is canonized, he or she is recognized as a Christian saint. In the early years of the church, saints were most often people who became martyrs* for their faith. Local people claimed miracles had occurred after the martyrs' deaths and began to make offerings at their tombs. Such rituals often took place without official approval from church authorities.

As the Middle Ages progressed, regional church officials such as bishops began to become involved. They arranged for saints' bodies to be moved to decorated sepulchers* and for saints' names to be entered on regional church calendars, giving them an official saint's day*. These rituals gave official approval to a saint and were the earliest form of church canonization.

Beginning in the 900s, bishops of the Roman Church* asked the pope to recognize and approve local saints. A special commission was organized by a bishop to investigate the life and miracles of a possible saint. Then the pope was asked to approve the suggestion. Increasingly, canonization became a papal responsibility. By the early 1200s, only the pope was allowed to declare someone a saint.

From that time on, canonization began with local approval and claims of miracles. If popular enthusiasm was sufficiently organized and powerful, the pope would call for an investigation. At first, miracles were the major concern. In the later Middle Ages, however, rules for canonization became more complex, and the emphasis changed from miracles to proof of a virtuous life.

The culmination of the Investiture Controversy took place when Henry IV submitted to Pope Gregory VII at Canossa. This page from the 11th-century chronicle of the life of Matilda of Tuscany shows Henry begging the countess to intercede with the pope on his behalf. Abbot Hugh of Cluny is also present.

C anossa was a castle in northern Italy where a dramatic showdown took place in 1077. The dispute was between the pope and the Holy Roman Emperor and has become known as the Investiture Controversy. At Canossa, the emperor was humbled but also avoided a possible disaster.

Pope GREGORY VII had decreed that the emperors should no longer appoint their own bishops in Germany. However, the emperors needed a close relationship with their bishops to control the powerful German dukes. Emperor Henry IV refused to obey Gregory's order. He had the German bishops accuse Gregory of disloyalty and declare that Gregory was no longer the pope. In response, Gregory excluded Henry from the rites of the church and ordered the German dukes to replace Henry with a new emperor.

The dukes took up arms against Henry. They invited Pope Gregory to come to Germany to judge their disagreements with the emperor and demanded that Henry must obtain the pope's forgiveness. Henry sent letters to the pope promising to repent, but he did not withdraw his bishops' accusations. So Gregory rejected Henry's letters and set out for Germany. Henry crossed the Alps to try to stop him, but Gregory took refuge in Canossa, a mountain castle belonging to a powerful supporter, Countess Matilda of Tuscany.

It was winter, but Henry went to the castle and stood outside the gate for three days, reportedly barefoot in the snow. Matilda encouraged Gregory to forgive Henry in accordance with his priestly duty. The pope granted Henry forgiveness and let him join the church again. Canossa was a symbolic victory for the church. It implied that the pope rather than the emperor was head of the church. But Henry IV remained in power. (*See also* **Church-State Relations; Holy Roman Empire.**)

* **archbishop** head bishop in a region or nation

* **pagan** word used by Christians to mean non-Christian and believing in several gods

See color plate 6, vol. 2.

C anterbury is to the east of London, on the main route leading inland from the ports of the English Channel. It is the cathedral city of the leading archbishop* in England. In the later Middle Ages, it was an important pilgrimage site.

Before 500, Canterbury had been a Roman settlement when Britain was a Christian province of the ancient Roman Empire. However, the British Isles turned largely pagan* as a result of ANGLO-SAXON invasions from northern Europe. Only Ireland, which was sending missionaries to England, was still a center of Christianity. Canterbury had become capital of the non-Christian kingdom of Kent. In 597, a monk named Augustine was sent by the Church of ROME to convert the Anglo-Saxons to Christianity. He chose Canterbury as the center of his missionary work and converted Ethelbert, the king of Kent. Augustine became the first archbishop of Canterbury.

At first, it was uncertain whether England would follow the traditions of Irish Christianity or those of Rome, but a meeting known as the Synod of Whitby in 664 settled the question in favor of Rome. By 700, Canterbury's powers extended far beyond the kingdom of Kent. Churches in all seven English kingdoms were under its guidance, even those that had been established from Ireland.

Canterbury Cathedral (interior view shown here), is the principal cathedral of England and the home of the archbishop who heads the English church. After the murder of Archbishop Thomas Becket in 1170, Canterbury became an important pilgrimage site. Many buildings were constructed in the city during this time to accommodate travelers.

During the next 300 years, Canterbury became an important center of learning. It was also the site of several meetings among rulers of all regions of England. In the middle 900s, Archbishop Dunstan helped many of the kings formulate and conduct their policies. In 973, he anointed the first undisputed king of all England, Edgar the Peaceable.

Canterbury was one of the issues behind the Norman invasion of England. The English church had chosen an archbishop of whom the pope did not approve, so William of Normandy claimed that he was carrying out the will of the Roman Church when he won the Battle of HASTINGS in 1066. He installed the first Norman archbishop of England, LANFRANC OF BEC. Lanfranc was followed by the celebrated ANSELM, who defended the church's rights against the Norman kings.

In 1170, the murder of Thomas BECKET, the archbishop of Canterbury, brought about a new era in Canterbury's history. Shortly after Becket's death, there were reports of miracles occurring at his tomb. As a result, Canterbury quickly became an important pilgrimage site. The city responded to the crowds of pilgrims with a burst of building activity; many medieval hospitals* and inns were built to accommodate the increasing numbers of people who came there. The pilgrimages to Canterbury were immortalized by Geoffrey CHAUCER in his book *Canterbury Tales*.

There were other famous archbishops of Canterbury. Stephen Langton played an important part in developing the MAGNA CARTA (1215), which guaranteed English liberties. Henry Chichele supervised the suppression of the LOLLARD heresy* in the early 1400s.

---

* **hospital** originally, a place of hospitality provided by the church for those in need, travelers, and the poor as well as the sick

* **heresy** belief that is contrary to church doctrine

* **relic** object cherished for its association with a martyr or saint

Canterbury Cathedral, which holds Becket's relics*, has vivid stained glass windows showing some of the miracles after Becket's death. It was remodeled several times during the Middle Ages. Canterbury itself became a royal city during the reign of King Henry VI.

Capet, Hugh

ca. 938–996
King of France
and founder of the
Capetian dynasty

Hugh Capet was the first of the line of kings that created FRANCE from the western part of CHARLEMAGNE's Frankish Empire. Since 840, that portion of the empire had been falling apart as different noble families gained power in local areas.

The Capets were one of the most powerful of these families. Owning lands around PARIS and in other nearby regions, some of Hugh Capet's ancestors had already been elected as West Frankish kings in place of Charlemagne's descendants. When the CAROLINGIAN king Louis V died without children in 987, the nobles and church leaders elected Hugh Capet to the throne instead of Louis's brother.

* **consecrated** declared sacred during a church ceremony, in this case as the future king

During the reigns of Capet and his descendants, nobles in regions such as BURGUNDY and FLANDERS had great power, but they began to feel the king's authority through his links with the church. Hugh Capet was crowned by the church, and he started a custom by having his son consecrated* as future king during his own lifetime. He also played an important part in choosing bishops and other church leaders throughout the kingdom. In these ways, he strengthened royal influence all over France. His family ruled until 1326.

Cardinals, College of

In the Middle Ages, the college of cardinals was a group of clergy who helped the pope manage the Western Church. It included the head priests of churches in Rome itself, bishops from areas around Rome, and some lower officials. The college became a powerful body that advised popes and chose their successors. The number of cardinals varied from a low of 18 to a high of 30 or more.

Originally, the church was guided by the pope and by the synod, or assembly, of all the bishops. As the church grew, it became harder to arrange a meeting of the full synod. As early as 1059, the cardinals were identified as the group for selecting a new pope. By 1100, a body called the consistory, made up of cardinals and other papal advisers selected by the pope, was helping to govern the Roman Church.

At first, bishops resented the cardinals' power. The cardinals claimed that they, rather than bishops, were the true successors of the apostles (the original 12 followers of Jesus). Cardinals began to wear robes of imperial red and miters, hats that symbolized the bishops' authority. Gradually, they began to outrank the bishops.

The power of the college of cardinals was made clear at two church councils in the later Middle Ages. A church constitution issued in 1179 set the principle that any candidate who won two-thirds of the cardinals' votes became the new pope. A century later, another constitution spelled out the process even more clearly. The cardinals were to be kept in a room until they elected a new pope. The longer the cardinals took to do so, the less food would be served at the meeting. The cardinals were opposed to this new constitution, but it became part of church law.

Cardinals also helped the pope with administrative, diplomatic, and legal matters. They were papal assistants, judges, and representatives when the pope could not be present. In the papal courts, they had large staffs of legal advisers. Cardinals were consulted about a wide range of political, administrative, and financial matters.

Though popes rarely acted on important matters without seeking the cardinals' advice, this advice never had legal force. Several times in the 1300s, the cardinals tried to gain power to govern, but the popes always prevented this. However, in 1378, the cardinals did take the step of deposing a pope they had selected. When the papacy returned to Rome from AVIGNON, they had second thoughts about Pope Urban VI and replaced him with Clement VII. (*See also* **Christianity.**)

Carmina Burana

The *Carmina Burana* (Songs of Beuren) is an important collection of some 300 medieval songs and a few plays. They are remarkable because so many of them are about nonreligious subjects.

The battered manuscript of the collection was discovered in 1803 in the monastery of Benediktbeuren in Germany. Many of the songs are in Latin, but German, French, and Greek appear in some sections, reflecting the authors' international origins. They were probably copied down in Bavaria or southern Austria between 1225 and 1230.

The manuscript begins with a set of songs about morality and fate, including such varied topics as the crusades, politics, and exorcisms. There is a large group of laments and love songs of many different types. A third group of verses covers courtly life, drinking and gambling, and other disreputable activities. Many of these are scornful or humorous, of the types written by GOLIARDS, the wandering scholars of the time. In addition, the manuscript contains material from two religious plays.

Although most of the selections in the *Carmina Burana* are anonymous, some of the poets can be identified from other sources. They range from the ancient world to the 1200s and come from many different places. The Roman poet Ovid is included; so is Hugh of Orleans, France; Geoffrey of Winchester in England; and the poet from the Rhineland in Germany who was known as the Archpoet.

Some of the songs are for dancing or drinking. Some tell stories and others are dialogues between two characters. Some are rhymed and others are not. In some, the languages are mixed—for example, Latin and Old French. Some songs include markings intended to indicate the musical notes.

The musical markings are difficult to read. However, by comparing other manuscripts that include music for a few of the songs, scholars have been able to reconstruct the melodies for about 40 songs in the *Carmina Burana*. In 1937, Carl Orff, a modern German composer, produced a musical setting of these poems. This work has helped familiarize modern audiences with the medieval anthology. (*See also* **German Language and Literature; Music.**)

See
color plate 8,
vol. 3.

* **succession** the transmission of authority on the death of one ruler to the next

* **Low Countries** flat coastal lands west of Germany, now occupied by Belgium and the Netherlands

The Carolingians were a royal family who ruled over the FRANKS for almost 250 years. CHARLEMAGNE, recognized by the pope as the first western emperor since the 400s, was a Carolingian. His empire was hard to hold together because of raids from outside peoples such as the VIKINGS and because of internal rivalry between the rulers and other nobles. The succession* customs of the Franks added to these problems: Charlemagne's descendants often divided up the realm. Under the later Carolingians, some of the main divisions of present-day Europe began to take shape.

The First Carolingians.   In the early 600s, the MEROVINGIAN family of Franks was the most powerful ruling family in western Europe. They controlled most of modern France, the Low Countries*, and the western part of Germany. There were three kingdoms, each with its own ruler.

The ruler of the northeastern kingdom, which was called Austrasia, was Queen Brunhilde. She had lost the support of her nobles because she tried to set up a strong government. The nobles, led by Carolingian ancestors named Pepin and Arnulf, gained help from the western Frankish king Chothar II. In 613, Chothar had Brunhilde executed and took control of her kingdom. He rewarded Pepin and Arnulf by putting them in positions of power at his palace, with responsibilities for Austrasia.

A grandson of these early Carolingians, another Pepin, became the most important Frankish leader in the late 600s. The Merovingian kings by now were quite weak, and Pepin succeeded in destroying the power of the other Frankish nobles at the palace. This gave him control of the whole combined Frankish kingdom. Pepin allowed the Merovingians to remain as figurehead kings. Though his titles were only mayor of the palace and duke, his power was such that he was later called Pepin II as though he and his grandfather had been kings. Pepin died in 714.

Pepin's son CHARLES MARTEL fought for and gained his father's titles and power. He gave high positions throughout the kingdom to loyal Austrasian nobles and began to organize the church leadership under his own control. Like his father, Charles Martel never took the title of king. At his death in 741, he divided responsibility for the kingdom between his sons, Carloman and Pepin. They worked together under the last Merovingian king, Childeric III, strengthening themselves against other family members and lessening the power of rivals. In 747, however, Carloman entered a monastery and gave the whole kingdom to his brother.

Early Carolingian Kings.   After Pepin gained control of Carloman's lands, he deposed Childeric III and claimed the kingship for himself. This made him the first real Carolingian ruler, Pepin III. To gain as much support as possible, Pepin had himself anointed* king twice—first by his own bishops and then by the pope. This was important because of the respect in which medieval nobles held the church.

In relying on the pope's authority to support his rule, Pepin continued the strategy his father had used. The early Carolingians had adopted the church service used in Rome and were making the church a unifying influence within the kingdom. Pepin developed further links with the church, using clerics* to work in the royal administration and to help restructure it. By this demonstration of how important Christianity was to his

* **anoint** to put holy oil on a person at a religious ceremony or coronation

* **cleric** church official qualified to lead church services

* **dynasty** succession of rulers from the same family or group

rule, Pepin helped create an alliance between the Carolingian dynasty* and the popes.

In 768, Pepin's kingdom passed to his sons, Charles and Carloman. When Carloman died in 771, his brother took over the whole kingdom and became Charles I, known as Charles the Great or Charlemagne.

Carolingian Rule Under Charlemagne. Charlemagne gained power over his nobles by involving them in military conquest. He defeated the Lombards in Italy, the Saxons and Bavarians in Germany, and the Muslims at the Spanish border. These conquests allowed him to reward the nobles with land and booty. However, he also made changes in the government structure that would give him more control over his nobles while still keeping their loyalty.

The empire was divided into some 400 counties. Each county was ruled by a COUNT, a noble from an important family whose main job was to carry out the king's commands, to make rulings, and to judge disputes. The counts were also responsible for maintaining the peace. The king's power was based largely on these nobles.

Charlemagne kept in contact with the counts by means of special agents who visited the counties to perform special assignments, bring the words of the king to the people, and collect revenues. He also called an annual assembly of the counts and other important officials of his government. His advisers were chosen from the most trusted noble families and from the church leaders, including Charlemagne's chief

Charlemagne's vast empire went to his only surviving son, Louis the Pious. Louis the Pious had three sons—Lothar, Louis, and Charles—and upon his death, civil war broke out over inheritance of the empire. The Treaty of Verdun (843) settled the dispute. Lothar received the central kingdom, Louis the lands in the east, and Charles the lands in the west.

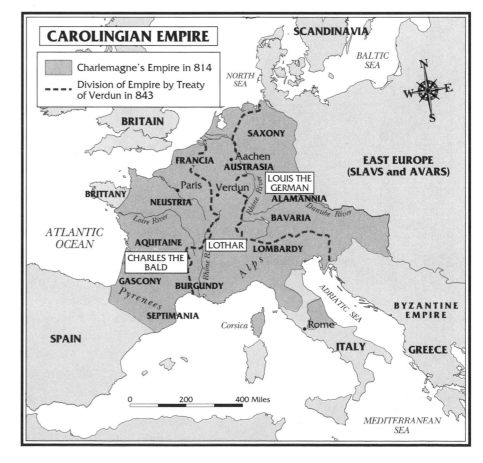

* **patron saint** saint held as guardian of a family's spiritual life

* **bishopric** office of or area governed by a bishop

religious officer, the capellanus. The capellanus was one of the most influential people in the empire: he and his assistants were responsible for looking after the family's sacred relics, such as a cape that had belonged to their patron saint*. Because of their superior education, they also prepared royal documents.

Charlemagne strengthened the church in many ways. He established parish churches in rural areas throughout the empire. These churches brought Roman Christianity into many areas for the first time. Charlemagne also strengthened the structure of the church by establishing new bishoprics* in recently converted areas. Such reforms not only increased the influence of the church; they also expanded royal control over the clerics, who owed much of their power to Charlemagne. Charlemagne's reforms, and the military power of his empire, were among the factors that led the pope to crown Charlemagne as emperor in 800.

The Successors of Charlemagne.   At Charlemagne's death in 814, his throne went to his surviving son, Louis, who became known as Louis the Pious. Louis involved the church still more deeply in government. He replaced advisers from the Frankish nobility with others of his own choosing, including even more people from the church. He summoned the national assembly several times a year rather than just once so that he could be better informed about the state of the empire and maintain closer control of it. Louis also attempted to reform the church by requiring a review of all religious institutions by his own government. Most nobles opposed these reforms because they lessened the nobles' power, putting the church, and thus the Christian population, under even greater royal control.

Louis's plans for his succession also caused problems. Wanting the empire to remain centrally united under his eldest son, Lothar, he decreed that his two younger sons would have lands of their own but would always be subordinate to their older brother. This was against Frankish custom and divided the family. The birth of a third son led to internal struggles between the heirs-to-be, who looked to the discontented nobles for support. When Louis died in 840, a civil war broke out between Lothar and the other two surviving sons, Louis and Charles. Warfare was ended with the Treaty of Verdun in 843.

At Verdun, Lothar surrendered his claim to a unified empire and agreed to follow the old custom, sharing the empire equally with his brothers. Lothar received the central lands of the kingdom, extending north-south from the Low Countries through Burgundy and into Italy. Louis received the eastern part of the empire and became known as Louis the German. Charles, nicknamed "the Bald," received the western portion, most of present-day France.

When Lothar died, his central kingdom was divided among his three sons, who all died without heirs. Lothar's southern lands then became separate kingdoms, Burgundy and Italy. The northern lands were divided between the other two Carolingian branches.

The Eastern Carolingians.   East Francia, the kingdom of Louis the German, grew increasingly Germanic as the king allied himself with the local nobles. Louis strengthened his ties to these nobles by marrying his sons to

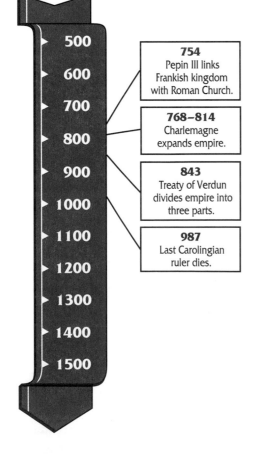

500

600

700

800

900

1000

1100

1200

1300

1400

1500

754
Pepin III links Frankish kingdom with Roman Church.

768–814
Charlemagne expands empire.

843
Treaty of Verdun divides empire into three parts.

987
Last Carolingian ruler dies.

Lorraine

The northern part of Lothar's kingdom became known as Lotharingia, or Lorraine. Throughout the Middle Ages and up until modern times, Lorraine has sometimes been French, sometimes German. Its coastal areas grew into the independent nations of Belgium and Holland, but the inland area is now a county of France, Alsace-Lorraine. Alsace-Lorraine was still being fought for by France and Germany during the world wars in the 20th century.

* **vassal** person given land by a lord or monarch in return for loyalty and services

their daughters, but his sons often fought with the nobles and with each other. Louis himself also had disputes with his brother Charles the Bald about the northern territories of Lothar's old kingdom. As a result, royal power diminished and that of the nobles grew.

Following Louis's death in 876, East Francia was divided among his three sons—Louis III, Karlmann, and Charles the Fat. Louis and Karlmann died within a few years, leaving no heirs. As a result, the eastern kingdom was united again under the youngest son, Charles the Fat. Charles also became king of the western kingdom for a time. However, he was not a strong king, and in 887 he was deposed by his increasingly powerful nobles. These nobles chose Arnulf of Carinthia, the illegitimate son of Charles's brother Karlmann, to be king. Arnulf was a capable and successful king who was able to protect his kingdom against raids from Slavs in the east and Vikings in the north.

When Arnulf died in 899, he was succeeded by his six-year-old son, Louis the Child. During Louis's reign, the nobles fought constantly among themselves, uniting only rarely to resist Slavic raids. When Louis died in 911, the nobles chose a non-Carolingian Germanic duke named Conrad as king. This set the stage for the accession of OTTO I THE GREAT of Germany in 936.

The Western Carolingians.   Carolingian power in West Francia, Charles the Bald's kingdom, was also weakened by outside raids and by the growing power of his nobles. Charles looked to the church for support, giving it an increased role in the affairs of the kingdom. However, the nobles were able to gain power because Charles was often distracted by negotiations with the pope.

During the brief reigns of Charles's sons, Louis II (the Stammerer) and Carloman, royal power continued to decline. Following the death of Carloman, the West Franks elected Charles the Fat of East Francia to be their king also. However, Charles had even less power in the west than he did in his own territory. When he was deposed, the West Frankish nobility passed over the legitimate west Carolingian heir, Charles the Simple, and elected the count of Paris, Odo. Odo, a member of the powerful Robertinian family that began to challenge the Carolingians for the western crown, had successfully defeated Viking raids on Paris in the preceding years.

Odo's success against the Vikings did not continue, however. This gave the supporters of the Carolingians more power. To win them over, Odo named Charles the Simple as his successor. Charles came to an agreement with the Vikings. He allowed their leader Rollo to settle in Normandy as a vassal* of West Francia. Charles also accepted the accession of Duke Conrad as the first non-Carolingian ruler of East Francia. Nevertheless, Charles the Simple was eventually deposed and imprisoned by his enemies.

Two rulers from the Robertinian family of Count Odo next took the throne, but then the Carolingian heirs were recalled, ruling until the later 900s. Louis V, the last Carolingian ruler, was killed in an accident in 987. After that, the nobles elected yet another Robertinian, Hugh CAPET, as their ruler. Capet succeeded in consolidating his power and became the first of the Capetian line of kings of France.

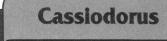

Cassiodorus

ca. 490–ca. 583
Statesman and scholar in
Ostrogothic Italy

* **psalms**   sacred songs from the Old Testament
of the Bible

Flavius Magnus Aurelius Cassiodorus, Senator, was born at the end of a century during which the imperial city of Rome was twice sacked by tribes of barbarians. He came from a family that was experienced in the old traditions of Roman government and served the first non-Roman ruler of Italy, THEODORIC THE OSTROGOTH.

Theodoric began his rule of Italy when Cassiodorus was three years old. Theodoric respected Roman civilization but could not write, and so he brought educated people into his court. As a teenager, Cassiodorus began to prepare letters and other public documents for the king. A collection of these documents, called the *Variae,* still survives, showing that Cassiodorus was a highly persuasive writer.

After Theodoric's death in 526, Cassiodorus retired from public office and founded a school for religious studies on his family estates. He then traveled to Constantinople, where he seems to have devoted his efforts to his own religious writing. His most important religious work was about the psalms*. This very methodical and clear book was based on the work of AUGUSTINE.

Returning to Italy in 554, Cassiodorus became involved with the school he had founded. There he wrote other Christian texts and a reference handbook for copying manuscripts. He also wrote an instructional manual for the educational program at his school. Throughout the Middle Ages, Cassiodorus's works were viewed as models for excellent writing.

Castellan

* **hereditary**   passed on from parent to child

* **heretical**   characterized by a belief that is
contrary to established church doctrine

* **ministerial**   class of people in medieval
Germany; administrators below the rank of
knight whose power depended on the power
of their lord

Castles in the Middle Ages were not always very strong or well staffed. Nevertheless, those who commanded them, the castellans, often had wide-reaching rights in surrounding towns and fortified areas (castellanies). Frequently, these rights were hereditary*, granted by a king or powerful noble. COUNTS used castellans to maintain control over areas of their counties. Royal castellans represented the king on royal lands. Some castellans had authority only over their own castles.

To keep order, experienced castellans were needed in border areas and in regions where military power was essential. They had many knights in their service to help enforce the laws. Such castellans also acted as judges in local disputes. The most powerful castellan in France in the late 1200s and early 1300s was that of Montréal in southern France. He was directly responsible to the king and had to keep the unruly and sometimes heretical* region of Carcassonne under control. Strong castellans were also found in northeastern France, where powerful towns resented interference.

In peaceful areas, castellans might have few duties except such special tasks as guarding the royal forest. Their castellanies gave them extra income and a headquarters for their work but little responsibility.

Castellans were found primarily in France, the Low Countries (the Netherlands, Belgium, and Luxembourg), and Spain. In Germany, their role was often taken by ministerials*. In countries without castellans, such as England, holders of castles did not administer local justice and often had no hereditary rights. They were appointed by the king and could be dismissed at the pleasure of the monarch. (*See also* **Castles and Fortifications; Count, County; Nobility and Nobles.**)

Castile

See map in Aragon (vol. 1).

Castile, or the "land of castles," was a remote frontier area in the old Spanish Christian kingdom of ASTURIAS. These castles were built as a defense against Muslims to the south and against the neighboring Christian kingdom of NAVARRE. The Muslims had invaded Spain and forced the Christians back into the mountains of the north coast, but they then withdrew from the northern river valleys to be closer to their capital at CÓRDOBA. In the early 800s, settlers moved down from old Castile into this more fertile plain and began an expansion that did not stop until Castile had taken over a large part of the Spanish peninsula, including Asturias. Only PORTUGAL and ARAGON remained separate, and at the end of the Middle Ages, Castile united with Aragon to become the new kingdom of Spain.

From County to Empire.   In the 800s, the kingdom of Asturias included three regions: Galicia, León, and Castile. Castile was a rough inland frontier far from Oviedo, the capital of Asturias. This may explain Castile's independence from the other two regions of Asturias. Even the languages differed; Castilian was later to become the official language of all Spain.

From the start, there were rivalries between the regions, and the seat of power often changed. People from all three areas spread southward to farm valleys that the Muslims had ignored because of internal struggles. Free peasants occupied and worked the empty land under Asturian counts, for monasteries, or on their own.

In the 900s, a count named Fernán González pushed the Castilian frontier ever closer to Córdoba in Muslim territory, making Castile an almost independent county. However, in the last decades of the 900s, Castile suffered losses at the hands of the Muslim leader of Córdoba, al-MANSUR. Still, Castile lost less than Galicia and León, and Sancho Garcia, grandson of Fernán González, expanded Castile again in the early 1000s.

King Alfonso X of Castile earned his title *el Sabio* (the Learned) because of his interest in the arts and learning. He is shown here, surrounded by his court musicians. The illustration is from the *Songs to the Virgin Mary,* a 13th-century collection of troubadour music.

After Garcia, González's male line died out, and rule over the county ended with Ferdinand, who was Garcia's grandson and a son of Sancho III of neighboring Navarre. Ferdinand moved quickly against the rest of Asturias, defeating its king to become Ferdinand I of León and Castile. Under Ferdinand, the expanded Castile was pushed farther into Muslim lands to the south. Ferdinand's kingdom also included the shrine of SANTIAGO DE COMPOSTELA in Galicia. Pilgrims and merchants from France and beyond added to the prosperity of his reign.

The 100 years following Ferdinand's death were marked by wars and further expansion. The drive against the Muslim kingdoms pushed as far south as TOLEDO, and the weakened Muslims had to call in fierce allies from North Africa called the Almoravids to stop the advance. The king of Castile assumed the title of emperor of Spain. In addition, the nation became more closely aligned with the rest of Europe, accepting the Roman Church rather than the old Mozarabic* rite and expanding trade northward by land and sea.

This was the era of the Spanish hero the CID. It was the time when the Muslim wars in Spain became crusades*, supported by the pope and by knights from the orders of CHIVALRY. The Muslim kingdoms were forced to pay large amounts of tribute* to the Christians. Other Muslim invaders from North Africa weakened the Muslim kingdoms by attacking them from the south. The major Christian nations of Spain made joint plans for further advances on the Muslim frontier. In 1147, combined Christian forces led by Castile's Alfonso VII temporarily captured the Muslim town of Almeria on the southern coast of Spain. Christians occupied two-thirds of the Spanish peninsula.

Conquering the South. When Alfonso VII died in 1157, Castile had grown to include a large part of northern Spain and was poised to expand even farther into Muslim lands. However, Castile could no longer claim to be the Empire of Spain. Not only had Aragon combined with the eastern county of CATALONIA to become a powerful trading nation in the Mediterranean, but Portugal had left Castile and become a separate kingdom. In addition, Castile itself was split between Alfonso's two heirs. Once again there were two nations, León and Castile, which often fought between themselves.

The people still formed a largely rural society of landholders and peasants. However, merchants and artisans from France and beyond had set up towns on the pilgrimage route in the north. As the Christian border moved south, more and more Jews and defeated Muslims also entered the society. This enriched the culture, though it also produced new tensions. The dominant form of agriculture became ranching, and towns with wealth based on livestock grew in the south. Urban influence on government increased through the cortes*, which negotiated taxes with the kings. Though Castile remained somewhat backward compared to its eastern neighbor Aragon, considerable wealth began to pour in from the sale of wool. In addition, a considerable amount of Muslim tribute was still being paid to Castile.

After a period of fighting between the Christian kingdoms, during which Castile made an alliance by marriage with the English monarch Henry II, huge Muslim troop preparations in Morocco made the kings set

* **Mozarabic** form of Christian worship practiced by Spanish Christians who had adopted some aspects of Arab culture

* **crusades** holy wars declared by the pope against non-Christians. Most were against Muslims, but crusades were also declared against heretics and pagans.

* **tribute** payment made to a dominant foreign power to stop it from invading

* **cortes** advisory parliaments of the Spanish kingdoms

their differences aside. An international army, including four of the five Spanish Christian kings, their armies, and perhaps as many as 70,000 crusaders from outside Spain, met the Muslims at Las Navas de Tolosa on July 16, 1212. The Muslim invasion force was destroyed in one of the most famous battles of the Spanish Middle Ages. Spain's remaining wealthy Muslim kingdoms were open to further Christian conquests.

Under a new king, Ferdinand III, León and Castile were reunited again, and their combined armies pushed toward the south. In 1236, they captured Córdoba, the old Muslim capital. Twelve years later Seville was in their hands; they had conquered all of the south except Granada. Castile was without doubt the largest kingdom in Spain.

Disarray, Culture, and Unity. The advance to the south brought unexpected problems to Castile. There was great apparent wealth, due to booty captured from the Muslims, but land—the source of real wealth—suffered. The wars caused agriculture to collapse, both in the south, where Muslim farms had been destroyed, and in the north, where farmers left their land to find new wealth in the south. The result was inflation*, other economic problems, and even some famines. In addition, the king of Castile had received large amounts of tribute from the Muslim nations, but he could not collect so easily from his own nobles, who were the new tenants of the captured territories.

These problems faced Ferdinand's son, Alfonso X el Sabio. Alfonso was able to take advantage of the influx of Muslim scholarship that conquering the south had made available. He developed a new, tolerant, and enlightened code of laws and was able to support a fine literary court, enriched now by three cultures: Christian, Arabic, and Jewish. It was partly due to his court that Castilian became the official language of Spain. However, Alfonso was not able to solve the financial plight of the nation.

His successors, too, though they had adequate personal wealth, were rarely able to pull the nation together. This situation was made more difficult by two circumstances. Quite often during the next 100 years, kings died leaving heirs who were too young to rule, making it necessary to appoint regents*. There were also fierce rivalries between heirs, often complicated by struggles between the increasingly independent nobility.

An example of these trends was the minority* of Alfonso XI, who became one of the most competent kings of Castile. His grandmother Maria de Molina acted as regent for 13 years, just managing to keep the nobles under control. However, Alfonso took power as a teenage king in 1325, tamed the nobility, and set up a tax system that restored some royal control over finances. He completed the legal program of his great-grandfather, Alfonso X, making it the law of the land. He also won several victories over the Moors and laid siege to Gibraltar in 1350; but there he died of the Black Death.

Alfonso XI made many contributions to the future of Castile, but he left a succession problem. In addition to his son Pedro I, he had five illegitimate children to whom he left great power. The eldest of these, Henry of Trastámara, was exiled and gained support from the kings of Aragon and France. Pedro called in England's heir, Edward the Black Prince of Aquitaine (southern France), and together they were victorious. Then they argued about their alliance, and Pedro was killed by Henry, who became Henry II of Castile.

* **inflation** economic trend in which money declines in value for buying goods

* **regent** person appointed to govern a kingdom when the rightful ruler is too young, absent, or disabled

* **minority** time before a child comes of age and takes on adult responsibilities

See color plate 15, vol. 3.

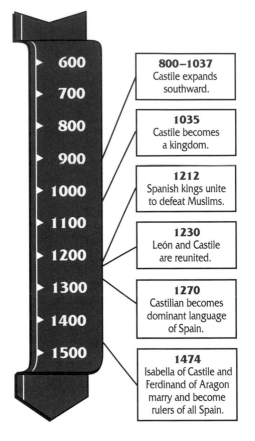

800–1037
Castile expands southward.

1035
Castile becomes a kingdom.

1212
Spanish kings unite to defeat Muslims.

1230
León and Castile are reunited.

1270
Castilian becomes dominant language of Spain.

1474
Isabella of Castile and Ferdinand of Aragon marry and become rulers of all Spain.

The final chapter of Castile's history is the history of Henry's Trastámara dynasty. Under attack from Pedro's supporters and from the other Spanish kingdoms, members of the dynasty weathered outside challenges from Portugal and from England's JOHN OF GAUNT, as well as internal strife that included religious violence against Jews who had entered Spain from Muslim areas. The Jews were pressured to convert to Christianity, and many did, becoming so-called CONVERSOS. Those who did not convert ultimately suffered expulsion from Spain.

The longest reign of a Trastámara was that of John II. John became king at the age of two under the regency of his mother, Catherine, and his uncle Ferdinand. The two regents kept the peace until John came of age. (Ferdinand was elected king of Aragon in 1412 after the throne there became vacant.) John himself later came under the influence of a powerful politician, Alvaro de Luna, who worked hard to strengthen the king's position against the nobles and cortes.

In the end, it was Ferdinand's heir in Aragon, also called Ferdinand, who benefited. John II's son and grandson both struggled against the still rebellious nobility of Castile, but his granddaughter Isabella was made of a different mettle. She dominated her half brother, Castile's King Henry IV, and gained control of the nobles. Henry declared Isabella as his heir but then changed his mind, naming instead his illegitimate daughter Juana. Isabella started a civil war, aided by her new husband, Prince Ferdinand of Aragon. She and Ferdinand were victorious and became rulers of all Spain. (*See also* **Cortes.**)

Castles and Fortifications

During the Middle Ages, especially in western Europe, warfare changed considerably. At the beginning, much of it was tribal, as different peoples were displaced from their lands and searched for new places to settle. Later there were power struggles between local lords, many of whom had independent power and wanted more. Toward the end of the period, wars were most often between powerful dukes or national kings, who could amass great resources for battle. Throughout the period, however, fighting was a common part of the way of life.

Fortifications were therefore very important. Leaders who waged war, especially those in the feudal* west of Europe, needed strongholds or castles where they could protect their supporters and their own possessions if a strong enemy attacked. Country dwellers in all areas needed a safe haven in which to take shelter if their lands were being pillaged. Towns, a good target for attack because of the combined wealth of their inhabitants, also needed strong walls to keep away greedy marauders.

Because any fortified area was subject to attack, more than strong walls was needed. Supplies of food and water had to be stored in case the fighting was drawn out. It was useful to have different ways to counterattack, to drive an enemy away and shorten the siege* if possible.

Constructing fortifications was a major undertaking, however. Many factors had to be considered. What was the nature of the site to be protected? What types of attacks might be expected? What building materials were available? How much labor and what other resources could be used?

* **feudal** referring to the social, economic, and political system that flourished in western Europe during the Middle Ages

* **siege** long and persistent effort to force a surrender by surrounding a fortress with armed troops, cutting it off from aid

Because all these factors differed in different places and at different times, medieval fortifications were of many types.

Early Fortifications and Castles. Before cannons began to be widely used in the 1400s, one of the most important factors in locating and building a fortification was elevation. The best sites were those that were higher than the surrounding land. If defenders were high up, projectiles launched against them, such as arrows and stones, would have less range and less impact because they would be pulled back down by gravity. The defenders' missiles, on the other hand, would travel farther, accelerate, and do more damage. High ground and steep approaches were therefore chosen wherever possible. If these were not available, they would be arranged by human labor.

In flat countryside, the usual type of early medieval fortification began with an earth mound called a motte, surrounded by a ditch as large as 50 feet wide and 50 feet deep. The earth was usually mixed with stones or

By the end of the 1300s, cannonballs could penetrate castle walls. Fortifications were then designed with thicker walls and reinforced with banks of earth, where cannonballs might lodge themselves. The fortress of Salces, shown here, was the first fortification to use this new type of military architecture.

A Medieval Castle

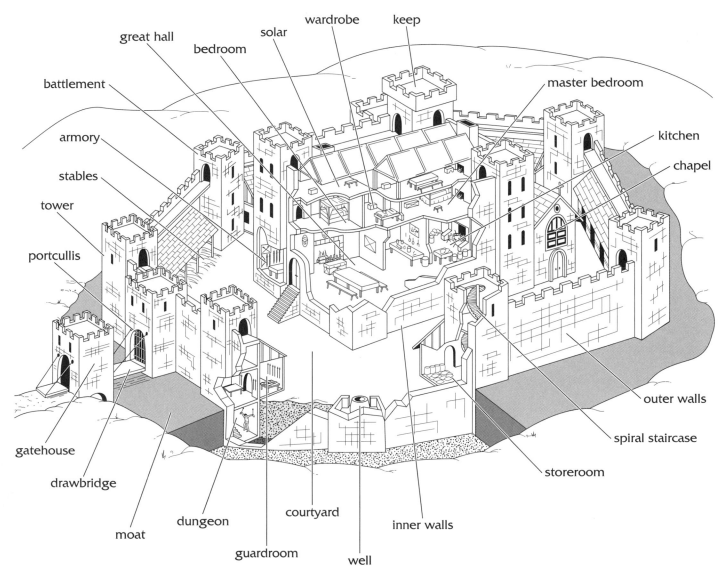

pieces of wood and branches as reinforcement. Such materials allowed for steeper sides that were harder to climb but would still not collapse or erode. The slopes were usually topped by a wall called a bail or bailey built of wood or hardened earth. A single tower or several buildings would be erected inside the bailey.

This motte-and-bailey design was the basic form for forts built between the end of the Roman Empire and the 1100s. The remains of early mottes, some dating from the 700s, are numerous in France and England. Some of the wooden castles that followed this design were quite large and impressive. Some had main towers that were three stories high and several other buildings for supplies and living quarters. They required an enormous amount of wood and were built on very large mounds. Such wooden castles remained common throughout the early Middle Ages wherever timber was abundant.

One advantage of wooden castles was that they could be built quickly. One hundred men working 8 hours a day might take 20 days to erect a typical motte. The buildings could be built in even less time. If a castle was destroyed, it could be easily rebuilt. In the early 1100s, King Louis VI of France had to besiege and destroy the same castle three times in seven years because its rebellious owner was able to rebuild it so quickly.

In addition to wooden castles, the ancient Romans had already built many military structures to defend their empire. Some of these had been temporary, with simple wooden walls and towers built on high ground. However, the Romans also built permanent stone walls with towers around cities, at frontiers, and in other places of particular importance. Some of these were enclosed behind ditches, traps, or other earthworks that made them hard to approach. During the early Middle Ages, these Roman structures were sometimes repaired or rebuilt, but elaborate stone forts and walls were rarely built in northern Europe until the end of the 1000s.

Changes in Building Materials and Design. During the 1100s, new weapons and methods of warfare made wooden castles more vulnerable to attack. Wood also became more scarce as the population grew and began to use it for other purposes. At the same time, new tools and techniques that made building with stone more efficient came into use.

Many of these developments were related to the crusades, which brought western Europeans into contact with the Byzantine and Islamic civilizations of the East. The Byzantines had preserved many techniques of the ancient Romans. They had elaborate ARTILLERY weapons, based on the sling or bow-and-arrow principle, that could hurl large rocks with considerable accuracy. They also had an invention called Greek fire, which involved lobbing large pottery containers that burst into flame on impact. This made it easy to set wooden buildings on fire. The crusaders returned home with many of these weapons. Because their local enemies had done likewise, however, they found it necessary to strengthen and fireproof their home fortifications.

The crusades had also made wood more scarce. Building the crusading ships required a great deal of wood. Contact with the East also led to trade, which demanded still more ships. Trade also created greater wealth, leading to the growth of cities and a need for wooden houses. Finally,

> **Remember:** Words in small capital letters have separate entries, and the index at the end of Volume 4 will guide you to more information on many topics.

From his castle, a nobleman managed his business affairs and defended the surrounding countryside. The castle also provided a home for his family and a refuge for his tenants during an enemy attack. The medieval castle was protected from attack by its location—such as on a hillside or near a river—and by thick, high walls and battlements.

wood was a trading commodity in itself—the wealthy Islamic world in particular was willing to pay good money for timber.

Because of the scarcity of wood, Eastern civilizations became more practiced at building with stone. The crusaders learned some of their building techniques and also copied their tools. Islamic craftsmen in particular made superior steel and developed ingenious devices, such as a stone-cutting saw that was operated by a water mill. This allowed stones to be more accurately shaped and used to build very sturdy structures.

The process of change that resulted from these influences was gradual. When a noble or a nation adopted a new offensive or defensive technique, foes would try to find countermeasures. This often led to new fortification methods. For example, stone walls were fireproof, thus a stronger defense than wood, but they could be made to collapse more easily than structures built of wood. Attackers would dig short tunnels or mines below the wall's foundation, making a wooden roof to support the weight above. They did not use the tunnel to enter the castle one person at a time because this would have been too slow. Instead, they would set the roof on fire, causing the whole wall to collapse from the weight of the stones. Later they filled the mine with gunpowder and blew up the wall. These techniques, called sapping, were discouraged by making the stone foundations deeper and heavier and by putting a ditch or moat, often filled with water, around the wall. In this way, fortification methods changed.

The battle of ideas did not end here. Moats were also useful in stopping attackers from reaching the wall itself, which they could assault by using hook ladders or large wooden siege towers wheeled up to the wall. When attackers tried to fill the moats with earth, logs, or debris, defenders began to build overhanging platforms with openings through which they could drop heavy stones, hot oil, or Greek fire onto the attackers. At first, the platforms were temporary structures built of wood, but later they were often permanent structures built of stone.

A simple castle in the early Middle Ages was no more than a single, solid tower. In the 1000s, larger castles often consisted of a similar solid tower, called a keep or dungeon, where the lord lived, but the dungeon usually had extra fortification. A strong outer wall surrounded the dungeon, also enclosing storage buildings and places for men-at-arms to sleep. The wall generally had towers at intervals along it and at the corners. These towers, smaller than the dungeon but taller and stronger than the linking "curtain" walls, had slit windows in their sides and crenels* around the top. They were spaced according to the minimum range of defensive weapons so that the lord's soldiers could stay in the towers and defend the entire wall. If the curtain walls were broken, the dungeon was a second line of defense.

As needs changed, however, so did design. In the late 1100s, King PHILIP II AUGUSTUS of France built several royal castles in which the dungeon was joined to the outer walls and could also be used in the initial defense. These castles were no longer residences; they were military fortifications designed to defend the kingdom as Philip fought to drive the English out of Normandy. Later still, in the 1200s, such castles might have no dungeon tower at all. Sometimes another complete wall with towers was built inside the first. At the same time, other buildings inside the original wall were moved up to or even into the walls, leaving an open courtyard in the middle. Storage rooms inside the walls were harder for enemy artillery to damage, and the open courtyard provided space for defensive artillery that could hurl missiles back over the walls at the attackers.

Beginning in the 1200s, many castles, especially those of kings and great lords, were built by special teams of architects and military engineers. Such fortifications became very elaborate, requiring financial resources that only the wealthiest individuals or towns could afford. They included many carefully planned features to combat siege techniques of the day.

Earlier castles were intended largely for defense. Defenders would crowd into the castle, hurl missiles at their enemies, fight them off if they tried to enter, and wait for them to give up and leave. Now means of counterattack were developed. Gates that could quickly be closed with a drawbridge were built. This enabled besieged defenders to mount a sudden sortie or exit, using the open courtyard as a place to muster the troops. In 1429, JOAN OF ARC led a sortie from Orleans that destroyed England's temporary headquarters fort and broke the siege.

Because a gate or entrance door was especially vulnerable to attack by battering rams, it was reinforced by an iron grill called a portcullis, operated with heavy chains. In some castles, drawbridge and portcullis were linked: the grill automatically rose as the bridge was lowered. In others, the two operated separately, each with its own counterweights.

In one design, a narrow footbridge led to another, smaller entrance near the main one. The large drawbridge was used only for horsemen, carts, and troops. It could thus be kept raised most of the time to provide added security. Sometimes, too, the far end of the main drawbridge rested on a high wooden ramp that could be destroyed in case of a siege. This made it more difficult for attackers to reach the castle entrance.

Behind the main gate, there might be another entrance guarded by a second door and portcullis. This feature made it easier to check on

* **crenels** narrow gaps along the tops of walls and towers from which bowmen could attack the enemy and still have maximum protection

All in a Knight's Work

One of the chronicles from the late 1100s tells how the lord of Bourbourg, near Calais in France, built a complete castle in a single night. His carpenters used prefabrication techniques, making parts of the structure before assembling them. Though the castle was erected hastily, the lord's enemy, Arnold of Guines, had to mount a full-scale siege in order to capture it.

Remember: *Consult the index at the end of Volume 4 to find more information on many topics.*

people entering the castle. A group of unwelcome visitors could be trapped between the two entrances and dealt with by guards in the fortified towers above. By the 1200s, such entrances were often like miniature forts themselves.

When large castles or towns were besieged, the attacking force would switch its attacks to different places on the walls. The defenders therefore had to be able to move quickly from tower to tower and from place to place. Walkways were built along the upper, interior walls of castles or along the platforms that projected outward from them. Sometimes these walkways were protected by crenels and sometimes by heavy, steeply sloping wooden roofs. However, because such roofs could catch fire or be crushed by heavy projectiles, they were usually left uncovered so they would remain clear.

Fortifications and Castles in the Late Middle Ages.   In the late Middle Ages, large siege weapons were developed to hurl large projectiles weighing as much as 650 pounds. Continued blows by such weapons could break down the outer layers of castle walls. The walls were therefore reinforced to resist such blows. Exposed walls up to 33 feet thick were built, and towers were rounded because a circular design made them more resistant to repeated hits.

Just as the design and techniques of medieval fortification were reaching their high point, the cannon was invented. This new technology suddenly made medieval styles of fortification less effective. By the end of the 1300s, cannonballs were able to penetrate the walls of many castles and other fortifications. Their range was so great that elevation became much less of an advantage. Though it took time for cannons to become accurate and safe, they clearly posed a great threat to traditional defenses.

The first response was to make town and castle walls thicker. It was soon apparent, however, that new types of fortification were needed. High towers became a liability—if they fell they could do a great deal of damage. They were replaced by low, wide bastions* reinforced with earth. Instead of square or round walls, bastions were usually pointed, making direct hits less likely. Slits for archers were replaced by larger openings for cannons, which could be moved to cover a broader range of fire. Other military considerations led to carefully designed star-shaped plans in which each wall could be protected by a neighboring wall. In front of these walls or the ditches around them, builders constructed long slopes where cannonballs might lodge in great masses of earth. The first example of this new type of military architecture was the fortress of Salces, begun in 1497, on the border between France and Spain.

With the development of efficient cannons and firearms, the castle lost its basic military character. Instead, it became simply a residence for the wealthy. Even so, tall fortified castles were still useful against robbers, gangs of ruffians, and rebellious peasants. Many of these medieval castles have therefore been preserved as private homes in their original state, especially in parts of France and Germany. Most old city walls, however, were destroyed as towns and cities expanded. Among those that still survive are the city walls of Chester in England, Carcassonne in France, Nuremberg in Germany, and Avila in Spain. (*See also* **Warfare.**)

* **bastion** reinforced corner of a fort that enabled defenders to fire at attackers from several angles

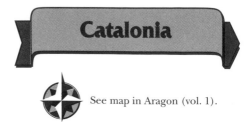

See map in Aragon (vol. 1).

* **dynasty** succession of rulers from the same family or group

Catalonia was a region on the Mediterranean coast of Spain and France, stretching southward and also westward from the Pyrenees mountains. In the time of CHARLEMAGNE, it was a frontier area organized against the Muslims in Spain. Later, feudal rivalries lessened the French territories, but the Spanish lands, centered on BARCELONA, became the heart of the great Mediterranean nation called the crown of ARAGON. Barcelona itself grew to be one of the most important cities of Spain.

Early History of Catalonia. In the early Middle Ages, Christians and Muslims fought over the land that became Catalonia. At first a part of Christian VISIGOTHIC Spain, it was overrun by the Muslims in the early 700s, when they invaded Spain and advanced their frontier into southern France. However, the Frankish emperor Charlemagne pushed the Muslims back to the Pyrenees and then, in 801, as far south as Barcelona. In this campaign, he was greatly helped by his cousin Count William of TOULOUSE, whose story is told in the CHANSONS DE GESTE of the TROUBADOURS. (In the chansons, he was called William of Orange.)

William's sons inherited the conquered lands of Catalonia, but they were soon replaced by a family from Carcassonne, a town that rivaled Toulouse in southern France. The members of the Carcassonne dynasty* were Visigoths and ruled Catalonia for more than 500 years. One of the first, Guifred "the Hairy," controlled all the major sections of Catalonia by 878.

Coexistence with Muslim Spain. Farmers from the Pyrenees and farther north were attracted to fertile but deserted inland valleys in southern Catalonia. The Christian church was able to expand there and founded several monasteries. However, the political situation grew more complicated as CAROLINGIAN power in the south of France faded. Catalonia's counts became more involved with Muslim Spain. A thriving trade began between the Muslims and the Catalans (Catalonians). There were also Muslim raids, during one of which, in 897, Guifred was killed.

Under Guifred's sons, Catalonia was divided into several counties and became peaceful and prosperous. This was partly due to a treaty negotiated with the Muslims in the 950s. The Catalonian church developed close ties with the papacy in Rome and attracted famous teachers. Barcelona became the most important city in the area. Then, in the years around 1000, the Muslim leader al-MANSUR launched another series of unexpected raids—against which the Catalonians fiercely counterattacked—that reached as far as Córdoba, capital of Muslim Spain.

Once again the war brought benefits. For a time, the Muslims made tribute payments, further adding to Catalonian prosperity. Yet the Muslim trade still continued. Important items, including cloth, horses, weapons, and slaves, were exchanged. Catalonian AGRICULTURE adopted new methods of farming poorer soil, many of which came from the Muslims.

By the time of al-Mansur's raids, Catalonia had settled into a form of FEUDALISM, with many castellans* protecting the local population and serving the regional lord or count. The law they administered was based on the old Visigothic customs of the region, which had survived since the start of the Middle Ages. Most of the counts were still from the family of

* **castellan** lord of a castle who provided basic protection for local inhabitants and who owed allegiance to a higher noble

Guifred. However, they functioned independently, owing their allegiance to the distant and by now weak Carolingian kings.

Growth of a Nation.   In the 1010s and 1020s, the situation changed. Local castellans had benefited greatly from the campaign against the Muslims. When it was over, rivalries among them led to local wars. During these wars, the castellans tightened their hold over farmers who served them, treating them more like serfs* than independent farmers. The church and the counts tried to maintain peace, but the farmers often rebelled and the rule of law broke down. Then two powerful leaders of Barcelona brought their county back under control. They also extended their influence through all of Catalonia, including part of southern France, and made an alliance with princes from NORMANDY, who were establishing themselves as a Mediterranean power.

The first of the two leaders, Count Ramon Berenguer I, ruled from 1035 to 1076. He forced the castellans of his county to swear personal loyalty to him and updated and reinforced the laws in his territory. He went on to establish his authority over the original seat of his family, the town of Carcassonne, north of the Pyrenees. He also had his son marry a daughter of Robert Guiscard, the powerful Norman conqueror of Sicily.

Ramon's grandson, Ramon Berenguer III (1096–1131), gained control of other major counties in Catalonia, confirmed the ties with Carcassonne, and married the heiress of PROVENCE. These actions gave him control of the Mediterranean coast from Barcelona all the way east to the Italian border. He also led a group of crusaders that seized Majorca in 1115, temporarily gaining power over western Mediterranean sea routes and crushing a Muslim pirate base.

Union with Aragon.   While the counts of Barcelona were gaining power in Catalonia, Christian regions to the northwest had also strengthened their positions as independent nations. Neighboring

* **serf** rural worker with little or no freedom who was sometimes sold along with the land he worked

Some Christians joined monastic orders, where they could devote themselves better to God and the spiritual life. The monastery at Poblet is one of several Christian monasteries founded in Catalonia during the Middle Ages.

Aragon had achieved unity under several strong kings and was now a dominant power in the area, even taking some lands from Catalonia. Castile, farther to the west, had also become a strong force, claiming for its king the historic title of emperor of Spain. Under the leadership of Aragon's Alfonso I the Battler, both nations were pursuing a holy war against the Muslims.

However, there was also a fierce rivalry between the rulers. When Alfonso died childless in 1134, the king of Castile tried to claim the throne of Aragon as well. This was unacceptable to the nobles of Aragon, who arranged for Alfonso's infant niece and heir to be married to Catalonia's Count Ramon Berenguer IV.

Thus began a new phase in the history of Catalonia. The union of Aragon and Catalonia, under the title of the Crown of Aragon, became an even more important force in the Mediterranean world, both in trade and in warfare. While Catalonia's French possessions were later lost to the counts of Toulouse, it gained large parts of Spain and put together a far-flung empire, including Naples and Sicily as well as Majorca. For most of the 1300s, there were also independent Catalonian states in Greece. These were founded by soldiers from Catalonia who had fought on the advancing Christian frontiers against Muslim Spain.

Cathars

* **heretic** person who disagrees with established church doctrine

Cathars were Christian heretics* in France, northern Italy, and parts of Germany during the 1100s and 1200s. They rejected the Christianity of Rome and founded their own church. Catharism was preached throughout western Europe and gained a large following. However, a CRUSADE was declared against it, and by the middle 1300s, Catharism had been destroyed in western Europe.

The Cathars believed in dualism, an ancient idea that the universe is divided between two conflicting forces, good and evil. Cathars argued that the human body and the material world are evil: only the human spirit can become pure and achieve goodness. As part of their rejection of the material world, Cathars frequently fasted and were strict vegetarians.

Dualistic beliefs first appeared in medieval Europe in the Balkan peninsula among a religious group known as the Bogomils and became popular in France and Italy in the late 1100s. Believers became known as Cathars from the Greek word *katharos,* meaning pure, because of their efforts to purify themselves. The city of Albi, near Toulouse in southern France, was a center of Catharism. For this reason, Cathars were also called Albigensians.

Catharism attracted converts among the nobility, the clergy, artisans, townspeople, and peasants. It was not unusual for entire communities to become Cathar. Larger towns sometimes appointed Cathar bishops. The Cathar hierarchy had two levels: perfects, who followed the strictest Cathar principles, and believers, whose self-denial was less demanding.

To the Roman Church, it was heresy to believe that the human body, created by God, could be evil. Heretics who refused to admit the errors of their thinking were usually excommunicated*, and local rulers were urged to imprison them and confiscate their property. However, Cathars were so

* **excommunicate** to exclude from the rites of the church

The Papal Police

The inquisitors after the Albigensian crusade were very thorough. As full-time investigators, they took complete records of all confessions, which had to be given under solemn oath. When a Cathar stronghold fell in the year 1244, 200 leading heretics were questioned, then burned. For years, their records were used to help track down other Cathar sympathizers. In spite of this pressure, however, castellans in the south of France continued to help Cathars into the 1300s.

* **recant**   to state in public that one's beliefs are wrong

numerous in parts of Europe and had so much support that these usual ways of dealing with them failed. Missionaries were sent into Cathar towns to debate and preach against them. St. DOMINIC, founder of the Dominicans, joined the campaign against the Cathars in southern France.

In 1208, a papal ambassador to the count of Toulouse was murdered. Pope Innocent excommunicated the count, offering his lands and goods to anyone who would join a crusade against Catharism. The Albigensian crusade began. Crusaders pillaged southern France, captured the lands of local nobles, and replaced bishops sympathetic to the Cathars with supporters of the pope. The once independent nobles of southern France were ultimately brought firmly under the authority of the French king.

The crusade itself ended in 1229, and Cathars began to return to their old homes. Four years later, Pope Gregory IX began a papal INQUISITION against the heretics. The pope gave Dominican friars the authority to judge cases of heresy in southern France. The trials were held in secret, and torture was sometimes used to gain confessions. People who admitted their heresies and recanted* could be imprisoned, but those found guilty who refused to recant could be burned to death. Campaigns against the Cathars were launched many times; others besides those in the Albigensian crusade also used force. Many Cathars fled from France to Spain and Italy, but the inquisition followed them there. The last Cathar bishop in western Europe was seized in northern Italy in 1321.

Cathedrals and Churches

See color plate 15, vol. 2.

In the Middle Ages, many new churches, including impressive cathedrals, were built. Church construction was financed in many ways. In the Byzantine East, the early large religious buildings were often paid for from imperial funds. Later churches were smaller and usually funded privately, by members of the emperor's family and other aristocrats. In the West, noble families also often built their own churches, which they then viewed as their own property. The greatest effort went into the cathedrals, however. Kings, nobles, and townspeople joined the bishop in financing construction, which could take 30 to 100 years to complete. Architects, stonemasons, and sculptors sometimes spent their entire adult lives working on one cathedral.

Christian churches varied from region to region and from period to period. Early Christian churches were modeled on the Roman public hall or basilica. They were large but simple rectangular buildings with an apse (a semicircular area with a vaulted ceiling) for the altar at one end. Variations on this type included churches with galleries and churches with several apses. Other early churches were circular or octagonal in shape.

The cross was a popular ground plan. Early Byzantine churches sometimes formed a cross with arms of equal length, known as the Greek cross, in a basically square design. The plain Greek cross design, developed in the 400s and 500s, had a central dome and often a dome above each arm of the cross. The cross-in-square church, with a small central dome and additional domes over the corners of the square, became the most common Byzantine design after 800. There were many variations of it, but all tended to be squarish and covered by domes. Many such churches still exist in the eastern Mediterranean. Russian church design often follows these models.

Churches in the West tended to be more rectangular. They were often designed as a Latin cross, with one arm (the nave) longer than the others. Double-ended churches were built during the CAROLINGIAN period, with an apse at each end. Pilgrimage churches had many apsed chapels for the relics* of different saints. There were also hall churches, shaped like long boxes and built mostly in Germany. In Scandinavia, there were wooden stave churches, with steeply pitched roofs. A stave church from the mid-1100s still exists in Borgund, Norway.

Early Byzantine architects based their churches on Roman designs, then developed the use of domes and interior mosaics* in different ways, creating feelings of great space and color or feelings of calm and somber intimacy. Western ROMANESQUE-style churches of the 1000s and early 1100s

* **relic**   object cherished for its association with a martyr or saint

* **mosaic**   art form in which small pieces of stone or glass are set in cement; also refers to a picture made in this manner

Rheims Cathedral, begun in 1211, is one of France's finest examples of Gothic architecture. It was the traditional coronation church of the French kings from 1179 until the early 1800s.

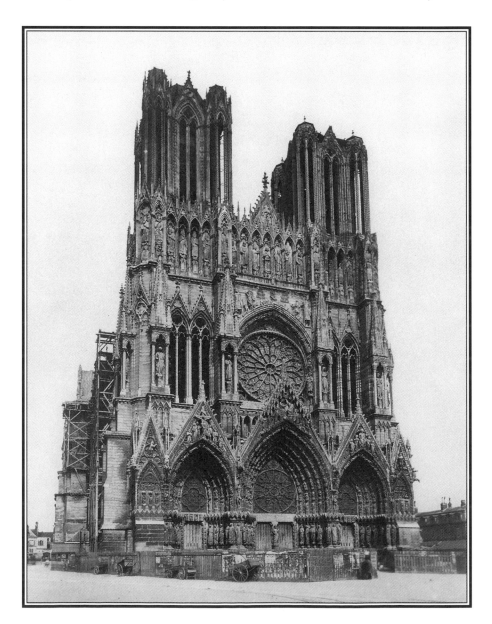

also resembled Roman models in their rounded arches and thick walls. These were used in larger and larger buildings, with structural sections called bays divided by sturdy columns. Such columns could be topped with heavy stone vaults* rather than wooden ceilings.

GOTHIC churches, built in the West between 1150 and 1300, were taller and lighter than Romanesque buildings. Stone arms called flying buttresses helped support the weight of the vaults from the outside. Architects could therefore make the columns and walls thinner and higher, constructing large windows filled with stained glass. These windows, like the arches in the doorways and inside the church, were tall and pointed, creating a sense of upward movement. French Gothic cathedrals such as the one at CHARTRES were an inspiration for Gothic churches elsewhere.

Cathedrals are churches that house a bishop's cathedra, or throne. They are usually the largest church in a diocese*. In the Byzantine world, the most impressive example of a cathedral is Constantinople's HAGIA SOPHIA, a vast domed church from the early Middle Ages, richly decorated with mosaics inside. The Western Church eventually had several cathedrals to rival this magnificent building, including NOTRE DAME in Paris.

Western cathedrals typically have an imposing west front and may have three towers, including one over the center of the Latin cross. As in pilgrimage churches, aisles* and ambulatories* often lead to many side chapels. There were regional variations on this basic style; for example, English Gothic cathedrals like those in York and Salisbury were lower, and longer, to allow for different types of rituals and processions.

Cathedrals were often run by CHAPTERS, groups of priests called canons, who were in charge of maintaining and repairing the cathedrals. The bishop and a chapter worked together to raise funds to manage the cathedral. After a fire badly damaged Chartres's cathedral in 1194, the chapter and bishop pledged a sizable portion of their own incomes for three years to finance the cathedral's reconstruction.

Many medieval churches and cathedrals are kept in good repair and are still being used for worship today. They are also popular attractions for visitors. (*See also* **Byzantine Architecture; Christianity; Clergy.**)

* **vault** section of a three-dimensional arched ceiling of stone

* **diocese** church district under a bishop's authority

* **aisles** passages on either side of a church parallel to the nave, set off by columns or stone supports

* **ambulatory** passageway circling the choir and altar sections of a church

See color plate 12, vol. 2.

Catherine of Siena, St.

1347–1380
Mystic, teacher, and religious activist

* **lay order** religious group organized by friars for laypersons who did not wish to take full vows

Catherine was the daughter of a dyer who lived in the Italian city of SIENA near the church of St. Dominic. When she was 16, she joined the lay order* of the DOMINICANS and strove to follow Christ's example by helping the sick and the poor and the prisoners of the city. She worked especially hard to bring peace to Siena by ending the family feuds and political disputes that divided it. Her active social work and reform efforts in the city and in the Dominican order attracted people to her and won her a large following.

At the age of 20, Catherine experienced a mystical dedication to Christ. Her works include *The Dialogue*, or *Book of Divine Providence*, composed as a dialogue between her soul and God, and many letters and prayers. These works show her as a woman of great intelligence and holiness, indicating why she had such an influence on other people. Her confessor, Raymond Capua, who later became the master general of the Dominican order, wrote her life story. His book and Catherine's own writings became known throughout Europe.

During the time when the popes moved from Rome to AVIGNON on the border of Burgundy and France, Catherine was a leader of the movement to have the popes return to Italy. Her sincerity, zeal, and piety won her many admirers, though the return of the popes was followed by the Great SCHISM of the Western Church.

Catherine died in Rome in 1380 at the age of 33. In 1461, the church declared her a saint. She is now a patroness of Italy.

Caxton, William

ca. 1415–1492
First English publisher

* **guild** association of craft and trade workers that set standards and represented the interests of its members

* **Low Countries** flat coastal lands west of Germany, now occupied by Belgium and the Netherlands

When William Caxton was still a boy, he was apprenticed to a fabric vendor in London. Because fabric vendors, or mercers, were members of an influential guild* with connections overseas, Caxton learned about finance and foreign trade. At the end of his apprenticeship, he became a merchant and traveled between England and BRUGES, an important European market for cloth and other items. Moving to Bruges around 1462, he was elected governor of the English Nation of Merchant Adventurers there, an organization of traders.

In addition to fine fabrics, the Low Countries* produced manuscripts that were much sought after because of their quality. Caxton began to market these. He also decided to buy a printing press, a new technology developed in Germany by Johannes GUTENBERG, to publish books in English. Caxton teamed up with John Veldenen, a printer in COLOGNE. He bought a press there and produced the first book printed in English. The book was a retelling of the story of the Trojan War, which Caxton himself translated from French.

Caxton moved his press to Bruges to be closer to England. However, because he found it hard to run an English bookstore from Bruges, he moved to London and set up shop near parliament. As a publisher, he chose the books to be printed and had them dedicated to important people so they would sell well. Among the hundred or so books he published were a book on chess, the works of Geoffrey CHAUCER, and the Arthurian tales of Sir Thomas MALORY. Caxton often included his own opinions of the works he published in the dedications and thus was also the first English literary critic. (*See also* **Wynkyn de Worde.**)

Celtic Languages and Literature

See color plate 8, vol. 2.

Before the Romans established their empire, speakers of Celtic lived in a wide area from the Balkan peninsula in southeast Europe to Spain and the British Isles in the west. They were the dominant peoples of northern Europe. In the first century B.C., Celtic BARDS, or singing poets who specialized in songs of praise, were described. Under the Roman Empire, many Celts adopted Christianity as their religion and began to use Latin as a second language. Then, after Rome fell in the 400s, Germanic MIGRATIONS began to displace the Celts.

Celtic languages are a branch of the Indo-European language family, which also includes Germanic languages, such as English and German, and languages of the Mediterranean, such as Latin, Spanish, and Italian. Today the Celtic branch of the family exists only in the extreme western area of Europe. Celtic languages, called the insular languages, include the Brythonic or British group—Welsh and Breton—and the Goidelic or Irish group—Irish and Scottish Gaelic. Brythonic is sometimes referred to as p-Celtic and Goidelic as q-Celtic because "four" is *petguar* in Old Welsh and *qethair* in Old Irish. Each group produced its own literature in the Middle Ages.

Brythonic Literature

The earliest surviving written words from the Brythonic language group are Celtic names found in Latin inscriptions from the 400s to the 600s. The literature itself included a strong oral* tradition. The few written works that exist come from late manuscripts, the originals of which were probably written much earlier.

* **oral** by word of mouth rather than in writing

Wales. Welsh literature dates from the 500s, by which time the Celtic language had developed a distinctive Welsh version. Anglo-Saxons were invading Wales and southern Scotland at this time, but Celtic bards still composed verses of praise for their local rulers. The poetry is complex in structure, pithy in style, and includes striking imagery. Two of the most famous writers were Taliesin and Aneirin. Taliesin became the subject of later poems, being described as a magician who could change his shape.

The bardic tradition was highly organized, especially from the 1000s to the 1200s, when Wales became politically consolidated. A group of professional court bards called the Gogynfeirdd used the old language to write moving elegies, religious poems, and songs of praise. Later, after Wales lost its independence in 1282 to England's EDWARD I, a new school of poets arose. Their work was more personal and natural and written in a more modern Welsh. Most notable among these poets was Dafydd ap Gwylym. His work has proved hard to translate, but scholars view him as a master, with a keen sense of humor, full of wonder at nature and the love of God. He has been called one of the greatest medieval poets.

In addition to Welsh poetry, there was a tradition of Welsh literary prose, which included an important work called *The Mabinogion*. This collection preserves some tales of King Arthur, a major topic of Welsh literature.

Brittany and Other Areas. In the Middle Ages, Brythonic also survived in other parts of the British Isles, including Cumberland and Cornwall. From Cornwall, the language and its literature spread back to Brittany in France and became the Breton language. Brittany's oral tradition in the Middle Ages is thought to have popularized much ARTHURIAN LITERATURE in France and the rest of Europe, leading to important works such as the romances of CHRÉTIEN DE TROYES and some of the ballads of MARIE DE FRANCE.

Goidelic or Gaelic Literature

The earliest records of the Goidelic language group are also names in inscriptions, written in an Irish adaptation of the Roman alphabet. These names date from the 300s to the 600s and are found in parts of Britain and in Ireland.

Remember: *Words in small capital letters have separate entries and the index at the end of Volume 4 will guide you to more information on many topics.*

Ireland. The earliest datable piece of Irish literature is an elegy on the death of St. Columba in 597, attributed to a poet named Dallan Forgaill. It is significant as a poem written in the old Celtic tradition but about a Christian saint. While oral poetry continued outside monasteries, Christian monks became involved in writing down Irish literature, both religious and secular*. Only after 1100 were manuscripts written by learned laymen.

Most medieval Irish literature was quite conservative. Verses were written in praise of the ruling kings. However, some early lyrics were fresh and innovative, written as light relief from the serious business of scholarship. For example, in a famous poem from the 800s called "The Scholar and His Cat," the writer playfully comments on similarities between his white cat hunting around the scriptorium* and his own work as a scholarly monk copying Latin hymns and notes on astronomy.

One of the greatest of all Irish poems may come from the same time period. It is the "Lament of the Old Woman of Beare." In it, a magical princess finally grows old after being queen to seven kings and can no longer renew herself to marry a new king of the people. The poem can be seen as a lament about old age and lost royalty.

After this "classical" period of Old Irish poetry, a far-reaching change took place. Storytelling focused on tales of the distant past, and writing was less fresh and more scholarly. Celtic writers no longer enjoyed the respect or income they had once commanded, and their children began to learn English rather than Irish. Celtic literature and learning as they had been understood were ending.

Scotland. The Goidelic version of Celtic also spread through Scotland. Once again, one of the earliest poems is about St. Columba, by a biographer named Adamnan. As in other Celtic areas, bards flourished; their staple product was praise poetry. Long-lasting lines of hereditary poets and traditional historians worked for certain ruling families. They acted as both custodians of learning and servants and mentors of their patrons.

At the end of the medieval period, we find the earliest surviving popular Gaelic verse: folk songs. They are concerned with personal feelings and local incidents, early battles, and heroes. These songs usually use different rhythms from those of the professional bards, but there are indications that the rhythms are also ancient, used throughout the Middle Ages. (*See also* **Minstrels; Troubadour, Trouvère.**)

* **secular** nonreligious; connected with everyday life

* **scriptorium** workshop in which books were written or copied, decorated, and bound

Chamberlain

Many of the titles of great officers of state have their origin in humble work. The term *chamberlain* at first meant a household serf or domestic servant in the king's private chamber. Because this was where the royal treasure was originally kept, the term came to mean royal treasurer in many nations. It also described other officials who handled finance, whether for a town, a cathedral, or a monastery.

The authority of the chamberlain varied from place to place in Europe. In France, the chamberlain was never the official treasurer. He was restricted to the care and supervision of objects and revenues connected with the personal needs of the monarch and his household. During the

Anglo-Saxon period in England, the chamberlains (clerks) ran the personal chamber and the king's treasury, but under the Normans the office of EXCHEQUER was created to control finance. However, in time of war, the Exchequer raised money and turned it over to the king's chamber. As commander in chief, he could call upon his chamberlains to pay the expenses of the fighting. In the kingdom of Bohemia, the chamberlain performed duties by the late 1100s that have led at least one historian to call him a minister of finance.

The original meaning of the title *chamberlain* survived in England in the office of the lord great chamberlain. Unlike the chamberlains who monitored the king's personal finances, the lord great chamberlain's main duty during the Middle Ages was ceremonial, to serve water to the king at his coronation and perhaps on the great feast days as well.

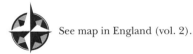

Champagne, County of

* **fief** under feudalism, property of value (usually land) that a person held under obligations of loyalty to an overlord

See map in England (vol. 2).

During the 1200s, the county of Champagne was one of the most powerful regions in the kingdom of France. Its counts were notable crusaders, and Champagne became an important economic center because of its large county FAIRS. Rheims, an ancient cathedral city in Champagne, was where the French kings were usually crowned.

Lying directly east of Paris in northern France, Champagne is an area of fertile open country that was on the early medieval routes that linked the North Sea with the Mediterranean. In the 1000s, it consisted of many independent fiefs* that owed allegiance to different rulers, including the dukes of BURGUNDY, the archbishops of Rheims, and the French kings.

In 1093, Hugh of Troyes, the son of a count of Blois in central France, inherited one of the fiefs in Champagne and acquired two others by marriage. This gave him considerable power in the area. He founded the important monastery of Clairvaux but then left to fight in the First Crusade. Deciding to stay in the Holy Land, he joined the Knights Templars and gave his lands to his nephew Thibaut, who had become count of Blois.

Thibaut, seeing that Blois was surrounded by aggressive neighbors such as Normandy and Anjou, devoted much attention to his new territory. He set up regular yearly trade fairs in several of its towns, and merchants began to travel the rivers of Champagne rather than use routes farther north. Thibaut also confirmed his ties to all his various overlords in Champagne to ensure that each would help him protect his rights.

Thibaut's eldest son, Henry, inherited Champagne in 1152, leaving Blois to a younger brother. Henry, who had fought in the Second Crusade with King Louis VII, married Marie, daughter of Louis and ELEANOR OF AQUITAINE, thus forging a long-term alliance that benefited both Champagne and France. Count Henry also strengthened Champagne by reorganizing local government, making it easier to rule by setting up smaller districts.

Beginning in Henry's time, Champagne had 150 years of sustained economic and population growth. The great fairs continued. Immigrants moved into the region, merchants from other parts of Europe established branches in the main towns, and local industries were developed.

The crusading tradition of the counts of Champagne continued. This meant that the counts' wives and widows were sometimes in control in Champagne. One powerful countess, Blanche of Navarre, helped make Champagne one of the best-governed counties in France. She arranged for all feudal* relationships to be written down and kept in archives. Maintaining these records greatly strengthened the central government in Champagne.

In the late 1200s, Champagne came increasingly under royal control. The heiress of Champagne married into the royal family, and when her son Louis X became king of France in 1314, Champagne was incorporated into the royal domain. After this time, however, the region began to suffer. Trade with the Mediterranean began to move along the Atlantic coast rather than through the rivers of Champagne. The BLACK DEATH ravaged the region in 1348. English military campaigns during the HUNDRED YEARS WAR further devastated the county in the 1370s. By the 1400s, Champagne was no longer the power it had been 100 years earlier. (*See also* **France.**)

* **feudal** referring to the social, economic, and political system that flourished in western Europe during the Middle Ages

Chancery

During the Middle Ages, official paperwork was prepared by a ruler's chancery, or secretarial department. Such departments wrote letters and documents for emperors, popes, and kings. Nobles, bishops, cities, and other authorities also had chanceries. Special procedures and styles were used to make forgery difficult. Keeping records was also often the job of chancery workers.

The original chancery was kept for the Roman emperors. By the Middle Ages, this had moved to CONSTANTINOPLE, and its official language had changed from Latin to Greek. In the 300s, the popes organized their own chancery in Rome. Many chancery customs and practices, including the use of Latin, were adopted by CHARLEMAGNE's Frankish Empire and later Western kingdoms.

Under Charlemagne, the head of the chancery was called the *cancellarius,* or chancellor. Under later rulers, this person, who read all official documents, acted as royal private secretary or even as chief adviser. Thomas BECKET, for example, was a very powerful chancellor in England. Like Becket, other chancellors and chancery workers often had church training.

As governments grew, chanceries developed efficient techniques to keep up with all the paperwork. For example, a specialist would make a rough draft to plan what was to be written. To do this, he might look at another document of the same type or use a book with examples to follow. Then a notary or scribe would make a fine copy of the document. Finally, another copy might be made and kept in the official register or archive.

Chanceries developed many ways to discourage the forging of documents. In addition to keeping an official register, they often used a special style of writing. Some chanceries even had hidden codes of word rhythms; if a document did not use these rhythms, it could be spotted as a forgery.

The use of chanceries helped increase the efficiency of governments and enabled them to grow. It also allowed governments to expand their control over more and more aspects of public life.

Chansons de Geste

The chansons de geste are medieval popular poems about French heroes. More than 100 manuscripts survive. Some of these give different versions of the same hero's deeds. They were among the first works written in French rather than in Latin, which meant that more people could understand them.

The best-known chanson de geste is the *Chanson de Roland (Song of Roland)*, a story of heroism and betrayal in the time of CHARLEMAGNE. Another one, *Charlemagne's Pilgrimage*, tells how the Frankish king goes to the Holy Land because his wife doubts he is the greatest Christian ruler. He and his knights make boasts about their bravery to the Byzantine emperor, but they can only live up to their words with the help of God.

The chansons de geste primarily describe early Carolingian times (around 800), though they were written down between 1000 and 1300. They were often grouped in cycles about the same person. If a hero was popular, there might a poem about his childhood and other poems about his own children. The language is not polished, and there is often a comic element.

The chansons may have been written by court poets called trouvères, or they could have been traditional oral poems, passed on by wandering MINSTRELS. Many of the details in them are fictional, but the people who listened to them thought of them as history. The same details are sometimes included in French histories that were written at the time. The stories were often translated into other languages and were heard from Italy to Scandinavia. (*See also* **Arthurian Literature; Troubadour, Trouvère.**)

Wise Guy

A group of chansons de geste tells about a hero named William of Orange. He was the same person as Count William of Toulouse, who helped Charlemagne repulse Muslim raids in the early 800s. One of the songs tells how William and his young nephew Guy enter a Muslim city in disguise to court a beautiful Islamic princess named Orabel. They get into many dangerous situations, and William is often at a loss about what to do. Guy, however, always has a humorous or sarcastic comment ready for his uncle.

Chaplain

* **Mass** Christian ritual commemorating Christ's Last Supper on earth, also called Communion or Eucharist

* **rector** priest in charge of a parish

* **endow** to provide money for an activity in a will or gift

Originally, the term *chaplain* simply meant a priest in charge of a chapel. However, during the Middle Ages, the term widened to cover confessors in private households, parish assistants or curates, and chantry priests as well.

Chaplains were allowed to say mass* but usually could not baptize, perform marriages, bury, or give the last rites of the dead. Unlike the positions of priests who were parish rectors*, chaplains' positions were rarely endowed*. Chaplains usually worked for a relatively low wage. Even those who had special positions—in the private chapels of the wealthy or in cathedrals or monasteries—were often treated as servants.

In the late Middle Ages, chantry priests became more common. A chantry was an endowment to support masses for the soul of a deceased person, for a limited time or perpetually. Chantry priests were paid to chant the masses at a particular altar in a church. The pay was usually better than that of chaplains, and the position was independent of the rector. Many chaplains left other jobs and became chantry priests instead. (*See also* **Benefice; Clergy.**)

Chapter

* **prior** second most important monk in an abbey (after the abbot); leader of a priory or small monastery

* **laypersons** nobles or common people who were not official clergy in the church and had not taken vows as monks or nuns. Some monasteries accepted lay brothers and sisters to help them with their work.

Each morning, the monks in a medieval monastery met to hear a chapter from the Bible or from the rules of their monastery. The abbot was not present at the meeting, which was run by the prior*. A comment on the reading would be followed by monastery business, including perhaps decisions about its lands, accepting a layperson* into the monastery, or even the election of a new abbot. This daily meeting became known as the chapter, and the meeting room was called the chapter house. Eventually, the word *chapter* came to refer to the group itself.

Cathedrals and some churches also had chapters, headed by an elected dean. However, cathedral chapters could rarely elect their bishop or archbishop; usually local kings wanted to choose their own church leaders.

In medieval law, the chapter often had a unique status. Its property was not listed as belonging to an individual but to the whole chapter. Chapters made decisions about this property, and they were the first organizations allowed to own property. Modern corporations owe their right to own property to the chapters of the Middle Ages.

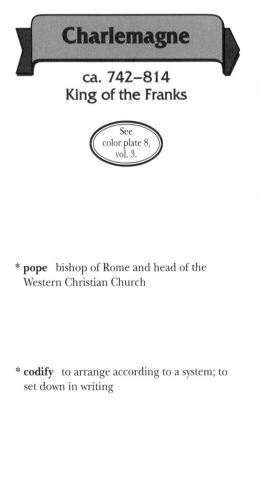

Charlemagne

ca. 742–814
King of the Franks

See
color plate 8,
vol. 3.

* **pope** bishop of Rome and head of the Western Christian Church

* **codify** to arrange according to a system; to set down in writing

Charlemagne, or Charles the Great, was the grandson of CHARLES MARTEL and successor to PEPIN III THE SHORT, the first Carolingian king of the Franks. Under his rule, the Frankish kingdom expanded to include Lombardy (northern Italy) and other areas. He was the first medieval emperor in western Europe.

When his father died in 768, Charlemagne shared rule with his brother Carloman, as was the custom among the Franks. Carloman died three years later. From that point on, Charlemagne ruled the entire kingdom. Between 771 and 804, he conquered Lombardy, Saxony, Bavaria, and parts of northern Spain. This made him undisputed ruler of almost all western Europe—half of the Christian world. Only Britain, southern Italy, and Muslim Spain were outside his control.

Southern Italy was ruled by the Byzantine emperors who, as descendants of the old Roman Empire, ruled the Eastern Christian world. Rome, seat of the popes*, was a part of Byzantine Italy; however, the pope often disagreed with Byzantine policies. Charlemagne, by uniting the Western Christians and occupying northern Italy, now had great influence in Rome.

Charlemagne's conquests gave him wealth and independence from the Frankish nobles. He let his conquered peoples keep many of their own laws and codified* them, expanding his own influence in their affairs by using written decrees. He also strengthened his position as ruler by sending personal representatives on regular visits to distant areas. In his new capital at AACHEN, he invited distinguished scholars to teach him and the people who ran his administration.

Charlemagne arranged for one of his sons to marry the daughter of Empress Irene, the Byzantine ruler. However, he also presented himself as representative of the West and thus a rival to the Byzantine Empire. On Christmas Day in 800, Pope Leo III crowned Charlemagne as emperor. By this act, the pope recognized Charlemagne as ruler of the western

Charlemagne was one of the great military leaders of the Middle Ages. He devoted his reign to the expansion of the Frankish kingdom and became ruler of most of western Europe. He helped to revive education and the arts in his kingdom.

* **province** Roman term for an area controlled by the empire

provinces* of the old Roman Empire and separated Rome from the Byzantine sphere of influence.

Despite his new title, Charlemagne never changed the basis of his rule. He continued to govern as king of the Franks and Lombards. Because he spent much of his wealth on Aachen and on defenses around his empire, he again became more dependent on the Frankish nobles. He also arranged for his succession in the traditional Frankish manner, with his lands to be divided equally among his three sons. However, two of them died before he did, so the empire remained under one ruler after his death.

Charles V of France

**1338–1380
King of France**

* **fief** under feudalism, property of value (usually land) that a person held under obligations of loyalty to an overlord

See color plate 13, vol. 3.

Charles V, known as Charles the Wise, became France's acting ruler while still a teenager. He reigned as king of France from 1364 to 1380. Under his rule, France recovered from the first onslaught of a war with England. Charles also supported the antipopes who established themselves at AVIGNON.

Born the year after his grandfather Philip of Valois had claimed England's European fief* of Gascony, Charles grew up during the early English invasions of the HUNDRED YEARS WAR. When his father, King John, was captured by the English at the Battle of Poitiers in 1356, Charles had to assume the leadership of France.

It was a difficult time. The country was defeated and had no money to ransom the king or pay its soldiers. Many unpaid soldiers became outlaws, terrorizing the countryside. Leading nobles were under attack for corruption. Other nobles opposed the government, wanting a more efficient and less centralized administration. Citizens of the country had a growing resentment against all nobles.

By 1358, however, Charles had successfully defeated riots and rebellions in Paris and had put down an uprising against the nobles. He made a number of reforms that won over his political enemies. When the English invaded once again in 1359, he managed to avoid a direct battle. Helped by Pope Clement VI, who was based at Avignon on the French border, Charles also signed the Treaty of Brétigny in 1360 and arranged for his father's ransom.

King John returned to France and helped set up some regular taxes. These not only provided money to pay off his ransom but also lessened the problem of the unpaid soldiers. A regular army was established to deal with the outlaws and also to defend the country. Then John died and Charles became king.

As king, Charles made useful allies. He persuaded Flanders and Brittany to support France rather than England, and he helped the growing Spanish nation of Castile. He also supported Gascon lords against the English principality of Aquitaine, thus reactivating hostilities in the Hundred Years War. However, helped by a navy from Castile and, once again, by avoiding direct battles on land, Charles made impressive gains over the English.

Nevertheless, Charles's reign left some problems for France. Charles was called "the Wise" because he was a patron of the arts and learning. He founded a royal library and made improvements to the Louvre palace and other buildings. However, the expense involved in some of his efforts put a severe strain on the economy. Then, during the last years of his life, Charles sided with Pope Clement VII, the first antipope of Avignon, against Pope Urban VI and was largely responsible for the papal SCHISM that resulted. This led to neighboring nations' greater hostility toward France.

Finally, as he lay dying in 1380, Charles canceled the important taxes needed to maintain the army because the nobles disliked them. At his death, he therefore left behind a troubled government that his 12-year-old son and heir, Charles VI, made even worse. This led to new opportunities for England, and the war continued for many more years. (*See also* **France; Papacy, Origins and Development.**)

Charles VII of France

1403–1461
King of France

* **disinherit** to deprive of an inheritance or the right to inherit

* **vassal** person given land by a lord or monarch in return for loyalty and services

When Charles was the dauphin, or heir to the throne of France, he was disinherited* by England's HENRY V. By the end of his life, however, Charles had not only regained the throne but also driven the English from France, ending the HUNDRED YEARS WAR.

Charles was the youngest son of King Charles VI of France, but both of his brothers died in the 1410s. During this decade, Henry V of England also launched a powerful attack against France, recapturing England's old duchy of Normandy. To make matters worse, the duke of BURGUNDY, a powerful vassal* of the French kings, became allied with the English. These events gave Henry of England power to arrange for his own marriage to France's Princess Catherine in 1420, and he was made dauphin instead of Charles.

Two years later, Charles VI died—but so did Henry. This left the nine-month-old heir of Henry and Catherine as king of France as well as of England. Although young Charles also claimed the French throne, his claim was less effective because the English had control of Rheims, where French kings were traditionally crowned. Charles was accepted as king of France in areas south of the Loire River, but the English and Burgundians mocked him as "king of Bourges," the small city where he had set up his headquarters.

At first, Charles had little success on the battlefield against the English, who attacked as far south as the city of Orleans. His fortunes changed, however, when a peasant girl named JOAN OF ARC helped break the siege of Orleans, saving the city from the English. She then led a heroic march to Rheims through lands held by the English, and in 1430 Charles was finally crowned king as Charles VII of France.

The coronation at Rheims did not drive away the English. They still had control of much of France and many powerful allies. Charles's nobles were also arguing among themselves, weakening the French. However, Charles succeeded in settling the arguments and also signed a peace treaty with Philip of Burgundy. This took away England's most important ally.

Once Burgundy had been won over, France was able to reverse the tide of war with England. Paris was recovered in 1436, and taxes that had not been collected since 1418 began to be collected once again. The taxes gave Charles funds to pay his soldiers and strengthened the French so much that the English were relieved to have a truce in 1444.

Charles did not disband his soldiers, however. So many unemployed soldiers would add to the problem of outlaws roaming the countryside once more. (This had been happening since before the reign of his grandfather CHARLES V.) Instead, Charles arranged a campaign against the Swiss and then, in the following year, established a force of 9,000 mounted troops on regular salary that became the first "standing army." The standing army solved many problems. It employed soldiers who would otherwise have become outlaws. It gave Charles's restless nobles positions as army commanders working for France. It also provided a trained force that, after 1449, quickly drove the English from France, thus ending the Hundred Years War.

By the time he was 50, Charles VII was a victorious and respected king. He had become a skilled leader and politician and had established France once again as a peaceful and powerful kingdom. (*See also* **France.**)

During his reign, Charles VII drove the English from France and brought the Hundred Years War to an end. He became a highly respected king.

Charles Martel

ca. 688–741
Father of the line of
Carolingian kings

* **mayor of the palace** under the late Merovingians, a leading noble who held the power behind the throne

Charles Martel was mayor of the palace* for the last MEROVINGIAN king. Under his leadership, the Franks stopped the Muslims in SPAIN from extending their power northward. Though his king died before he did, Charles never named an official successor to the Frankish throne. As a result, his son was able to claim the throne for himself and became the first CAROLINGIAN ruler.

The Merovingians were kings over a large part of western Europe but had lost most of their power to leading nobles. One of these nobles was Charles's father, known as Pepin II, who was mayor of the eastern part of the kingdom, then took control of the western part. In 714, Charles inherited Pepin's office, and though he was not king, he led all of the Franks.

He also inherited a major problem. Muslims had taken the Spanish peninsula in 711 and crossed the Pyrenees Mountains into southern France. From there, they conducted their raids, one of which swept 200 miles north of the Spanish border. Charles repulsed this raid at the town of Poitiers in 732.

For help in his Muslim wars, Charles made an alliance with the Lombard king in northern Italy. This displeased the pope, whom the Lombards often threatened. Charles also used church revenue for his own purposes. Nevertheless, because the pope was weak at the time and Charles was leader of the most powerful state in western Europe, the pope issued nothing more than warnings.

When Charles died, he had named no successor to the Frankish throne. His elder son, Carloman, became a monk, but his younger son took his father's office. Then, in 751, with the pope's approval, he became King PEPIN III.

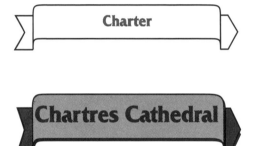

Charter

See *Seals and Charters.*

Chartres Cathedral

* **crypt** underground room of a church or cathedral, often used as a burial place

* **vault** section of a three-dimensional arched ceiling of stone

The GOTHIC cathedral at Chartres, a town southwest of Paris, is perhaps the most famous in all of France. The cathedral was constructed after a fire in 1194 destroyed all but the crypt* and west end of an older ROMANESQUE cathedral. On that foundation, a new church was constructed in a different style, light and graceful. The pioneering design techniques first used at Chartres were later employed in many other church buildings. The nave vaults* are more than 120 feet

These flying buttresses support the nave wall of Chartres Cathedral. The purpose of their massive half arches is to counteract the outward pressure of the cathedral's high vaults.

* **clerestory** upper part of a church wall that rises above an adjoining roof and contains windows

* **guild** association of craft and trade workers that set standards and represented the interests of its members

high and appear to float over a clerestory* of large stained glass windows that fill most of the upper walls. To support the vaults, the builders used flying buttresses: massive half-arches on the outside of the building that support the points where the thrust of the vaults is strongest.

Most of the medieval stained glass windows are still in place. Many were donated by the guilds* of Chartres and depict craftsmen at work, as well as stories of the lives of Christ and the saints. Outside the church, three sculpted porches hold statues representing Old Testament kings, saints, and scenes of Jesus Christ and the Virgin Mary.

Most of the cathedral was built in less than a generation. This gives it a stylistic unity that was unusual in the Middle Ages. Like all medieval cathedrals, however, portions of this one, including one of its two spires, were added later. (*See also* **Construction, Building.**)

Chaucer, Geoffrey

ca. 1340–1400
Greatest English writer of the Middle Ages

* **satiric** referring to humor that criticizes or makes fun of something bad or foolish

* **patron** person of wealth and influence who supports an artist, writer, or scholar

Geoffrey Chaucer, author of the *Canterbury Tales,* was the greatest English writer before William Shakespeare. Records of his early life are few. He was the son of a prosperous London wine merchant, probably went to a good London school, and by the age of 17 was a page in one of England's princely households. For about six years starting in 1359, he was involved in the HUNDRED YEARS WAR: King EDWARD III paid a ransom to free him from the French in 1360, and he brought important letters back from France in the same year. He may also have helped EDWARD THE BLACK PRINCE during his campaign in Spain.

During this period, Chaucer probably met his future wife, Philippa, a lady-in-waiting to the wife of King Edward. A marriage to one so well placed may have speeded Chaucer's rise at court. In 1367, shortly after his marriage, the king awarded him an income for life.

Early Life and Poetry. Chaucer probably learned French, the language of the wine trade, while working for his father. He apparently read a great deal of French poetry. When he began writing himself, many of his early poems were in the French tradition of COURTLY LOVE. He also translated the *ROMAN DE LA ROSE (Romance of the Rose),* a popular French poem of the time that is full of satiric* humor, delights in intellectual activity, and discusses major issues in medieval thought. This work seems to have appealed to Chaucer's sensibility and to his curiosity about philosophy, science, and religion.

Chaucer's most original early work is *Book of the Duchess.* Written in honor of the dead wife of JOHN OF GAUNT, another prince of England who became Chaucer's patron*, this poem describes a dream about a knight mourning the death of his lady. Written with great subtlety and tact, it shows a talent for mixing images, themes, incidents, and even lines from earlier writers to produce a work that was wholly fresh at the time. In it, Chaucer uses a rather simple-minded first-person narrator, a device that became a feature of some of his later poems.

Chaucer was soon traveling overseas on royal business. One of his trips was to Italy, where he surely encountered the works of the great Italian storyteller Giovanni BOCCACCIO. The poets PETRARCH and DANTE also influenced Chaucer, but it was Boccaccio who introduced him to the ideas of the Italian Renaissance. This period in Italian history (1300s–1500s) was noted for individual expression in the arts, increased knowledge of ancient Greek and Roman manuscripts, and celebration of worldly pleasures.

Customs Controller Period.   In 1374, Chaucer was sworn in as a customs controller in the port of London. His job was to keep records of exports in the wool trade. Though busy all day, he still found time to write. This was probably when he translated Boethius's *Consolation of Philosophy,* a dialogue in verse and prose between the author and Philosophy, personified as a woman. This well-known Christian work in Latin describes God as the source of goodness and happiness. Chaucer's translation emphasizes the ability of humankind to rise above the harshness and unfairness of life.

Another work from this time, *House of Fame,* is a highly original poem about a bookish dreamer who is carried away by a golden eagle to the House of Fame, a castle situated on a hill of ice. The eagle praises the dreamer as a person who pores over books in the evening after spending his days "making reckonings"*—probably a description of Chaucer's own daily routine. He also wrote a work called *Parliament of Fowls,* a lovely, if puzzling, poem in praise of love written for St. Valentine's Day. The narrator is in awe of love but explains that he is also ignorant of it.

Chaucer's most notable poem from his years as a customs controller is *Troilus and Criseyde,* one of the great works of English literature. Troilus is a hero in Troy's war against the Greeks. An idealist with a high regard for honorable conduct, he falls in love with Criseyde, a lovely young widow and a complex character. She seems shy and withdrawn, yet forthright and confident of her beauty. Her motives are often unclear, adding to her aura of mystery.

Aided by Criseyde's uncle Pandarus, Troilus declares his love for Criseyde, and she returns it. However, her father, a defector to the Greeks, arranges for her to join him in the Greek camp. There she is wooed by a Greek hero, whose love she also returns. Throughout the poem, Criseyde is so charming that when she betrays Troilus, her treachery is hard to believe. Chaucer lets the reader share Troilus's experience; we understand his inability to reject Criseyde despite her infidelity.

During this middle period of Chaucer's work, Edward III's grandson RICHARD II succeeded his grandfather on the English throne. The tale of Criseyde's unfaithfulness drew criticism from the ladies of the royal court. One of them, probably the new queen herself, demanded that Chaucer write a poem celebrating female fidelity. *Legend of Good Women* was the result. In this story of legendary women, Chaucer's narrator is straight-faced, but he sometimes clearly changes historical facts (as in the legend of Cleopatra) to fit the theme.

Later Life and Works.   Political developments in England and Chaucer's own life are scarcely mentioned in his work. We do know from official records that he left the customs department in 1385 and was appointed justice of the peace in a rural area southeast of London. He returned to the city four years later as clerk of the works for royal estates such as the Tower of London. During this time, he was robbed three times in four days.

* **reckoning**   calculations, including accounting that Chaucer would have done as a customs recorder

Geoffrey Chaucer was one of the great storytellers of the Middle Ages. He did much to advance the prestige of English as a literary language. His most famous work, *Canterbury Tales,* is told within the framework of a pilgrimage to the shrine of St. Thomas Becket at Canterbury. His characters, who range in social status from a knight to a plowman, are a microcosm of medieval society.

A Plea for Money

One of Chaucer's final poems does reflect an event in his life. In 1399, Richard II was deposed by a new king, Henry IV. This caused Chaucer's royal income to lapse. With his usual irony, he wrote a ballad, *To His Purse*, lamenting the loss of his money as though it were a lady he loved who had deserted him. He sent this ballad to Henry, and Henry apparently reinstated his income.

* **reeve**   administrative assistant or steward

Most of the last decade of Chaucer's life was probably dedicated to writing. Always interested in science and in ASTROLOGY in particular, he based *Treatise on the Astrolabe* (1391) on an Arabic work and dedicated it to his son Lewis, a student at Oxford University. His major work from this period was his masterpiece, the *Canterbury Tales*, which follows a model provided by Boccaccio.

A first-person narrator on a pilgrimage to CANTERBURY describes his fellow pilgrims and records the tales they tell each other as they travel. Chaucer makes fun of the narrator by having him tell by far the worst story. The characters of the other pilgrims are also well drawn, as are the story characters. Each level adds richness and humor to the whole work.

The group, which has stopped at the Tabard Inn on its way to Canterbury, reflects the full range of medieval society. A knight and his son represent the aristocracy. A parson, a prioress, and other religious figures represent the church. There are also members of the learned professions, including a doctor of physic, and upper-middle-class characters such as a merchant and a widow, the so-called Wife of Bath. A miller, a reeve*, a plowman, and other characters represent the lower-middle and working classes.

The host of the Tabard Inn organizes the storytelling with splendid self-assurance. The pilgrims argue with one another and are described with a careful selection of details. Their tales encompass themes of piety and romance, morality and bawdy humor. When the final tale, that of a parson, is told, it provides a dignified end to a rich experience. Chaucer even apologizes for the wicked works he has written in the past. However, the rich tapestry of the *Canterbury Tales* embodies, even more than his earlier works, Chaucer's gusto for life and his impressions of medieval society. (*See also* **English Language and Literature; French Language and Literature; Italian Language and Literature.**)

Children's Crusade

See map in Crusades (vol. 2).

The Children's Crusade became a legend in its own time. The story went that a boy prophet led thousands of German and French children southward to the Mediterranean coast, promising that the waters would divide and allow them to walk to Jerusalem. However, the sea did not part, and the children, who were given free passage on merchant ships, were shipwrecked. According to one version of the story, they were sold to the Muslims as slaves.

The truth behind the story seems to be different. There were probably two popular movements, both of which arose in 1212, one in Germany and the other in France. In the first one, a boy from Cologne named Nicholas led a crowd up the Rhine River and over the Alps into Italy. After nearly half a year, 7,000 people reached the Mediterranean port city of Genoa but could go no farther. Some may have wandered as far west as Marseilles and could indeed have been sold as slaves. Others went south to Rome and beyond. Few returned home.

The French movement appears to have been led by a French shepherd boy from near Orleans named Stephen, who claimed he had a letter

The legend behind the Children's Crusade has overshadowed the historical facts. This print from the 1800s is a sentimental portrayal of the Children's Crusade showing young children with swords riding toy horses.

from Jesus Christ for the king of France. Stephen set off for the royal court at St. Denis, north of Paris, eventually attracting about 30,000 followers. While at St. Denis, he is said to have performed many miracles. The king, advised by scholars at the University of Paris, ordered the crowd to return home, which most of them did. The French crusade caused less commotion than the one from Germany.

Historians now believe that most of the followers in these movements were not children but people drawn from the lower classes of rural society. The early 1200s saw the beginning of religious reform movements that valued childlike innocence, poverty, and piety. There may have been a feeling that the unarmed poor could accomplish what wealthy, well-armed, and powerful knights and kings were unable to do in the Third and Fourth Crusades. Supported only by divine aid, they would purge the crusading movement of more materialistic motives, such as greed for land and booty.

Other movements of the same type occurred later. For example, there was a shepherds' crusade later in the same century. There were also several religious community movements in the later Middle Ages that sought to bring back the simple life of the early Christian church. (*See also* **Beguines and Beghards; Brethren of the Common Life; Cathars; Friars.**)

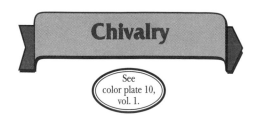

Chivalry

See color plate 10, vol. 1.

Today *chivalry* means considerate manners toward others, especially toward people who are weak or defenseless. The word gained this meaning in the Middle Ages. Chivalry was a code of honor that developed for armed knights on horseback, the most powerful fighters in medieval warfare. The word is related to cavalry and to the French word *chevalier,* which means horseman.

To the knight's basic role as a warrior, chivalry added ideas about social rank, manners, Christian virtues, courage, and honor. Knights began to pursue high standards of chivalrous behavior in their own lives. Religious groups of knights called chivalric orders were formed to fight during the CRUSADES. Later, national monarchs began to honor notable subjects by granting them knighthood in reward for valor and loyalty.

Knights and Chivalry. Throughout the Middle Ages, knights were closely associated with warfare and power. Power meant wealth; wealth enabled people to own horses and heavy ARMOR; and these provided the ability to gain greater wealth and power. Knights trained themselves to fight in full armor and to excel in battle. They could cause brutal damage to opposing forces. In the later Middle Ages, when not on the battlefield, knights practiced their skills in hunts and tournaments*. Tournaments provided an opportunity to practice and display military skill, an important part of chivalry.

Other qualities also became associated with chivalry. Medieval romance literature often involved stories of COURTLY LOVE, in which a knight devoted himself to the service of a lady. Courtly love became part of the concept of chivalry. Christianity, too, had an important influence on chivalry. Beginning in the 900s, the church tried to civilize the knights' brutal style of warfare. Limits were imposed upon battles, and knights were expected to respect the church, protect the weak, and preserve the peace.

As chivalry continued to develop, Christian values such as charity tempered the knights' ferocity. A moral, religious, and social code arose, one based on values of fidelity, piety, and service to God. Knights who adopted these Christian values were known as knights of Christ. The church created purification rites for knights and ceremonies to bless their swords.

The concept of religious chivalry was most significant during the crusades. Crusading provided an outlet for both military valor and devotion to a religious cause. Large numbers of knights now went into battle to defend the church. This led to the development of chivalric orders.

Chivalric Orders. During the 1000s and 1100s, several groups of crusading knights founded military orders to protect Christian pilgrims in the Holy Land. These orders embraced the ideals of Christian chivalry. Members also took vows of poverty and obedience, like Christian monks.

The first chivalric order was the Knights of St. John of Jerusalem, also known as the Knights Hospitalers. The order was founded in 1070 by a group of Italian knights to protect a pilgrim's hospital in Jerusalem. When the Muslims drove the crusaders from the Holy Land in 1291, the order moved to island fortresses in the Mediterranean Sea. There they fought Turkish pirates, becoming known as the Knights of Rhodes and the Knights of Malta.

A second great chivalric order was the Knights Templars. The Templars were mostly French. The order was founded in 1119 to defend the Holy Sepulcher (Christ's tomb) in Jerusalem, protect pilgrims, and fight the Muslims. The order grew rapidly and became rich and powerful. In 1307, the Templars moved to France, where their wealth and power aroused envy. When King Philip IV ordered the Templars arrested, their estates were confiscated, and many were put to death. A few years later, the order was abolished by the pope.

A third great chivalric order was the Teutonic Knights. This group of German knights, originally formed to protect a pilgrims' hospital in Jerusalem, became a major power in northeast Europe, helping to convert pagan tribes in the BALTIC COUNTRIES to Christianity. Besides these three

* **tournament** contest between knights that was staged in peacetime as a sport

 See map in Crusades (vol. 2).

Military skill played an important part in the code of chivalry. Knights were trained to excel in battle. When not on the battle-field, they practiced and displayed their fighting skills in tournaments. People from all social classes enjoyed watching tourna-ments, and these competitions became a popular form of public entertainment.

major orders, there were other important orders of knights in Spain, Por-tugal, and Hungary that fought to defend the church.

Knighthood as an Honor.   After the Christian loss of the Holy Land, Muslim authorities still permitted pilgrims to come to Jerusalem—but travel to the area was more hazardous. To encourage would-be pilgrims, the king of Cyprus honored many of those who made the journey as Knights of the Holy Sepulcher or Knights of the Sword of Cyprus. This started a tradition of secular, or nonreligious, orders of knighthood. Peo-ple so honored did not have to take monastic vows.

Other feudal monarchs saw that awarding such knighthoods would help maintain the loyalty of their vassals and subjects. One of the first sec-ular orders was England's Order of the Garter, founded in 1348 by King Edward III and modeled on the legendary Knights of the Round Table. Other orders included the Order of the Golden Fleece, awarded by the dukes of Burgundy and honoring the wool trade and the idea of making chivalrous quests; and Denmark's Order of the White Elephant, so called because elephants were believed to be careful not to harm defenseless creatures such as ants. (*See also* **Arthurian Literature; Knights, Orders of.**)

Chrétien de Troyes

late 1100s
French poet

* **Holy Grail** cup that Jesus supposedly drank from at the Last Supper

Chrétien de Troyes was a poet who wrote for the aristocratic courts of northern France. He was one of the first medieval romantic poets. His five most important works tell stories of King Arthur and his knights, especially Yvain, Lancelot, and Perceval. The poems were widely read and provided inspiration for poets across Europe through the 1300s.

Chrétien's Arthurian romances are among the earliest and most prized versions of these stories. They are based on Celtic legends about Arthur and his followers, and they deal with chivalry, courtly love, religious faith, and the quest for the Holy Grail*. The poems tell about the knights' adventures and crises and what they learn through their struggles. The works include comic scenes, such as Perceval's blunders while he is learning proper court behavior. The major themes, such as Perceval's deepening religious understanding as he searches for the Grail, influenced many other medieval poets.

Chrétien was trained in Latin and worked as a clerk. One of his innovations, however, was to write in the French of his day, making the stories readable by knights who did not know Latin. At the French court, his noble patrons included Countess Marie de Champagne, for whom he wrote his poem about Lancelot, *Le Chevalier de la Charrette.* He dedicated the *Conte du Graal,* based on the adventures of Perceval, to Count Philip of Flanders. He also wrote some other minor poems and translated works of the ancient Roman poet Ovid into French. (*See also* **Arthurian Literature; French Language and Literature; Tristan, Legend of.**)

Christianity

T he church of the Middle Ages may be said to have begun in 312, when Roman emperor CONSTANTINE I recognized the Christian religion as an equal to other religions in the empire. Later in the same century, Emperor Theodosius I outlawed paganism* and made Christianity the imperial state religion.

Constantine also founded a new capital of the Roman Empire at CONSTANTINOPLE. By doing so, he planted seeds for a later division of the church into two churches—a Western Church headed by the bishop of Rome (pope) and an Eastern Church headed by the Byzantine emperor and the patriarch of Constantinople.

* **paganism** word used by Christians to mean non-Christian religions that believe in several gods

See color plate 7, vol. 2.

* **apostles** early followers of Jesus who traveled and spread his teachings

The Early Church

To understand medieval Christianity, it is necessary to start well before the Middle Ages. The history of the early church set the scene for many of the radical changes that occurred later. These changes affected both what the Christians believed and how their church was organized.

Beliefs.   The men and women of the early Christian church believed that Jesus Christ would set up a divine kingdom within their lifetimes. When they saw this was not so, they decided it was their duty, as the church, to spread Christianity and thus prepare the world for Christ's second coming. To preserve Christ's message, they compiled the Christian Bible, expanding the Jewish Scriptures by adding the four Gospels, accounts of Christ's life and teachings. They also included letters by Christ's apostles* that had been circulated among the early Christian communities. The Christian Bible became the basis of the church's teaching mission.

However, disagreements grew up between Christians in different areas about what the Bible meant and what they should believe. A serious question facing the church in the 300s concerned the nature of God. Christians agreed that God had three aspects: God the Father, Jesus Christ the Son, and the Holy Spirit. But they did not agree about the relationship between the Father and the Son. Was Christ subordinate to God or his equal? Many Christians in Syria followed a teacher named

See color plate 2, vol. 3.

* **theological** pertaining to the nature of God, the study of religion, and religious beliefs

* **heretic** person who disagrees with established church doctrine

* **excommunicate** to exclude from the rites of the church

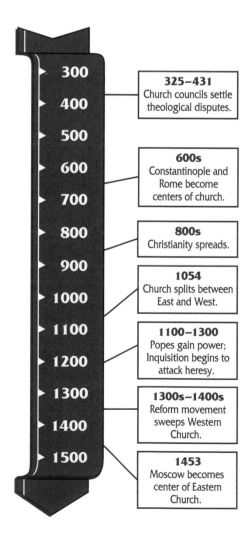

300

400

500

600

700

800

900

1000

1100

1200

1300

1400

1500

325–431
Church councils settle theological disputes.

600s
Constantinople and Rome become centers of church.

800s
Christianity spreads.

1054
Church splits between East and West.

1100–1300
Popes gain power; Inquisition begins to attack heresy.

1300s–1400s
Reform movement sweeps Western Church.

1453
Moscow becomes center of Eastern Church.

Arius and held that God the Father was the most important aspect of the Trinity.

Emperor Constantine, though not yet a Christian, was disturbed by this rift in one of the most powerful religions in the empire. He called a council of the church together at Nicaea (325). Christians accepted this because they were glad that the Roman emperor was now finally protecting rather than persecuting them. At Nicaea and at a later council in Constantinople (381), the church leaders decided that the Father, Son, and Holy Spirit were three equal aspects of one God and that God and Christ were equal.

Other councils were called later to decide other theological* issues. Most of the theologians who discussed these issues wrote in Greek, the accepted intellectual language of the day. Their decisions did not please everyone, but they defined Christian belief and preserved the unity of the church. They also led to the exclusion of some people. Those who did not accept the majority ruling of these councils were often denounced as heretics* and were excommunicated*. The followers of Arius's beliefs, for example, became known as Arian heretics. HERESIES and EXCOMMUNICATIONS continued throughout the Middle Ages.

Organization. Leaders of the early church were called bishops. Christians believed the first bishops had been blessed by the apostles. Because later bishops were blessed by their predecessors, they were considered spiritual successors of the apostles and of Christ himself. One of the most famous bishops of the early church was St. AUGUSTINE, from Hippo in North Africa. Noted for his carefully reasoned theological works in Latin, he had a great influence on the Western Church.

Under the bishops were priests, who led day-to-day worship for the people. In addition, there were movements in which Christians renounced the world by living alone in the desert as hermits or else lived together monastically as monks or nuns, with strict rules of poverty, chastity, obedience, and prayer.

Bishops were responsible for spreading and protecting Christian beliefs. They authorized monastic communities, managed the churches in their districts, and settled church disputes at meetings. These meetings were called synods when a few neighboring bishops met together and councils when bishops gathered from throughout the Christian world.

Three centers were at first recognized as dominant in the church: Rome, the capital of the Roman Empire; Alexandria in Egypt; and Antioch in Syria. Alexandria and Antioch played leading roles in theological controversies of the 300s and 400s. When Constantinople was founded and became the capital of the empire, it too was viewed as a center. Jerusalem also gained influence as a center of pilgrimages. The bishops of these five cities were often called patriarchs, and those of Rome and Alexandria were sometimes called popes.

Rome was unusual for a number of reasons. It had been the old capital of the Roman Empire. The bishop of Rome, or pope, was believed to have been appointed by St. Peter, the leading apostle whom Christ had called the "rock" on which the church should be built. The bishop of Rome was also the only patriarch in all the West. So Rome was often viewed as the head patriarchate. However, the Roman Church used Latin, whereas the Eastern Church used Greek and local languages. Also, Rome ceased to be the empire's capital in 330 and fell to barbarian invasions in the 400s.

* **papacy** office of pope and his administrators

The Roman papacy* was not destroyed, however. Barbarian leaders often married Christian women from among the peoples they conquered and established their own churches. Clovis, for example, king of the MEROVINGIAN Franks, married a princess from Burgundy named Clotilda and converted to Christianity. Other rulers were also influenced by their Christian wives. The popes were able to remain as rulers of parts of Italy. Pope GREGORY I (590–604), the first strong medieval pope, took an active interest in converting the barbarian invaders to Roman Christianity. After Gregory I, the Roman Church sent missionaries to distant parts of Europe and won the support of new Christian rulers.

Meanwhile, in the 600s, the Eastern Church faced a disaster. Arab armies swept across the Byzantine provinces of Palestine, Syria, Egypt, and North Africa, engulfing the patriarchates of Alexandria, Antioch, and Jerusalem. The Arabs allowed bishops to continue looking after Christians in these areas, but only two of the five patriarchates were still free: the one in Constantinople and the one in Rome.

A Church Divided

Though the Eastern Church had lost three of its patriarchates, the Byzantine patriarchate was still supported by its powerful Christian emperor. Byzantine Christians regarded the emperor as co-responsible for the church. Though the patriarch of Constantinople was the church's spiritual leader, the emperor was viewed as Christ's secular* representative, with the task of managing the church and spreading its message. Of the two men, the emperor had more power. He appointed his own successor and also soon took responsibility for choosing new patriarchs from a list of three candidates submitted to him by high church officials.

* **secular** nonreligious; connected with everyday life

By contrast with the patriarchs, popes frequently assumed governmental as well as religious responsibilities, and the method of choosing them was more variable. After Gregory I, prospects for the Western Church still looked grim. The Muslim armies that took Antioch, Jerusalem, and Alexandria also conquered the western provinces of Africa and most of Spain. In Britain, pagan Germanic invaders called Anglo-Saxons enslaved, drove away, or killed most of the island's Christian inhabitants. The Germans who lived to the east of the Franks were also pagan.

Lombards invaded Italy and advanced on Rome. Though Christian, they were Arian heretics fiercely hostile to the Roman Church. In addition, the Byzantine emperor held on to his influence in Italy and pressured the pope to obey him. When Pope Martin I defied his will, Emperor Constans II had him arrested and brought to Constantinople for trial. Martin was declared guilty of treason and exiled in 655.

New Tensions.   In the 700s, the Eastern Church faced a new problem. A bitter debate broke out about the use of sacred images called ICONS. Prompted by the success of Islam, which allowed no images of God or humans in mosques, Byzantine emperor Leo III promoted a policy of iconoclasm*, ordering images of Christ, the Virgin Mary, and saints

* **iconoclasm** removal or destruction of icons (images of Christ and the saints) in churches

At the Council of Clermont in 1095, Pope Urban II issued a plea to all Christians to make a pilgrimage to the Holy Land. The purpose of the pilgrimage was to fight against the Muslims, who were considered enemies of the Christian faith. This began the age of the crusades, a period that lasted for nearly 200 years.

removed from churches and public places. John of Damascus and some other Byzantine theologians defended the veneration of icons, as did the Roman pope, who thought icons helped people understand church teachings. After more than a century of dispute, Byzantine empress Irene finally accepted icons back into Eastern churches, but the controversy shook the Christian community.

At the same time, the papacy was able to grow stronger. The popes began to stand up to the Lombards and to the Byzantine emperors as well. They fortified the walls of Rome against attack and developed closer ties with the FRANKS, who were now the most powerful force in the West. Pope Zacharias helped the CAROLINGIAN family become rulers of the Franks by approving the election of Pepin (later known as Pepin III) as king.

Pepin's son Charles (later called CHARLEMAGNE) strengthened the organization of the kingdom, expanded its boundaries, and allowed Christian missions from Rome and other Christian areas in the lands he conquered. The papal-Frankish alliance began to be seen as an empire of the West that balanced the Byzantine Empire. During Charlemagne's long reign (768–814), he promoted Christianity throughout his empire. The alliance reached its climax in 800, when Charlemagne traveled to Rome and Pope Leo III crowned him "emperor of the Romans" in St. Peter's church on Christmas Day.

Unfortunately for the Roman Church, the empire soon began to fall into smaller units. In Italy, popes became corrupt and incompetent, elected by Roman nobles rather than the church. Elsewhere in Europe, the church's independence and integrity were weakened by its association with FEUDALISM. Feudal lords gained control of church property, taxing it for revenues and appointing unqualified bishops and clergy. New rulers emerged, including kings of Germany, who claimed the title Holy Roman Emperor.

In the Byzantine Church at this time, a great missionary movement was taking place. In the 800s, two brothers, CYRIL AND METHODIOS, went north and converted the SLAVS in the Balkan peninsula and beyond to Christianity. Because the Slavs had no written language, the brothers created a new alphabet, using Greek and Hebrew letters, and new words that allowed them to translate the Bible and services into the Slavic language. However, the Western Church, especially in Germany, objected to this expanding Eastern influence and also to the use of languages other than Latin and Greek to teach the Christian faith.

Reform and Schism.   In 909, a reform movement began at a monastery in Cluny, France, and spread to other monasteries and church institutions in the West. They gained independence from feudal control by putting themselves directly under papal authority. Then in the mid-1000s, the German emperor, HENRY III, restored greater power to the papacy by appointing the first of a series of German reform popes, ending the Roman nobility's control of the papacy. Similar reform ideas attracted the support of other reform-minded rulers and clergy.

The growing strength of the Western Church deepened disagreements and tensions that had already developed between the two halves of Christianity. The matter came to a head in 1054, when Pope Leo IX sent envoys to Constantinople. The two sides argued about an issue of wording in the main Christian statement of belief. Byzantine emperor Constantine IX had hoped the papal agents and the patriarch of Constantinople would settle their differences, but the tensions were too strong to overcome. The mission ended disastrously. Each church excommunicated the other, and the Western envoys barely escaped from an angry Byzantine crowd.

The Byzantine and Orthodox Churches

The Byzantine Empire itself, under attack from the forces of Islam, grew steadily weaker until the end of the Middle Ages, when Constantinople was sacked by the Ottoman Turks. However, the influence of the Byzantine Church remained strong, especially in the Slavic countries of eastern Europe.

Byzantine theology tended to be more spiritual and mystical than the rational theology of the Western Church. Byzantine church law also placed greater emphasis on the spirit rather than the letter of the law and was more flexible than church law in the West. The Eastern liturgy—especially the Eucharist*—was one of the great splendors of the Byzantine Church. When Prince Vladimir of Russia went to Constantinople in 987, he described it as "heavenly." Byzantine music, with its roots in the Jewish synagogue of the early Christian period, was magnificent. There was also a strong tradition of monasteries. The communities of Mount Athos in Greece were a center for monks from all over the Byzantine Christian East.

In 1204, during the Fourth CRUSADE, Christians from the West sacked Constantinople. This was not the first setback for the Byzantine emperors, nor was it the last. They managed to retake their city in 1261, but from then on they continued to lose ground to the forces of Islam. The Slavic Christian countries in the Balkans were overrun, as both Serbia and Bulgaria fell to the Ottoman Turks.

Russian churches such as those in KIEVAN RUS remained independent, however, and loyal to the Byzantine patriarch. At the end of the Middle Ages, the center of the Russian church moved north first to Vladimir, then Moscow. After Constantinople fell to the Turks in 1453, the Russians called Moscow the "third Rome," successor to ancient Rome and Constantinople.

The Roman Church

During the later Middle Ages, the Western Church became a powerful institution with its own government, laws, courts, and tax system. Its teachings and worship influenced everyone from king to peasant. Several waves of reform also brought considerable changes, leading up to the Protestant Reformation in the 1500s.

Growth of the Papacy. In 1073, the monk Hildebrand was elected Pope GREGORY VII. An able reformer who served several of the German reform popes who preceded him, Gregory threatened to excommunicate any emperor, king, prince, or other ruler who took it upon himself to appoint a bishop or any other church officer. Such appointments could only be made by the church.

* **Eucharist** Christian ritual commemorating Christ's Last Supper on earth, also called Communion

Split by a Word

The final schism between the Eastern and Western churches revolved around a single word: *Filioque.* Christians in the West, especially in Germany, were adding this word to the Christian creed or declaration of faith. It means "and the Son" in Latin and was held to reflect the equal nature of the Trinity, stating that the Holy Spirit resided in Christ as well as in God the Father.

The Eastern Church would not accept such a change in its ancient statement of faith. Although this may seem like a technicality, given the strong beliefs and tensions of the time, it caused the final break between the two churches, which had been coming for a long time.

* **Lateran**   referring to several councils of the Western Church, named from the Roman palace in which they originally took place

* **mendicant**   begging; depending on charity for a living

This action and other reform moves led to several crises in CHURCH-STATE RELATIONS. Gregory himself had a serious argument with German emperor Henry IV that led to a dramatic showdown at CANOSSA in 1077 and later resulted in an agreement called the CONCORDAT of Worms. At both places, it was Gregory who won the victory, at least in the short term.

The papacy continued to grow stronger in the 1100s and 1200s. It gained independence from control by the emperor and the Roman nobility by giving the College of CARDINALS responsibility for the election of new popes. The papacy also expanded the number of its agents, codified church law, deposed bishops and abbots, and developed a large papal court called the curia. In 1123, it called the first of a series of Lateran* Councils, the first church councils held in the West under the pope's authority.

Popes used their new power to wage war against the heretical CATHARS in southern France and to launch a series of crusades against the Turks in the Holy Land. They also started the INQUISITION, a special church court designed to deal methodically with HERESIES. By 1300, the papacy and its large curia had taken over administration of almost the entire Western Church. The papacy had become as powerful as any monarchy.

The Western Church also developed new types of religious orders. Earlier in the Middle Ages, life in a monastery or convent meant withdrawal from society. It revolved around prayer and hard work. However, during the crusades, orders of CHIVALRY were founded. Their members were medieval knights and monks at the same time. They followed a strict religious rule and also went into battle against nonbelievers.

In the early 1200s, new mendicant* orders of FRIARS emerged. FRANCISCANS traveled the countryside to help the poor, surviving on charity. DOMINICANS concentrated on preaching and teaching and set up schools in university and other towns. These friars also set up lay orders for men and women who wished to follow a religious life without taking full monastic vows. Other independent lay groups began to appear, including the BEGUINES AND BEGHARDS and later the Sisters and BRETHREN OF THE COMMON LIFE. Associated with these new groups was a growing tradition of Western mystics, prominent among whom were CATHERINE OF SIENA, Meister ECKHART, and St. BIRGITTA of Sweden.

The Great Schism and New Reformers.

In the 1300s and 1400s, European rulers challenged the political power of the papacy, and reformers once again called for changes in the way the church was governed. Kings objected to church courts that competed with royal courts. They resented papal interference in their political and personal affairs. They also saw how taxes on the large amounts of land the church owned went to Rome rather than to the royal treasury.

When King Philip IV of France tried to tax the French clergy, Pope BONIFACE VIII ordered the clergy not to pay the tax. In 1309, Philip engineered the election of a French pope, who moved the papacy to AVIGNON on the border of southern France. In 1377, Pope Gregory XI returned the papacy to Rome, but after his death the following year, the church faced a new problem when two new popes were elected, one in Avignon and one in Rome. This new crisis—called the Great SCHISM—lasted for 40 more years. During these scandals, the papacy lost some of its prestige and power. The spectacle of rival popes, each claiming to be head of the church, upset many Christians.

Church reformers saw councils as a way to counter papal power and respond to the widespread demand for effective change. In the early 1400s, councils at Pisa and Constance met to solve the problem of the Great Schism. Other councils were held at Pavia, Basel, and Florence, addressing such questions as reform of the papacy and reunification with the Byzantine Church. However, these councils did not satisfy a radical movement that criticized the church for its wealth and the worldliness of its clergy.

One of the most outspoken critics of church abuses in the 1300s was John WYCLIF, an English priest who taught theology at England's Oxford University. He questioned the authority of the church itself, claiming that the supreme religious authority was the Bible, not the church. The church condemned him as a heretic and persecuted his supporters.

In BOHEMIA, another priest, Jan HUS, a theologian at the University of Prague, preached against corruption in the church. He too declared that the Bible was a higher religious authority than the church and asserted that the state had both the right and the duty to supervise the church. In response, Hus was executed, and the pope authorized a crusade against Hus's supporters in Bohemia. Despite such severe punishments against those who criticized the church, calls for reform grew louder in the late Middle Ages. In the following century, Martin Luther changed the face of Western Christianity by ushering in the movement known as Protestantism.

Christine de Pizan

ca. 1363–ca. 1429
French author

* **patron** person of wealth and influence who supports an artist, writer, or scholar

Christine de Pizan was an influential writer at a time when there were few women writers. Born in Venice, Italy, she grew up in the court of France's King CHARLES V, for whom her father was a resident scholar. She became one of the best-educated women of her time. In 1379, she married Étienne du Castel, a secretary to the king.

Within a space of ten years, the king, Christine's father, and her husband all died. She was a widow at the age of 25, with a mother and three children to care for and no one to support her. She had to go to court to gain her inheritance. For comfort, she turned to study and writing.

Christine's earliest works were love poems, though she stated that she wrote them for her patrons* only; she herself still mourned her husband and father. Christine also wrote about religion, history, politics, and morality for men and women. One of her works describes her own life and urges sympathy for the plight of widows.

A major theme of her writing was the position of women in the Middle Ages. She wrote a book about famous women of the past and criticized the famous ROMAN DE LA ROSE for its negative view of women. In a late poem, she celebrated the victory of JOAN OF ARC. Christine wrote with wit on the prejudices of her day. A man said to her once that educated women were unattractive because there were so few of them. She retorted that ignorant men were even less attractive because there were

Christine de Pizan wrote on a variety of subjects. One of her major themes was the position of women during the Middle Ages. She is shown here presenting a book of her poetry to a patron.

so many of them. She was held in great esteem by her contemporaries, and her works were translated into several languages. (*See also* **French Language and Literature.**)

Chronicles

Chronicles were the histories written during the Middle Ages. They were based on many sources: retellings of past events and reports of current events, tales from distant places, and eyewitness accounts. Facts were often mixed with legend. Nevertheless, chronicles provide many vivid descriptions of life in the Middle Ages.

One of the earliest medieval chroniclers in western Europe was Isidore of Seville. Isidore lived in the early 600s, before the Muslim conquest of Spain. He wrote a history of the ruling VISIGOTHS and how they had become heirs to the Spanish part of the old Roman Empire. Though there is no proof that Isidore was a monk, other early historical writers, such as GREGORY OF TOURS and the venerable BEDE, wrote in a monastic setting. Gregory told the history of the French church, and Bede wrote a history of the Anglo-Saxons.

The church, and the BENEDICTINES especially, regarded history as important because it was the record of God's works. Monks had access to many books as well as the time to devote to assembling histories. Many sets of annals, year-by-year records of local and international events, were attributed to different monasteries. Many unnamed monks would contribute to these annals as the years went by.

In addition, named writers often compiled histories based on annals and other sources, including lives of saints, epic songs, historical traditions, and their own experiences. One important chronicler was Matthew of Paris, a monk who lived at the monastery of St. Albans in England. He wrote the *Chronica Majora* in the 1200s, describing events that took place across Europe in his lifetime. Matthew allows his own concern about the growing power of the monarchy to show through as he writes about politics.

* **abbey** monastery under the rule of an abbot or abbess

In France, the abbey* of St. Denis became a center of chronicle writing, as monks kept notes about historic events. From these notes developed the *Grandes Chroniques de France,* which became the official history of France. In Germany and Italy, where many cities were very independent, urban histories became important. These chronicles include the views of rich merchants and local rulers and provide fuller accounts of different levels of society than most other historical sources do.

A new kind of eyewitness chronicle appeared in the later Middle Ages, one written by nobles actually involved in important events. In the *Conquest of Constantinople,* Geoffrey de Villehardouin, the marshal of Champagne, tells about the Fourth Crusade. He was one of the crusade's leaders and supported the decision to attack Constantinople instead of Jerusalem. He weaves his own views into the chronicle and glorifies the decision as heroic.

See color plate 6, vol. 3.

Other authors wrote about important people they knew well. In the early 1300s, Philippe of Comines compiled his personal memories of King Louis IX of France during the Seventh Crusade, also known as the Crusade of Louis IX. Later in the same century, author Jehan Froissart, born in France, traveled extensively with England's Queen Phillipa of Hainaut, wife of Edward III. His account of the earlier part of the Hundred Years War between England and France includes his own descriptions of many important leaders on both sides of the long struggle.

Church-State Relations

In the eastern parts of the old Roman Empire, Roman civilization survived as the Byzantine Empire of the Middle Ages. Emperor Constantine I and his successors ruled over the Eastern Church, and its leaders, the patriarchs, were largely under his control. The West, however, had no similar overlord.

Barbarian invasions had forced the western part of the empire to collapse in the mid-400s. The Roman Church under the pope became the main symbol of Latin laws, learning, and traditions. This led to later contests for power between emerging local rulers and the popes and other Western bishops. At issue was the question of whose authority was greater—the spiritual authority of the church as represented by the pope or the secular* authority of the kings and emperors of the different states.

* **secular** nonreligious; connected with everyday life

In the Holy Roman Empire, which included both Germany and Italy, the contest was most severe. The empire had started when Pope Leo III

* **invest** to confirm someone in office by giving the robes and symbols of that office

crowned CHARLEMAGNE as Holy Roman Emperor of the West in 800, and emperors were usually crowned by popes. However, at times, the emperors tried to control the choice of later popes and the local bishops who headed the German church. When Pope Gregory VII finally asserted that the church should invest* its own bishops, Emperor Henry IV resisted. Thus began what has become known as the Investiture Controversy. Henry made his local bishops depose Gregory as pope, and Gregory excommunicated Henry. Henry finally gave in to Gregory at CANOSSA, Italy, in 1077, but the struggle continued until 1122, when the CONCORDAT of Worms was agreed upon.

In Italy, the issue was more complex because the popes were local rulers themselves, controlling land and wealth. The church-state conflict occurred at a regional level as towns and cities took different sides. Two parties, calling themselves GUELPHS AND GHIBELLINES (the Guelphs were supporters of the pope), developed. By the 1200s, lords and cities on both sides formed alliances, leading to intense conflict. The empire's struggles resulted in independence for cities in both Italy and Germany.

Church-state conflicts also occurred in England and France. King Henry II of England feuded with Thomas BECKET, archbishop of the English church, and Becket was murdered in Canterbury Cathedral in 1170. Henry was later forced to repent and come to an agreement with the church. In 1296, when France's Philip IV the Fair asserted a right to tax the church, Pope BONIFACE VIII responded by forbidding taxation of the church without papal permission. This led to the election of a new French pope, who left Rome and took up residence at AVIGNON on the French border.

Supporters of papal power in the later Middle Ages often used an argument called the doctrine of the two swords. Based on quotations from the Bible, the doctrine claimed that the pope had final authority over *both* church and state. The spiritual sword represented the pope's own religious authority over the church; the pope granted the secular sword, authority over a state, to other rulers.

In the 1300s, however, several important writers took the side of royal power. These included the poet DANTE and writers John of Paris and Marsilius of Padua. Their works anticipated the growth of royal power in Europe in the centuries that followed.

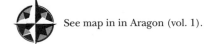

Cid, The

ca. 1043–1099
National hero of Spain

See map in in Aragon (vol. 1).

* **vassal** person given land by a lord or monarch in return for loyalty and services

The Cid was a Spanish Christian hero. His real name was Rodrigo Díaz de Vivar. He was known for his stormy relationship with King Alfonso VI of León and CASTILE and for his many victorious battles against the Muslims in SPAIN. His conquest of VALENCIA in 1094 halted Muslim expansion in the Spanish peninsula. At times, however, he fought *for* Muslim princes.

Rodrigo was already an admired general when Alfonso came to the throne. In fact, he had successfully fought against Alfonso for the previous king, Alfonso's brother Sancho. Fearing Rodrigo's enmity, King Alfonso made Rodrigo his vassal* and gave him his niece's hand in marriage. Alfonso also tried to stop Rodrigo from using his military talents, but in 1081

Rodrigo attacked a nearby Muslim fortress without the king's permission. Alfonso was furious and banished Rodrigo from his kingdom.

During his exile, Rodrigo offered his services to Muslim rulers in the eastern part of Spain, who were fighting among themselves and against the Christians of ARAGON and CATALONIA. It was there that he earned the name of the Cid, which comes from the Arabic word *sayyid,* meaning lord.

In 1086, a new Muslim threat developed in the south. The Almoravids, a fierce Muslim people from Morocco, crossed into Spain to help the kingdom of Seville against a combined Christian force led by Alfonso. Alfonso's army was destroyed, and he asked Rodrigo to return from exile. The two soon argued, however. In 1089, Rodrigo went back to his Muslim allies. Although he had to fight hard, he succeeded in regaining his former influence.

Alfonso continued battling the Muslims in the south. The Cid again helped him, but again they argued. In 1092, Alfonso planned an attack against the Cid, but he failed because of poor organization. He lost another army against the Almoravids. Rodrigo was the only Spanish leader the Muslims had not defeated.

In the same year, Almoravid sympathizers took the city of Valencia. Rodrigo laid siege to the city for two years, fighting off major Muslim relief efforts. After retaking Valencia, he ruled it himself as a Christian lord surrounded by Muslim kingdoms. He successfully defended the city several times against heavy Muslim attacks and never campaigned against Alfonso. The Cid remained undefeated until he died.

The Cid: The Myth and the Man

Minstrels throughout Spain sang "El cantar de mio Cid," an epic poem composed in the 1100s. In it, the two-year siege of Valencia ends dramatically with Rodrigo chasing the Muslim leader on horseback and then slaying him.

The reality was even more surprising, however. When the Muslim leader came to relieve the siege of Valencia, he was unable even to get near the city. The Cid had rechanneled waters intended for irrigating the fields and flooded all approaches to the city. He was helped in this endeavor by torrential rains.

Cistercians

* **habit** costume of a particular group, such as a religious order

* **scapular** long wide band of cloth with an opening for the head, worn front to back over the shoulders

Prompted by the reform papacy of GREGORY VII and a desire for a simpler life, the Cistercian order swept across western Europe in the 1100s. It began in 1098, when a French abbot and 21 of his monks left their rich abbey to start a new monastery on donated land. The word *Cistercians* comes from Citeaux, the name of the swampy forest in BURGUNDY where the monks built their monastery.

Cistercian monasteries were situated in isolated areas: forests, marshes, rocky places. The monks worked hard and lived simply, away from the distractions of society. They were called white monks because they wore a white habit* with only a black scapular*. By 1150, they had nearly 350 monasteries spread across Europe, from England to Austria and Scandinavia to Spain.

The white monks arrived on the scene at a time when Europe needed new agricultural land. They cleared wilderness by cutting trees and draining swamps. They grew crops, mined, made wine, and kept bees for honey. To carry out their work, the monks hired thousands of peasants for manual labor. Many peasants in Europe escaped poverty by becoming Cistercian lay brothers. At first, the order was against admitting women, but a number of Cistercian nunneries were founded in the 1200s.

Even though the Cistercian order was not committed to formal learning and education, Cistercians made important literary contributions during the Middle Ages. They wrote about the lives of saints, historical chronicles, and sermons for monastic audiences. The sermons, letters, and treatises of Cistercian BERNARD OF CLAIRVAUX helped make him a powerful religious influence in France. An English Cistercian named Ethelred of Rievaulx wrote works that were popular across Europe, especially his treatise *On the Soul* and a dialogue *On Spiritual Friendship*. Cistercians established colleges and universities in Paris, Oxford, Bologna, and elsewhere.

Cistercians were also practical administrators. Popes and kings employed them as ambassadors, judges, and missionaries. Many Cistercians became bishops. In 1145, a monk from Clairvaux became Pope Eugenius III.

By 1300, however, the Cistercian order was in decline. The HUNDRED YEARS WAR isolated Citeaux from its daughter houses. The BLACK DEATH wiped out more than half the monks. Because Cistercian houses were wealthy, powerful lords began to prey on them for their revenue.

Cities and Towns

During the Middle Ages, cities and towns changed dramatically. Ancient settlements were adapted to the needs of medieval life, and new towns sprang up as the paths of wealth and power shifted. At various times and places, some cities grew poorer while others blossomed. Perhaps most striking were the differences between towns and cities in Europe and those of the Islamic world.

Byzantine Cities and Towns

During the early Middle Ages, the cities of the BYZANTINE EMPIRE looked much like ancient Greek and Roman cities. CONSTANTINOPLE was the greatest city of the age, with a population of about 300,000. In the city center rose the vast domed church of Hagia Sophia, built by the emperor Justinian in the 530s. Nearby was the senate house and imperial palace. These great public buildings were all lavishly decorated in marble, mosaic, and fresco. They were the center of Constantinople's political life, which, like that of other Byzantine cities, was dominated by the church and the emperor. Broad boulevards radiated from the city's large central square, and churches and houses clustered together along streets lined with shops. Open squares served as marketplaces where artisans made and sold their wares.

Of course, not all Byzantine towns and cities were as grand and wealthy as Constantinople. Many were small and poor. Some ancient cities, such as Athens, had fallen into a state of decline. Others, such as Ephesus in ANATOLIA, became a blend of ancient and medieval building on a much less elaborate scale than Constantinople. The plan of ancient Ephesus remained, along with many of its great monuments. Because the medieval city was Christian, however, ancient temples fell into ruin and churches were built in their place. Some of the old public buildings were abandoned, and open spaces were often cluttered with poorly built structures.

Beginning in the 600s, Islamic invasions destroyed or severely damaged many Byzantine cities. As a result, a new type of urban life emerged.

Few medieval cities could match the wealth and splendor of Constantinople, the greatest city in Europe in the Middle Ages. It became a major trading port and a great religious and cultural center. This map of the city dates from the 1500s.

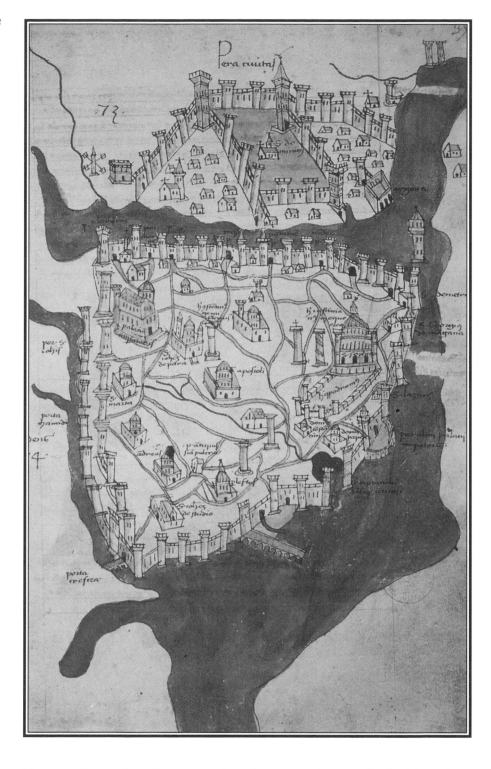

Most public services disappeared, and construction was limited largely to churches and fortifications. Some cities were reduced to mere fortresses. In others, houses and industrial buildings were densely huddled around a dilapidated cathedral. Byzantine towns and cities began to recover and expand somewhat in the late 800s and 900s, but they never recaptured the scale or grandeur of the earlier age. Few had the independence to improve their own situations. They relied on the central government of the empire.

* **crusader** person who participated in the holy wars against the Muslims during the Middle Ages

* **dynasty** succession of rulers from the same family or group

Although, for a time, Constantinople remained the greatest city in the world, its population probably expanding to more than 700,000, the city became increasingly shabby. Parts of it fell into ruin. New palaces and many new churches were built, but none were as magnificent as Hagia Sophia. Gradually, the city became more subject to western European influence, and crusaders* from the West conquered it in 1204. After that time, the city never recovered, even though the Byzantines recaptured it some 50 years later. Under the PALAIOLOGOS dynasty* of emperors, some magnificent new structures were built, but large parts of the city lay in ruins. By the time the OTTOMAN forces finally destroyed the walls, the city's population had dropped below 75,000.

Islamic Cities and Towns

The medieval Islamic world was largely a world of cities. Although the religion of Islam emerged in the desert, cities and towns became the centers of Islamic culture. Many new cities were created during the early centuries of Islam, including BAGHDAD in Iraq, CAIRO in Egypt, and CÓRDOBA in Spain. At its height, Cairo may have had 500,000 inhabitants. Baghdad's population was estimated at nearly a million.

Islamic cities and towns were often the seats of government and centers of religious learning. Military power was also based in cities. Agricultural produce flowed into the cities to feed the expanding population. Urban markets grew and the economy thrived, stimulating trade and industry. In general, cities throughout the Islamic Empire showed remarkable similarities, stemming from their shared religious and cultural traditions.

Mosques were a central feature of the Islamic city and served a number of public functions. In addition to being sites for prayer, they were all-purpose buildings in which worship, religious education, general administration, and public assembly took place.

Located next to the central mosque, the market served as a center of trade and manufacturing, as well as an area for public gathering and socializing. People from different parts of the city, along with merchants from many lands, could meet in the market. Islamic markets were organized according to trades and professions, with sellers of the same merchandise in adjacent stalls. Less prestigious occupations, such as tanning and dying, were located farther from the mosque than others. Many towns had inns and warehouses to accommodate merchants and their merchandise.

In most medieval Islamic cities, residential areas were separate from the marketplace. They were divided into neighborhoods made up of distinct family, ethnic, or religious groups. The primary cohesive forces in these cities were religion and family ties. Powerful ruling families and their military followers gave the city a sense of relative security. The rest of an individual's needs were provided for by the mosque, the market, and the family home.

Western European Cities and Towns

The ancient Roman towns and cities of western Europe were declining at the start of the Middle Ages as a result of barbarian invasions. Most shrank considerably in size and population. Later invasions such as those of the

VIKINGS in the 800s and 900s further damaged Europe's old urban culture. A more peaceful climate returned, however. The economy improved, cities began to flourish once again, and new towns sprang up. During the 1100s and 1200s, towns and cities experienced enormous growth and population increases. This revival reached its peak during the early 1300s, but then famine, plague, and war devastated western European towns. Urban life did not fully recover until the late 1400s.

The Early Middle Ages. Beginning in the 300s, Christianity had a profound influence on towns and cities. The cathedral was often the most important building. Close by was the bishop's palace. Monasteries generally were located in the suburbs, but early medieval towns also contained a large number of small parish churches.

* **Frankish** referring to the Germanic tribe called the Franks, who dominated western Europe in the early Middle Ages

The Frankish* kings and noble families of the MEROVINGIAN dynasty preferred to live in rural palaces and estates in the countryside. During the 600s and 700s, the church took over more and more urban land, and public property disappeared almost entirely. By the end of the period, many towns were controlled by bishops.

The intellectual life of the town also was controlled by the church through schools run by cathedrals and monasteries. During the later, CAROLINGIAN dynasty of the Franks, the Western Church further expanded its influence in towns. Larger churches were built, and more church schools and hospitals were established. The dynamic new cathedral quarter became the center of the town.

See color plate 1, vol. 1.

Then Vikings and other barbarians once again invaded western Europe. They burned towns, destroyed buildings, and ravaged the suburbs. As a result, towns and cities in the 900s strengthened their fortifications. Old Roman walls were restored, and new walls were built to protect the suburbs. Other aspects of the towns, however, were relatively unchanged. The church remained the largest landowner; in fact, the power of the church increased as monasteries also moved within the town walls to escape the barbarians.

The Later Middle Ages. As the era of invasion came to a close, various factors led to a period of urban growth in western Europe. Warmer weather and improved agricultural methods created more food, which could support larger urban populations. In the late 900s, important trade links began to develop between the Mediterranean towns of western Europe and Byzantine and Islamic markets. This burst of commercial activity stimulated the growth of Italian and Spanish towns such as Venice, Genoa, Pisa, and Barcelona. The CRUSADES against the Muslims and the foundation of Western "crusader states"* in the East also opened up new trade routes.

* **crusader states** states established in the East by Western Christians during the crusades. They included Jerusalem and Antioch.

By the late 1100s, large annual FAIRS were held in several towns in the Champagne region of France. At these fairs, products from northern Europe were exchanged for goods from the Mediterranean region. One of the most important products was cloth manufactured in such northern towns as Bruges, Ypres, and Ghent.

Economic recovery drew more people into towns and cities from the countryside, and urban populations expanded greatly. By 1300, towns such as Florence, Venice, and Milan had populations of more than 100,000 people. Paris may have had as many as 200,000. Though monks and clergy still made up a significant portion of the population, there were now many more merchants and artisans conducting their businesses.

New towns began to develop in this thriving economy, often at important crossroads or other favorable sites. Royal and noble patrons founded some of these towns because the founder of a town could gain control over a region, as well as profit from taxes paid by the town.

As urban populations increased, towns and cities gained intellectual and cultural importance. During the 1200s, UNIVERSITIES were established in some European towns, producing an educated elite who could assume leading roles in urban society. At about the same time, professional merchant or craft GUILDS began to dominate town life. Guild members sought to control the town government and achieve independence from bishops and local lords. Many towns adopted a more democratic, COMMUNE form of government.

A Time of Crisis.   The 1300s and 1400s were a period of crisis for western Europe. Overall, the urban growth of preceding centuries came to an end, though individual towns suffered in varying degrees. Towns began to organize into leagues and maintain armed militias. Violent conflicts sometimes erupted as urban groups struggled for control. In 1302, for example, tradespeople in the town of Bruges massacred French officials and their noble supporters. Similar revolts occurred in southern France during the 1300s. Some European towns were at odds with territorial princes. Others warred among themselves as urban leaders tried to expand their influence and bring smaller towns under their control.

The HUNDRED YEARS WAR also affected western Europe's urban environment. Towns and cities built up their fortifications. Monarchs raised town taxes to pay for the war. Internal urban violence and regional warfare took a toll on the economy. By the early 1300s, there were food shortages. Lack of transportation and poor methods of food preservation made it difficult to ship food or stockpile it. As a result, food prices rose. This caused great hardship, malnutrition, and even starvation for the urban poor. The health of urban populations weakened, leaving them vulnerable to disease.

The BLACK DEATH reached Europe in late 1347 and recurred at intervals throughout the 1300s and 1400s. Populations declined dramatically. Throughout western Europe, towns were abandoned as people died or fled to the countryside. A few towns, such as Rostock in north Germany and Milan in Italy, actually grew during the period, but these were in the minority.

However, while towns and cities lost much of their populations to the plague, their social and economic structure remained relatively unchanged. By the end of the 1400s, the great age of world exploration and discovery had begun. This led to economic recovery and population increase, and western European cities began entering the modern age.

Growth and Development of Cities and Towns

Medieval towns had many forms, shaped by such circumstances as history, geography, and economy. Each culture's customs led to a different type of town environment. Yet Byzantine, Islamic, and western European cities and towns also shared certain common elements.

See map in Black Death (vol. 1).

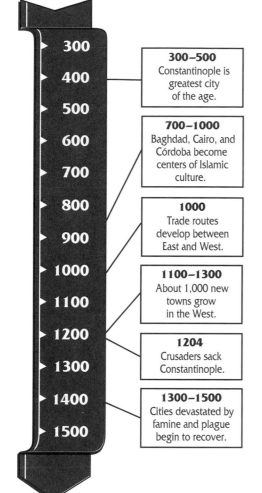

300–500
Constantinople is greatest city of the age.

700–1000
Baghdad, Cairo, and Córdoba become centers of Islamic culture.

1000
Trade routes develop between East and West.

1100–1300
About 1,000 new towns grow in the West.

1204
Crusaders sack Constantinople.

1300–1500
Cities devastated by famine and plague begin to recover.

Types of Cities and Towns. Some medieval towns developed from ancient towns of Roman or Greek origin that had been carefully planned and laid out. When they were threatened by invaders, these towns built defensive walls for protection. The new walls defined the limits of many towns for centuries to come. The wall and moat around Constantinople, for example, could hold up to a million people and resisted assault for 1,000 years.

Even within the walls of cities that fell to Muslim or Germanic invaders, many Roman and Greek buildings survived because they were too difficult to remove. New buildings were often erected on old foundations. Pathways continued to follow ancient streets. Ancient public buildings were fortified, or their materials were used to build other structures. Over time, the accumulation of rubble and debris raised the ground level and caused streets to narrow and curve. Yet, for the most part, these towns reflected the ancient patterns upon which they were established.

The new towns that developed during the early Middle Ages grew at favorable locations, such as an easily defended hilltop, a crossroads of major trade routes, or a river ford. For example, Southampton, in Britain, was built on the coast by the Anglo-Saxons as a trading town. Other towns grew up around castles, monasteries, or churches. Settlers built close to the existing buildings, which became the center of the town. Roads led from the town center like the spokes of a wheel, and most new development occurred along these spokes. Towns also developed on a linear plan, along a single street or road, such as a section of a major pilgrimage route. The focus of such towns was always the main street and its major crossroads.

Other new settlements were planned towns, built according to a specific design. In the Byzantine Empire, the city of Justiniana Prima was built in this way. It was located near the birthplace of the emperor Justinian and followed a plan similar to the ancient cities of the region, with broad squares and streets lined with columns.

Many Islamic rulers planned their own cities. Baghdad, for example, was founded by the reigning ABBASID dynasty in the 700s. Two hundred years later, the FATIMID dynasty established its authority in Egypt by building the city of Cairo.

In western Europe, town planning began in the 1100s. The most common plan for new European towns of the time was a rectangular grid. This plan varied in the number of intersecting streets, the number of blocks, the size of the area, and the amount and location of open space within the grid. Sometimes the plan was modified to suit the geography of the site. In most planned towns, streets were laid when the town was founded, but buildings were not erected until later. Among the earliest planned towns in western Europe was the BASTIDE Montauban in southwest France, which was established in 1144. During the next two centuries, close to 1,000 new towns were built in western Europe.

Basic Characteristics of Medieval Towns. All but the smallest towns were divided into neighborhoods, based on administrative or religious units, family ties, or ethnic or national background. In most middle-sized towns, there was a great mix of social classes within these districts, and rich and poor often lived side by side. In Europe, especially in the 1400s, Jews were often restricted to their own areas.

The houses of medieval towns were extremely varied. Their size, shape, plan, and building materials differed from region to region, depending on local customs and resources. In European towns, it was the custom for houses to front on the street, so most houses were narrow and deep. The width of a house was also limited by the size of available wooden cross beams. The upper floors of many houses were used as living areas and storage space. Kitchens were often placed at the top of the house to allow cooking smoke to escape and lessen the risk of fire. The ground floor might be used as a shop, workroom, or storage space, and it had its own street entrance. In Islamic cities, however, privacy and security were the residents' main concerns. Houses faced away from the street and toward inner courtyards. Residential streets were narrow and winding. This helped restrict access to the neighborhood.

Streets in medieval towns were used primarily by pedestrians. Wheeled traffic was usually restricted to a few wide, major streets. These streets were often lined with covered walkways that offered protection from rain and sun and provided space for shopkeepers to display their wares.

Open space was considered important. A variety of activities took place in streets and squares. Streets were used as processional routes, markets, front yards, and playgrounds, as well as thoroughfares. Squares served as markets, religious centers, courtrooms, meeting places, theaters, and military assembly grounds. In Ephesus, for example, the ancient squares were used in medieval times for the civic center and the marketplace.

Important buildings were usually set off by open space. In Europe, cathedrals, in particular, frequently had open space on several sides where people gathered for celebrations and other events. Aside from churches, the most important public buildings were often those that housed the civic government. Impressive town halls were built, beginning in the 1200s. Town halls and churches often occupied opposite sides of the main public square.

In Islamic cities, the mosque and market were built side by side. Placing the market at the center of the city was an Islamic innovation because pre-Islamic cities of the same regions did not have markets in the center of town. In the Islamic plan, both the mosque and the market became lively meeting places.

By the late Middle Ages, a shortage of open space forced some towns to regulate and protect those spaces that still existed. At the same time, they regulated such things as the heights of buildings, the widths of balconies, and the size and position of market stalls.

One of the basic characteristics of all medieval towns was the defensive wall. Wooden palisades or defenses of wood and earth were used early on, especially in northern Europe, where wood was readily available. Whenever possible, however, walls were built of stone or masonry because they were stronger and offered greater protection. Town walls were tall, continuous structures, marked by rectangular or semicircular towers and several sturdy gates. Up to the 1000s, the walls and towers were generally the tallest structures in the town.

Town life did not end at the walls. There was always a close relationship between town and countryside. Markets and other commercial activities sometimes concentrated outside city gates to avoid tolls required by

Remember: Consult the index at the end of Volume 4 to find more information on many topics.

town officials. Sanctuaries and monasteries were often located outside the town, as were mills, slaughterhouses, and tanneries. To isolate the sick, hospitals were set outside the walls of some towns. As a service to travelers, inns and hostels were built at town gates because the gates closed at sunset. (*See also* **Byzantine Architecture; Islamic Art and Architecture; Markets; Trade.**)

Classical Tradition in the Middle Ages

* **Hellenistic** referring to Greek history, culture, or art after Alexander the Great

* **scriptoria** workshops in which books were written or copied, decorated, and bound

* **pagan** word used by Christians to mean non-Christian and believing in several gods

* **Byzantine** referring to the Eastern Christian Empire that was based in Constantinople

Books and manuscripts do not last forever. Ancient Greek and Roman authors owe the survival of their works to medieval scholars in Europe and the Muslim world, who studied, copied, and translated them. Without these scholars, the thinking of ARISTOTLE and Ptolemy, the epics of Homer, the speeches of Cicero, the poetry of Virgil, and many other works, might be unknown today.

Ancient Greek literature flowered in Athens and the independent cities of Greece during the 400s and 300s B.C. It was treasured by the Hellenistic* world and by the Roman Empire that succeeded it. Writing and rhetoric were taught on the basis of the old Greek models, and libraries and scriptoria* made many copies of the works of famous authors. Alexandria in Egypt was the center of this tradition of learning. Rome supported the same practices and preserved its own authors as well. Saving classic works for study was felt to be vital to the education and humanity of citizens of the Roman Empire.

After the rise of Christianity and Islam, conflict was felt between the old pagan* studies and the new religions. During the Middle Ages, the value of ancient works was still generally accepted, but Christians argued that they were only the beginnings of a true Christian education.

This was the attitude of the Byzantine* emperors of Constantinople. After the fall of Rome (476) and of Alexandria (616), Constantinople was the main Christian heir to the Hellenistic tradition. Ancient Greek works were preserved, especially after Greek became the official language of the empire. Literature, philosophy, medicine, and other subjects remained popular though not always well understood. Especially in the 800s and 900s, many old manuscripts were copied and studied, and contemporary writers produced imitations and adaptations. Some of the manuscripts were brought to western Europe and translated into Latin, particularly after the Fourth Crusade in 1204, when crusaders from the West sacked Constantinople.

The Arabs, into whose hands Alexandria fell, also played an important part in preserving classical thought. Many of the manuscripts of Alexandria were taken to Syria, which, though in Arab hands, had a large Christian population. A tradition of translating these works into Arabic, especially the works on medicine, science, mathematics, and philosophy, grew up in the 800s and 900s. In fact, many texts lost in the original Greek have survived in Arabic translation. The translations had great influence on Muslim thought and were also passed on to western Europe through Muslim Spain during the 1200s and 1300s.

The western part of the old Roman Empire was far less able to preserve the old traditions once Rome had fallen to the Germanic tribes.

Latin survived as a language, but at first it was used largely for religion and reading the Bible. Only the papacy, and later the monasteries, guarded the traditions by preserving some of the ancient texts. Focus was less on the literature and thinking of the ancients, however, and more on the Latin language: its grammar, style, and vocabulary. Greek works were largely ignored, except for a few that had been translated into Latin.

Gradually, the tradition of learning in Latin developed among the rulers of the West, but it was not until the reign of CHARLEMAGNE around 800 that there was any real support for ancient learning outside the church. Earlier, Latin was most effectively studied in the religious houses of Ireland and England, notably by BEDE and by ALCUIN OF YORK.

The work of the Latin authors of Rome began to be valued. Cicero, the great Roman orator, was always popular; his work had been approved by St. AUGUSTINE as a model for persuasive speaking. Virgil, who wrote the Roman epic poem about Aeneas, the fall of Troy, and the birth of Rome, was studied for grammar. Virgil was also approved because one of his poems appeared to prophesy the birth of Jesus and became very popular during the 800s. Ovid, who wrote poems about myths and about love, was valued for his skill at poetry and for his ideas about love. His work was a major influence behind the tradition of courtly love and reached its peak of popularity in the 1100s. However, it was not until the following century that contact with the Byzantine and Islamic worlds brought the full influence of Greek science and philosophy into western Europe. (*See also* **Alchemy; Astrology and Astronomy; Medicine; Plato in the Middle Ages.**)

Clement VI, Pope

ca. 1291–1352
Pope, monk,
and theologian

See map in Black Death (vol. 1).

Clement VI was one of the AVIGNON popes. Born Pierre Roger, he became a monk, a theologian, and an admired preacher. He was archbishop of Rouen and chancellor to King Philip VI of France before he was elected pope in 1342. Clement had the difficult job of being pope during the BLACK DEATH.

Charming, generous, and interested in helping people, Clement had as his main goal making the papal court the most magnificent court in Europe. With a financial surplus left by his predecessor, Pope Benedict XII, he bought the town of Avignon from the queen of Naples and finished building a new papal palace. He also lent large sums of money to the French king and nobles.

Clement tried unsuccessfully to end the HUNDRED YEARS WAR. He was unable to restore order in Italy, where unrest prevented the popes from returning to Rome until 1377. However, he managed to arrange a European naval alliance that cleared the eastern Mediterranean of Turkish pirates.

When the Black Death struck in 1347, Clement urged priests and doctors to help the sick and dying. He provided land so the dead could be buried more quickly and took action to prevent the further spread of the plague. Many Jews were blamed for the Black Death and killed by Christians, but Clement sheltered Jews at Avignon and in the PAPAL

* **excommunicate** to exclude from the rites of the church

STATES, excommunicating* anyone who caused them harm. He also suppressed a growing anti-Jewish group in Swabia who called themselves flagellants. This group urged people to whip themselves for 33 days (a day for each year of Jesus' life) in order to purify their souls.

* **ordain** to bless, dedicate, and appoint to a particular level of the clergy. Ordination is performed by a bishop in the Roman Catholic and Eastern Orthodox Churches.

* **sacrament** religious ceremony of the Christian church, considered especially sacred, such as Communion and baptism

I n the Christian religion, clergy are those who have been ordained* to organize and conduct church services and perform other religious rites for believers. There were three levels of clergy in the early church: bishop, priest (or presbyter), and deacon. Bishops were in charge of all the churches in a city or district; priests ran the individual churches and conducted sacraments* and other services; deacons were the assistants.

Five other levels were soon added: subdeacon, acolyte, exorcist, lector, and porter. At first, these positions were all considered vital jobs; for example, the exorcist brought holy water to priests at the altar and also expelled devils. Soon these jobs were regarded merely as stages of apprenticeship through which future clergy had to pass.

Qualifications.   In addition to having passed through the minor orders, people who wanted to join the clergy had to meet other requirements. Candidates had to be male; women were not allowed to be clergy. In the early church, deaconesses and widows had performed minor duties, and during the Middle Ages some women, especially heads of convents, preached and heard confessions. However, popes and church councils tried their best to curb the practice.

* **celibacy** state of being unmarried

By the beginning of the Middle Ages, there was a celibacy* rule, which differed in the East and the West. In the Eastern (Byzantine) Church, clergy could not marry after they joined a major order, but those already married were allowed to remain married. However, because bishops had to practice abstinence*, only unmarried clergy became bishops. In the West, bishops, priests, deacons, and subdeacons had to be celibate. A married candidate had to give up his wife to enter the clergy.

* **abstinence** avoidance of certain pleasures and activities, such as marriage

Bishops had to be at least 30 years old. The age limit for other members of the clergy varied: by the end of the Middle Ages, priests had to be 25, deacons had to be 20, and subdeacons had to be 18. The five minor orders were open to children, the only requirement being that the children had to be at least 7 years old.

Candidates were automatically disqualified if they had not been baptized or if they had certain kinds of what the church called "irregularities." These included illegitimate birth, physical handicaps, mental illness, and bigamy (being married to two or more people at the same time). A person was also disqualified for the commission of murder or other serious crimes, the mutilation of self or others, or attempting suicide.

Ordination.   The service of entrance into one of the levels of clergy was called ordination. The bishop cut a lock of hair from the candidate (called tonsure) and presented him with a surplice (church gown) and objects to symbolize his new duties. The porter, who rang the church bells and opened the doors of the church, for example, was given keys.

* **cruet** altar vessel for wine or water

The exorcist received the collection of formulas to cast out evil spirits. The acolyte—who carried candlesticks in the church procession, lit them on the altar, and brought bread and wine to the altar for the Mass—was given candlesticks and a cruet*. The deacon received his robes and book of Gospels, while the bishop was given his crozier (staff), ring, and miter (bishop's headdress).

Privileges and Obligations.   Clergy had some special legal protections during the Middle Ages. Anybody who hit a member of the clergy was punished with EXCOMMUNICATION, a sentence only the pope could forgive. A judge could not order a member of the clergy who was in debt to give up everything he owned; he was allowed to keep at least some of his income and property for living expenses. Also, clergy had to be tried in a church court. They could not be summoned before a lay court or condemned by a lay judge.

Another privilege was exemption from certain political and financial responsibilities. Clergy did not have to serve as magistrates or house troops on the march or pay taxes. Exceptions were made, however, if the clergy's talents were needed. During the MEROVINGIAN and CAROLINGIAN periods, the king called on the clergy to perform public duties because of their superior education.

The main obligations of the clergy were to look after believers and to recite the DIVINE OFFICE, either by themselves or with others. They did not live as strictly as monks, unless they *were* monks (which was possible). Clergy were not required to dress in any special way: the only requirement about the way they looked was the tonsure. However, they had to dress neatly; live decent, honest lives; and avoid anything that might shame the church. They were not allowed to gamble, hunt, join the military, perform surgery, go to the theater, or conduct business. (*See also* **Christianity.**)

Climate, Influence on History

Most historians believe that climate had an effect on the events of the past. Medieval society depended greatly on agriculture and trade, which were affected by local weather. Few historians would question that bad weather usually affected the economy. The extent of the influence, however, is hotly debated. Some historians hold that existing evidence can support only local short-term effects of the weather. Others argue that some major trends in history may have resulted from changes in climate. For example, they link the westward movements of the Turks and the MONGOLS into Syria, Anatolia, and eastern Europe to a growing dryness throughout central Asia. They associate the flourishing of western Europe between the 800s and 1200s with a warming trend in the weather there.

Two questions arise: how can we determine what the weather was like in the past, and how can we tell whether effects were due to the climate or to other events and trends that might have taken place at the same time?

Until recently, evidence about the weather in the Middle Ages came largely from CHRONICLES and other local historical records. Attempts to show that long-term weather patterns caused major trends in history were very controversial, viewed as interesting ideas and nothing more.

Recent scientific research techniques, often involving data from plant remains, have recently added to evidence about ancient climatic conditions. Plants respond to changes in weather. The techniques used include the study of tree rings, the study of links between climate and old records of plant flowering and harvest times, and the study of pollen and plant remains found in peat marshes in different areas. Radiocarbon dating can estimate the age of such materials by measuring how much they have decayed. Plotting the advance and retreat of glaciers also yields valuable information.

As a result of these techniques, data now being collected support the idea of broad changes in climate. According to this evidence, Asia did have an overall warming and drying trend in the early Middle Ages. Western European weather north of the Alps remained abnormally cold and wet until about 750, after which time it also became warmer and drier. This caused droughts in the Mediterranean area but led to better agricultural conditions in northern Europe. Then Europe's weather turned colder and wetter again between 1200 and 1350 and did not improve significantly for the rest of the Middle Ages.

How much these climate changes affected major trends in history is still open to interpretation, however. Though the center of European prosperity did move north between 750 and 1200, many other events were occurring at the same time, including the development of feudalism*. Similarly, there was a rural crisis in Europe after 1200, but other factors, including the Black Death, certainly contributed to this.

One important movement does seem to owe its progress to the weather, however. The westward voyages of the VIKINGS, to Iceland, Greenland, and Newfoundland, could not have taken place before the European warming trend because ice floes in the Atlantic blocked shipping lanes. Similarly, the end of the occupation of Greenland coincided with renewed bad weather in the North Atlantic. (*See also* **Agriculture; Feudalism.**)

* **feudalism** the social, economic, and political system of western Europe in the Middle Ages in which vassals gave service to their lord in return for his protection and the use of the land

Clocks and Reckoning of Time

Timekeeping in the early Middle Ages was a complex task. It was usually based on hours of daylight; the period of daylight was divided into 12 units, and thus the length of an hour differed in summer and winter and according to latitude. Hours were important for religion because prayers had to be said not only at dawn and dusk but also at various times in between. These variable hours were often called canonical hours. Other activities, such as military schedules and the meetings of law courts, were also linked to time of day. For most people, however, the exact time was not important because they worked alone or labored together as groups for most of the day.

For people who needed to keep track of time, sundials and water clocks were the principal means of doing so, though marked candles and sand glasses were also used. In the later Middle Ages, progress in clock making led to the development of the mechanical clock, which gradually became more accurate and less cumbersome. While more and more people came to depend on clocks and timekeeping, however, the vast majority did not need accurately planned schedules until the Industrial Revolution.

Sundials.   Sundials, used in the Roman Empire and even earlier, remained an important method of telling time in the early Middle Ages. They were adopted from the Roman and Byzantine world both by Muslims and by western Europeans. Islamic scholars developed and described many improved timekeeping devices. The earliest surviving Muslim sundial was made for the sultan of Syria in the 1100s. Portable sundials not only indicated the time for prayers but also pointed out the direction of Mecca so that Muslims could face the holy city when they prayed. Such sundials were closely related to astrolabes*, which were also used to tell time.

The earliest sundials in western Europe were more primitive. Called scratch dials, they were simply half circles scratched on the southern wall of a church. Hour lines radiated from a central rod, the shadow of which showed the hour. Scratch dials existed in England as early as 670. Later, they were created on slabs of stone, built into a tower for visibility.

Water Clocks.   Water clocks were another timekeeping device used in the Roman Empire. A water clock had a slowly filling water chamber that contained a float. The float was attached to a cord that ran over an axle to a counterweight. As the float rose with the water level, the counterweight dropped and the axle turned. The length of an hour could be altered by adjusting the water flow.

In some water clocks developed in the Muslim world, the axle was linked by gears to a visual indicator such as an adjustable model sun. In western Europe, however, clocks were at first simpler. They were most commonly used to operate an alarm bell to awaken one of the monks and start the day. A medieval manuscript from an Italian monastery describes a device in which the counterweight that turned the axle also struck a series of small bells hanging from a rod. The alarm had to be reset every time it was used.

Demand for these clocks grew quickly. By 1183, there was a guild for water-clock makers in the German city of Cologne. The only known picture of a European medieval water clock appears in a French manuscript from about 1285. This clock is quite elaborate, with a large water-powered wheel divided into 15 parts.

In 1198, a water clock played a part in a fire at the English abbey of Bury St. Edmunds. The fire started on a wooden platform holding a shrine of St. Edmund. When the clock sounded for morning prayer, a monk arose and saw the flames. He called out in alarm, and his fellow monks ran for water—some to the well and some to the clock—to put out the fire.

Mechanical Clocks.   A mechanical clock was built in China in 979 for one of the emperors, and some historians believe this was the model for mechanical clocks that were made in Europe some 300 years later. However, there is little evidence of other clocks in China and none of any along the trade routes. The first European clocks are described not in eastern Europe or in the trading centers of Italy but in the far west.

* **astrolabe** instrument used to observe and calculate the position of heavenly bodies, to navigate, and to tell time

The oldest known mechanical timepiece in Europe is the clock made for the tower in Salisbury Cathedral in England. It dates from the 1200s.

* **priory** small monastery or convent headed by a prior or prioress

* *jaquemart* large mechanical figure on the top of an old public clock that strikes a bell on the hour

The earliest descriptions of mechanical clocks in Europe were in England. A clock was erected in a priory* in Bedfordshire in 1283. Within ten years, similar clocks were reported at the Norwich Cathedral priory, the Benedictine abbey in Cambridgeshire, and Merton College, Oxford. New mechanical clocks were also built at Exeter Cathedral, Christ Church Cathedral in Canterbury, and St. Paul's Cathedral in London. The first public clock in Europe was installed on a church tower in Milan in 1309. Shortly afterward, clocks were displayed in public places in Padua, Modena, and other Italian cities. These Italian clocks often announced the time through use of bells and *jaquemarts**.

One of the most elaborate mechanical clocks was constructed between 1348 and 1364 by Giovanni de' DONDI, an Italian physician and professor at the University of Padua. It was a large brass machine with iron gears and many dials, including one for the rising and setting of the sun.

By the end of the Middle Ages, clock makers had achieved a high level of craftsmanship. Clock making required careful precision, which opened the way for the invention of new mathematical instruments. Such instruments, and more accurate timekeeping, made it possible for explorers to determine their position at sea. (*See also* **Astrolabe; Calendars; Divine Office; Islam, Religion of.**)

Clothing

Clothing styles differed greatly during the Middle Ages, across regions as well as through time. They were affected by climate, by religion, by requirements of work, and by the influence of other cultures. In general, the styles grew from older traditions: the tunics of Greece and Rome, the turbans and robes of Persia and Arabia, the heavier leggings and collared cloaks of the Germanic tribes of northern Europe. Fashion ideas and fabrics also flowed along the trade routes from India and China.

These influences led to a great profusion of styles. People could often tell at a glance where a person was from and usually the person's occupation as well. Resident foreigners from distant areas were likely to wear clothes similar to those of the host community, though they were frequently required to show some distinguishing marks.

In rural areas, the variety of styles might have appeared limited. In great trading cities such as Constantinople, Cairo, and Venice, however, an abundance of fashions would have been visible as people from all cultures of the medieval world did business together.

See
color plate 3,
vol. 3.

Byzantine Clothing. The cities of the BYZANTINE EMPIRE, and especially Constantinople, directly inherited the traditions of ancient Rome. The basic garment design was still the Greco-Roman tunic—long for women and officials, cut off at the knee for soldiers and workingmen. The Byzantines also inherited the Romans' heavy involvement in trade, and they had contact with distant cultures. Through Persia, for example, they had access to the silks of the Far East. Finally, they were also influenced by the dress of the barbarian tribes to the north, where jewelry was popular and where colder climates had led to the development of heavy trousers, sleeves, and collars.

These influences meant that Byzantine garments were increasingly made of luxurious materials and rich colors. Hems were often lined with elaborate embroidery and studded with gems and pearls. Men wore their tunics over Persian-style leggings. Women wore garments with softer lines and richly embroidered collars and hems. They also nearly always wore veils and headdresses: either simple cowls or, for special occasions, gem-studded turban crowns.

The most spectacular Byzantine clothing was the formal costume of the emperor and empress when presiding over their court. They wore gold, tight-sleeved long tunics, and over them shorter, loose-fitting tunics of gold or purple. In the 1200s, the emperor replaced the outer coat with a black garment called a sakkos, traditionally worn by priests, emphasizing his religious role. Over the entire outfit, the emperor and empress wore the Byzantine *loros:* a long strip of cloth (usually linen) richly embroidered and studded with gems, pearls, and enamel, wound over and around the shoulder. The emperor draped one end over his arm like an ancient Roman toga; the empress would wear it tapering down to her right ankle. Their headdresses were also a classic Byzantine type, a crested and enameled crown, ornately decorated with gold and with clusters of pearls hanging to shoulder length.

Priests wore a simple, long, straight-sleeved tunic, over which they wore either a sakkos or an even looser black cloak that was made like a poncho. For church leaders, this cloak was often studded with embroidered crosses. By the 1300s, other robes signified higher positions in the church. Around the neck, the patriarch* wore a richly embroidered stole, sewn together down the front to create a single ornate panel. Bishops wore a dramatic scarf with crosses at the ends, on the shoulders, and at the neck. Priests were bareheaded, but monks had heavy hooded black robes, and nuns wore black robes and tight-fitting headcloths.

Foreigners living in the Byzantine Empire usually wore clothing similar to that of the natives. Often, however, the clothes had distinguishing marks. For example, there were several specifically Jewish details of dress. One such detail was the "show fringe," or zizith, which had a special religious significance. In the early Middle Ages, the fringes were sewn on the corners of large cloaks. Later they were attached instead to prayer shawls and even smaller items of clothing.

Islamic Clothing.   Medieval Islamic clothing adopted features from three different areas: pre-Islamic Arabia, Greece and Rome, and the central Asian regions of Persia and the Turkish peoples. The original Arabs of Mecca were traders and already wore turbans and probably some Eastern-style robes. However, early Muslim thought of the 700s and 800s discouraged luxury. More than in any other Mediterranean culture, clothing was viewed mainly as a means of hiding the shame of nakedness and promoting modesty and piety.

The basic early Islamic outfit consisted of an undergarment; a body shirt, covered by a tunic; and then an overgarment, either a mantle, a coat, or a light wrap, depending on the season. Clothing became more luxurious and ornate as wealth accumulated. The UMAYYAD caliphs* of the early 700s began to wear finer clothes, silk robes, and splendid white royal garments. The ABBASID caliphs, who replaced the Umayyads in 750 and ruled from Baghdad for more than 500 years, chose black for their royal robes, but their clothing was just as rich and finely decorated.

Developing textile technology and the many fabrics available in Arab lands during the Middle Ages spawned an industry in finely embroidered fabric, or *tiraz,* from which magnificent robes and garments were produced. One of the most common, and most decorative, embroidered garments was the robe of honor. It usually bore embroidered or woven inscriptions with the name of the ruler or vizier* and other information about the making of the robe, along with quotations from Islamic texts.

In the period from 800 to 1000, under the Abbasids, Baghdad was greatly influenced by Persia. Several Persian garments became popular, such as a tall conical hat called the *qalansuwa* and the caftan, a fine robe with long sleeves and buttons down the front. Clothing styles were also introduced from distant cultures with which the Arabs traded—for example, a long sarilike shawl from India and a sturdy raincloak from China.

Muslims had always covered their heads out of modesty and respect; this was already the tradition in Arabia by the time of Muhammad. Women wore simple head coverings and veils. Turbans, worn by men, became more complex as the Middle Ages progressed; by the 1100s, they consisted

* **patriarch** head of one of the five major centers of early Christianity: Alexandria, Antioch, Constantinople, Jerusalem, and Rome

* **caliph** religious and political head of an Islamic state

* **vizier** Muslim minister of state

Clothing in the Byzantine Empire was derived from the tunics of Greece and Rome. Women and officials wore long tunics. Soldiers and workers had tunics cut off at the knee.

Medieval Islamic clothing incorporated styles from Greece, Rome, and pre-Islamic Arabia. The turban, known as "the badge of Islam," became an important article of clothing in Islamic society.

One popular item of European clothing in the 14th and 15th centuries was the houppelande, a loose outer garment worn by both men and women. It was tied at the waist for men, and higher for women.

Byzantine Clothing

Islamic Clothing

Western European Clothing

of one or two caps wrapped in a winding cloth. Known as "the badge of Islam" *(sima al-Islam),* the turban became one of the most important and characteristic articles of clothing in Islamic society.

No Muslim dynasty* was more concerned about clothing than the FATIMIDS, who ruled an empire centered in Egypt from 909 to 1171. Every official, from the caliph down to simple clerks, wore ceremonial costumes for public occasions. These were supplied by an official bureau. Later dynasties, the SELJUKS, AYYUBIDS, and MAMLUKS, began to wear garments introduced by the Turkish military. Among these were a stiff cap with a triangular front called a *sharbush* and a coat called a *qaba* with ample sleeves and a diagonal closing across the chest. The length of the sleeves indicated rank or social status. When the OTTOMAN Turks conquered the eastern Arabs in the 1500s, there was no abrupt change in costume in the Islamic world.

A significant influence on Islamic dress was the Muslim law of *ghiyar,* or differentiation. This law required non-Muslims to be identified and separated from Muslim society. They were forbidden to wear Arab-style headgear or garments that might be associated with the army or the nobility. Christians also had to wear a special outer belt, a *zunnar,* and any non-Muslim who wore garments popular among the Muslim population had to attach some distinguishing mark to them or wear only certain colors.

Jews adopted many Islamic garments, properly modified, as their own. They wore a special *tiraz* robe of honor, which had Jewish rather than Islamic inscriptions. The tall *qalansuwa* hat was also worn, though with distinguishing buttons attached to it front and back. Turbans were also adopted, but they had to be dyed a honey color, matching the mantles that Jews were allowed to wear. Jewish dress in Egypt during the Fatimid, Ayyubid, and Mamluk periods was as rich and varied as that of the ruling Muslims. However, from the mid-1200s on, the Muslim world became less tolerant, more interested in humbling unbelievers and in converting them, and more insistent that the law of *ghiyar* be strictly enforced.

Western European Clothing.   For the people of western Europe, both men and women, clothing had great social significance. Unlike members of early Christian and Islamic society, the barbarian tribes of Europe had no hesitation about wearing finery. They quickly adapted to Roman clothing, but they retained their own prized adornments—heavy jewelry and warm furs. The church disapproved of vain clothing and managed to control clothing finery to an extent, especially during the early medieval period. Later, however, people began to wear the finest clothing they could afford. Rich people bought fine textiles, lustrous colors, and splendid jewels, and poorer people created holiday costumes that were as artful as their wealth or the law allowed.

Until about the year 1000, clothing remained largely under the influence of Roman and barbarian Germanic styles. Harsh weather in western Europe led to outfits that included layered short tunics and ample cloaks, sometimes made of fur. Men would typically wear trousers or leggings. Women wore long, flowing dresses called kirtles that concealed the lines of the figure, with a shawl covering the head and most of the face. Courtiers of both sexes had elegant floor-length tunics with borders of embroidery or fur. Because they traveled from one court to another, their styles became increasingly similar, whatever area they were from.

* **dynasty** succession of rulers from the same family or group

See color plate 1, vol. 1.

* **sumptuary** regulating expenses, especially to control extravagance or waste

* **scarlet** fine wool that took red dye so well that its name became the name of the color

Sumptuary Laws

At various times in the Middle Ages, laws were passed regulating what people could or could not buy. These were called sumptuary laws, and many of them pertained to clothing.

Sumptuary laws usually applied to certain groups of people. Not only were foreigners, such as Jews, singled out. The laws could also apply to certain classes of natives. For example, a Portuguese law in 1340 forbade people who lacked "the wealth to possess horses" to buy furs and jewelry. This prevented poorer people from passing themselves off as aristocrats.

Fashions at this time might change as a result of a spectacular event, such as a particular royal marriage or famous entertainment. Changes were relatively slow, however, and involved detail—for example, the styles of sleeves or shoes—rather than radical changes of line. Simple styles remained popular until the later 1200s, partly because of sumptuary* laws and edicts issued by the church. There were also class-conscious power centers in society, such as the GUILDS, which also urged restraint in clothing.

However, another force, acting in the opposite direction, had begun to influence fashion. There was a general expansion of European trade in the 1000s, and this was enhanced by the CRUSADES to the Holy Land in the 1100s and 1200s. Merchants and crusaders brought silk and other fine textiles back to western Europe, and the people were clearly impressed by the craftsmanship and decoration of the Muslim and Byzantine clothing. The accumulating wealth and power of the aristocratic and merchant classes enabled them to buy more elaborate styles and more luxurious clothing.

Change first occurred in the fabrics that were used for clothing. Both men and women began to wear garments of damask, a fine decorated silk from Damascus, or of baldekin, a silk-gold mix from Baghdad. Other new fabrics included cloths of silver and gold, velvet, and scarlet*.

Sleeve styles also began to change more rapidly, from short to long, from frilled to pleated, with different types of cuffs. Garments were even made with detachable sleeves so that styles could be changed. New color schemes became popular. One surprising combination was called *mi-parti*, with fabrics of different colors to the left and to the right. The left leg might be patterned, for example, and the right leg plain or dotted. Heraldic coats of arms also began to be worn, identifying the wearer's class, religion, craft or profession, and geographic origin. Such clothing also showed a man's ancestry or his employer.

In the early 1300s, clothing styles for men and women started to change quickly and to show great variety. Men's garments, particularly, were shaped to show off the body. National styles also developed, as fashions caught on in some countries but failed in others. Nobles began to rush to their tailors and dressmakers to keep up with fashion. Fortunes began to be made, and lost, in the apparel industry.

In the late 1300s, a typical garment was the houppelande, an elaborately pleated robe with padded shoulders and of variable length. The houppelande was belted at the waist for men and above the waist for women. In the Low Countries in the early 1400s, this gave way to the pourpoint, a close-fitting shirt with buttons down the front and a pinched-in waist to accentuate the shoulders. This was worn with even closer-fitting tights.

The pourpoint was often accompanied by one of the most extreme shoe styles of the Middle Ages, called poulaines because the shoes were thought to have originated in Poland. These were soft leather shoes with extremely long toes. The tips protruded so far that, for safety, they had to have straps or even gold chains attached so they could be tied to the shins or thighs.

Everyone of every age wore hats indoors and out. Hoods, particularly, had always been popular head coverings. By the 1400s, they were designed with very specific emblems or decoration that signified social status. There were many unusual hat styles. The turbanlike chaperon was worn by men. Another turban-based construction was the woman's butterfly headdress, in which a transparent fabric was gracefully draped over a stiff frame pinned to her hair. Men could also wear tall brimless hats that looked like a Turkish fez. For women, there were tall cone-shaped hats of fine fabric, with a single point or a horned top. These hats were often worn with a long, sheer veil that hung from the peak to the shoulders, waist, or even the ankles. Given to a beloved as a favor or token of affection, the veil was worn on a soldier's armored helmet.

Hats were also significant to Jews in western Europe. Between the years 500 and 1200, Jewish dress was not very different from that of their Christian neighbors, though anti-Jewish feeling sometimes identified ostentatious clothing as typically Jewish. The most distinctive article of Jewish clothing was probably the blunt-pointed *Judenhut* (Jewish hat). At the Fourth Lateran Council of 1215, it was decreed that Jews and Muslims "of both sexes in every Christian province and at all times shall be distinguished . . . by the character of their dress." In France, Jews were required to wear a circular badge on their outer garments. In England, the badge took the form of a yellow taffeta cloth cut to resemble the tablets of the Ten Commandments. In Germany, the *Judenhut* was often the required marker. (*See also* **Armor; Cosmetics and Beauty Aids; Family; Fur Trade; Jewish Communities; Leather and Leatherworking; Silk; Social Classes; Textiles; Trade; Wool.**)

Clovis

ca. 465–511
Frankish king

* **Gaul** Roman name for the area that became France

* **romanized** influenced by and accepting the culture of the Roman Empire

See map in Migrations, Germanic (vol. 3).

Clovis united the Franks and expanded their rule to cover a large part of Europe. When his father died in 481, he became one of several Frankish kings who ruled in northeastern Gaul* and the Rhineland area of Germany. He was surrounded by potential enemies: Franks, romanized* Celts, the ALAMANNI, the Burgundians, and the VISIGOTHS. Clovis began to eliminate rival Frankish kings by force and treachery. He defeated Syagrius, the nearby ruler of the Christian Celts, which gave him control of most of northeast Gaul. He strengthened his position with the Celts by marrying a Christian princess of BURGUNDY in 493. Three years later he became a Christian himself.

Clovis's gains antagonized his neighbors, the warlike Alamanni. He crushed them at the Battle of Tolbiac in 506, and they accepted him as their king. It was said that Clovis prayed to the Christian God for victory. The next year he fought the Visigoths, longtime enemies of the Franks in the Loire valley, and won a decisive victory at Vouillé, near Poitiers.

Clovis's new kingdom was now overwhelmingly Celtic and Christian in population. This fact reinforced the role of the church and weakened the pagan Germanic element in the Frankish kingdom. Clovis marked the change by moving his principal place of residence to PARIS. As a Christian king, he gave gifts to churches and encouraged the growth of monasteries; he also probably encouraged the composition of the Frankish code of law. When he died, he divided his empire among his four sons, beginning the MEROVINGIAN dynasty of Frankish rulers.

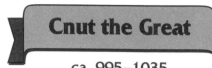

Cnut the Great

ca. 995–1035
King of England and Denmark

For a short while in the early 1000s, ENGLAND was part of the Danish Empire. Denmark had already settled lands in the English north during the 800s, but these had slowly been recaptured by sons of King ALFRED THE GREAT. Then Danish king Sweyn Forkbeard, with his son Cnut, mounted another successful attack, and Alfred's grandson Ethelred fled to NORMANDY. In 1014, Cnut was declared king of all England by the Danish forces. The English, too, accepted Cnut as their king after Ethelred and his son Edmund died in 1016.

Cnut the Great, king of Denmark, was also king of England from 1016 to 1035. He allowed the English people to continue to observe their own laws. He is shown here placing a gold cross on a church altar.

* **earldom** division of a kingdom that was usually ruled by an earl

* **royal domain** area of a kingdom that the king ruled directly, compared to lands granted to dukes or earls

Cnut divided England into four earldoms*: Northumbria and East Anglia, which had been under Danish law before, and Mercia and Wessex, which had just been conquered. Wessex became Cnut's royal domain*; he turned over the other areas to his leading supporters. To prevent action by Ethelred's heirs or by the Normans, he married Ethelred's widow, Emma of Normandy, and he allowed people in Mercia and Wessex to continue observing English laws. He also supported the English church with very generous endowments.

When Cnut's brother Harald died, Cnut became king of Denmark also, but he continued to rule from England. He introduced ideas to Denmark he had learned in England: for example, a system of coinage based on the English system, and English practices to follow in the Danish church. Rivals from SCANDINAVIA tried to drive Cnut from power in 1026, but he defeated them, adding parts of Sweden and Norway as well to the Danish Empire. Cnut died in 1035, and his sons briefly succeeded him. After his second son died childless, Ethelred's son EDWARD THE CONFESSOR inherited the English throne.

Cologne

 See map in Holy Roman Empire (vol. 2).

During the Middle Ages, Cologne grew into a major medieval religious, cultural, and economic center, one of the most important cities in the HOLY ROMAN EMPIRE. From the 900s, it was ruled by a series of German archbishops, who controlled city affairs. In addition, these archbishops were church leaders who became involved in electing and crowning the king of Germany. During the next 500 years, however, groups of merchants and the craft GUILDS increased in power and gained control of Cologne, making it the largest of all the independent cities of Germany.

Once an old Roman city on the Rhine River, Cologne declined after the FRANKS invaded it in the 400s. Destroyed by Vikings in 881, it had a rebirth in 962, when OTTO I THE GREAT of Germany became Holy Roman Emperor and made his brother, Bruno I, archbishop of Cologne. Bruno, also duke of the French duchy of Lorraine, became the first of the city's powerful ruling archbishops.

Cologne's location, at a spot where major land routes cross the Rhine, was ideal for commerce. Local industries began producing textiles, metal products, furs, and leather goods. A new merchant class formed in the city and traded in these goods, as well as in wine and metals.

Conflicts developed between the merchants and the archbishops. In 1074, Archbishop Anno II tried to claim a merchant's boat and its cargo. The merchants revolted, but after some initial success, their uprising was crushed. Relations between archbishop and city were mostly peaceful for the next 100 years, but another conflict occurred in 1180. While Archbishop Philip was away, the merchants built a wall around the city. Philip objected to this, demanding that his rights be respected. However, he left the wall standing and made the merchants responsible for its defense.

The merchants now began to control the city's institutions. They won important positions supervising the courts and property transfers. A group of wealthy merchants chose mayors and controlled business affairs, such as craft regulation. By 1200, the archbishop had achieved recognition as a key elector* of the German king, but his influence over city government had been reduced and Cologne was controlled by several powerful families. Religion and culture flourished as Cologne became more prosperous. New monastic orders were formed. A Dominican school was started by ALBERTUS MAGNUS in 1248, and the Dominicans also founded a university.

The ruling families were not always united, and the archbishop attempted to regain control of the city. In 1258, an agreement called the Great Arbitration Act was reached, setting a delicate balance between the archbishop and the merchants. The act held that all authority in the city came from the archbishop, but normal exercise of authority was in the hands of the townspeople. This left practical power with the merchants, and by the end of the 1200s, the archbishop had moved to Bonn. The only government function left to him in Cologne was the administration of justice. The focus of city government had shifted to the town council.

During the 1300s, groups of merchants and craftsmen vied for control of the city government. Finally, in 1396, an alliance of craft guilds and merchant corporations was formed. The new leaders issued a document that was the basis of government in Cologne through the 1700s.

Columbanus, St.

died 615
Monk, missionary

During the early Middle Ages, many missionaries traveled from Christian parts of the British Isles to pagan Europe. Columbanus was part of that tradition. Educated in Ireland, where he studied the Bible and early Christian authors in Latin, he set sail with 12 companions for the European mainland. There he spread Irish Christianity between 590 and 615.

Columbanus founded monasteries in BURGUNDY and gained many followers. However, he criticized the king and queen and the local church for moral looseness. Ordered to appear at a local church council at Chalon-sur-Saône in 603, he refused. Columbanus became so unpopular with the local clergy that he was expelled from the region.

In 610, he joined his companion St. Gall in the mountains of Switzerland and preached Christianity there. Then he crossed the Swiss Alps into Lombardy in northern Italy and established a famous monastery at Bobbio.

Columbanus was the first Irish writer whose Latin works—or at least a substantial number of them—have survived. These works include letters, sermons, poems, and other writings. His accomplished style suggests that he maintained a high level of reading and learning throughout his life. The main materials about his life are his letters and two books, one a life story written by Jonas, a monk at Bobbio. BEDE also wrote about Columbanus in his *Ecclesiastical History.*

Columbanus spent his final years at his monastery at Bobbio, where he died in 615. Bobbio became an important early medieval center of learning. (*See also* **Missions and Missionaries, Christian.**)

Commune

Communes were towns in western Europe that became self-governing in the later Middle Ages. They were often founded in reaction to local nobles who tried to govern as military rulers of rural estates. If a town's burghers, or inhabitants, could not persuade their overlord to govern differently, they often swore oaths of allegiance to one another, rebelled, and set up their own governments.

Origins. Ancient Greece and Rome were famed for democracy and urban life, but during the early Middle Ages democratic towns virtually ceased to exist. In the East, communities relied on the protection of large-scale government. However, western Europe, where the Roman Empire collapsed in the 400s, became by contrast an area ruled by local lords who lived on the efforts of farmers. Many of the old cities of the west were devastated by the fall of Rome. In Italy and other Mediterranean areas, only a few large communities managed to survive. North of the Alps, urban life virtually died, partly because of a lack of sufficient trade.

Power was held by FEUDAL lords of the countryside, who controlled their territory by force and by a very rough justice. Peasants needed their rulers' permission to relocate, to marry, and to pass on their possessions at death. Occasional local disputes were settled by lengthy and arbitrary means that included dueling and trial by ordeal*. Because of such customs, agricultural life moved slowly. Making a living through manufacture or trade became almost impossible because these occupations require mobility, quick decisions, and many more freedoms than peasants had.

By the 1100s, manufacturers and traders had slowly begun to assert themselves, creating markets and reviving towns. In the process, they brought wealth back to their areas. They still viewed the nobles as their overlords but began to organize themselves in guilds* to advance the interests of their different trades. In many places, they won permission to travel as they needed, to buy and sell goods without having to get approval, and to pay simple rent for their homes. Special courts were set up

* **trial by ordeal** method of judging a person's guilt or innocence by a physical test

* **guild** association of craft and trade workers that set standards and represented the interests of its members

From about 1337 to 1340, Italian artist Ambrogio Lorenzetti painted a series of frescoes showing the effects of both good and bad government in the commune of Siena, Italy. This fresco depicts Siena as a stable, busy, and prosperous city.

in the towns, with judges, fines, and other fixed penalties. Towns became freer than the countryside.

Guild members soon felt the need to make their own laws rather than appeal for permission from the nobles. At first, the lords were unwilling to allow this. As a result, some towns revolted as communities. Citizens would "swear to the commune" to fight to the death to protect each other and support one another's families. When such revolts succeeded, nobles might be forced to sign a legal "charter" listing the rights that the citizens had gained and how they were permitted to conduct their affairs.

Important Communes.   The earliest communes arose in northern Italy and parts of Germany, where conflicts between the Holy Roman Emperors, powerful local nobles, and the popes led to weaker rule than in other countries. VENICE, probably the first and most glorious of communes, may in fact never have had to deal with interference from outside lords; it had probably survived as an independent town from the 500s on. Protected from invasion by marshes and sandbars and by its canals, it became the most powerful city in the Mediterranean, and single-handedly it made treaties with nations and with crusader forces.

Other Italian communes, such as MILAN and PISA, formed in the climate of struggle between the Roman Church and the German rulers of the empire. In 1057, for example, Milan revolted against its ruling archbishop, and in 1080 the clergy of Lucca helped the people revolt against the imperial countess. Southern Italy, which at the time was firmly governed by Norman rulers, remained free of commune development, however.

Towns in parts of Germany and the Low Countries* also became communes relatively early. Once again, conflict among church, local rulers, and the emperors enabled towns to declare their independence. In 1074, COLOGNE rose against its archbishop, starting a struggle that led to civic freedoms and finally resulted in receipt of a civic seal from Emperor FREDERICK I BARBAROSSA. In Mainz, the town leaders won freedom from their archbishop because they helped solve a conflict between him and the emperor. Towns in Flanders such as BRUGES and GHENT also became free as a result of struggles between local rulers.

Where feudal rule was stronger, communes were slower to develop, but they were more often founded with the support of the local noble. In England and France, there were some early bitter struggles, as for example, in LONDON, Amiens, and Laon. New towns, called *villes neuves* in northern France and BASTIDES in the south, were also deliberately planned and founded. Rulers saw the wealth and stability that towns appeared to bring to an area. People were encouraged to come and settle in towns to strengthen frontiers, where profitable trade was as likely to occur as conflict.

Life in Communes.   Communes began in response to oppression by local rulers and their arbitrary laws. However, few communes actually rejected their former rulers. They had been granted special privileges by them and were protected by them. In return, the communes remained loyal and their inhabitants paid rent and taxes. This revenue provided great benefits to the local lords.

The rule of law also remained important in communes. Local laws were set by an elected council headed by a mayor (known as a burgermeister in Germany, a podesta in Italy). Council members were usually

* **Low Countries** flat coastal lands west of Germany, now occupied by Belgium and the Netherlands

selected from among the guild leaders of the town rather than from the lower ranks of workers. These council members were called ÉCHEVINS in Flanders and by the old Roman name CONSULS in Italy and the south of France.

Council meetings at first commonly took place in the leading guild headquarters. In addition to making laws, the councils collected money to pay taxes to their local lord, to improve the town streets and walls, and perhaps to build an impressive town hall for their meetings.

Not all communes survived the Middle Ages. In French-speaking areas especially, the rule of the nobles was often too strong. Either the councils bowed to nobles or appealed to the national king and became royal towns ruled by a CASTELLAN. In England, however, towns won representation at the national parliament and held on to their independence. In places with weaker overlords, such as Germany and Italy, towns also remained powerful, independent forces that contributed to the end of the feudal Middle Ages.

Concordats

In western Europe during the later Middle Ages, CHURCH-STATE RELATIONS were often troubled by the question of authority. Popes argued that the church could not be the subject of any state. Rulers claimed that each local church was a part of their state and should therefore be under their control.

Concordats were aimed at solving this basic disagreement. They were compromises between popes and different national rulers about the role of the state in managing national churches. They covered such matters as appointments to high church office, church authority over the clergy, taxation of local churches, and the makeup of the College of CARDINALS.

The first major medieval concordat was signed in the German town of Worms in 1122. In the Concordat of Worms, Pope Calixtus II and the Holy Roman Emperor, Henry V, settled the Investiture* Controversy. This issue had divided the papacy and the empire for decades. It was over who had the authority—pope or emperor—to choose bishops and abbots. The concordat settled the conflict by allowing *both* church and state to play a role in the selection of leaders of German churches.

Not all concordats were directly between popes and rulers. Some—for example, one with Portugal in 1289—were local agreements between rulers and bishops and were merely approved by the pope. At the Council of Constance in 1417, separate concordats were drawn up between the pope and each national church. In these, the pope agreed to different privileges for the clergy in the different nations of western Europe.

During the 1400s, the kings of England and Spain worked informally with their churches and so found little need for further formal agreements about church-state relationships. The French and German rulers, however, made official declarations about greater independence for their churches. In response, the popes made concordats that allowed them to retain a measure of influence over the churches and clergy. Nevertheless, the agreements in fact reflected the continuing decline of papal authority and the growing power of national rulers. The various churches still looked to Rome for spiritual guidance, but they were increasingly free of strong papal control.

* **investiture** act of installing a person in high office, such as a bishop

Church and Emperor

In the Concordat of Worms, both sides agreed to a compromise. Henry V guaranteed the free election of bishops and abbots in his empire and surrendered his claim to invest them with their ring and staff. In return, the pope granted the emperor the right to be present at investitures and church elections. That offered Henry an important advantage: even though he had no vote at such events, he could use his presence to influence the church's choice of its leaders.

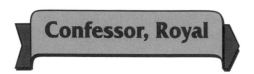

Confessor, Royal

* **absolution** forgiveness granted by a priest after a Christian has confessed to his or her sins

Confessing one's sins to gain forgiveness was important to Christians in the Middle Ages. All Christians, from king to peasant, wanted a priest who would hear them confess and give them absolution*. Royal confessors were the priests who heard a king's confession.

From the time of CONSTANTINE (ca. 288–337), first Christian emperor of the Roman Empire, Christian rulers had visited bishops and monks to seek forgiveness and ask for spiritual advice. In early medieval Europe, royal confessors were appointed to the different royal courts to hear the ruler's confession. By the 1200s, the royal confessor had become a permanent resident in the royal household.

A royal confessor was usually a member of a monastic order specially favored by the court. After the 1200s, these confessors were often DOMINICANS, but some were Augustinians, Carmelites, or members of other orders. Living in the royal palace, they were constantly on call to hear the king's confession. They also helped manage the king's household, represented the king's interests at court and in the kingdom, and often served as personal royal ambassadors for delicate diplomatic missions.

* **heretic** person who disagrees with established church doctrine

Royal confessors sometimes held other important posts. William of Paris, royal confessor of Philip IV the Fair of France, was appointed general inquisitor in France in 1303, to investigate heretics*. The influence and political experience confessors gained also led to promotion within their order, or elevation to the rank of bishop or CARDINAL.

Constable, Local

* **sanctuary** place of refuge or protection

In medieval England, three types of local government officials had the title of constable. The lowest in rank, township constables, performed basic police functions. Their duties included arresting people suspected of crimes, as well as those found carrying arms at fairs and markets, a practice that was strictly forbidden. Township constables could act independently, but they were also expected to carry out the sheriff's orders. Such orders might involve guarding people or property involved in legal disputes or supervising the guards appointed to watch a person who had claimed sanctuary*.

Another group of local officials was known as the hundred constables. This position originated in 1205 as part of a defense plan against the French. The hundred constable was captain of an armed force called a posse, which could be used against local individuals as well as foreigners. In the late 1200s and early 1300s, hundred constables received and recorded indictments* against people believed to have committed crimes. They also dealt with matters of public order. For example, they made sure local men did not carry weapons inappropriate for their rank.

* **indictment** statement charging a person with the commission of a crime

The highest-ranking local constable in England was the constable of a royal castle. This office was similar to that of CASTELLAN in some other countries but was not held by hereditary right. A constable of a royal castle had authority in the area surrounding his castle to obtain provisions for his troops and supplies to maintain the fortress. Often, this duty was combined with the office of sheriff. (*See also* **Law; Sanctuary, Right of.**)

Constable of the Realm

Aconstable was originally a high official in the court of a lord or king. The name comes from count of the stable, referring to the original purpose of the position: supervising the cavalry. The cavalry defended the lord's realm and contributed forces to larger armies. In addition to carrying out these military responsibilities, a constable often had certain judicial and ceremonial duties. Constables held a respected position in royal courts and the houses of great lords.

The position probably originated in the CAROLINGIAN period and may have been based on similar offices in the Byzantine Empire. Unlike the case in many other countries, the office of constable in France was not hereditary. However, it carried a great deal of military authority. Until the 1200s, the royal constable was subordinate to the SENESCHAL, the king's senior political official. After that time, French kings appointed a constable of the realm—the highest-ranking official in the nation.

In the late Middle Ages, the French constable of the realm governed regions that were causing the crown trouble. The office reached its peak in the 1300s, when the king's constable became the official head of the royal army. By the end of the Middle Ages, however, the position had lost a great deal of its importance as a result of disputes over the competence of its court and changes in military organization. The office was abolished in France in 1627. (*See also* **Constable, Local.**)

Constantine I the Great

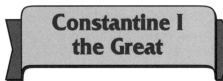

ca. 288–337
First Christian Roman emperor

Constantine I was the first Roman emperor to legalize the practice of Christianity. He built the city of Constantinople, which remained a great Christian center for more than a thousand years.

Though Constantine I lived well before 500, he is a key figure for the Middle Ages because of his relationship with CHRISTIANITY. He was the first Roman emperor to permit Roman citizens to be Christians. He also built the new capital of CONSTANTINOPLE, a city that endured as the center of Byzantine civilization and Christianity for more than 1,000 years.

Constantine was born in Serbia. His father, Constantius, was one of four contenders to become ruler of the Roman Empire. Upon Constantius's death in 306, Constantine was proclaimed emperor by his father's troops. After 16 years of struggling for the throne, Constantine finally claimed total mastery of the empire in 324.

In 312, on the eve of a battle with one of his rivals, Constantine supposedly saw a vision of a cross in the sky and the phrase "conquer with this." He commanded his soldiers to place crosses on their shields, and they won the battle the next day. Thereafter, Constantine publicly began to favor Christianity. In 313, he decreed that Christianity could be legally practiced in the empire.

Constantine gave money to build many new churches and arranged for the first council at Nicaea in 325. The council, which represented the Christian church throughout the world, was called to settle a disagreement about belief among church leaders. After supporting Christianity for much of his life, the emperor Constantine was baptized on his deathbed and became the first Christian emperor of the Roman Empire. About 50 years later, Christianity became the official religion of the Byzantine Empire.

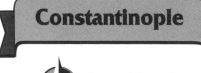

See map in Byzantine
Empire (vol. 1).

Constantinople was the capital of the BYZANTINE EMPIRE and of the Eastern Christian church. It was already a trading city during the time of ancient Greece, when it was called Byzantium. It reached its peak during the Middle Ages, after the Roman emperor CONSTANTINE I had chosen it as the "New Rome" of the East. Now called Istanbul, it is still an important city today.

Constantinople dominated the waterway that separates two large peninsulas in the eastern Mediterranean, Europe's Balkan peninsula and Asia's ANATOLIA (Asia Minor). These two land masses became the heartlands of Byzantine power after the rest of the Roman Empire was conquered by Germanic tribes of western Europe and the Islamic civilization of Arabia. The city itself, surrounded by water on three sides and by a massive wall, was an easily defended stronghold and a natural harbor on the important trade routes of the East. It survived as the Byzantine capital until 1453.

Constantinople in the Early Middle Ages.   When JUSTINIAN I became Byzantine emperor in 527, Constantinople was by far the largest city in the eastern Mediterranean. Its walls could contain up to a million people, although at the time, the city population was only some 500,000. Constantinople already contained the mighty church of HAGIA SOPHIA, a university, libraries that preserved many manuscripts from the ancient world, and an impressive palace to which Justinian and his successors made major additions.

The city grew to become a dense network of great private houses surrounded by large apartment buildings, workshops, and public baths. The streets were lighted at night to prevent crime. Ancient Roman customs survived. There was a huge hippodrome*, where chariot races took place. Racing teams attracted crowds of fans who sometimes rioted, taking sides in political debates as well as in the races. The Byzantine emperor also continued the Roman custom of distributing bread to citizens to keep the peace.

Constantinople was governed by a prefect, a high-ranking official with broad powers to run the city. Among his more important tasks were maintaining public order and ensuring that food could be distributed. He also enforced laws about building, about wills and inheritances, and about foreigners and immigration. The prefect's seal was used to authorize certain exports and to guarantee accurate weights and measures for trading purposes.

The Church in Constantinople.   Constantinople was the religious capital of the Eastern Orthodox, or Byzantine, Church. This church became the biggest landlord in the city, and it was also rich in estates and monasteries throughout the empire. Its great wealth was displayed in magnificent church buildings, decorated with paintings and mosaics of Christ and the saints, which were the envy of the Mediterranean world. The Byzantine patriarch* was the second most important person within the empire. He was also the most important Christian leader after the pope of Rome.

During the Middle Ages, the Byzantine Church underwent major changes and separated from the Christianity of Rome. In the 700s, a bitter dispute broke out in Constantinople over the issue of ICONS. Though the

* **hippodrome**   outdoor stadium used in ancient Greece and Rome for horse and chariot racing

* **patriarch**   head of one of the five major centers of early Christianity: Alexandria, Antioch, Constantinople, Jerusalem, and Rome

Roman Church disagreed, many Byzantine leaders became convinced that images of holy figures should not be displayed for public worship. In a movement called iconoclasm, Eastern churches destroyed or covered over their art for more than 100 years.

The emperors and patriarchs in the end abandoned this position, and Byzantine churches became more magnificent than ever. However, disagreements with the popes continued, and in 1054 the patriarch of Constantinople ceased to recognize the pope's seniority. At the same time, the pope began to ignore the opinions of the Eastern Church.

Constantinople and the Byzantine Empire.   As the site of the imperial palace and the seat of government, Constantinople was vital to the fortunes of the empire. It was the center of Byzantine culture. Great Byzantine scholars such as John the Grammarian and Leo the Mathematician exchanged knowledge with Iranian and Arab scientists. Future officials of the empire were trained in the university and in private schools all over the city. A tradition of government bureaucracy* flourished, and a law school was founded in 1045.

City government under the prefects also prospered. Industry and trade workers were supervised to prevent fraud. Goldsmiths and silver workers were strictly controlled. The SILK industry was highly specialized and regulated, and certain types of silk could not be exported. In the 900s, international trade was carefully supervised, taxes were imposed, and rules were made about where foreign visitors could stay and how they should conduct their business.

Byzantine nobles rarely invested in trade; their wealth came from landholdings. This created an opportunity for outsiders. By the end of the 1000s, many foreign traders, including Armenians, Syrians, Normans, and Italians, had moved into Constantinople. Powerful merchants from VENICE, GENOA, and Pisa were able to negotiate for tax exemptions and became unpopular with city natives. In 1182, the citizens massacred many Latin* merchants and looted their settlements. Order in the empire was beginning to break down.

The Byzantine Empire owed much of its long life to its carefully organized government. It also owed much to its powerful city walls, built before the Middle Ages in the early 400s. Constantinople was attacked by Persians and Slavs in 626, by Arabs in 674 and 717, by Russians in 860, and by Turks in the late 1000s. Each time, the walls stood between the emperors and destruction, and they proved unconquerable.

In 1204, however, the city was attacked by crusaders from the West, who were helped by a navy of ships from Venice. Venetian marines scaled the walls, and the crusaders succeeded in taking the city. Latin Christians took revenge for earlier massacres and controlled Constantinople for 57 years. Yet, though the city had fallen, Byzantine culture was not dead. A group of leaders who had retreated to Nicaea in Anatolia was able to reconquer Constantinople in 1261. The Byzantine Empire never achieved its former greatness, but it continued to be a political and cultural force for almost 200 more years.

In the early 1400s, the OTTOMAN Turks began invading the Balkan peninsula from Asia Minor. For several decades, they avoided a direct attack on Constantinople. In 1453, however, MEHMED II assaulted the old

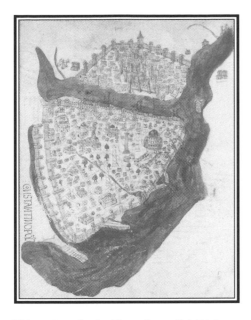

This watercolor by Florentine artist Cristoforo Buonelmonti shows Constantinople in 1420. The world's most important city in its time, Constantinople survived as the Byzantine capital until 1453, when it was conquered by the Ottomans and renamed Istanbul.

* **bureaucracy** large departmental organization such as a government

* **Latin** referring to western Europe and the Roman Church, which used the Latin language for its services

Roman walls with a new weapon of war, the cannon. The city and the Byzantine Empire were finally subdued. Constantinople was renamed and became the Ottoman capital of Istanbul.

Construction, Building

See color plate 15, vol. 1.

Medieval buildings ranged from humble homes to opulent palaces and religious buildings. During the Middle Ages, the design and construction of these buildings evolved. There were changes in materials, in the skills and knowledge of the builders, and in the building techniques they used.

Building Materials. During the early Middle Ages, western and northern Europe contained large forests. As a result, most early buildings there—whether houses, castles, or churches—were made of wood. Few of these survive. Over the centuries, most have been destroyed or replaced by stone structures. The Mediterranean region, on the other hand, had few forests. Buildings there were usually constructed of stone, brick, or earth mixed with straw, although wood was sometimes used for the frameworks of buildings.

Beginning in the 1100s, more and more buildings in western Europe were constructed of stone or masonry rather than wood. One reason was that fires became an enormous hazard in growing cities. In addition, lumber became less plentiful. As the population grew, wood supplies were depleted. People used wood at home for cooking and heating, as well as in industries such as metalworking, pottery making, and glassmaking. Farmers cleared forests to grow food for the expanding population, and more and more wood was needed for military purposes and shipbuilding. The result was that between the 700s and 1300s, the forests of western Europe were reduced by half.

One problem with constructing large buildings of stone was getting the stone from quarries to the construction site. Quarries were often far from where the stone was needed, and it was very expensive to move large quantities of stone by land. However, transport by water was easier and less expensive. One of the factors that contributed to the development of stone architecture in western Europe was the existence of many navigable rivers close to good quarries.

Builders and Craftsmen. Construction skills were passed down through generations of medieval builders. In the early Middle Ages, builders probably worked without any overall plans or blueprints. Instead, they relied on their basic knowledge of construction and the designs of existing buildings, as well as skills learned from years of practice.

From the 1000s on, these skills became more precise as builders worked more and more in stone. By the 1100s, building crews consisted of highly skilled teams of masons, stonecutters, glaziers*, sculptors, carpenters, and their assistants. The master mason generally was the person responsible for the overall design and for supervising construction. As a guide for the workers, the master mason produced design templates, full-scale drawings of stone shapes needed for the building. Stonecutters followed these templates as they cut and prepared the stones.

* **glazier** person who sets glass in windows and frames

Building crews consisted of highly skilled teams of workers, including masons, stonecutters, carpenters, sculptors, and glaziers. They generally worked under the guidance of the master mason.

Because the construction of a building was not based on a formal plan, innovations often came about through trial and error. This spirit of experimentation declined toward the end of the medieval era as the design and construction of buildings became more standardized.

Building Design and Techniques. Throughout the Middle Ages, builders gradually developed the basic techniques of earlier builders, adding their own ideas. They often used elements from important buildings of the past, including the monuments of ancient Greece and the Roman Empire. They also discovered new techniques in many areas of design and construction.

With the innovations introduced in the Middle Ages, small buildings such as houses became more comfortable. Large buildings became taller and more spacious, and their design changed dramatically, resulting in great palaces, impressive public monuments, and magnificent cathedrals.

In the early Middle Ages, the most common type of wooden construction was a simple framework of wooden poles that leaned toward each other in an upside-down V-shaped pattern. The tops of these poles were tied together along a horizontal beam called a ridgepole, while the bottoms rested on the ground. This framework supported the roof of the building and enclosed the living space. Inside, horizontal beams were used to keep the poles from spreading apart, and additional rafters* helped support the roof and its covering. The most common roofing material was thatch* because it was both plentiful and easily repaired or replaced. At first, this type of structure was often built over a pit dug into the ground. The pit made the interior space larger and provided protection

* **rafters** main and secondary vertical beams that support a wood-framed roof

* **thatch** plant material such as straw used to cover the roof of a building

from the wind and cold. Such half-buried buildings were common throughout Europe until about 1000. After that, they were used mostly in France, England, and Ireland.

In time, builders added additional floors within structures. Solid horizontal beams supported the upper floors and also helped strengthen the structure as a whole. Side walls were made of wood or else of such materials as bricks, broken pottery, earth, or plaster, packed between the upright posts and held together with mortar or plaster. The walls were often set on horizontal beams on the ground rather than directly on the ground itself to keep the vertical wall posts from rotting.

From the 900s to the 1200s, wooden structures became more economical and better designed. One reason for this was the development of new building techniques, such as the use of a mortise-and-tenon system* for joining walls and frames. Advances in metallurgy, the science and technology of metals, in the 1100s and 1200s also provided new tools—files, chisels, planes, and saws—that could shape wood more intricately and accurately.

The design and construction of stone and masonry houses were influenced by the design of wooden buildings. Wood was still used to provide a basic framework and also to create temporary scaffolding, but the walls were made of more carefully shaped stone, brick, or earth. Thatch roofs gradually gave way to roofs of tile, wooden shingles, or slate.

The great cathedrals and public buildings of the Middle Ages also combined ideas learned from earlier generations with new techniques. One of the main problems in constructing large buildings was finding a way to create large floor areas, support high ceilings, and provide enough light. Medieval builders solved this problem by developing new designs based on the principle of the arch. An arch is a set of wedge-shaped stones arranged in a curve. It can support itself as long as there is enough pressure from the sides, either from walls or other arches. Since Roman times, arches provided openings for doors or windows yet could support solid walls above them.

Medieval builders extended the principle of the arch to make elaborate vaults, three-dimensional arched stone structures that could form a ceiling and support the roof. Vaults were graceful yet strong and fireproof. They could be placed on separated columns rather than on solid masonry, allowing open floor areas and walls with large windows. Like arches, though, vaults need pressure from the sides, especially on tall buildings also subject to the wind. For this reason, stone supports called buttresses were used between windows on the outside walls. On later Gothic cathedrals, these became large, freestanding archlike structures called flying buttresses.

Such innovations enabled medieval builders in many parts of the world to construct larger and larger buildings of stone and masonry. In Europe, new features such as elaborate vaults and buttresses began to appear in castles, town halls, and especially cathedrals. The cathedrals at CHARTRES in France and CANTERBURY in England are just two examples of the many religious buildings completed in Europe during this time.

Byzantine builders used similar materials and techniques in their work and added their own innovations. For example, in the early but massive church of HAGIA SOPHIA, built in Byzantine Constantinople,

* **mortise-and-tenon system**   method for making joints in wood, with a narrow tenon slotting into a groove or mortise that was cut to fit it

See color plate 3, vol. 2.

there is an enormous vaulted nave and a huge dome. Moreover, Islamic builders used similar structural elements. In the palace of the ALHAMBRA in Spain, built for medieval Islamic rulers, arcades of slender pillars support the high central ceilings and low side galleries. In all of these places, builders skillfully used the materials available to them to create structures that were both durable and graceful. (*See also* **Byzantine Architecture; Gothic Architecture; Islamic Art and Architecture; Romanesque Architecture.**)

Consuls, Consulates

* **commune** town in the Middle Ages that established independence from its feudal ruler and formed its own government

* **guild** association of craft and trade workers that set standards and represented the interests of its members

Consuls were officials on the governing council, or consulate, of towns in northern Italy, southern France, and parts of Germany in the late Middle Ages. The office was associated with the development of communes*, though the name was borrowed from the chief magistrates in ancient Rome. Consuls first appeared in Italy in the late 1000s. By 1160, they led most towns of northern Italy and were spreading to southern France and Germany.

A number of factors contributed to the rise of consulates. They often appeared in new towns where local bishops were the only strong central authority. They also arose during power struggles between outside forces, such as the popes and the Holy Roman Emperors. Consulates often developed in towns with independent nobles and strong merchant and craft guilds*.

Italian consuls were most powerful from 1150 to 1250. During that time, many won independence for their towns and the surrounding districts. For example, the consuls of most of the Italian towns of Lombardy formed the Lombard League. This league was able to contest the rule of the Holy Roman Emperors Frederick I Barbarossa and Frederick II in their towns.

After 1250, consulates began losing authority. In some cases, single rulers rose to power. In other cases, there were competing groups of nobles or popular citizens' groups. By 1300, consulates had disappeared in much of Italy. In France, where consuls never had as much authority as they did in Italy, they became less important as towns came under the control of a centralized royal bureaucracy. (*See also* **Commune; Échevin; Holy Roman Empire.**)

Conversos

* **anti-Semitism** hostility toward and discrimination against Jews

Conversos were Spanish converts from Judaism to Christianity. Some conversos were Jews who converted to Christianity in late Roman and early Visigothic times because of religious persecution. From the early 700s, however, the Muslims occupied most of SPAIN and usually left the Jews free to worship as they wished. When Christian soldiers from the north slowly drove the Muslims out of Spain in the 1000s and 1100s, they at first continued this policy of religious tolerance. By the 1250s, however, the economies of the Christian kingdoms had begun to fall on hard times, and this led to a renewal of anti-Semitism*.

Violent persecution of Jews in the late 1300s and early 1400s led to thousands of new conversos. Many of these were at first favored by the church, gaining high positions among the ruling classes, particularly in the kingdom of CASTILE. However, the conversos' social, political, and economic success caused conflict with the "old Christians."

During the Spanish Inquisition*, conversos were investigated, and the sincerity of their faith was questioned. Racial hatred, social hostility, and jealousy at their success may have been important factors behind the expulsion of unconverted Jews from Spain in 1492. For the next 200 years, hostility between old Christians and the conversos lingered. Conversos were constantly under suspicion, and laws were passed to exclude them from military orders. (*See also* **Anti-Semitism; Jewish Communities; Jews, Expulsion of.**)

* **Spanish Inquisition** tribunal established in 1478 by the Spanish monarch to investigate and punish conversos whose faith was judged insincere

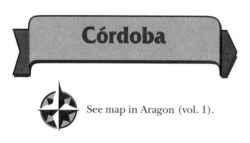

Córdoba

See map in Aragon (vol. 1).

The city of Córdoba is located in southern Spain. During the Middle Ages, when the Muslims held much of Spain for several hundred years, Córdoba became one of the great cities of the Islamic world. Much of its importance was due to its location on the flat plain of the Guadalquivir River, giving it rich agricultural lands and making it easy to reach but also easy to defend.

Early History. During Roman imperial times, Córdoba was an important commercial and cultural center. The Romans built a great 16-arch bridge

Córdoba flourished as an Islamic cultural center during the centuries of Muslim rule in Spain. The Great Mosque was built in the late 700s. The design of the interior arches shown here was made by the alternating use of stone and brick.

that still spans the Guadalquivir River. Early in the 400s, the Germanic VANDALS invaded and devastated the city, destroying its prosperity. In the 500s, the city became the center of religious struggles between the Roman Church and Christian heretics* known as Arians, whose views about the nature of Christ were denounced by the church. In 571, the city fell to the VISIGOTHS, another Germanic tribe, who maintained control until the Muslim conquest in the 700s.

Muslim Córdoba.   In 711, Muslim invaders sweeping into Spain from North Africa captured Córdoba from the Visigoths. The Muslims called southern Spain Andalusia, and they made Córdoba the seat of government for Andalusia. For the next few decades, the region was torn by internal strife as a result of tribal rivalries.

When the Abbasids defeated the UMAYYAD dynasty* of Syria in 750, a surviving Umayyad prince, Abd al-Rahman, fled to Spain. In 756, he overthrew the governor of Andalusia and made Córdoba the capital of his new emirate*. During his rule, a new palace and the Great Mosque were built in the city. Abd al-Rahman also extended the city walls, enlarged the old Roman bridge, improved and fortified the aqueduct, and built a new administrative building. Córdoba became the political, military, religious, and cultural capital of the emirate.

However, during the 800s, there were conflicts in the region between the Arabs, their Christian subjects, and Christian converts to Islam. Revolts erupted, and the power of the emirate steadily declined. By 912, its territory was reduced to the immediate area around Córdoba.

In 912, Abd al-Rahman III came to power. Under the rule of this energetic monarch, the Muslim conquest of Spain reached its fullest extent, and Córdoba became a great center of Islamic culture. The city during this period was clean and well paved, and it had an abundant supply of water. It was also huge, occupying an area of about 24 by 6 miles and containing a million people. The city was known throughout the Muslim world for its great numbers of mosques, mansions, public baths, and shops.

Córdoba at this time was perhaps most important as an intellectual center. The city had many free schools and large libraries. Its scholars translated ancient texts from Greece and other old Eastern cultures, making major contributions in music, geography, alchemy, chemistry, medicine, surgery, astronomy, philosophy, botany, and mathematics. The arts and crafts also flourished. The city boasted some 13,000 weavers, and its woolens, silks, and brocades were famous. Córdoba was also known for its leatherwork, gold and silver jewelry, and carved ivory.

Non-Muslims played an important role in Córdoba's achievements at this time. Christians served as administrators, financiers, physicians, artists, and master craftsmen. They maintained their own churches, schools, and libraries. The city was also the center of a brilliant Jewish culture, with numerous Jewish scholars, poets, and philosophers.

After the last Umayyad ruler died in 1031, there was no central leadership, and Muslim Spain gradually split into a number of separate principalities called *taifas*. Córdoba now became a republic. During the late 1000s and the 1100s, the city was controlled by several very repressive and puritanical regimes. These years, which were dominated by internal strife,

* **heretic** person who disagrees with established church doctrine

* **dynasty** succession of rulers from the same family or group

* **emirate** office and lands of an emir, a Muslim prince

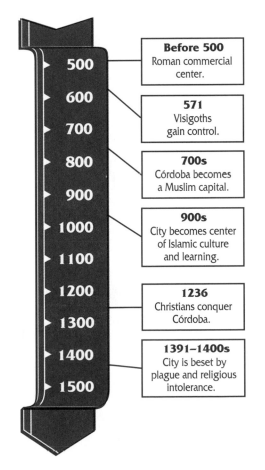

| Before 500 |
| Roman commercial center. |

500
600

| 571 |
| Visigoths gain control. |

700
800

| 700s |
| Córdoba becomes a Muslim capital. |

900
1000

| 900s |
| City becomes center of Islamic culture and learning. |

1100
1200

| 1236 |
| Christians conquer Córdoba. |

1300

| 1391–1400s |
| City is beset by plague and religious intolerance. |

1400
1500

robbed Córdoba of its military and political importance. Yet the period also produced some of the city's greatest scholars, including the philosopher and physician IBN RUSHD (AVERROËS) and the great Jewish philosopher Moses MAIMONIDES.

The Christian Reconquest.

In the 1230s, Ferdinand III, the Christian king of León and CASTILE, began to reconquer parts of Muslim Spain. In 1236, he captured Córdoba, bringing an end to more than 500 years of Muslim rule. Under the Christians, the city served as an important military base in the war against the city of GRANADA, one of the last Muslim strongholds. Many Castilian noble and military families settled in Córdoba, and the church appointed a bishop to the city. Córdoba's prosperity declined, however, and it never recovered its former splendor. Yet the Christians did not destroy all traces of the city's Muslim past. Even today, Muslim influence is still evident in the city's architecture and design.

Under the Christians, the Jewish community in Córdoba continued to flourish for more than 100 years. In 1391, however, most of the Jews were massacred in a series of riots. During this period, other Jews suffered from the plague, as did the rest of the city's inhabitants. Throughout the 1400s, many Jews were forced to convert to Christianity. In 1492, unconverted Jews were expelled from Spain as a result of decrees by the Spanish monarchs. (*See also* **Islam, Conquests of; Jews, Expulsion of; Spain, Muslim Kingdoms of.**)

See color plate 15, vol. 3.